YUZU THE PET VET

2

By Mingo Ito
In collaboration with
NIPPON COLUMBIA CO., LTD.

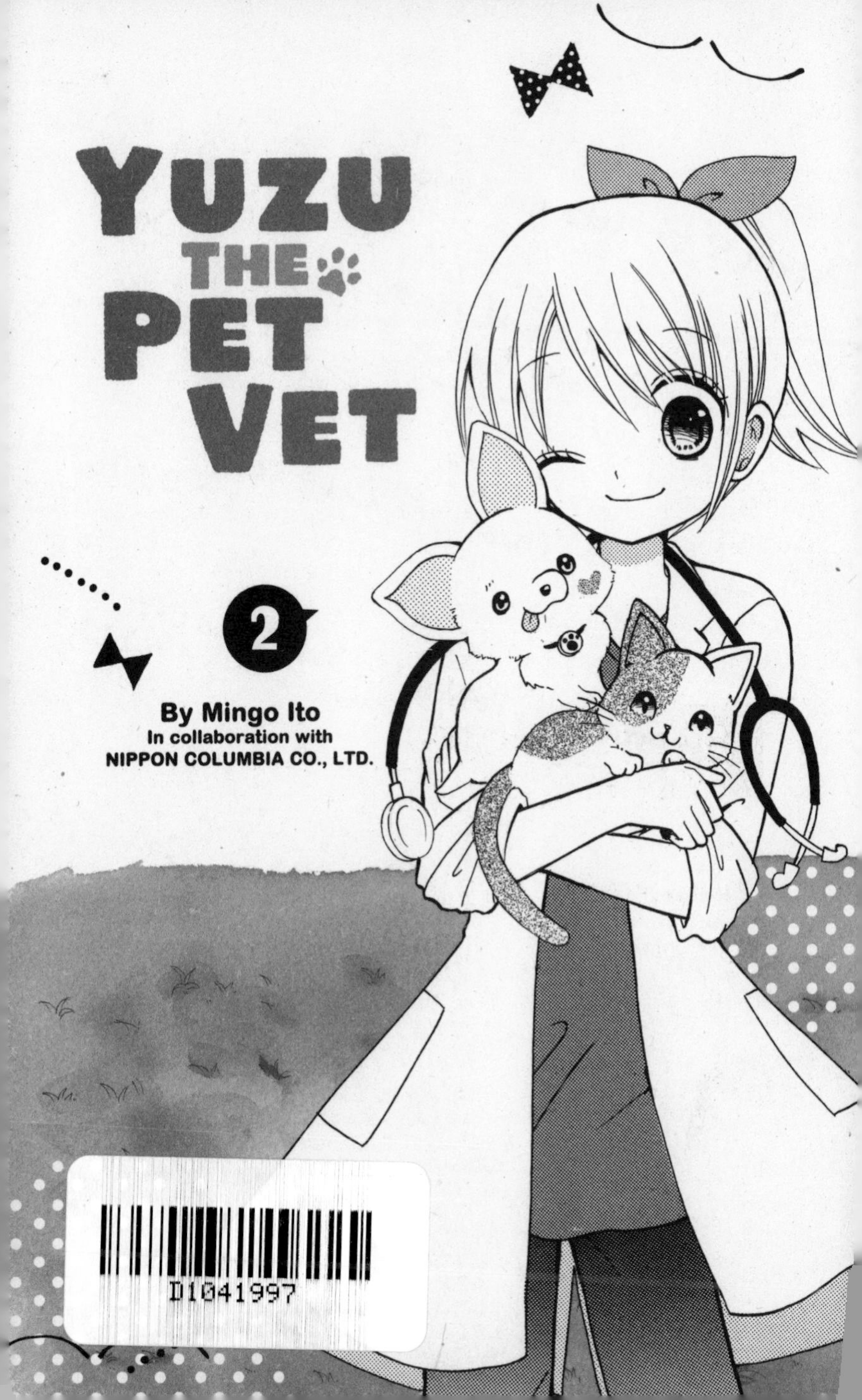

Patient 5! 🐾 Luke the Guide Dog ---------> 004

Patient 6! 🐾 Komachi, the Dog Who Cried Wolf ---------> 041

Patient 7! 🐾 Chacha the Rabbit Boss ---------> 077

Patient 8! 🐾 Peanut the Abandoned Cat ---------> 113

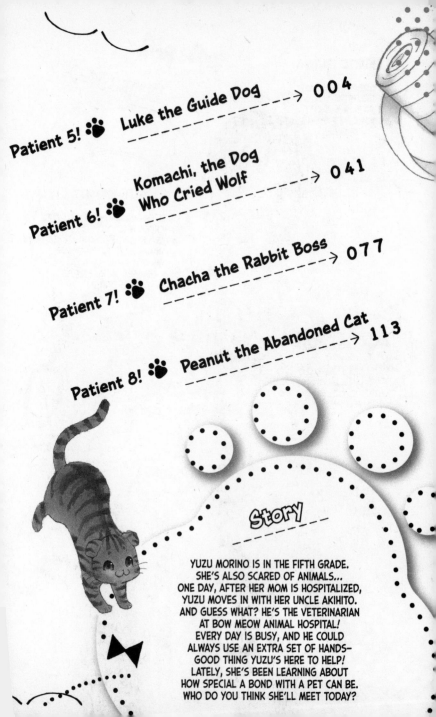

Story

YUZU MORINO IS IN THE FIFTH GRADE. SHE'S ALSO SCARED OF ANIMALS... ONE DAY, AFTER HER MOM IS HOSPITALIZED, YUZU MOVES IN WITH HER UNCLE AKIHITO. AND GUESS WHAT? HE'S THE VETERINARIAN AT BOW MEOW ANIMAL HOSPITAL! EVERY DAY IS BUSY, AND HE COULD ALWAYS USE AN EXTRA SET OF HANDS— GOOD THING YUZU'S HERE TO HELP! LATELY, SHE'S BEEN LEARNING ABOUT HOW SPECIAL A BOND WITH A PET CAN BE. WHO DO YOU THINK SHE'LL MEET TODAY?

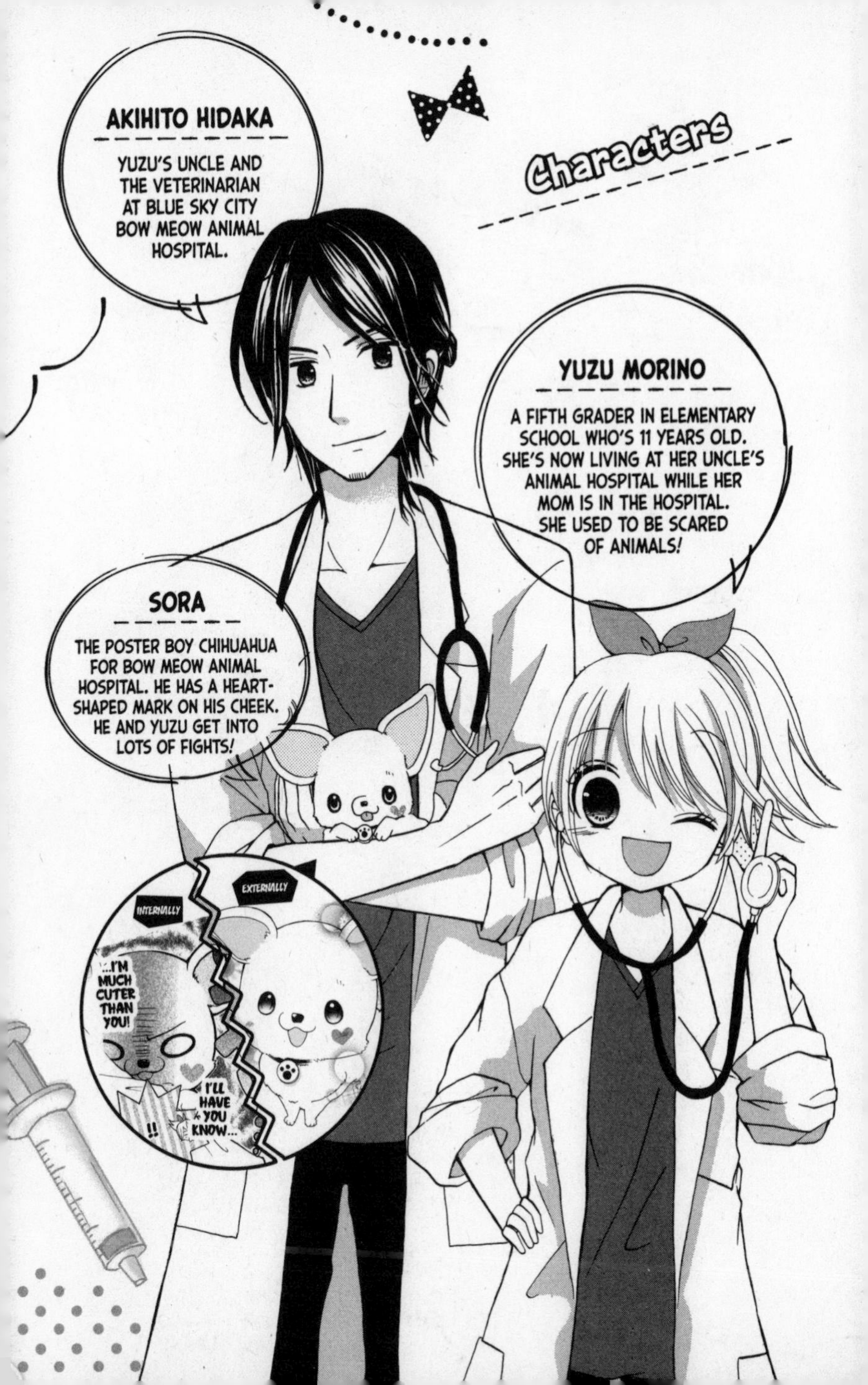
Characters
AKIHITO HIDAKA
YUZU'S UNCLE AND THE VETERINARIAN AT BLUE SKY CITY BOW MEOW ANIMAL HOSPITAL.
YUZU MORINO
A FIFTH GRADER IN ELEMENTARY SCHOOL WHO'S 11 YEARS OLD. SHE'S NOW LIVING AT HER UNCLE'S ANIMAL HOSPITAL WHILE HER MOM IS IN THE HOSPITAL. SHE USED TO BE SCARED OF ANIMALS!
SORA
THE POSTER BOY CHIHUAHUA FOR BOW MEOW ANIMAL HOSPITAL. HE HAS A HEART-SHAPED MARK ON HIS CHEEK. HE AND YUZU GET INTO LOTS OF FIGHTS!
EXTERNALLY
INTERNALLY
...I'M MUCH CUTER THAN YOU!
I'LL HAVE YOU KNOW...
!!

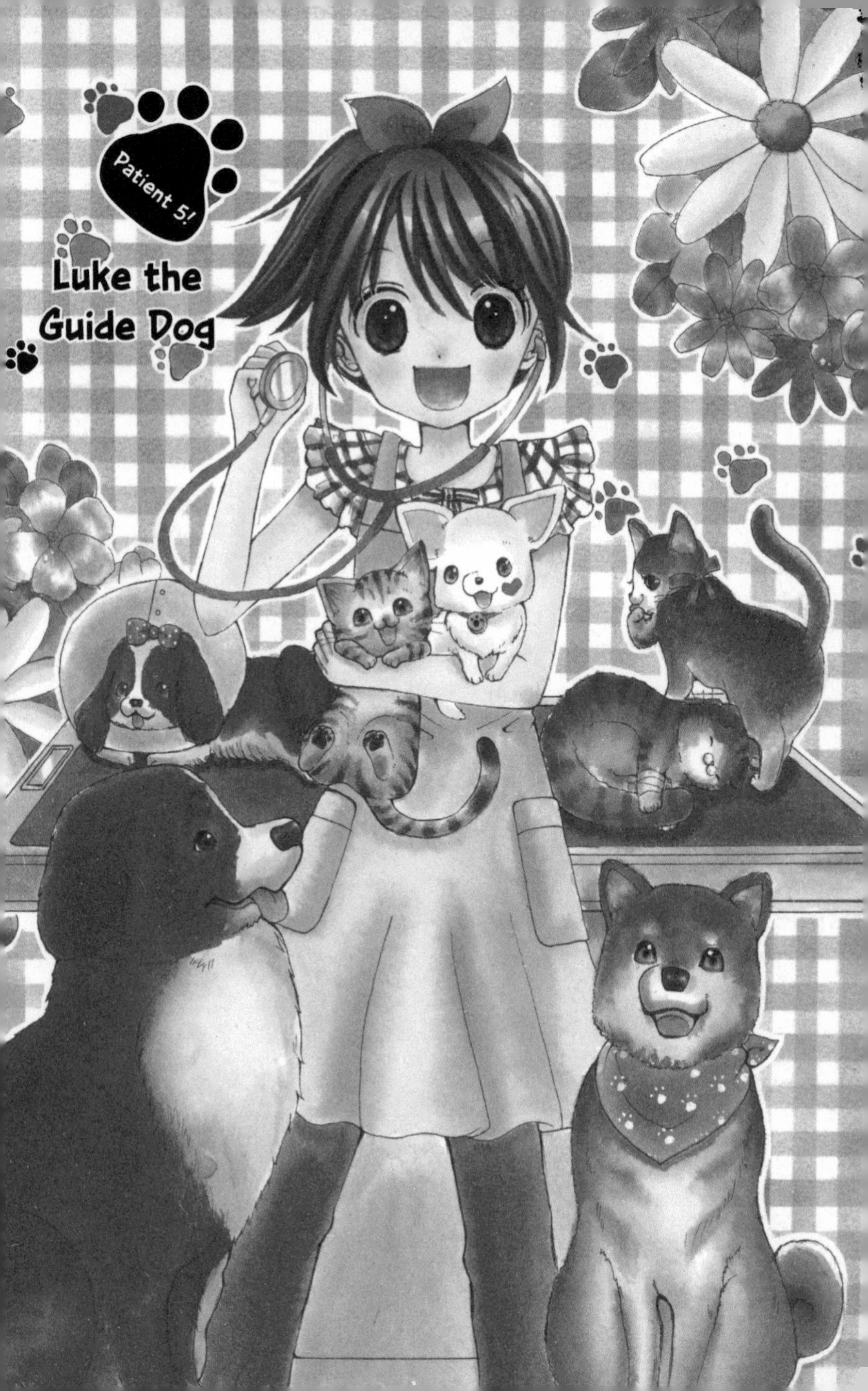
Patient 5!
Luke the Guide Dog

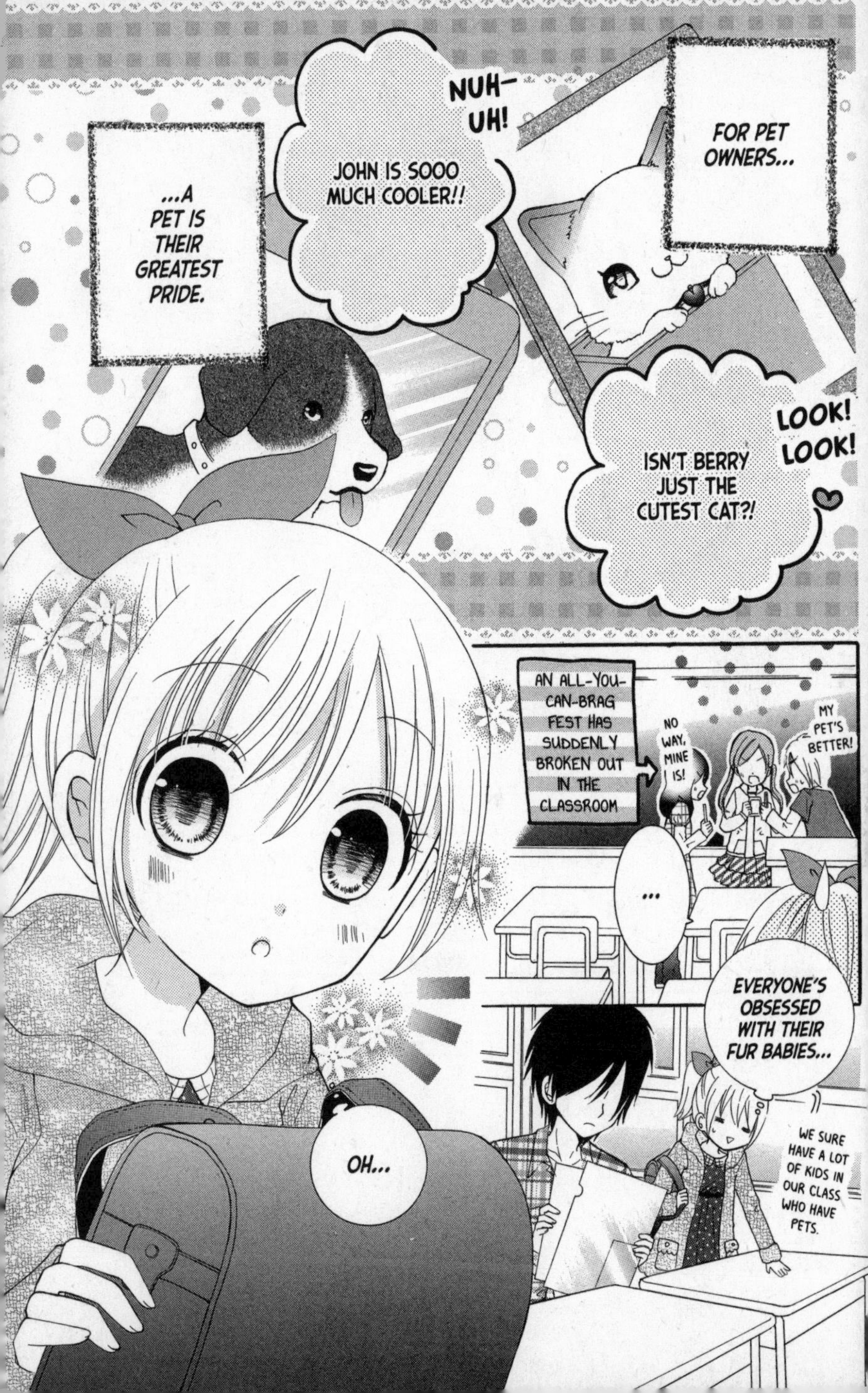

FOR PET OWNERS...
NUH-UH!
JOHN IS SOOO MUCH COOLER!!
...A PET IS THEIR GREATEST PRIDE.
LOOK! LOOK!
ISN'T BERRY JUST THE CUTEST CAT?!
AN ALL-YOU-CAN-BRAG FEST HAS SUDDENLY BROKEN OUT IN THE CLASSROOM
MY PET'S BETTER!
NO WAY, MINE IS!
...
EVERYONE'S OBSESSED WITH THEIR FUR BABIES...
WE SURE HAVE A LOT OF KIDS IN OUR CLASS WHO HAVE PETS.
OH...

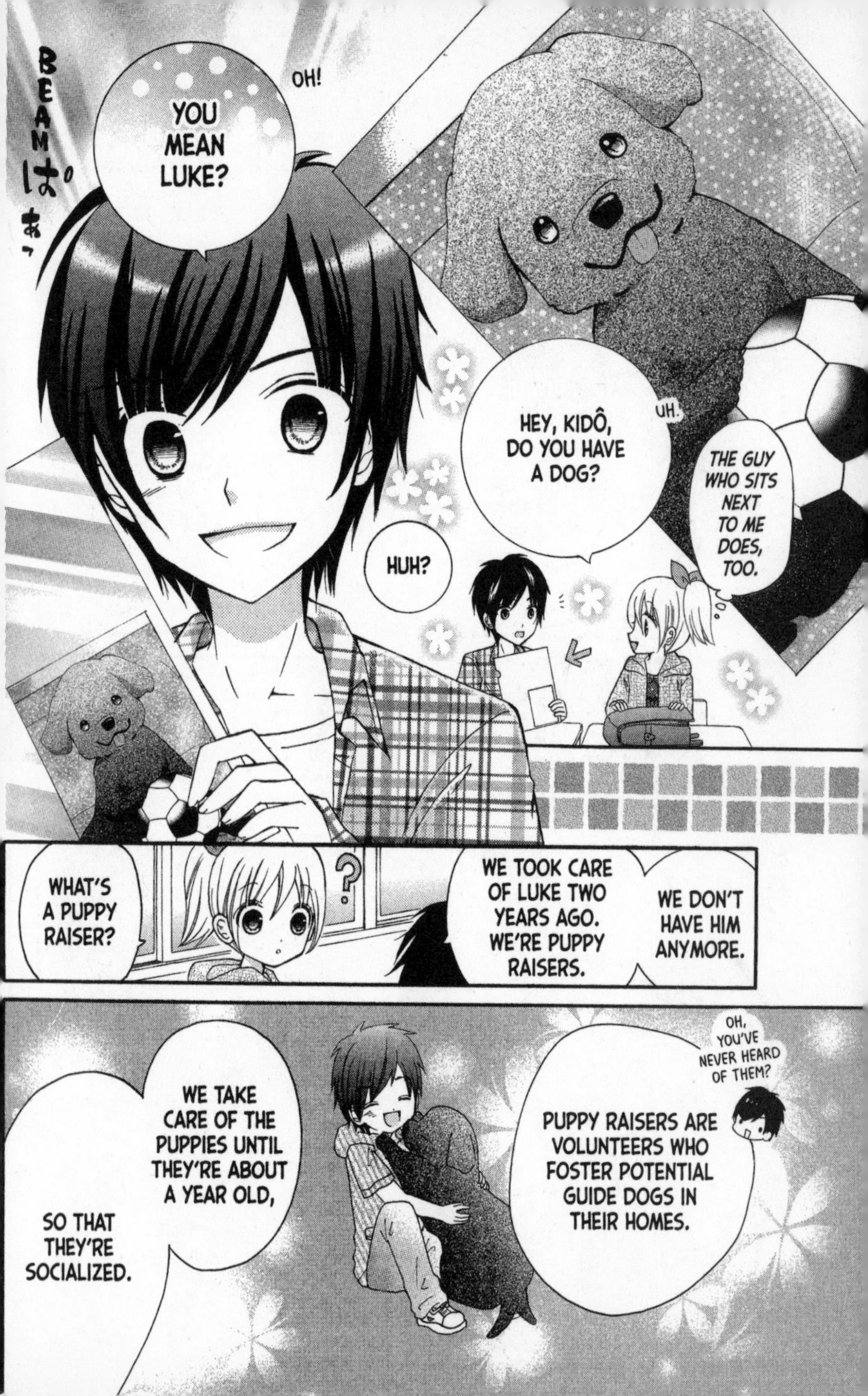

HEY, KIDÔ, DO YOU HAVE A DOG?
UH.
THE GUY WHO SITS NEXT TO ME DOES, TOO.
HUH?
OH!
YOU MEAN LUKE?
BEAM
WE TOOK CARE OF LUKE TWO YEARS AGO. WE'RE PUPPY RAISERS.
WE DON'T HAVE HIM ANYMORE.
WHAT'S A PUPPY RAISER?
OH, YOU'VE NEVER HEARD OF THEM?
PUPPY RAISERS ARE VOLUNTEERS WHO FOSTER POTENTIAL GUIDE DOGS IN THEIR HOMES.
WE TAKE CARE OF THE PUPPIES UNTIL THEY'RE ABOUT A YEAR OLD,
SO THAT THEY'RE SOCIALIZED.

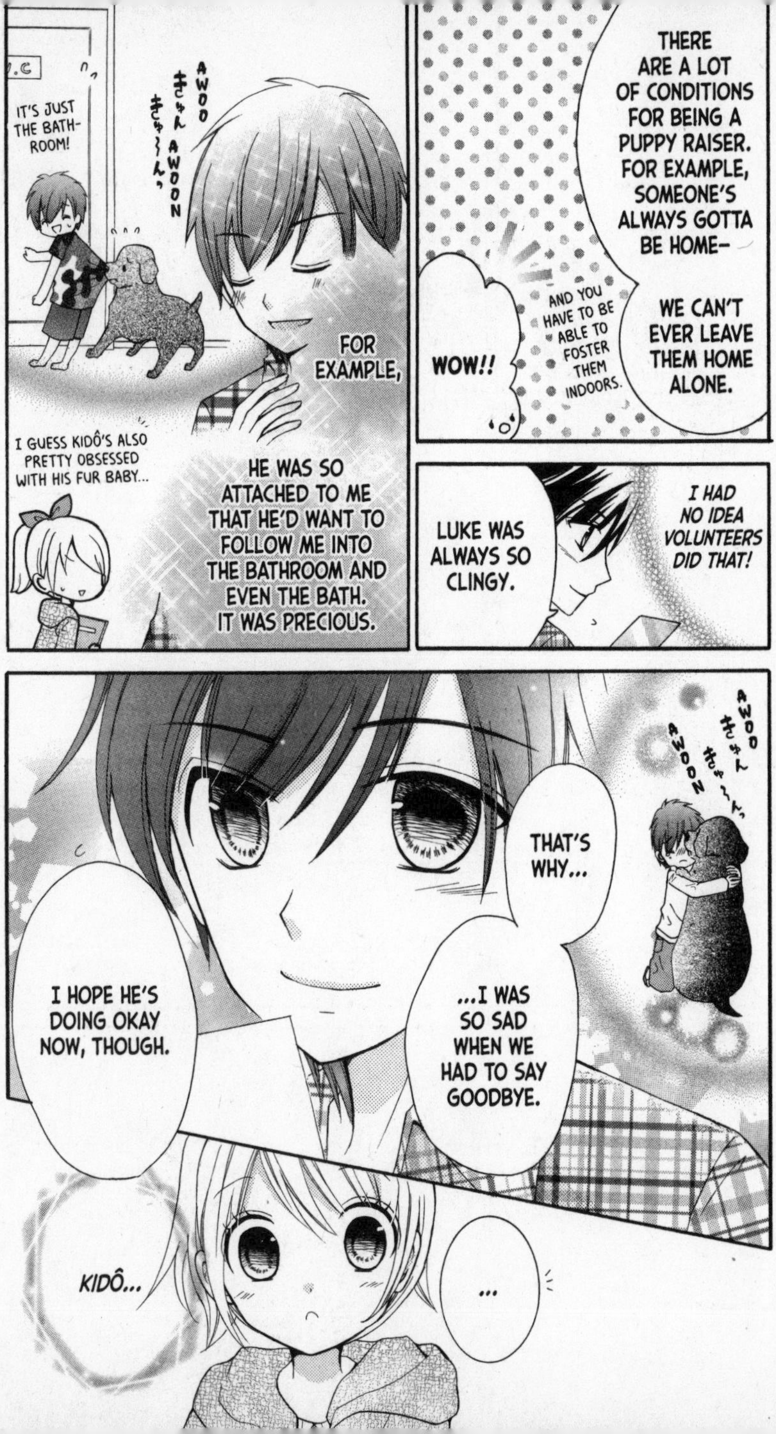
THERE ARE A LOT OF CONDITIONS FOR BEING A PUPPY RAISER. FOR EXAMPLE, SOMEONE'S ALWAYS GOTTA BE HOME—
WE CAN'T EVER LEAVE THEM HOME ALONE.
AND YOU HAVE TO BE ABLE TO FOSTER THEM INDOORS.
WOW!!
I HAD NO IDEA VOLUNTEERS DID THAT!
LUKE WAS ALWAYS SO CLINGY.
AWOO きゃん
AWOON きゅ〜んっ
FOR EXAMPLE,
IT'S JUST THE BATHROOM!
HE WAS SO ATTACHED TO ME THAT HE'D WANT TO FOLLOW ME INTO THE BATHROOM AND EVEN THE BATH. IT WAS PRECIOUS.
I GUESS KIDÔ'S ALSO PRETTY OBSESSED WITH HIS FUR BABY...
AWOO きゃん
AWOON きゃ〜んっ
THAT'S WHY...
...I WAS SO SAD WHEN WE HAD TO SAY GOODBYE.
I HOPE HE'S DOING OKAY NOW, THOUGH.
...
KIDÔ...

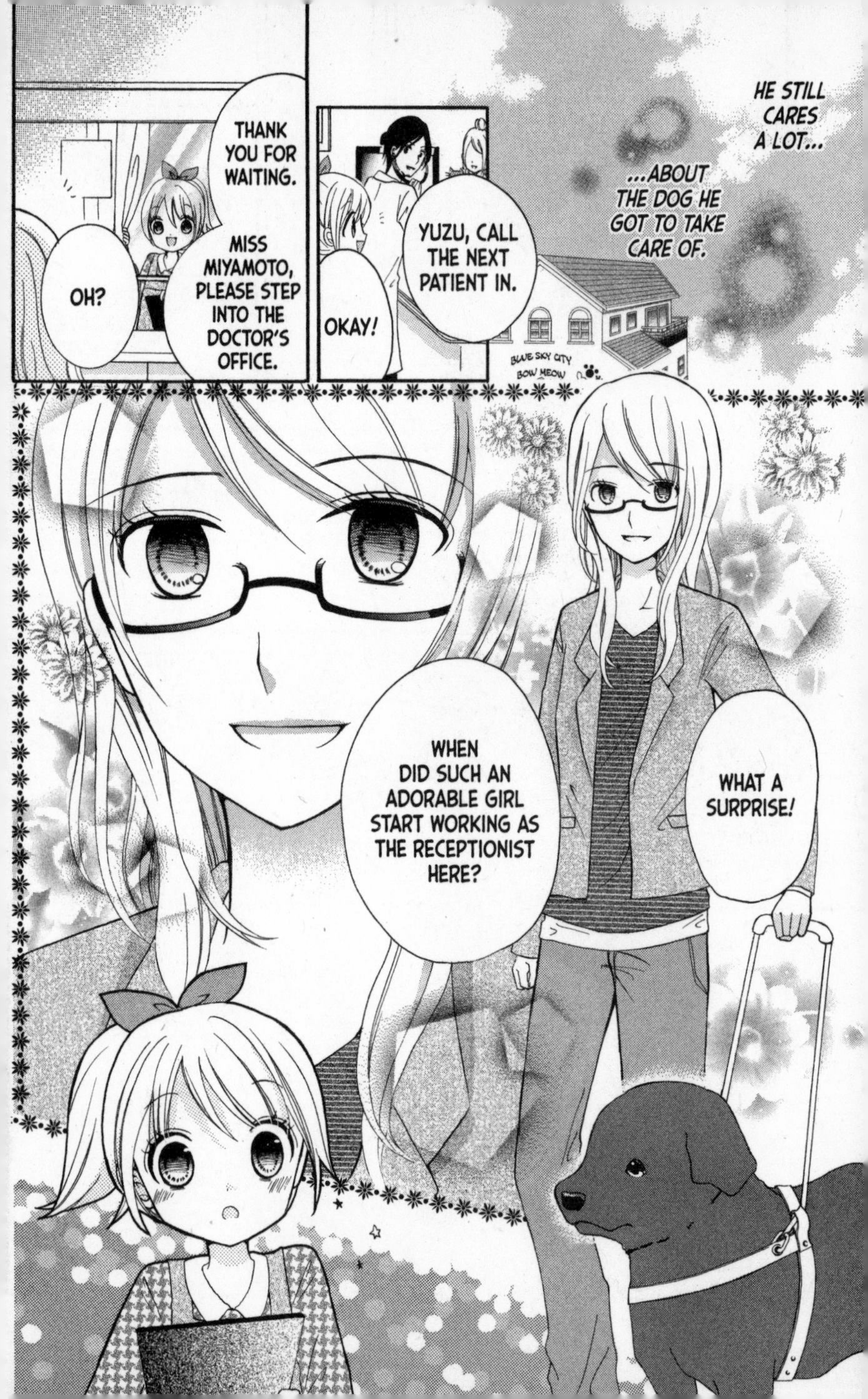
HE STILL CARES A LOT...
...ABOUT THE DOG HE GOT TO TAKE CARE OF.
BLUE SKY CITY BOW MEOW
YUZU, CALL THE NEXT PATIENT IN.
OKAY!
THANK YOU FOR WAITING.
MISS MIYAMOTO, PLEASE STEP INTO THE DOCTOR'S OFFICE.
OH?
WHAT A SURPRISE!
WHEN DID SUCH AN ADORABLE GIRL START WORKING AS THE RECEPTIONIST HERE?

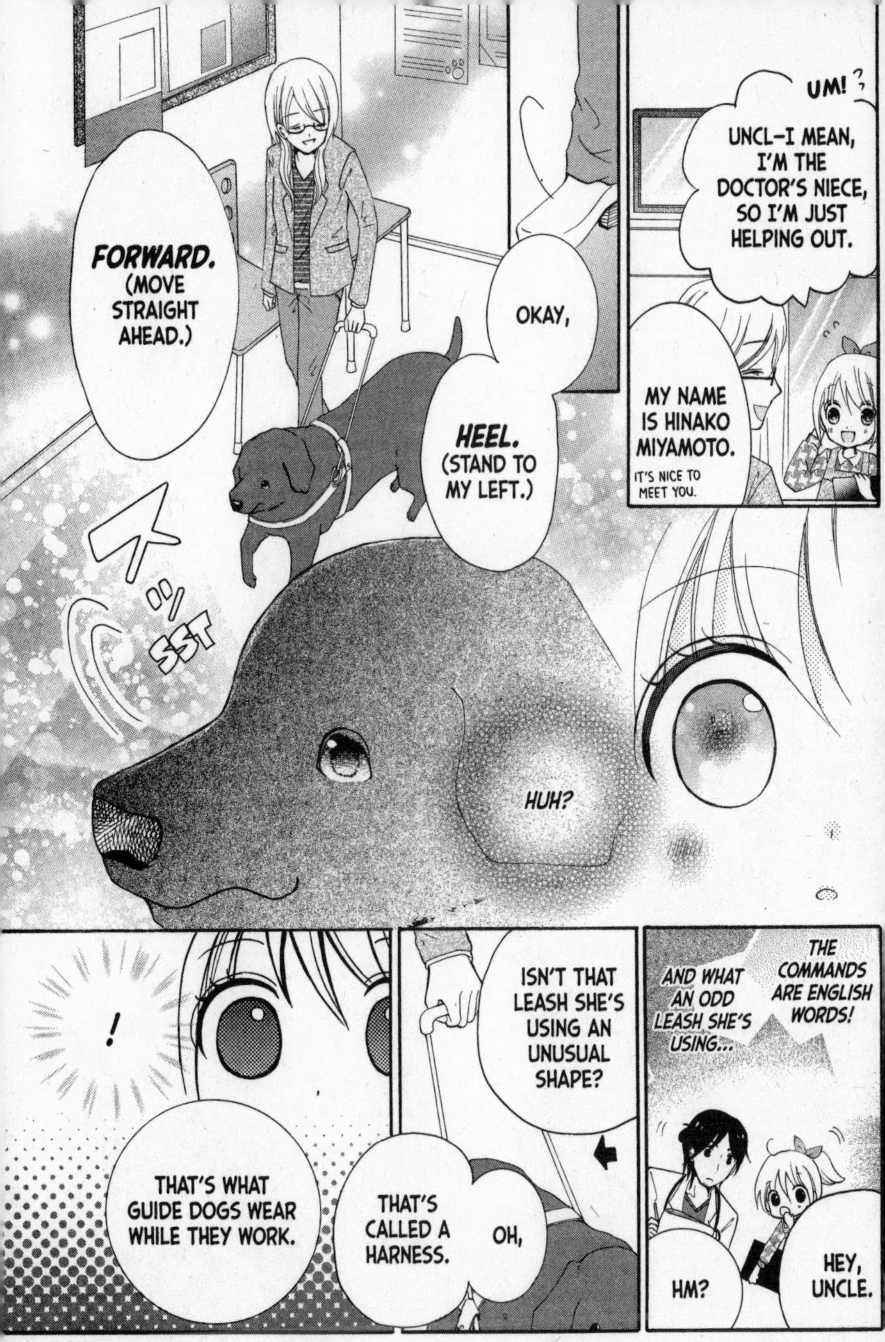

UM!
UNCL—I MEAN, I'M THE DOCTOR'S NIECE, SO I'M JUST HELPING OUT.
MY NAME IS HINAKO MIYAMOTO.
IT'S NICE TO MEET YOU.
OKAY,
HEEL. (STAND TO MY LEFT.)
FORWARD. (MOVE STRAIGHT AHEAD.)
SST
HUH?
THE COMMANDS ARE ENGLISH WORDS!
AND WHAT AN ODD LEASH SHE'S USING...
HEY, UNCLE.
HM?
ISN'T THAT LEASH SHE'S USING AN UNUSUAL SHAPE?
OH,
THAT'S CALLED A HARNESS.
!
THAT'S WHAT GUIDE DOGS WEAR WHILE THEY WORK.

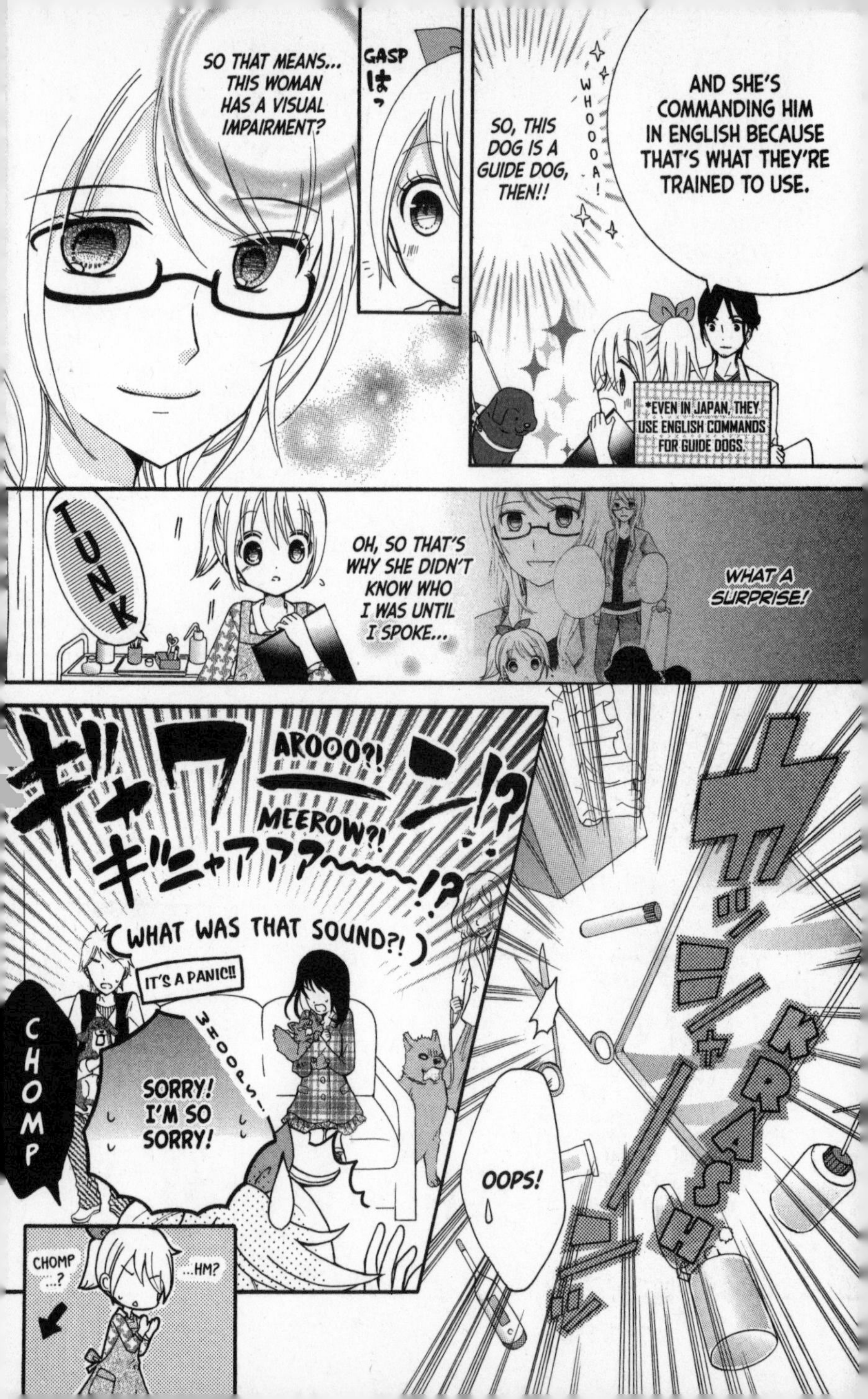
AND SHE'S COMMANDING HIM IN ENGLISH BECAUSE THAT'S WHAT THEY'RE TRAINED TO USE.
WHOOOA!
SO, THIS DOG IS A GUIDE DOG, THEN!!
*EVEN IN JAPAN, THEY USE ENGLISH COMMANDS FOR GUIDE DOGS.
GASP
はっ
SO THAT MEANS... THIS WOMAN HAS A VISUAL IMPAIRMENT?
WHAT A SURPRISE!
OH, SO THAT'S WHY SHE DIDN'T KNOW WHO I WAS UNTIL I SPOKE...
TUNK
KRASH
OOPS!
AROOO?!
ギャワーン!?
MEEROW?!
ギニャアアア〜〜!?
(WHAT WAS THAT SOUND?!)
IT'S A PANIC!!
WHOOPS!
SORRY! I'M SO SORRY!
CHOMP
...HM?
CHOMP ...?

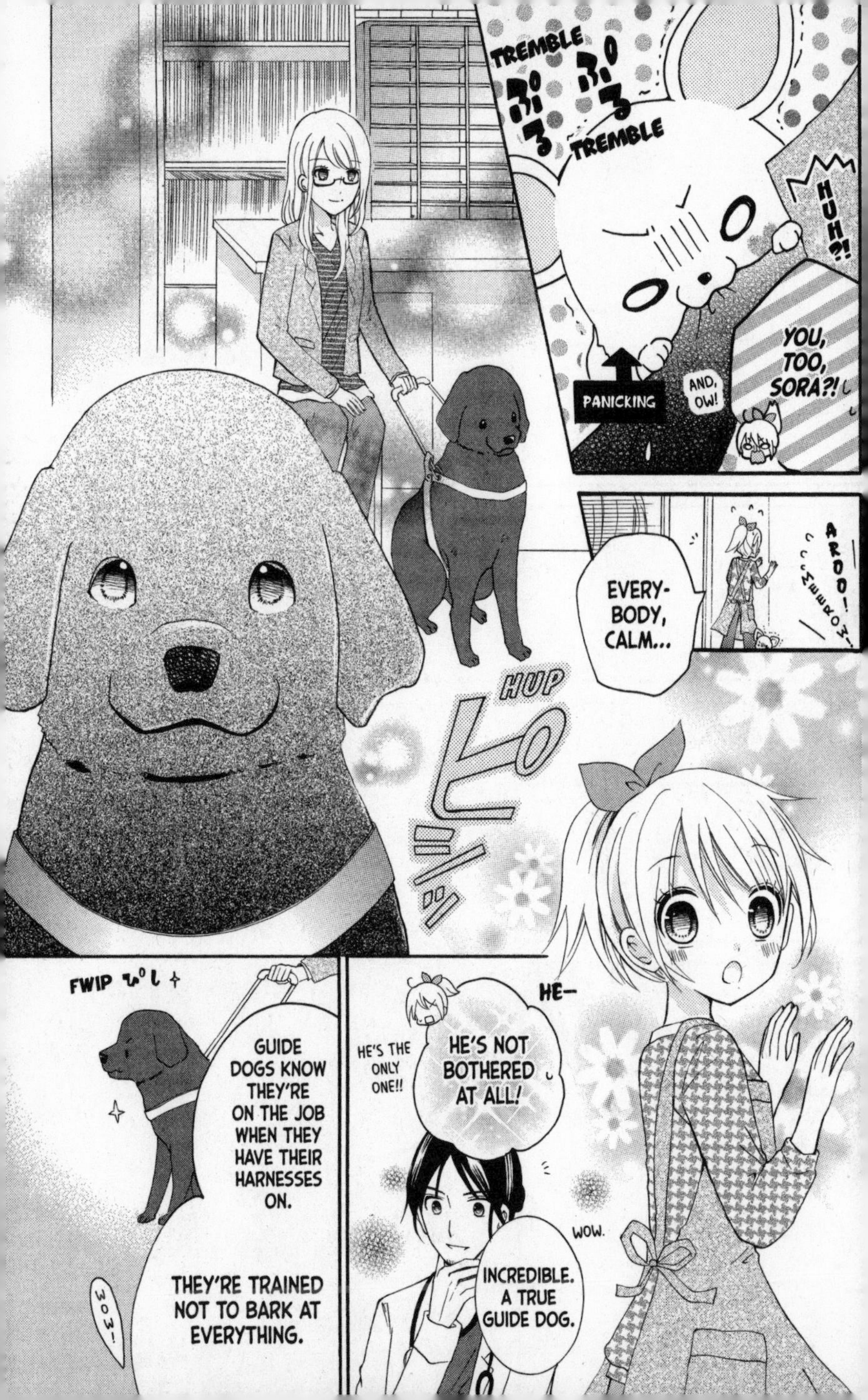
HUH?!
TREMBLE
TREMBLE
YOU, TOO, SORA?!
AND, OW!
PANICKING
AROOO!
EVERY-BODY, CALM...
HUP
HE-
HE'S NOT BOTHERED AT ALL!
HE'S THE ONLY ONE!!
WOW.
INCREDIBLE. A TRUE GUIDE DOG.
FWIP
GUIDE DOGS KNOW THEY'RE ON THE JOB WHEN THEY HAVE THEIR HARNESSES ON.
THEY'RE TRAINED NOT TO BARK AT EVERYTHING.
WOW!

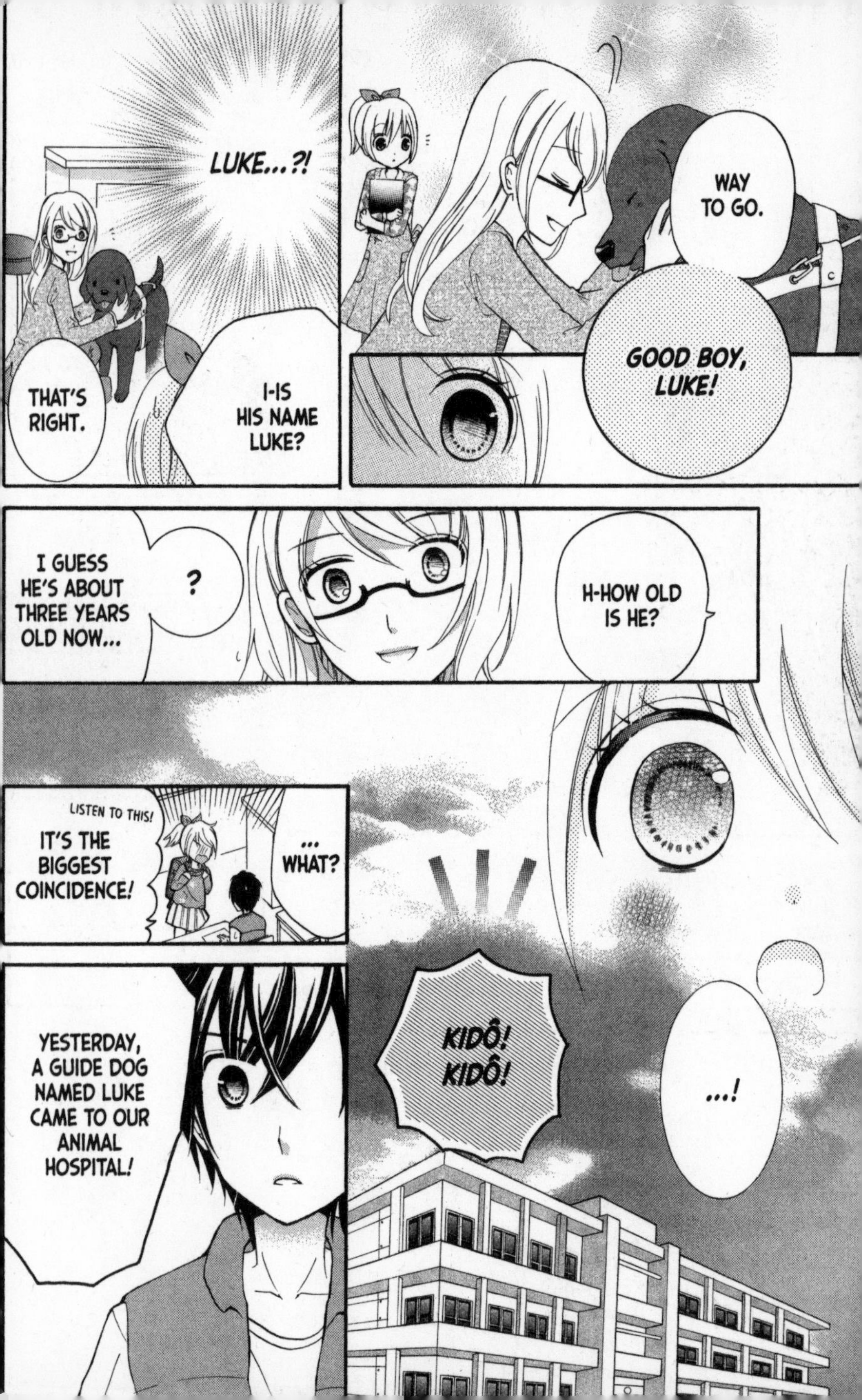
WAY TO GO.
GOOD BOY, LUKE!
LUKE...?!
I-IS HIS NAME LUKE?
THAT'S RIGHT.
H-HOW OLD IS HE?
?
I GUESS HE'S ABOUT THREE YEARS OLD NOW...
...!
KIDÔ! KIDÔ!
... WHAT?
LISTEN TO THIS!
IT'S THE BIGGEST COINCIDENCE!
YESTERDAY, A GUIDE DOG NAMED LUKE CAME TO OUR ANIMAL HOSPITAL!

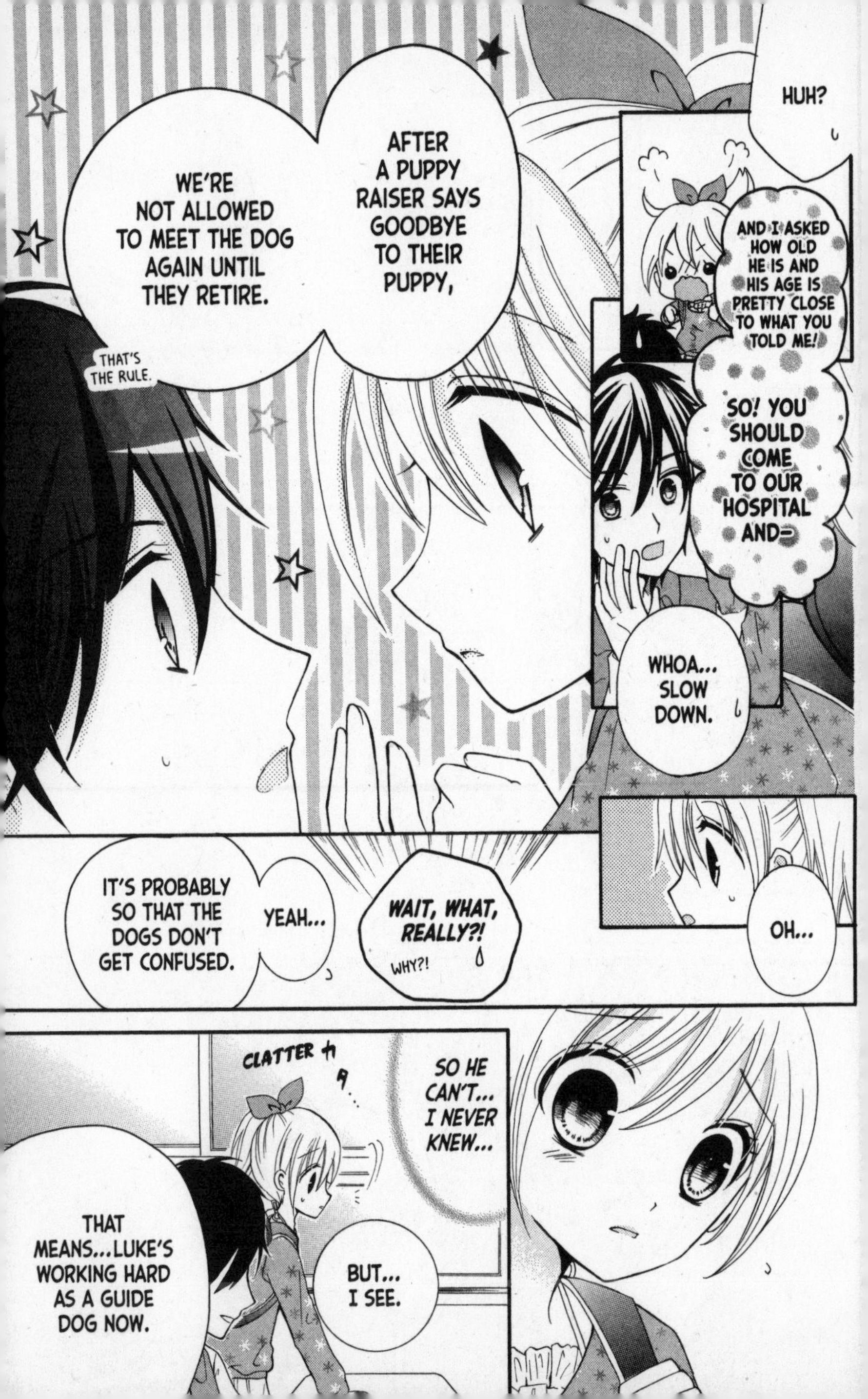
HUH?
AND I ASKED HOW OLD HE IS AND HIS AGE IS PRETTY CLOSE TO WHAT YOU TOLD ME!
SO! YOU SHOULD COME TO OUR HOSPITAL AND—
WHOA... SLOW DOWN.
AFTER A PUPPY RAISER SAYS GOODBYE TO THEIR PUPPY,
WE'RE NOT ALLOWED TO MEET THE DOG AGAIN UNTIL THEY RETIRE.
THAT'S THE RULE.
OH...
WAIT, WHAT, REALLY?!
WHY?!
YEAH...
IT'S PROBABLY SO THAT THE DOGS DON'T GET CONFUSED.
SO HE CAN'T... I NEVER KNEW...
CLATTER
BUT... I SEE.
THAT MEANS...LUKE'S WORKING HARD AS A GUIDE DOG NOW.

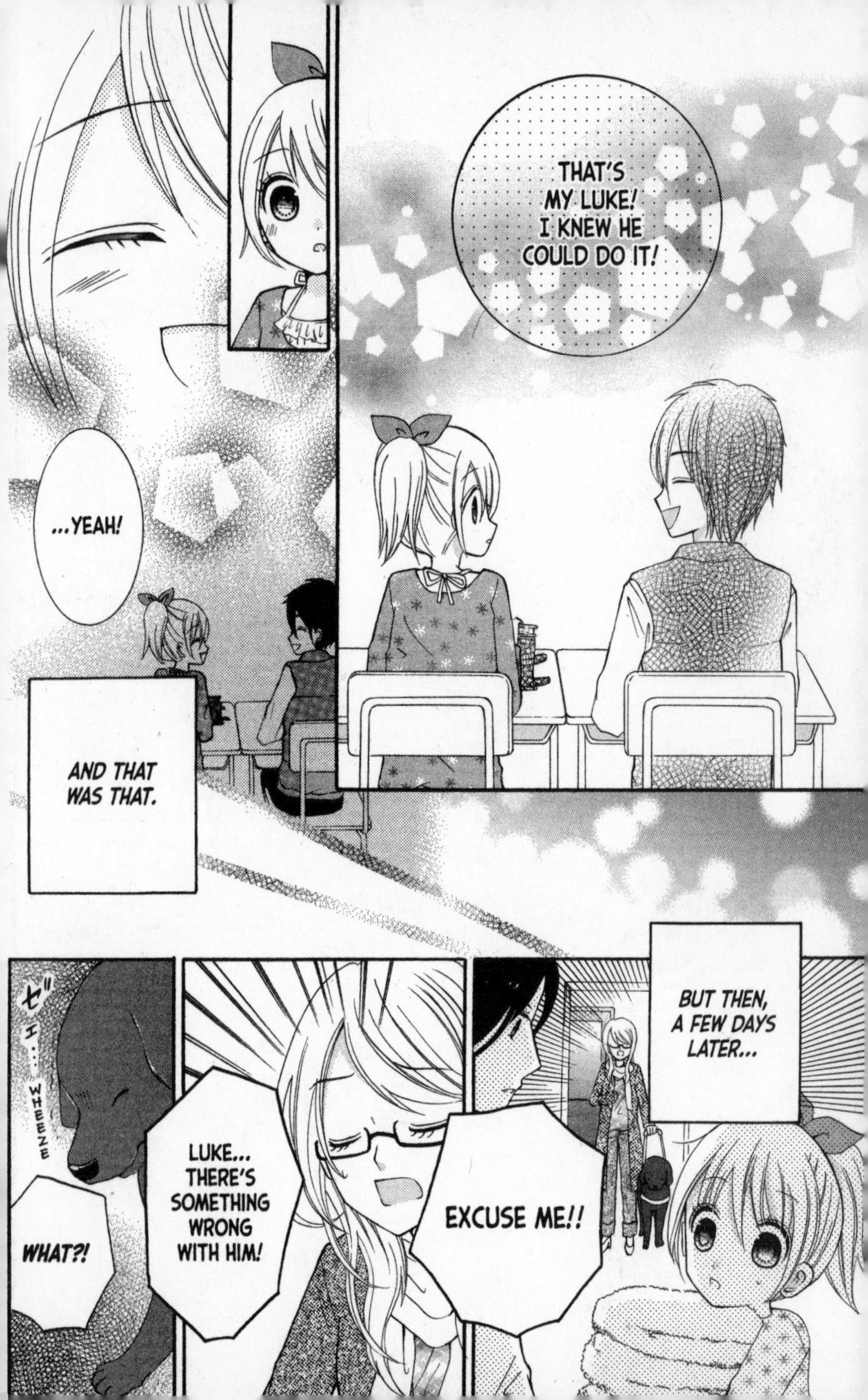
THAT'S MY LUKE! I KNEW HE COULD DO IT!
...YEAH!
AND THAT WAS THAT.
BUT THEN, A FEW DAYS LATER...
EXCUSE ME!!
LUKE... THERE'S SOMETHING WRONG WITH HIM!
ゼェ… WHEEZE
WHAT?!

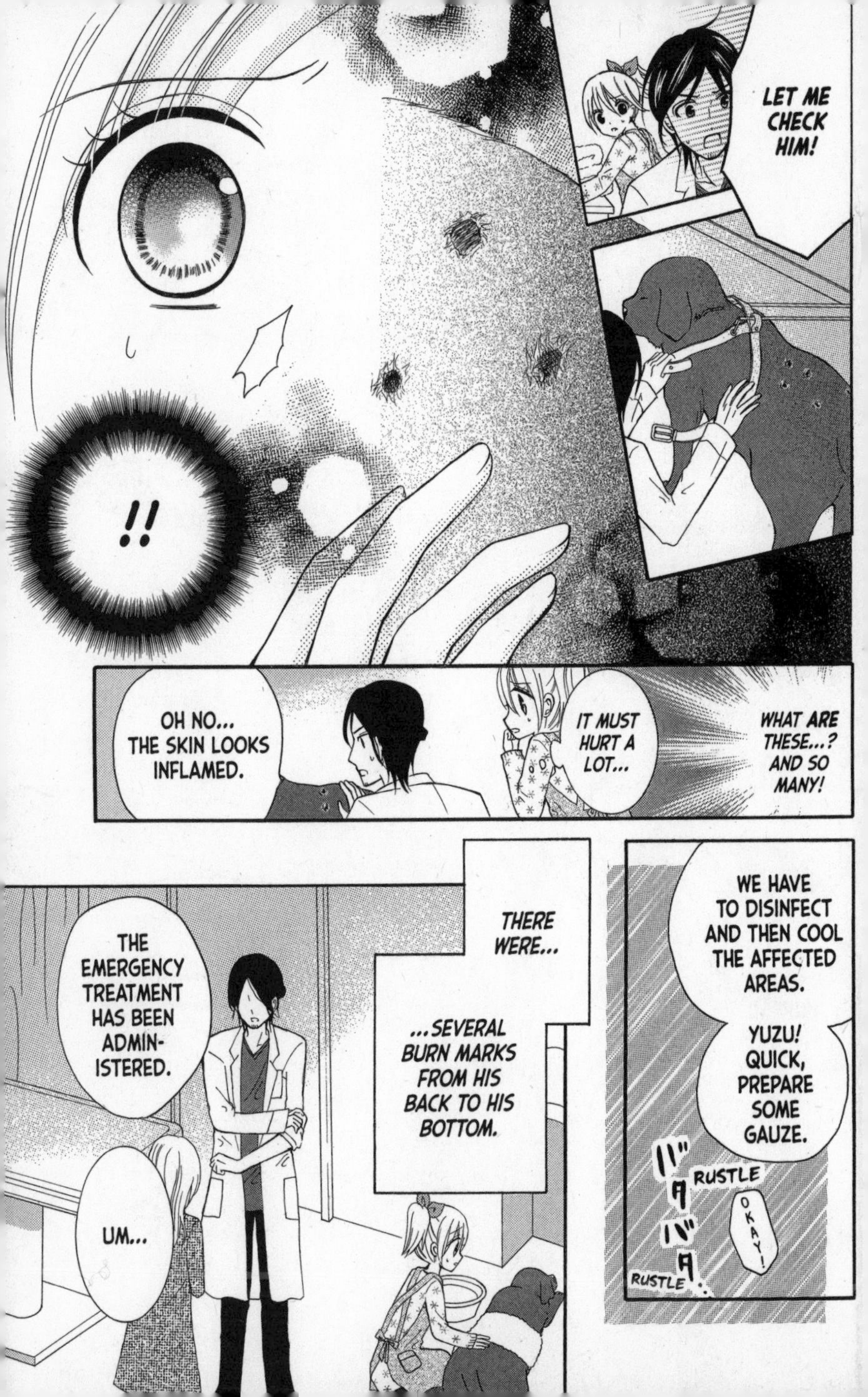
LET ME CHECK HIM!
!!
WHAT ARE THESE...? AND SO MANY!
IT MUST HURT A LOT...
OH NO... THE SKIN LOOKS INFLAMED.
WE HAVE TO DISINFECT AND THEN COOL THE AFFECTED AREAS.
YUZU! QUICK, PREPARE SOME GAUZE.
OKAY!
バタバタ
RUSTLE
RUSTLE
THERE WERE...
...SEVERAL BURN MARKS FROM HIS BACK TO HIS BOTTOM.
THE EMERGENCY TREATMENT HAS BEEN ADMIN-ISTERED.
UM...

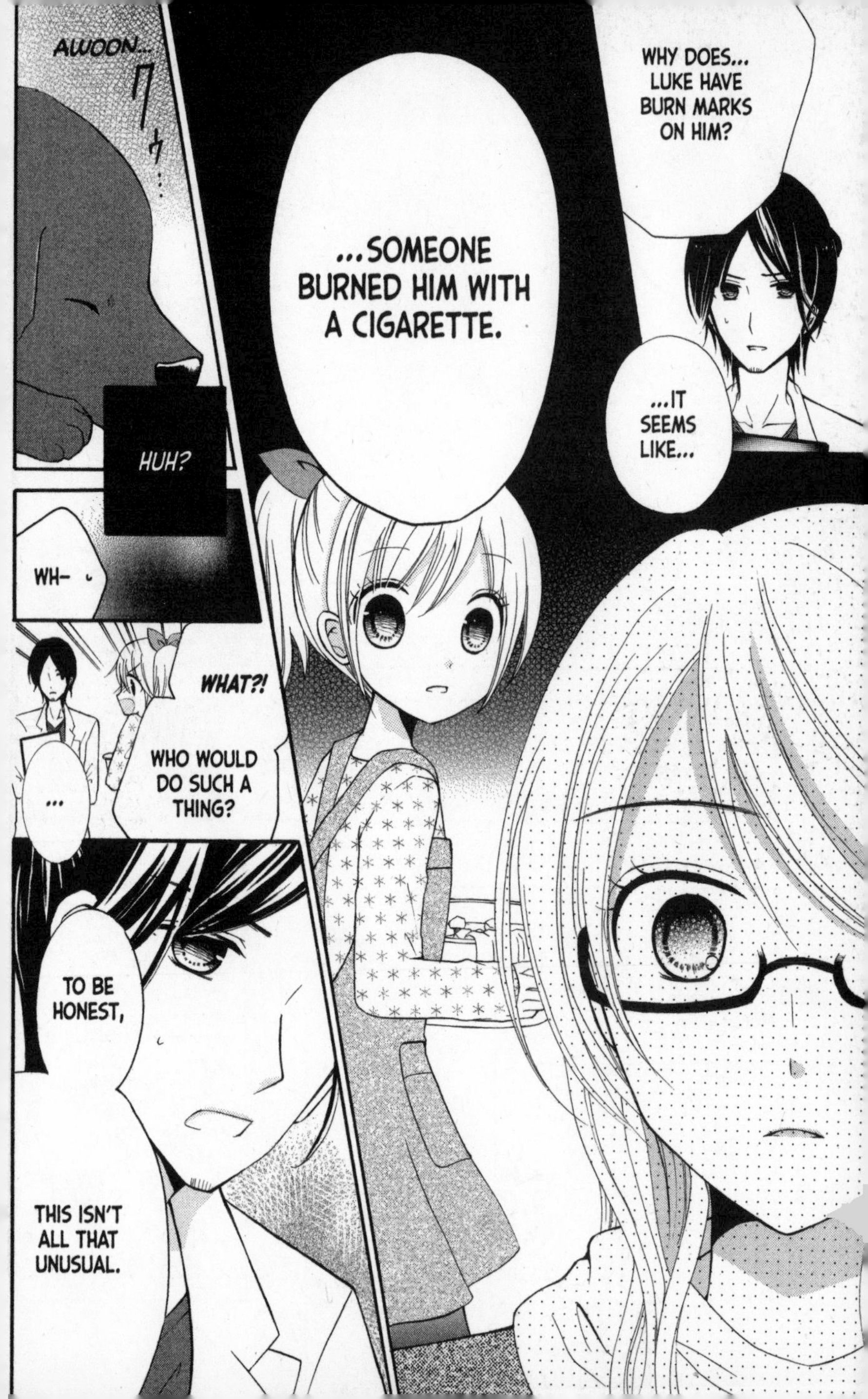
WHY DOES... LUKE HAVE BURN MARKS ON HIM?
...IT SEEMS LIKE...
...SOMEONE BURNED HIM WITH A CIGARETTE.
AWOON...
HUH?
WH-
WHAT?!
WHO WOULD DO SUCH A THING?
...
TO BE HONEST,
THIS ISN'T ALL THAT UNUSUAL.

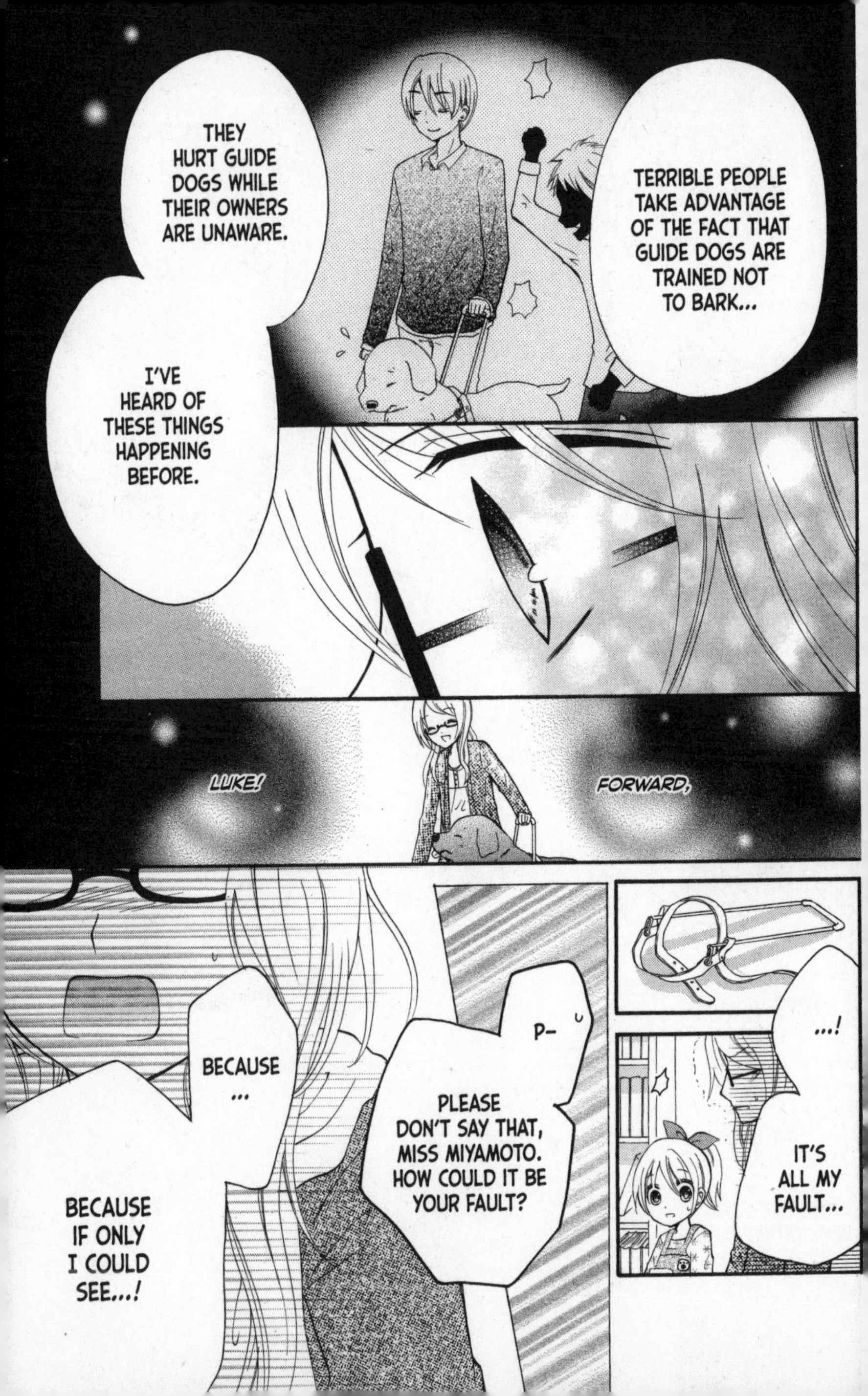
TERRIBLE PEOPLE TAKE ADVANTAGE OF THE FACT THAT GUIDE DOGS ARE TRAINED NOT TO BARK...
THEY HURT GUIDE DOGS WHILE THEIR OWNERS ARE UNAWARE.
I'VE HEARD OF THESE THINGS HAPPENING BEFORE.
FORWARD,
LUKE!
...!
IT'S ALL MY FAULT...
P-
PLEASE DON'T SAY THAT, MISS MIYAMOTO. HOW COULD IT BE YOUR FAULT?
BECAUSE ...
BECAUSE IF ONLY I COULD SEE...!

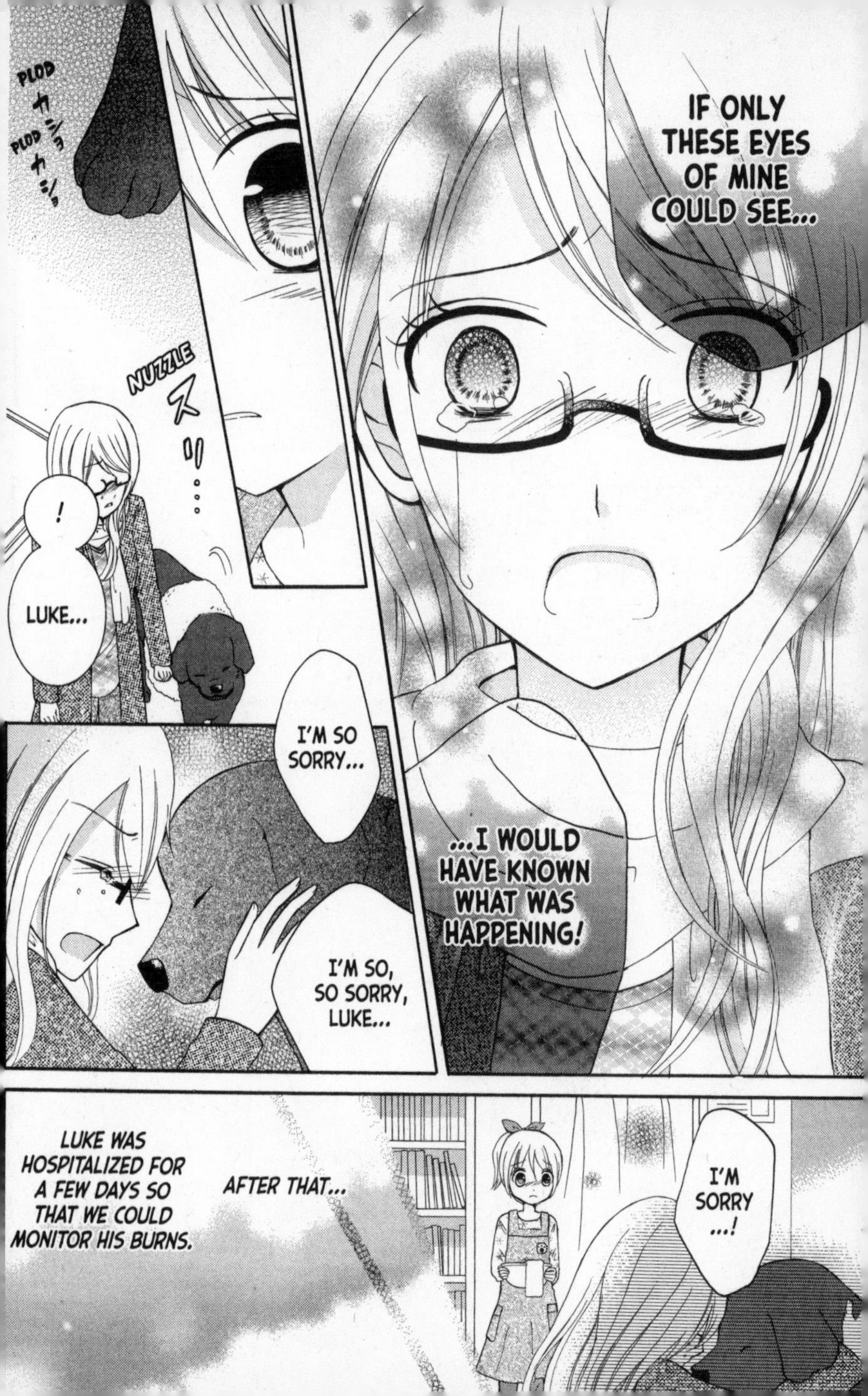
IF ONLY THESE EYES OF MINE COULD SEE...
...I WOULD HAVE KNOWN WHAT WAS HAPPENING!
PLOD
PLOD
NUZZLE
!
LUKE...
I'M SO SORRY...
I'M SO, SO SORRY, LUKE...
I'M SORRY ...!
AFTER THAT...
LUKE WAS HOSPITALIZED FOR A FEW DAYS SO THAT WE COULD MONITOR HIS BURNS.

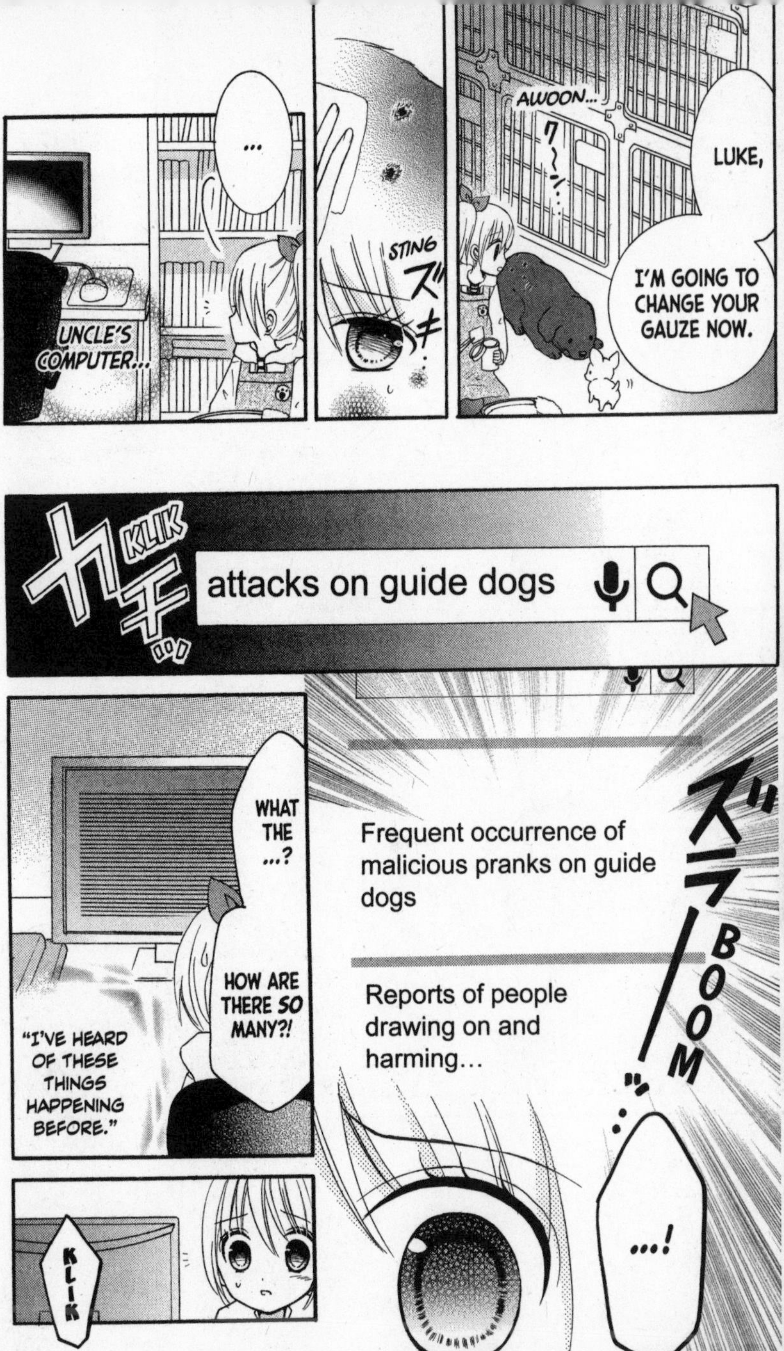
AWOON...
LUKE,
I'M GOING TO CHANGE YOUR GAUZE NOW.
STING
...
UNCLE'S COMPUTER...
KLIK
attacks on guide dogs
Frequent occurrence of malicious pranks on guide dogs
Reports of people drawing on and harming…
BOOM
...!
WHAT THE ...?
HOW ARE THERE SO MANY?!
"I'VE HEARD OF THESE THINGS HAPPENING BEFORE."
KLIK

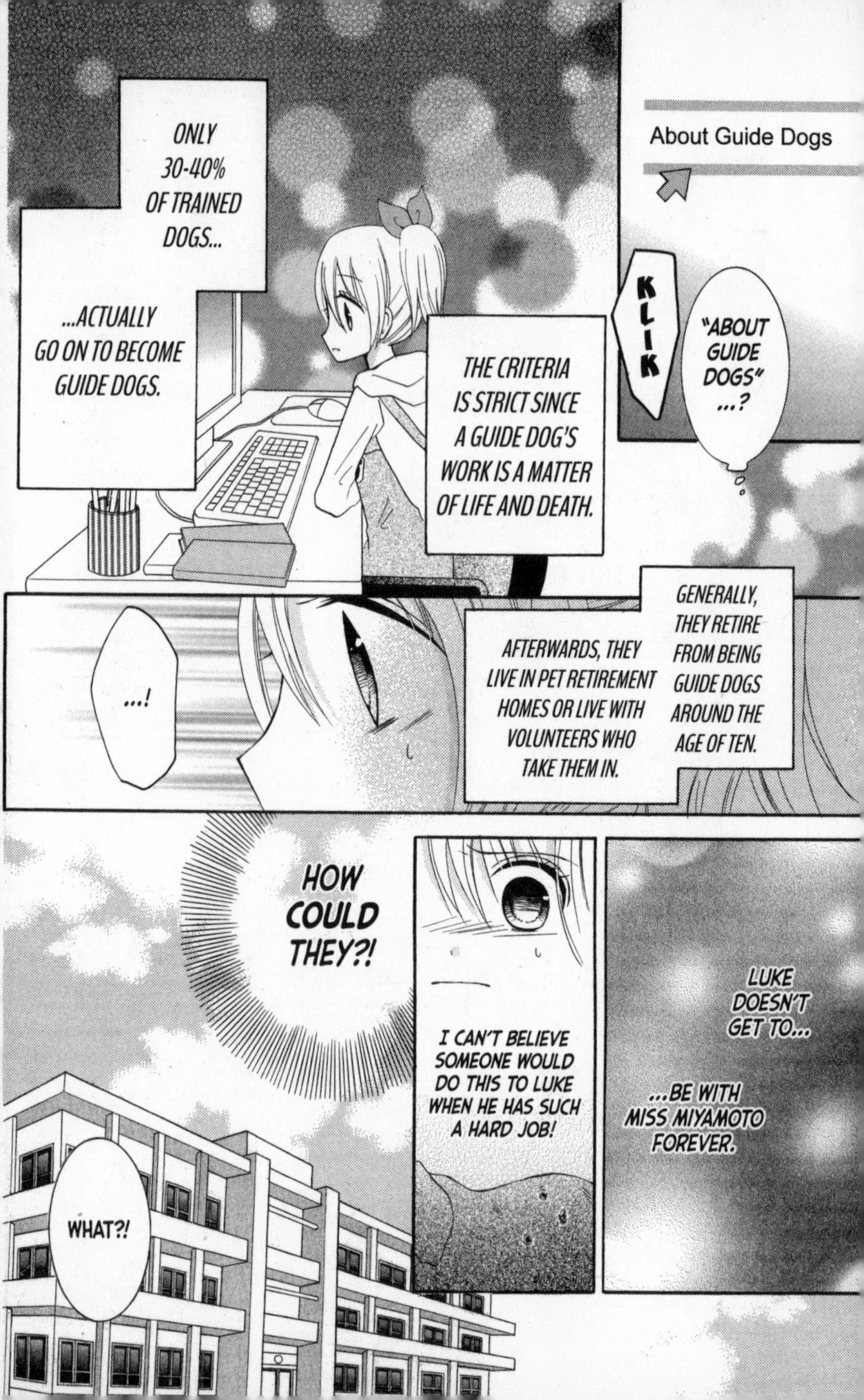
About Guide Dogs
KLIK
"ABOUT GUIDE DOGS" ...?
ONLY 30-40% OF TRAINED DOGS...
...ACTUALLY GO ON TO BECOME GUIDE DOGS.
THE CRITERIA IS STRICT SINCE A GUIDE DOG'S WORK IS A MATTER OF LIFE AND DEATH.
GENERALLY, THEY RETIRE FROM BEING GUIDE DOGS AROUND THE AGE OF TEN.
AFTERWARDS, THEY LIVE IN PET RETIREMENT HOMES OR LIVE WITH VOLUNTEERS WHO TAKE THEM IN.
...!
LUKE DOESN'T GET TO...
...BE WITH MISS MIYAMOTO FOREVER.
I CAN'T BELIEVE SOMEONE WOULD DO THIS TO LUKE WHEN HE HAS SUCH A HARD JOB!
HOW COULD THEY?!
WHAT?!

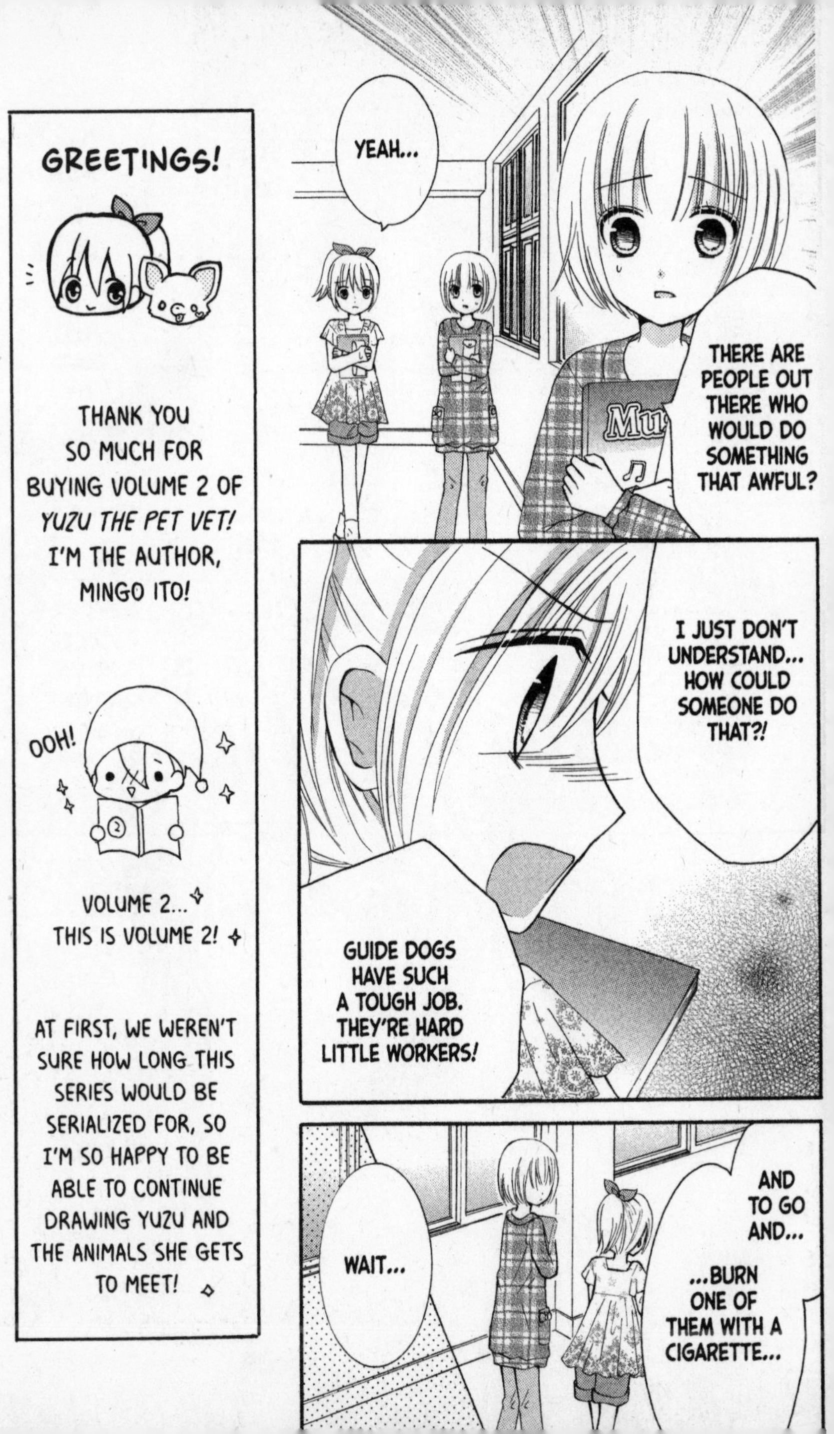
THERE ARE PEOPLE OUT THERE WHO WOULD DO SOMETHING THAT AWFUL?
YEAH...
I JUST DON'T UNDERSTAND... HOW COULD SOMEONE DO THAT?!
GUIDE DOGS HAVE SUCH A TOUGH JOB. THEY'RE HARD LITTLE WORKERS!
AND TO GO AND...
...BURN ONE OF THEM WITH A CIGARETTE...
WAIT...

GREETINGS!

THANK YOU SO MUCH FOR BUYING VOLUME 2 OF *YUZU THE PET VET!* I'M THE AUTHOR, MINGO ITO!

OOH!

VOLUME 2... THIS IS VOLUME 2!

AT FIRST, WE WEREN'T SURE HOW LONG THIS SERIES WOULD BE SERIALIZED FOR, SO I'M SO HAPPY TO BE ABLE TO CONTINUE DRAWING YUZU AND THE ANIMALS SHE GETS TO MEET!

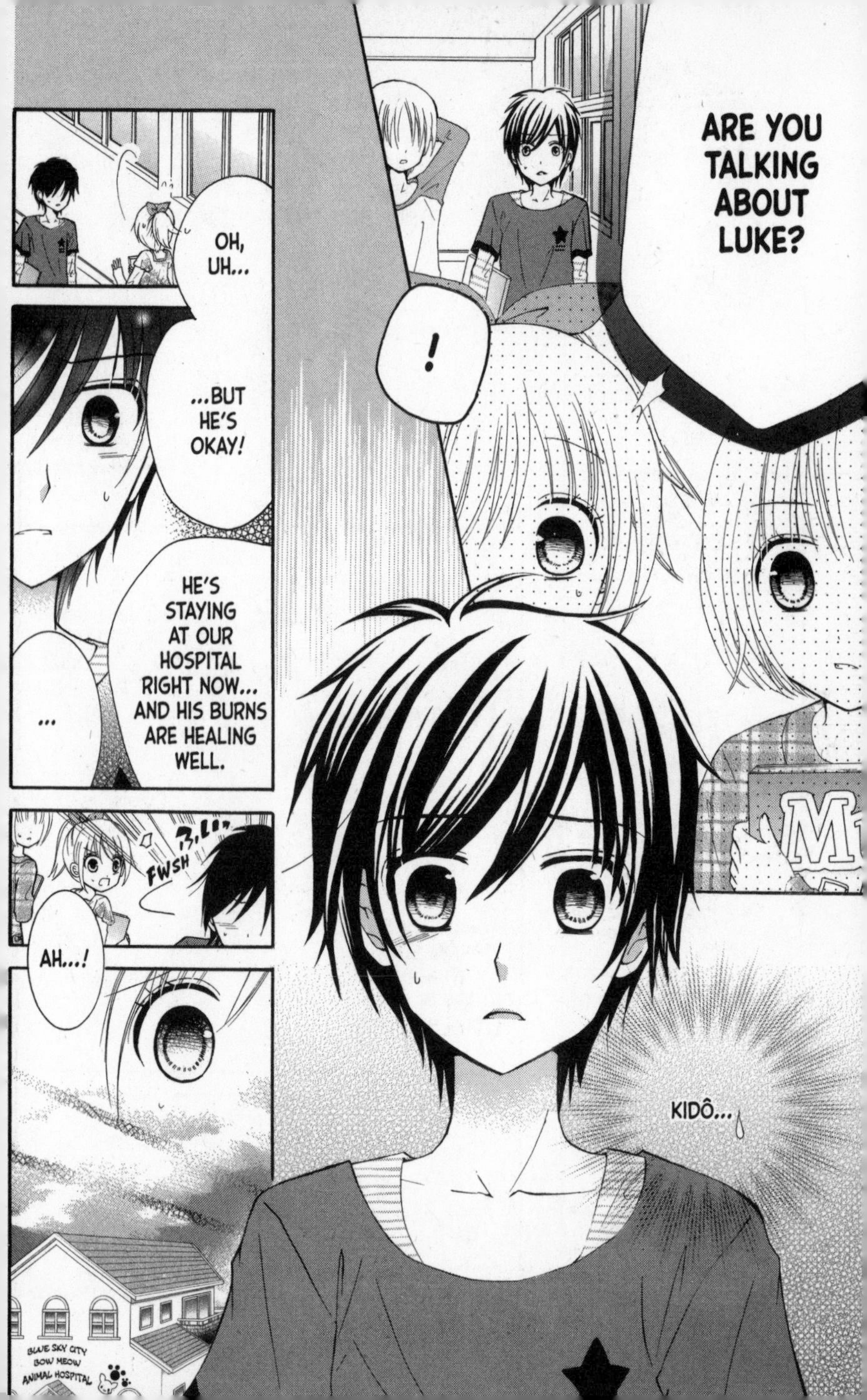
ARE YOU TALKING ABOUT LUKE?
!
KIDÔ...
OH, UH...
...BUT HE'S OKAY!
HE'S STAYING AT OUR HOSPITAL RIGHT NOW... AND HIS BURNS ARE HEALING WELL.
...
FWSH
AH...!
BLUE SKY CITY BOW MEOW ANIMAL HOSPITAL

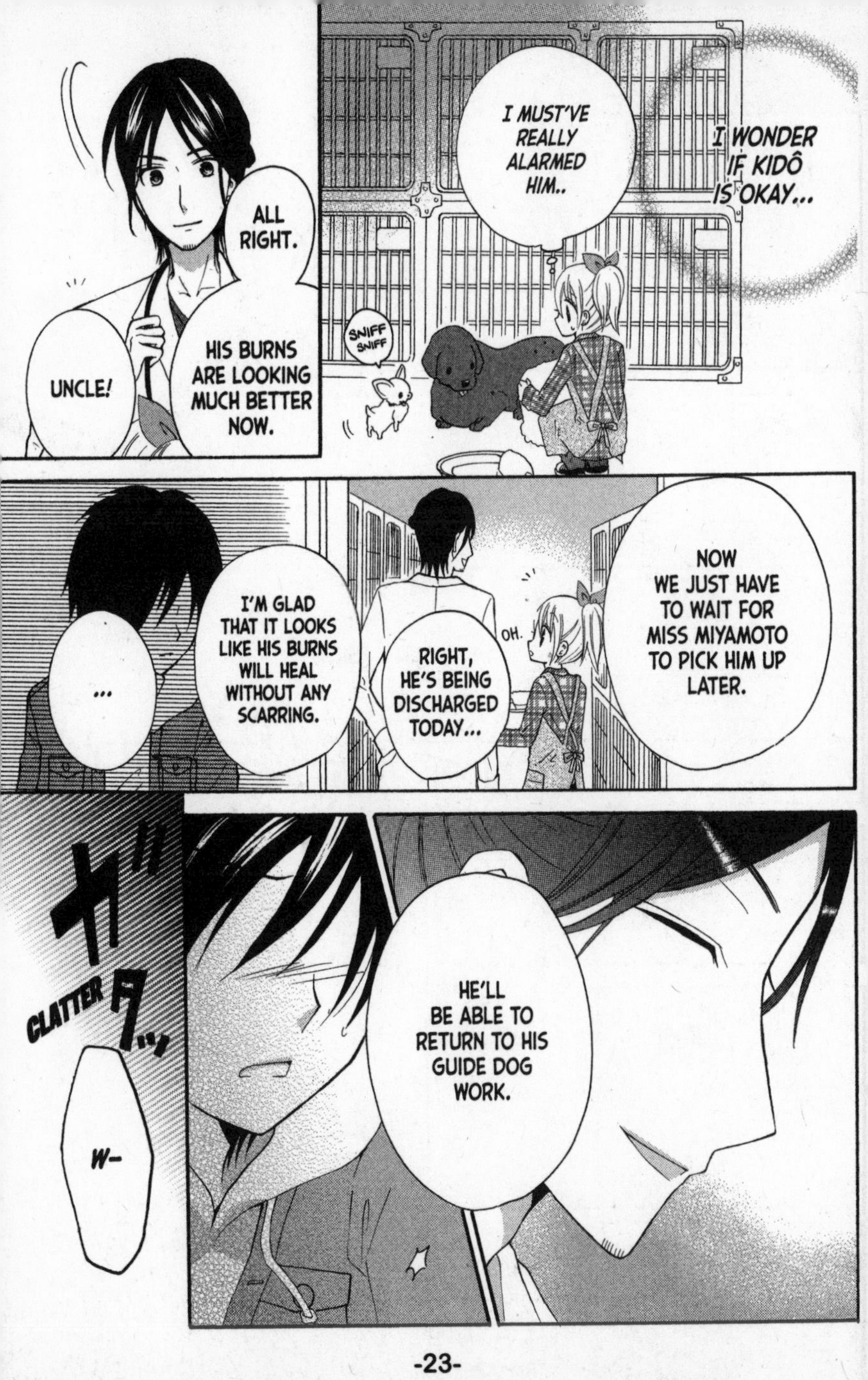
I WONDER IF KIDÔ IS OKAY...
I MUST'VE REALLY ALARMED HIM..
SNIFF SNIFF
ALL RIGHT.
HIS BURNS ARE LOOKING MUCH BETTER NOW.
UNCLE!
NOW WE JUST HAVE TO WAIT FOR MISS MIYAMOTO TO PICK HIM UP LATER.
OH.
RIGHT, HE'S BEING DISCHARGED TODAY...
I'M GLAD THAT IT LOOKS LIKE HIS BURNS WILL HEAL WITHOUT ANY SCARRING.
...
HE'LL BE ABLE TO RETURN TO HIS GUIDE DOG WORK.
CLATTER
W-

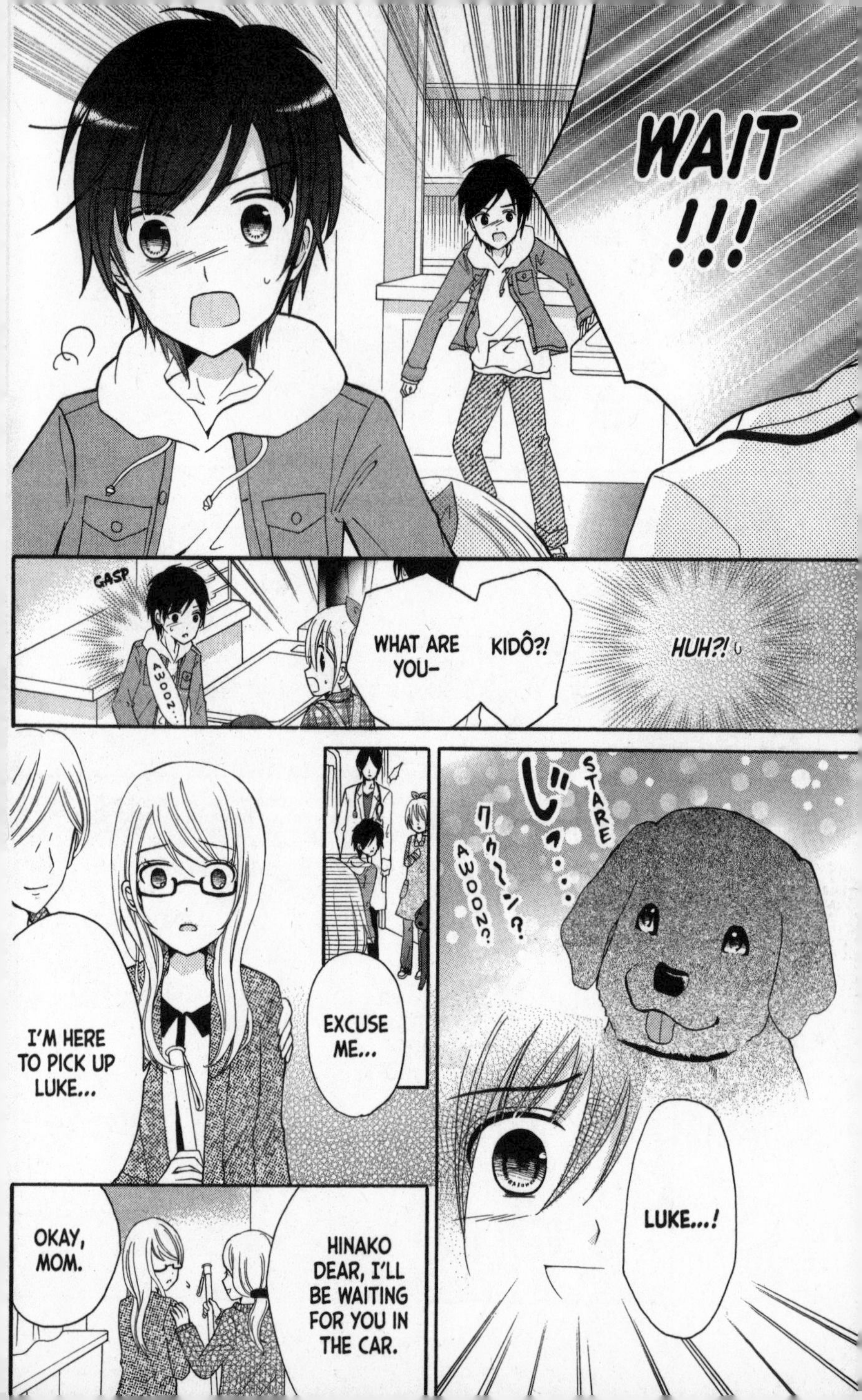
WAIT !!!
HUH?!
KIDÔ?!
WHAT ARE YOU-
GASP
AWOON...
STARE
じぃ…
クゥ～ン?
AWOON?
LUKE...!
EXCUSE ME...
I'M HERE TO PICK UP LUKE...
HINAKO DEAR, I'LL BE WAITING FOR YOU IN THE CAR.
OKAY, MOM.

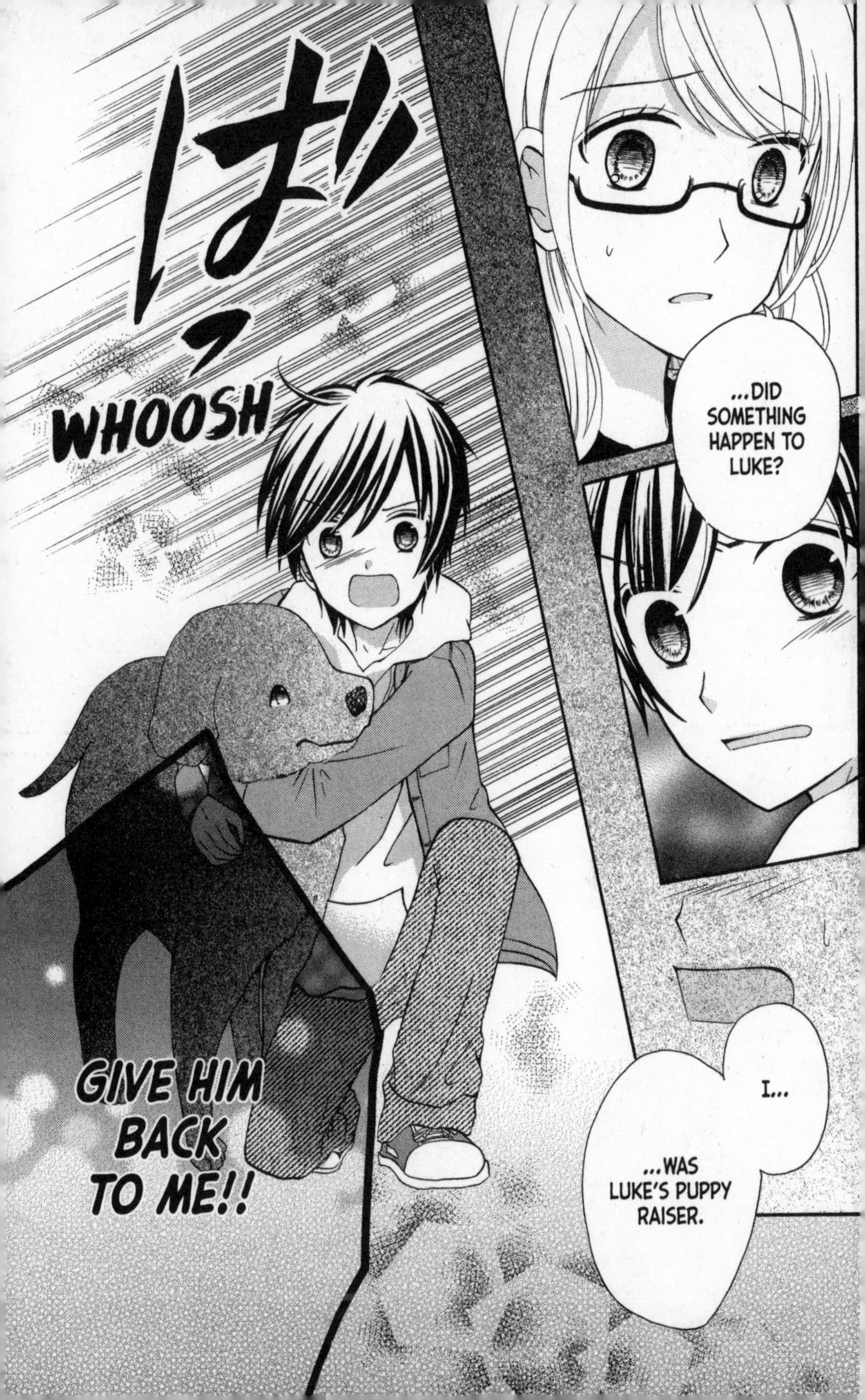
...DID SOMETHING HAPPEN TO LUKE?
I...
...WAS LUKE'S PUPPY RAISER.
はっ
WHOOSH
GIVE HIM BACK TO ME!!

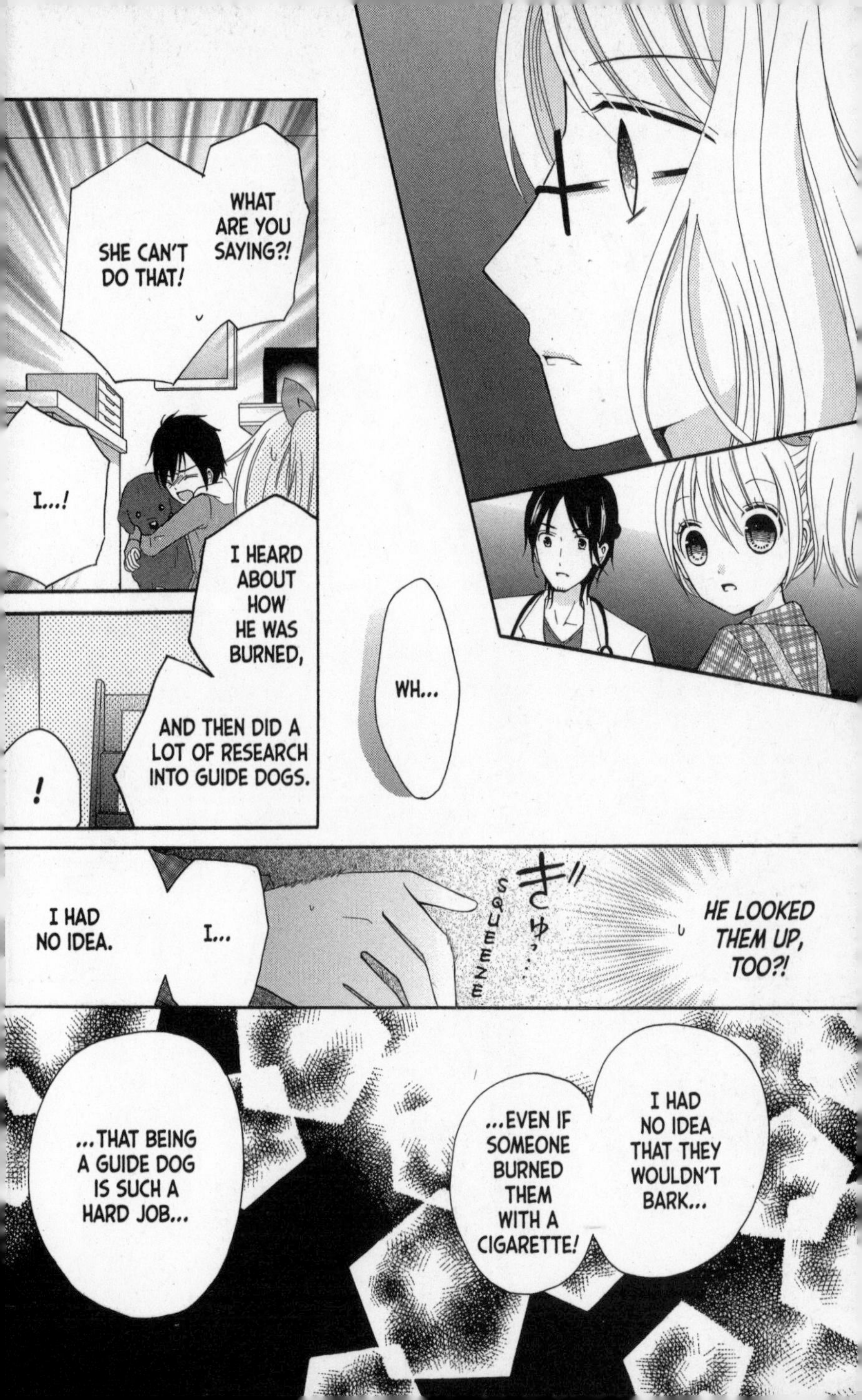
WH...
WHAT ARE YOU SAYING?!
SHE CAN'T DO THAT!
I...!
I HEARD ABOUT HOW HE WAS BURNED,
AND THEN DID A LOT OF RESEARCH INTO GUIDE DOGS.
!
HE LOOKED THEM UP, TOO?!
SQUEEZE
I...
I HAD NO IDEA.
I HAD NO IDEA THAT THEY WOULDN'T BARK...
...EVEN IF SOMEONE BURNED THEM WITH A CIGARETTE!
...THAT BEING A GUIDE DOG IS SUCH A HARD JOB...

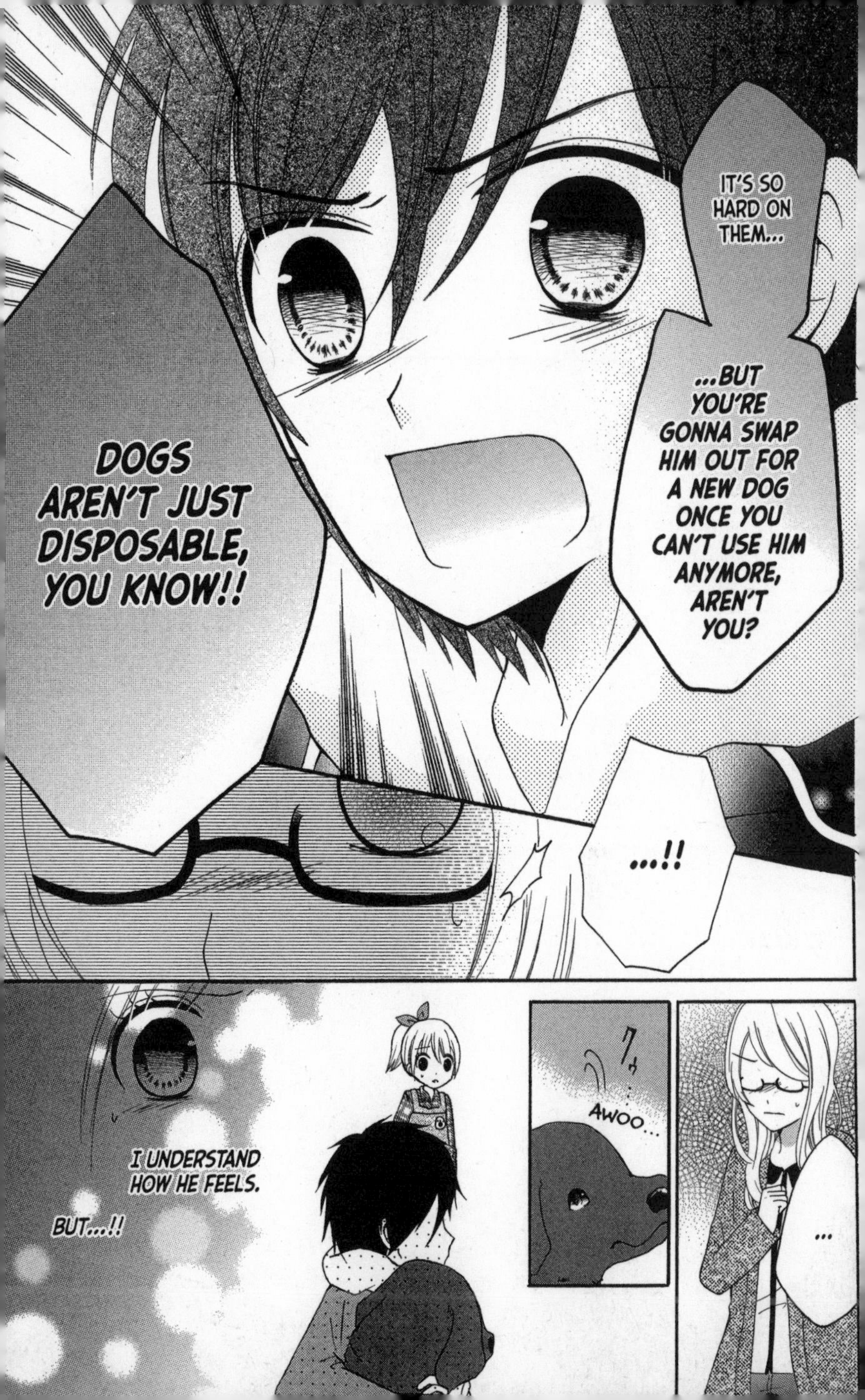
IT'S SO HARD ON THEM...
...BUT YOU'RE GONNA SWAP HIM OUT FOR A NEW DOG ONCE YOU CAN'T USE HIM ANYMORE, AREN'T YOU?
DOGS AREN'T JUST DISPOSABLE, YOU KNOW!!
...!!
...
AWOO...
I UNDERSTAND HOW HE FEELS.
BUT...!!

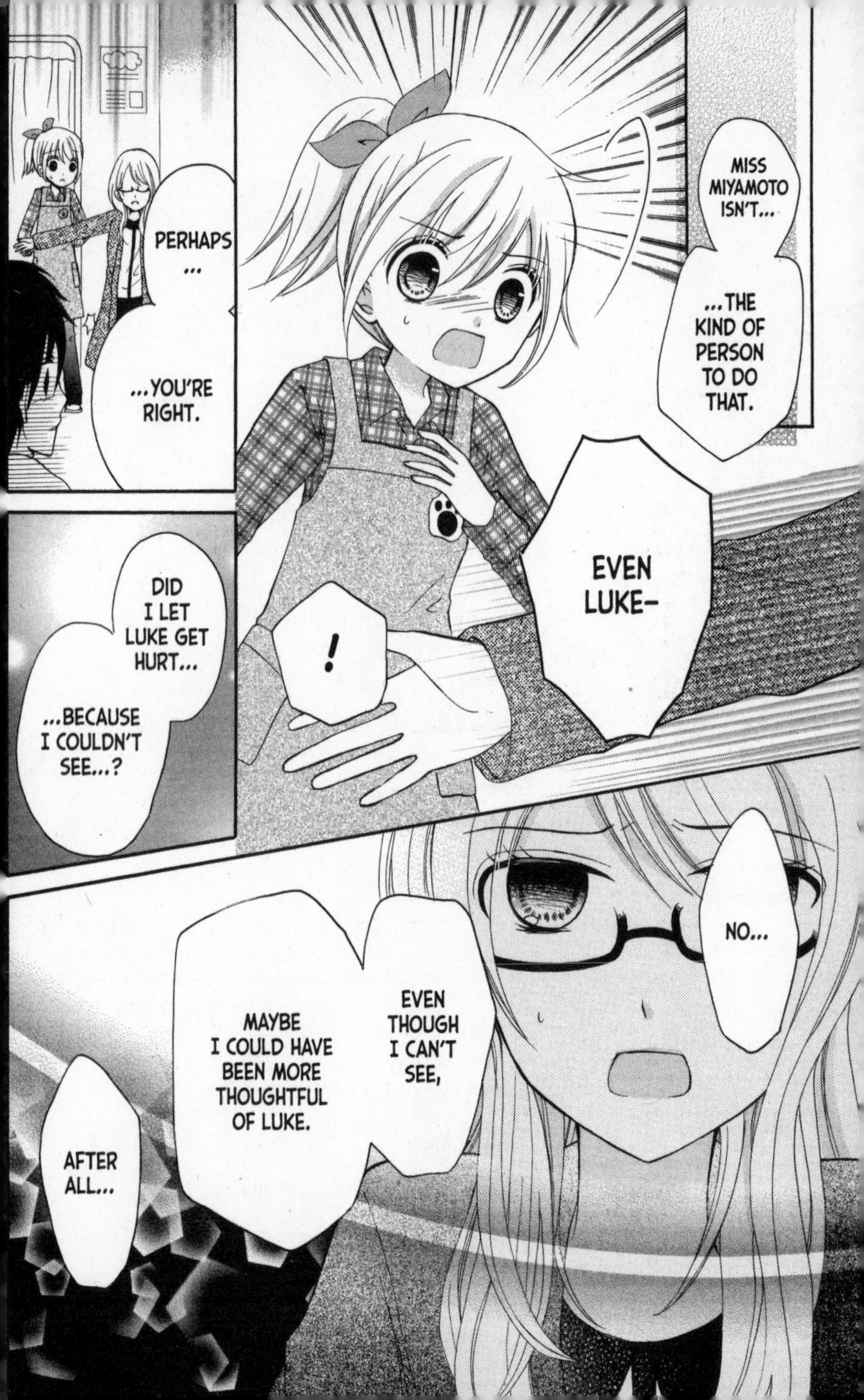

MISS MIYAMOTO ISN'T...
...THE KIND OF PERSON TO DO THAT.
EVEN LUKE–
!
PERHAPS...
...YOU'RE RIGHT.
DID I LET LUKE GET HURT...
...BECAUSE I COULDN'T SEE...?
NO...
EVEN THOUGH I CAN'T SEE,
MAYBE I COULD HAVE BEEN MORE THOUGHTFUL OF LUKE.
AFTER ALL...

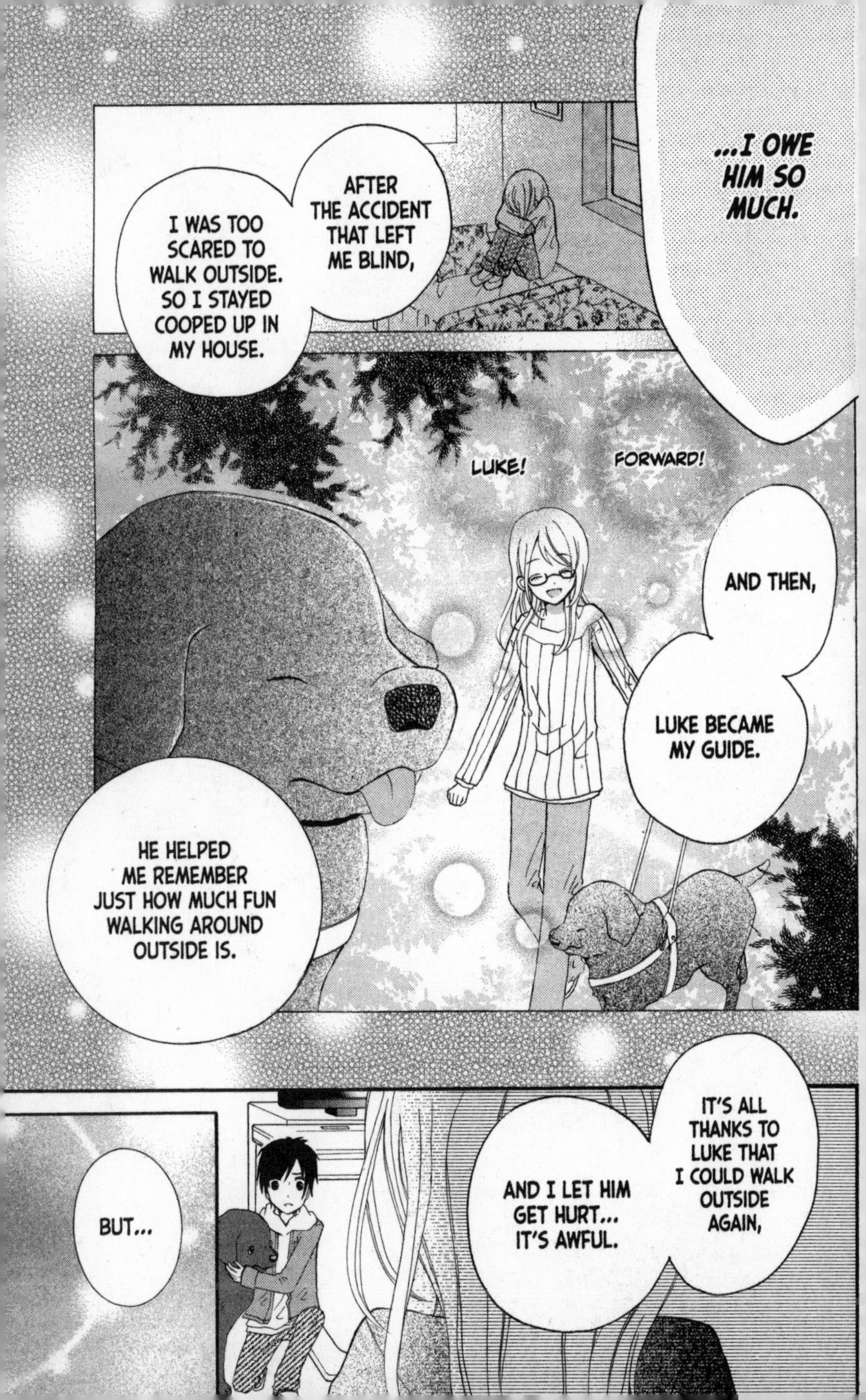
...I OWE HIM SO MUCH.
AFTER THE ACCIDENT THAT LEFT ME BLIND,
I WAS TOO SCARED TO WALK OUTSIDE. SO I STAYED COOPED UP IN MY HOUSE.
FORWARD!
LUKE!
AND THEN,
LUKE BECAME MY GUIDE.
HE HELPED ME REMEMBER JUST HOW MUCH FUN WALKING AROUND OUTSIDE IS.
IT'S ALL THANKS TO LUKE THAT I COULD WALK OUTSIDE AGAIN,
AND I LET HIM GET HURT... IT'S AWFUL.
BUT...

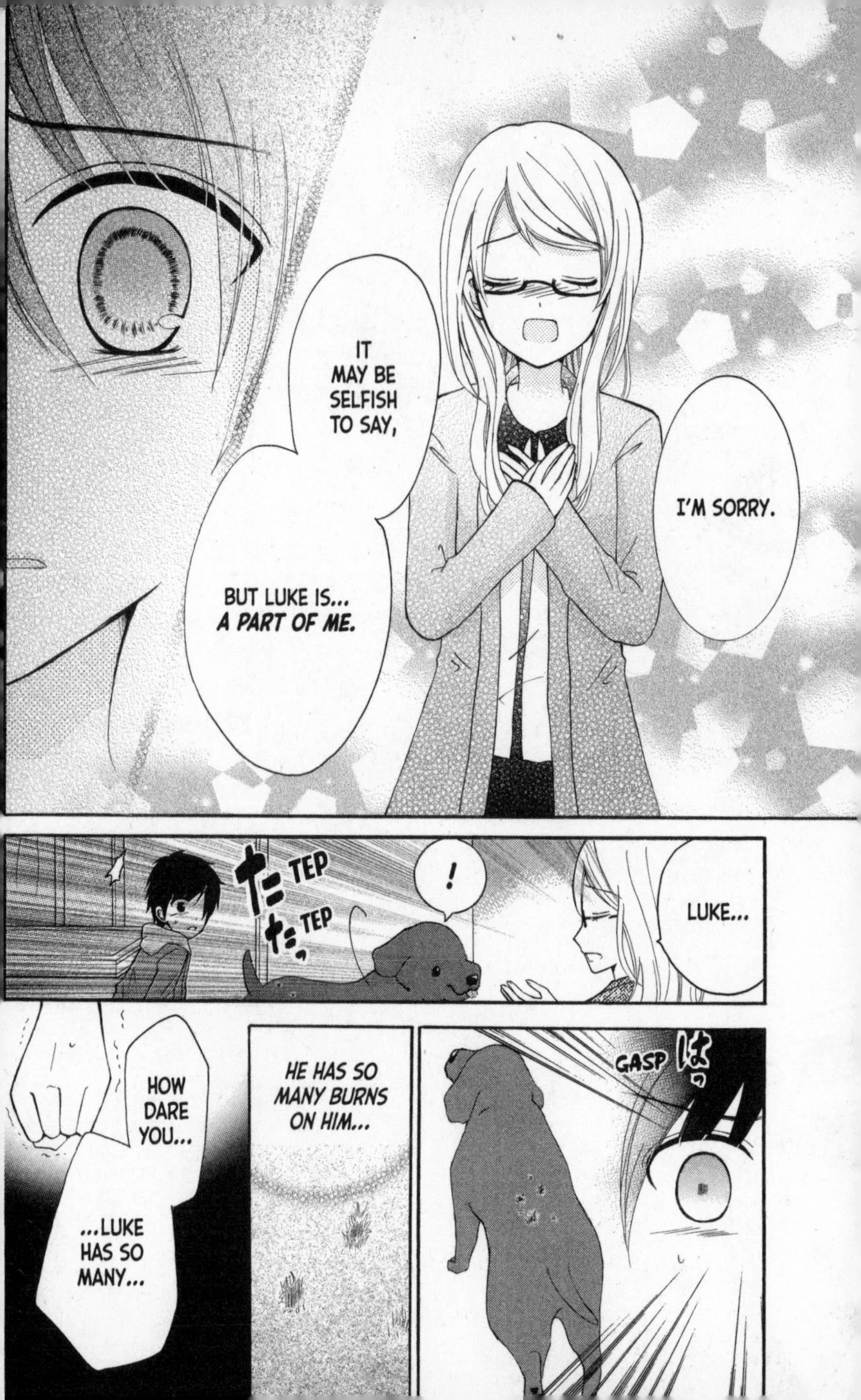
I'M SORRY.
IT MAY BE SELFISH TO SAY,
BUT LUKE IS... *A PART OF ME.*
LUKE...
!
TEP TEP
GASP はっ
HE HAS SO MANY BURNS ON HIM...
HOW DARE YOU...
...LUKE HAS SO MANY...

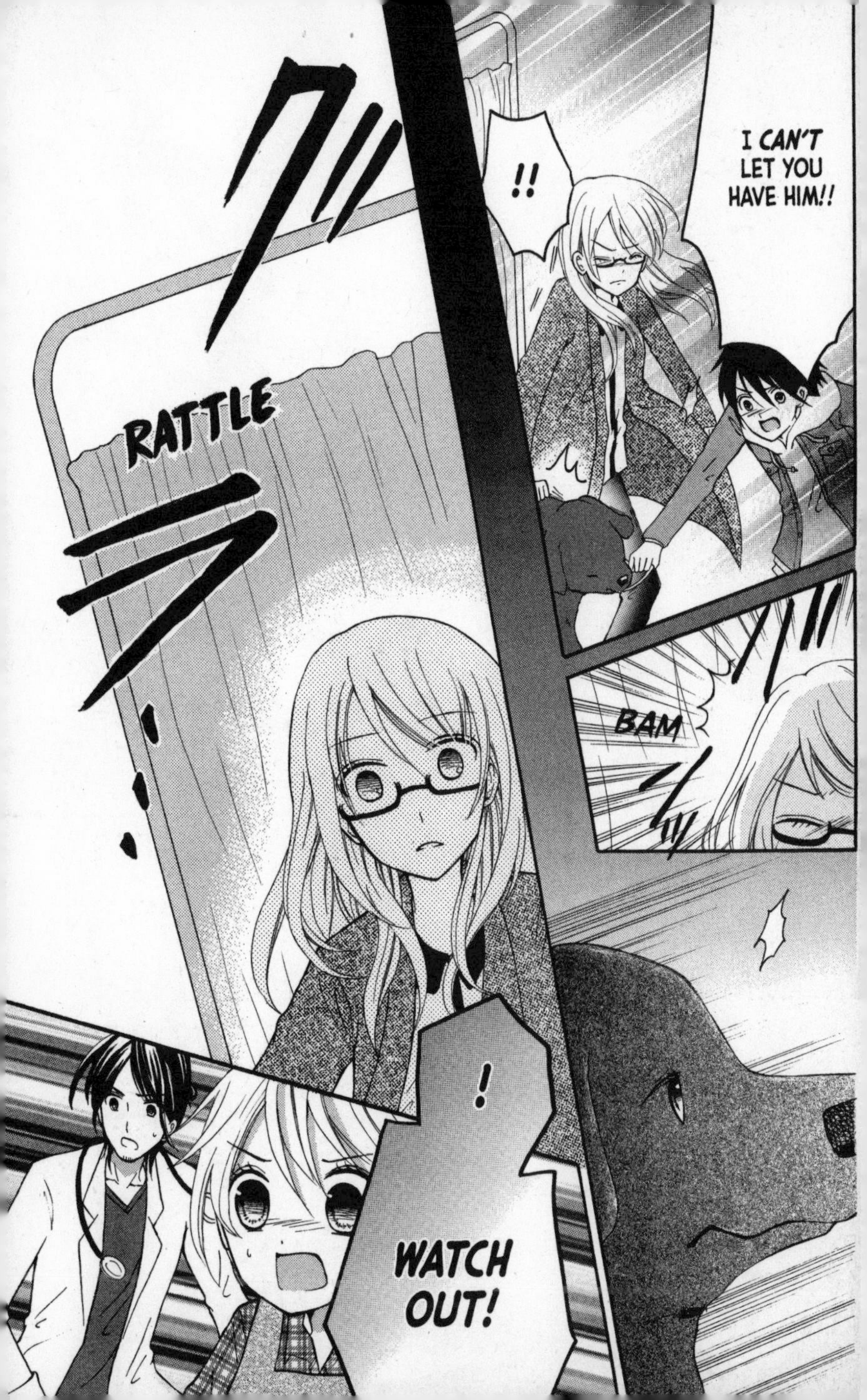
I CAN'T LET YOU HAVE HIM!!
!!
BAM
RATTLE
!
WATCH OUT!

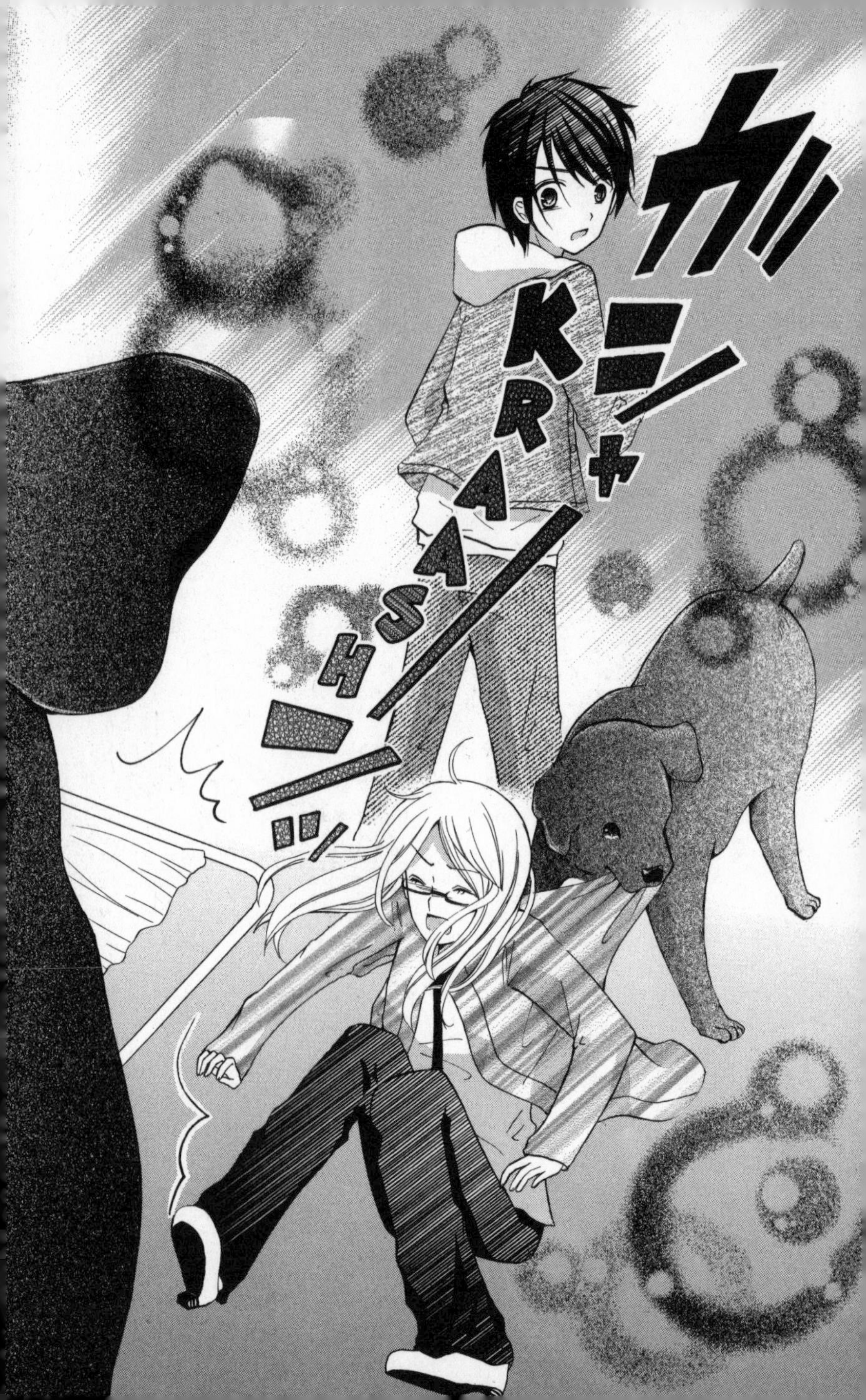

KRAASH

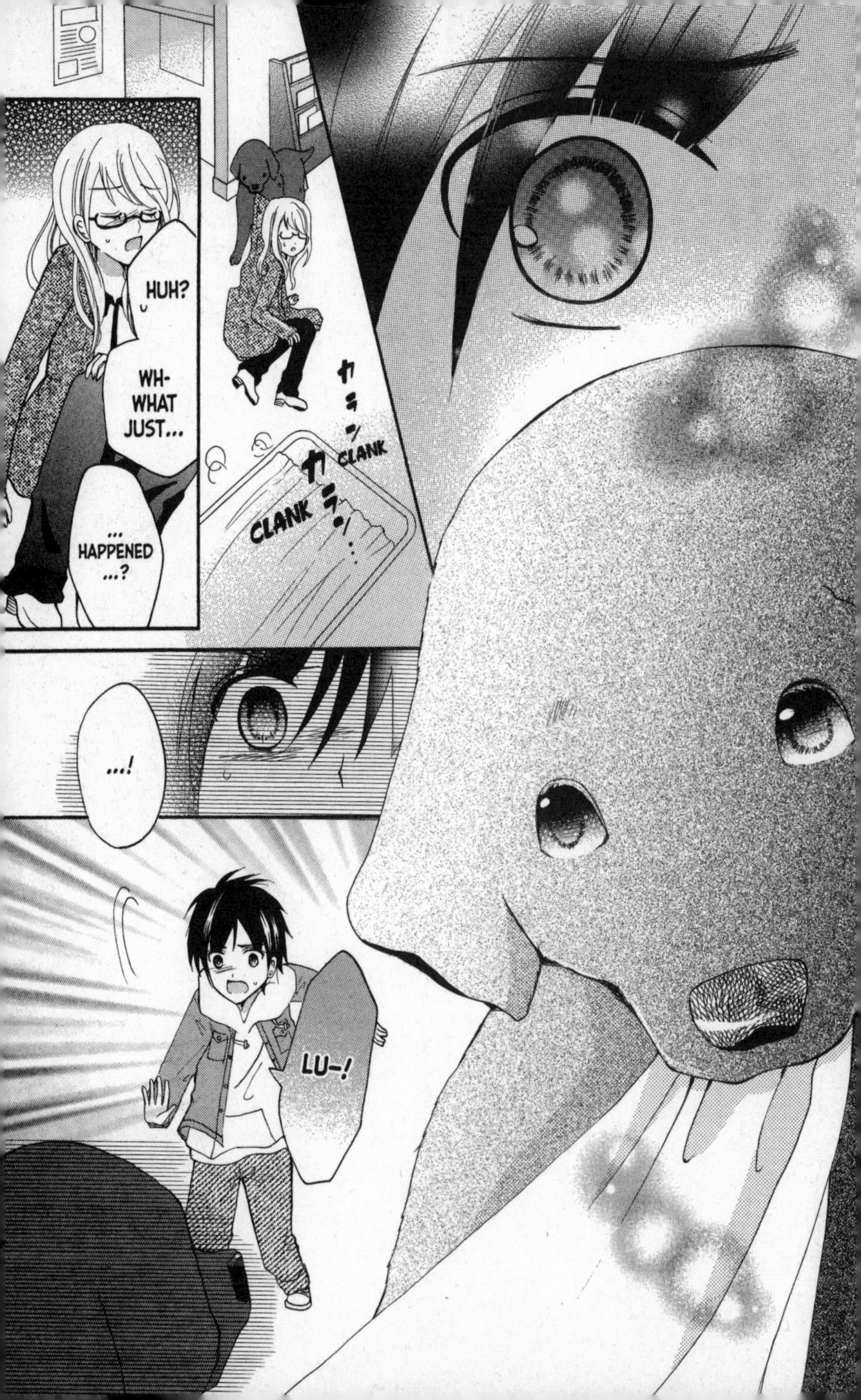

カラン
CLANK
カラ…
CLANK
HUH?
WH- WHAT JUST...
...HAPPENED ...?
...!
LU-!

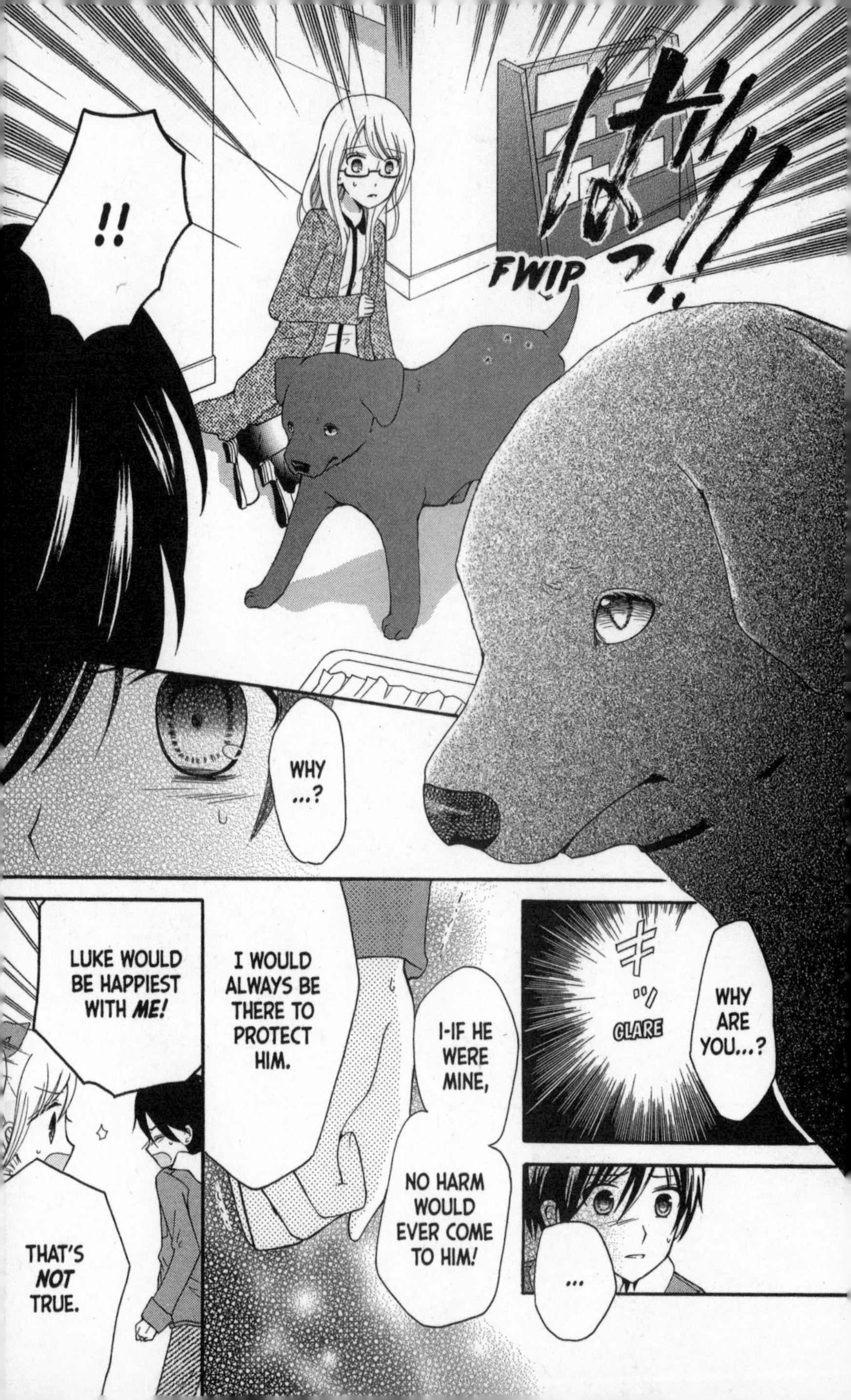
はっ!!
FWIP
!!
WHY ...?
WHY ARE YOU...?
キッ
GLARE
...
I-IF HE WERE MINE,
NO HARM WOULD EVER COME TO HIM!
I WOULD ALWAYS BE THERE TO PROTECT HIM.
LUKE WOULD BE HAPPIEST WITH *ME!*
THAT'S *NOT* TRUE.

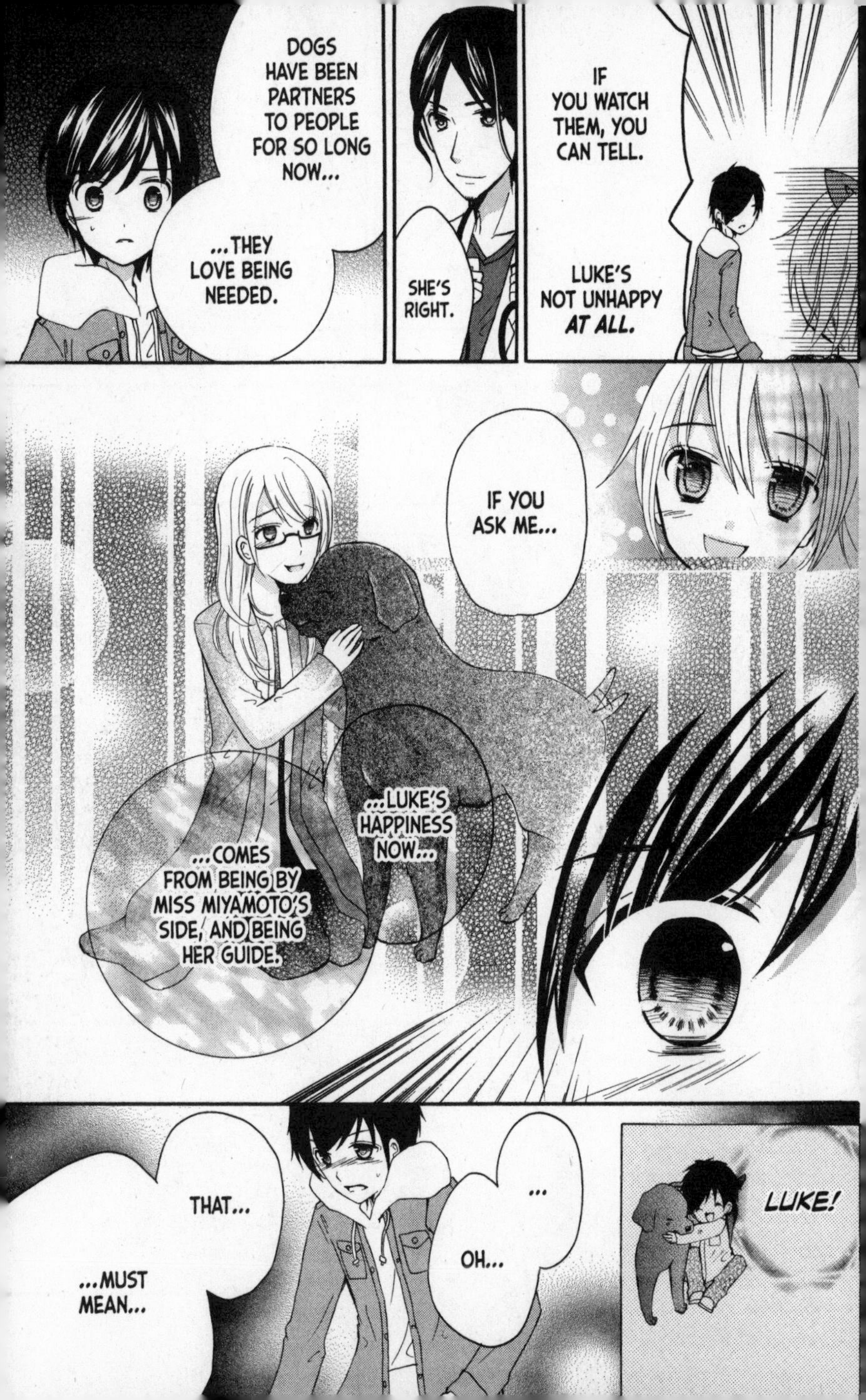
IF YOU WATCH THEM, YOU CAN TELL.
LUKE'S NOT UNHAPPY AT ALL.
SHE'S RIGHT.
DOGS HAVE BEEN PARTNERS TO PEOPLE FOR SO LONG NOW...
...THEY LOVE BEING NEEDED.
IF YOU ASK ME...
...LUKE'S HAPPINESS NOW...
...COMES FROM BEING BY MISS MIYAMOTO'S SIDE, AND BEING HER GUIDE.
LUKE!
...
OH...
THAT...
...MUST MEAN...

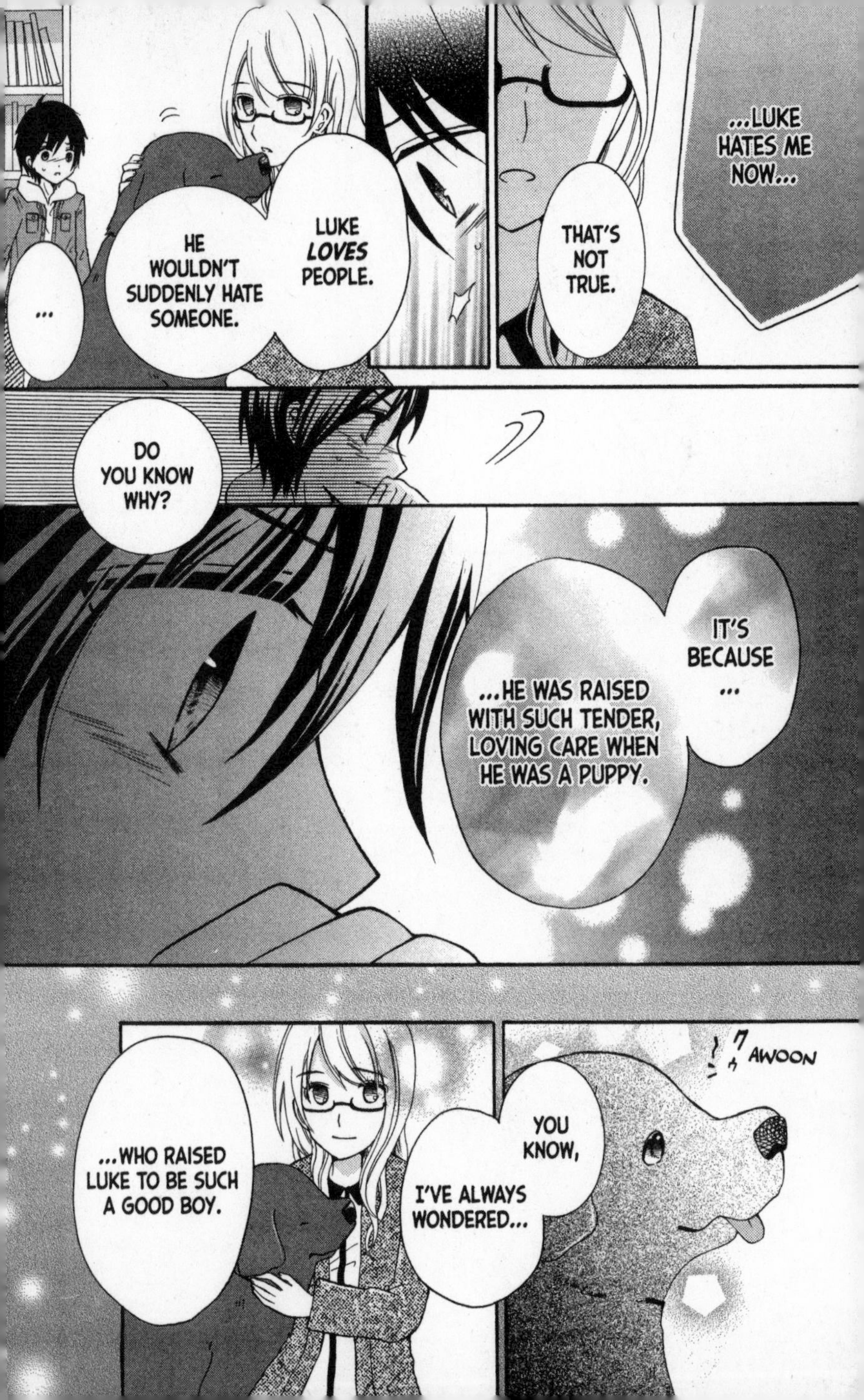
...LUKE HATES ME NOW...
THAT'S NOT TRUE.
LUKE *LOVES* PEOPLE.
HE WOULDN'T SUDDENLY HATE SOMEONE.
...
DO YOU KNOW WHY?
IT'S BECAUSE...
...HE WAS RAISED WITH SUCH TENDER, LOVING CARE WHEN HE WAS A PUPPY.
AWOON
YOU KNOW,
I'VE ALWAYS WONDERED...
...WHO RAISED LUKE TO BE SUCH A GOOD BOY.

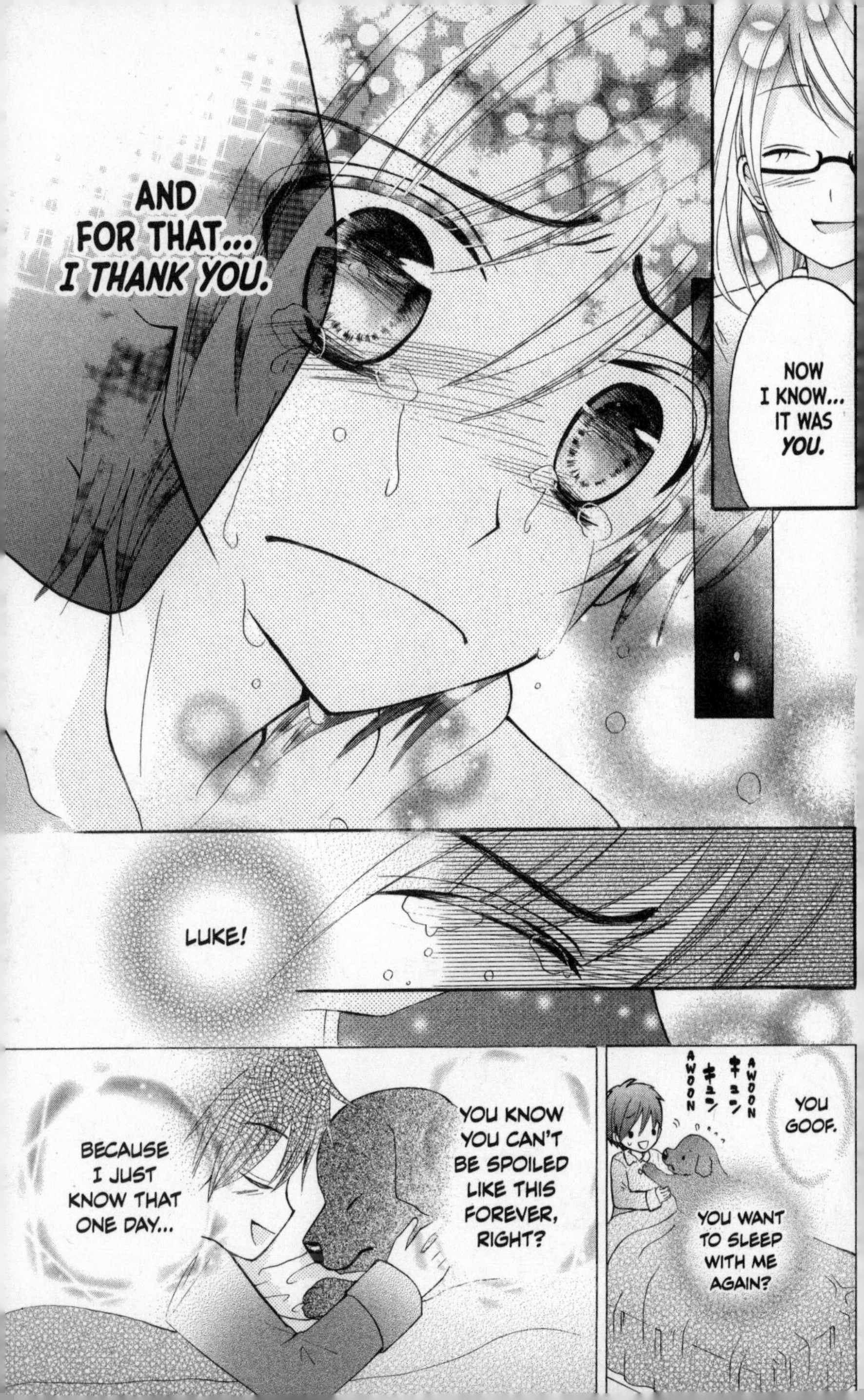
NOW I KNOW... IT WAS *YOU.*
AND FOR THAT... I THANK YOU.
LUKE!
キュン AWOON
キュン AWOON
YOU GOOF.
YOU WANT TO SLEEP WITH ME AGAIN?
YOU KNOW YOU CAN'T BE SPOILED LIKE THIS FOREVER, RIGHT?
BECAUSE I JUST KNOW THAT ONE DAY...

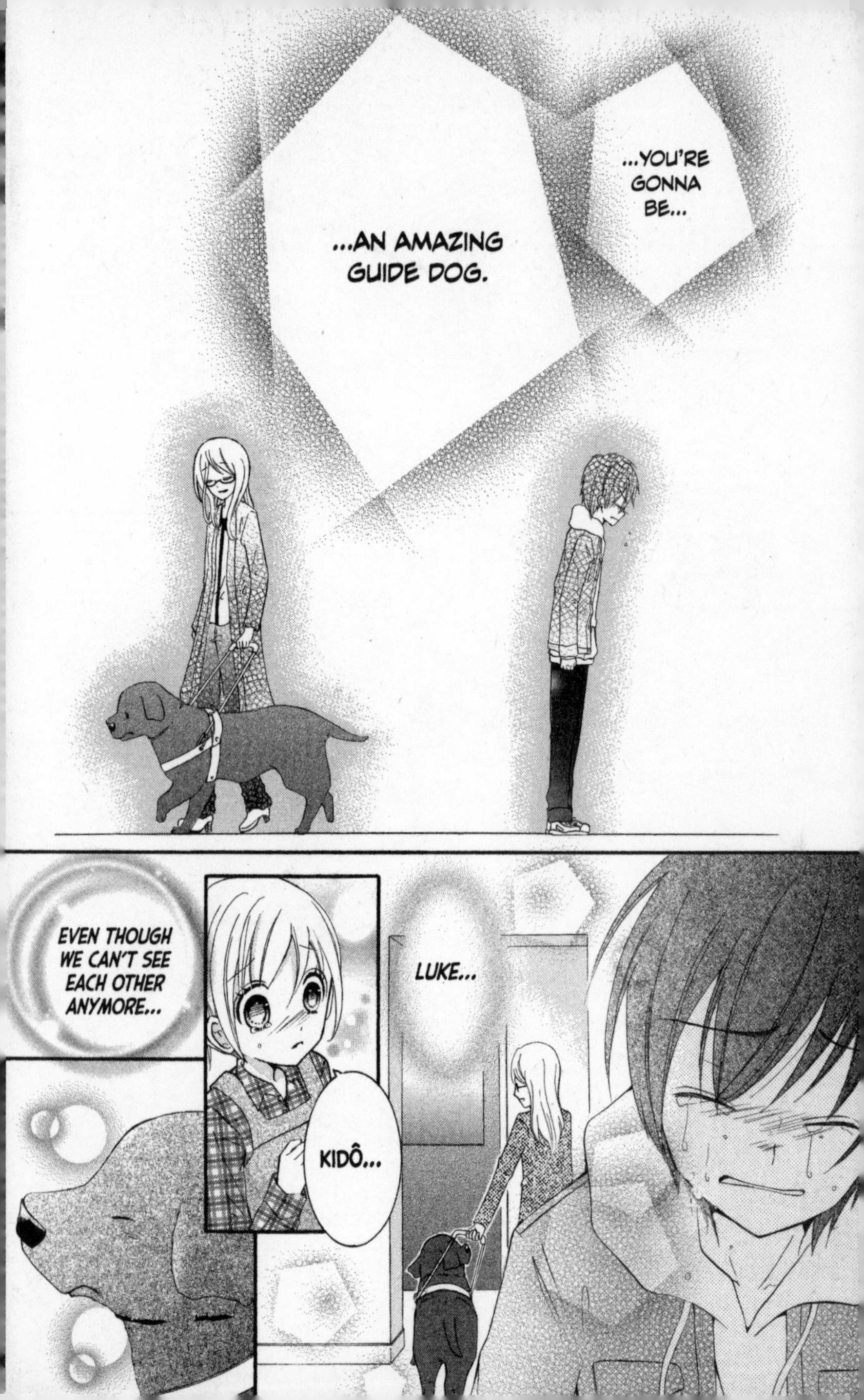
...YOU'RE GONNA BE...
...AN AMAZING GUIDE DOG.
LUKE...
KIDÔ...
EVEN THOUGH WE CAN'T SEE EACH OTHER ANYMORE...

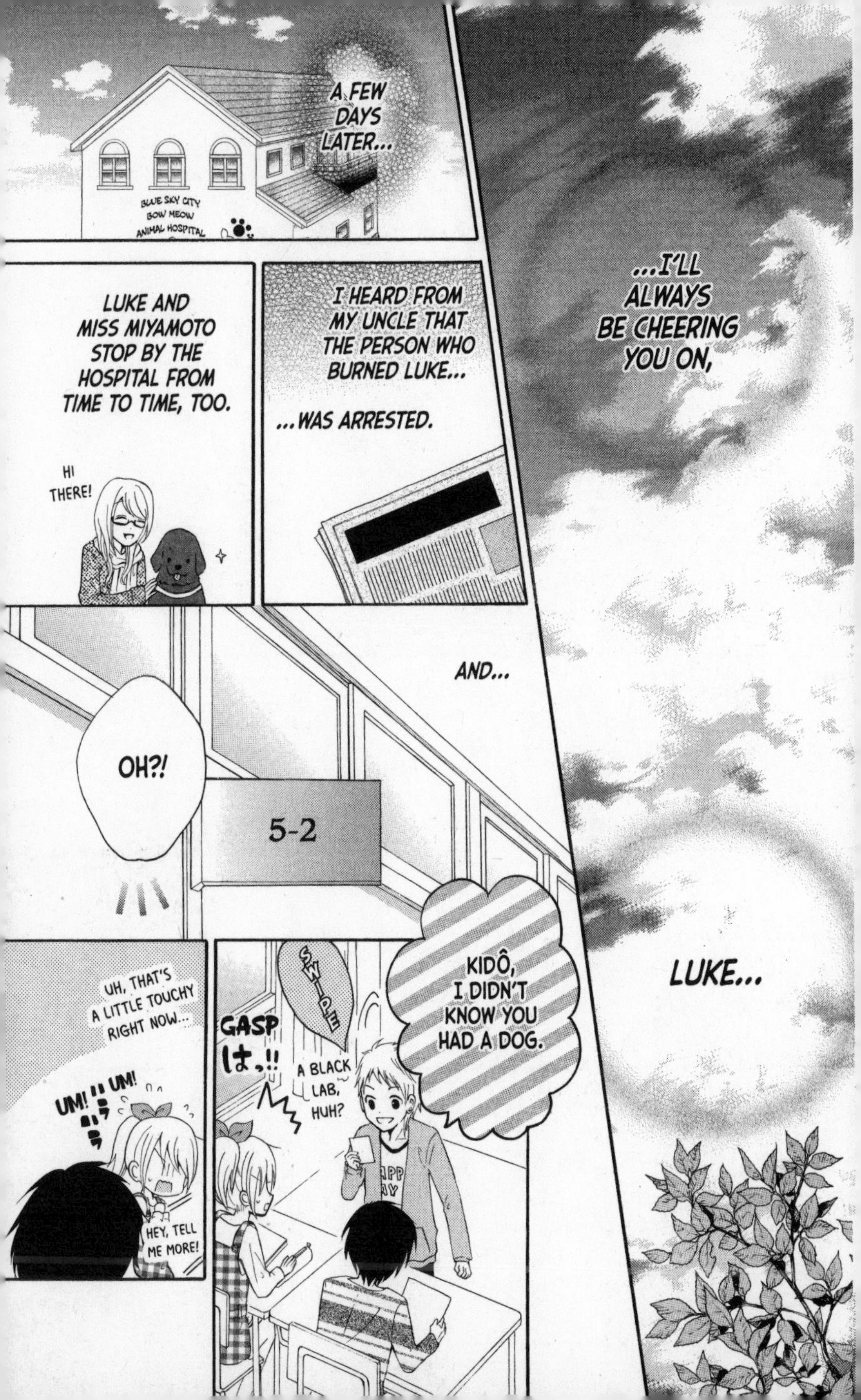
...I'LL ALWAYS BE CHEERING YOU ON,
LUKE...
A FEW DAYS LATER...
BLUE SKY CITY BOW MEOW ANIMAL HOSPITAL
I HEARD FROM MY UNCLE THAT THE PERSON WHO BURNED LUKE...
...WAS ARRESTED.
LUKE AND MISS MIYAMOTO STOP BY THE HOSPITAL FROM TIME TO TIME, TOO.
HI THERE!
AND...
OH?!
5-2
KIDÔ, I DIDN'T KNOW YOU HAD A DOG.
SWIPE
GASP は,!!
A BLACK LAB, HUH?
UH, THAT'S A LITTLE TOUCHY RIGHT NOW...
UM! UM!
HEY, TELL ME MORE!

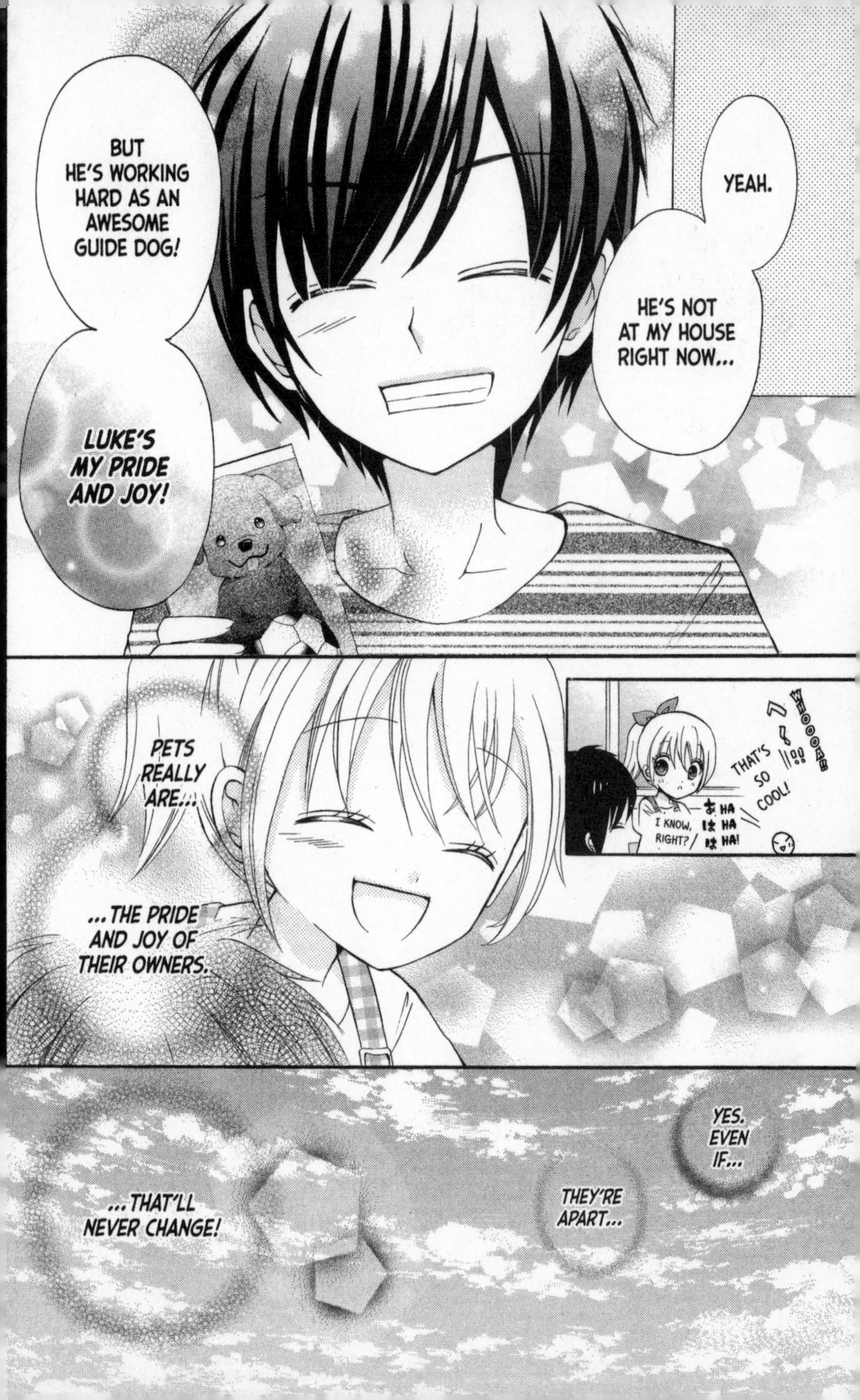
YEAH.
HE'S NOT AT MY HOUSE RIGHT NOW...
BUT HE'S WORKING HARD AS AN AWESOME GUIDE DOG!
LUKE'S MY PRIDE AND JOY!
WHOOOA!!
THAT'S SO COOL!
I KNOW, RIGHT?
HA HA HA!
PETS REALLY ARE...
...THE PRIDE AND JOY OF THEIR OWNERS.
YES. EVEN IF...
THEY'RE APART...
...THAT'LL NEVER CHANGE!

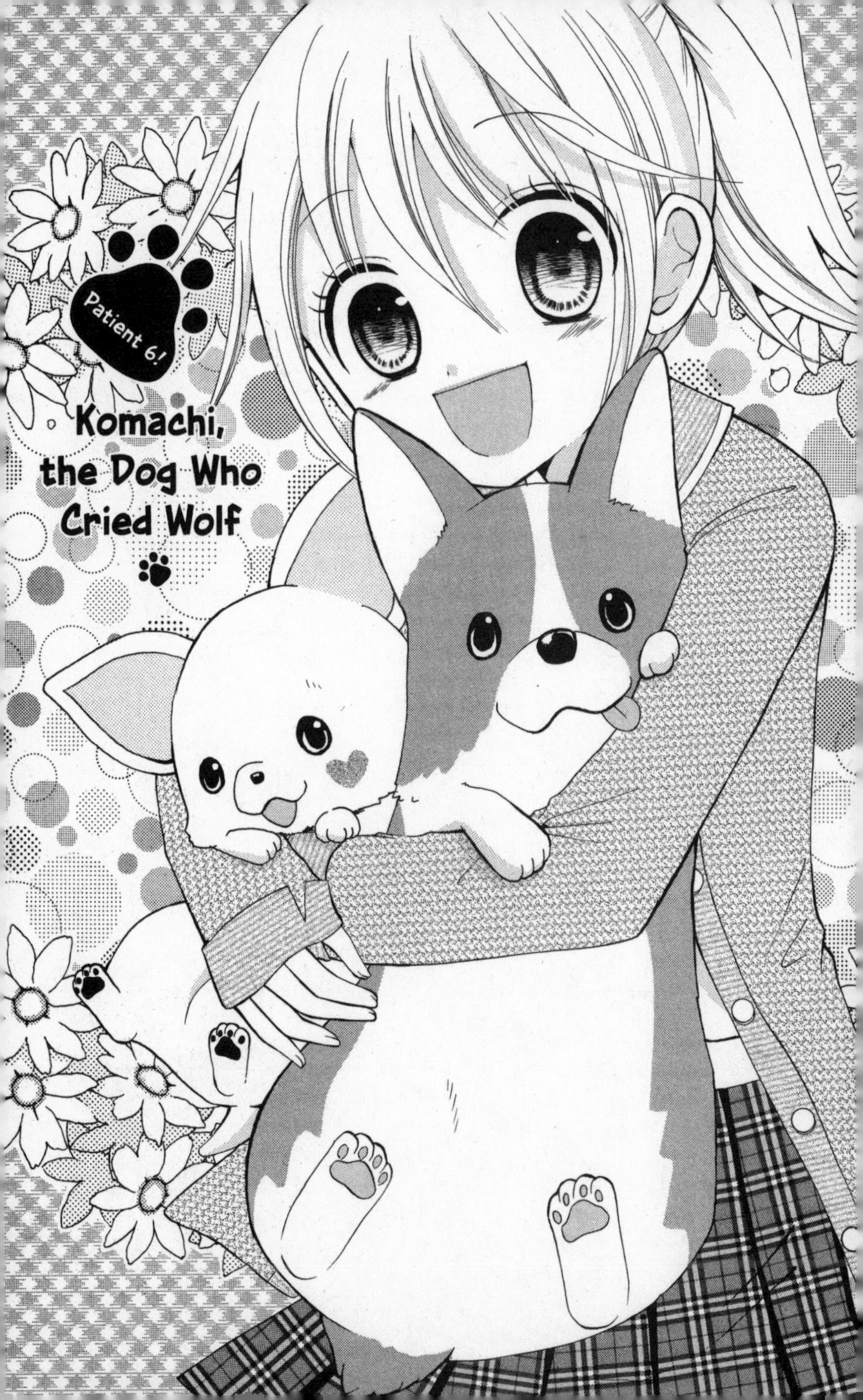
Patient 6!
Komachi, the Dog Who Cried Wolf

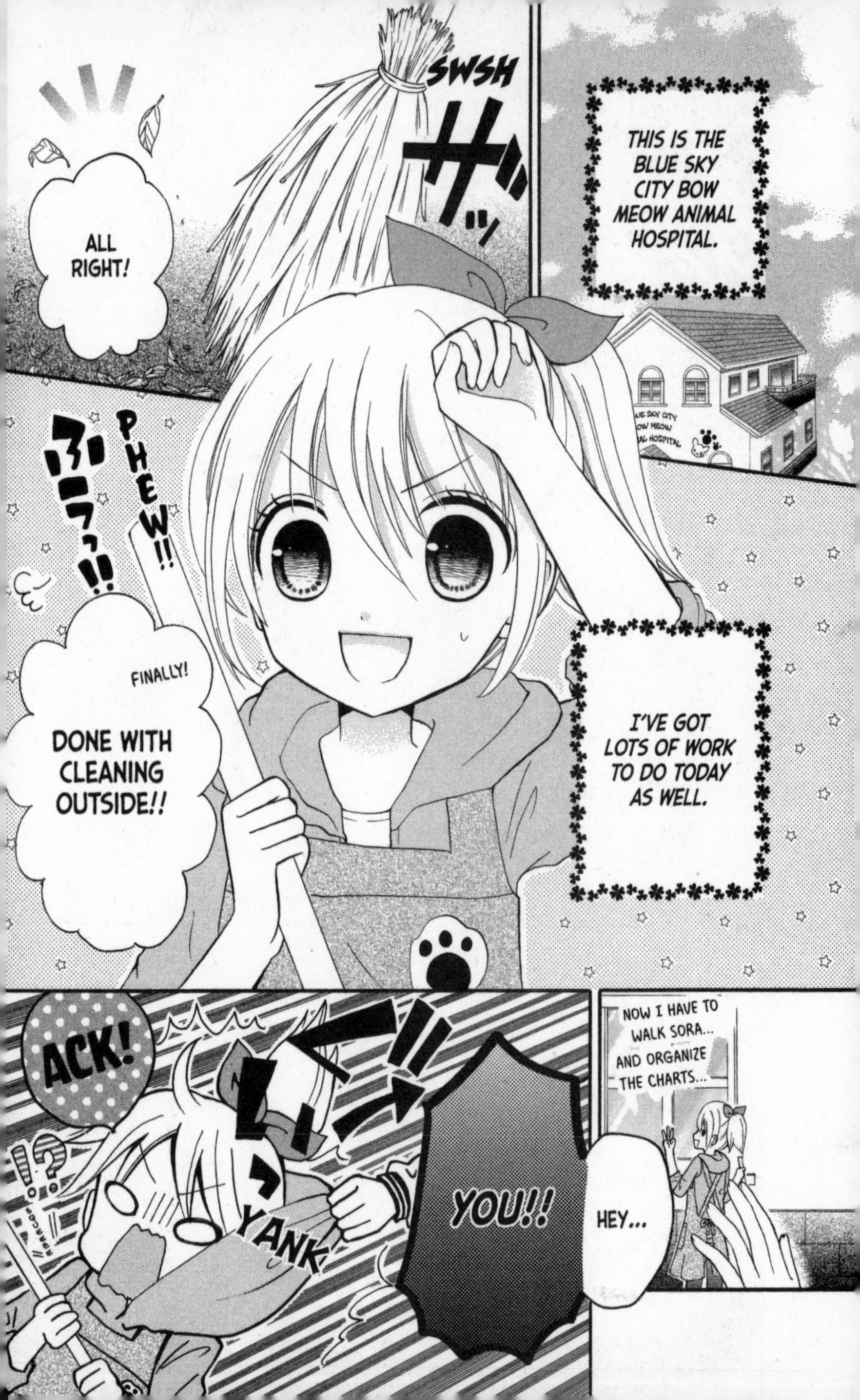

THIS IS THE BLUE SKY CITY BOW MEOW ANIMAL HOSPITAL.
SWSH
ALL RIGHT!
I'VE GOT LOTS OF WORK TO DO TODAY AS WELL.
PHEW!!
FINALLY!
DONE WITH CLEANING OUTSIDE!!
NOW I HAVE TO WALK SORA... AND ORGANIZE THE CHARTS...
HEY...
YOU!!
YANK
ACK!

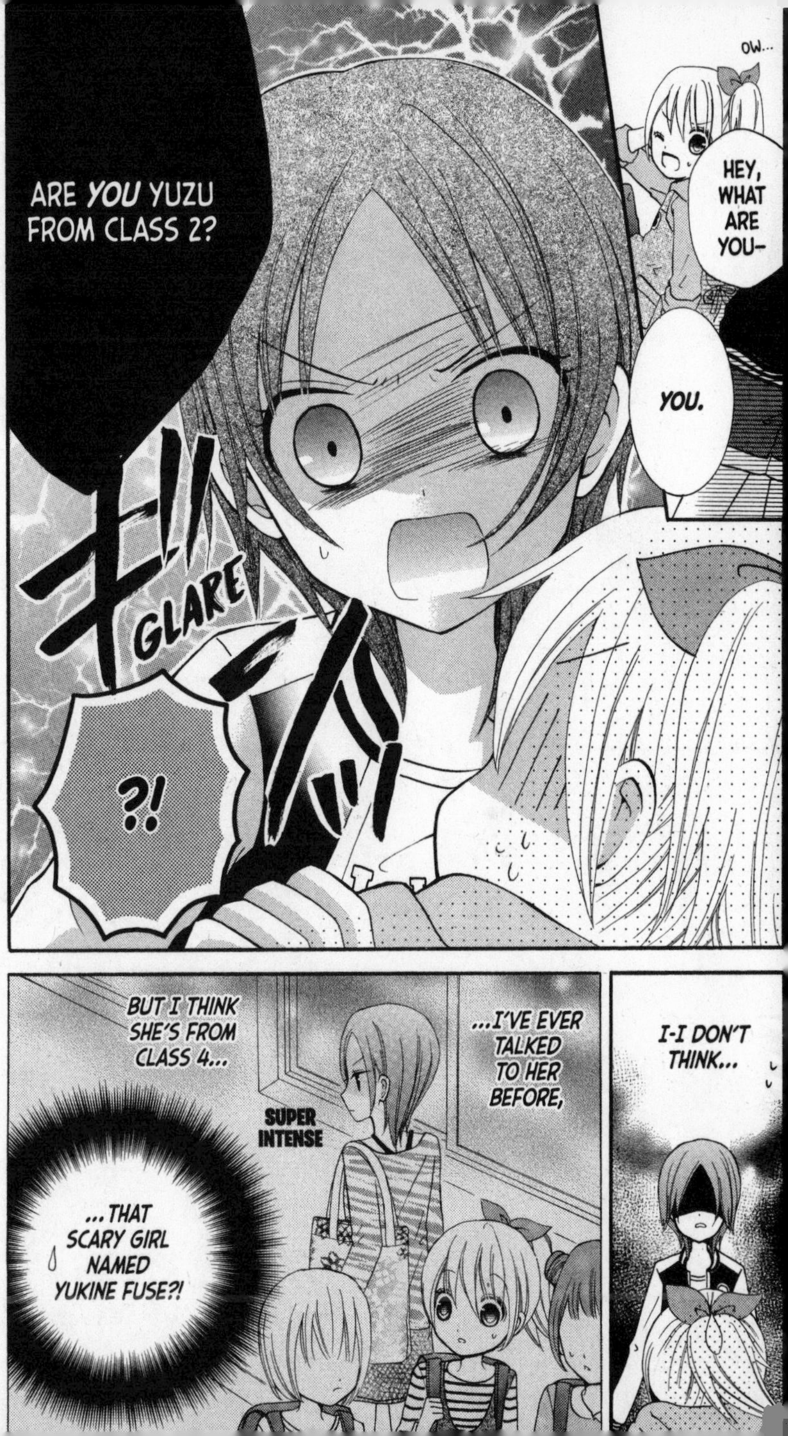
OW...
HEY, WHAT ARE YOU–
YOU.
ARE YOU YUZU FROM CLASS 2?
GLARE
?!
I-I DON'T THINK...
...I'VE EVER TALKED TO HER BEFORE,
BUT I THINK SHE'S FROM CLASS 4...
SUPER INTENSE
...THAT SCARY GIRL NAMED YUKINE FUSE?!

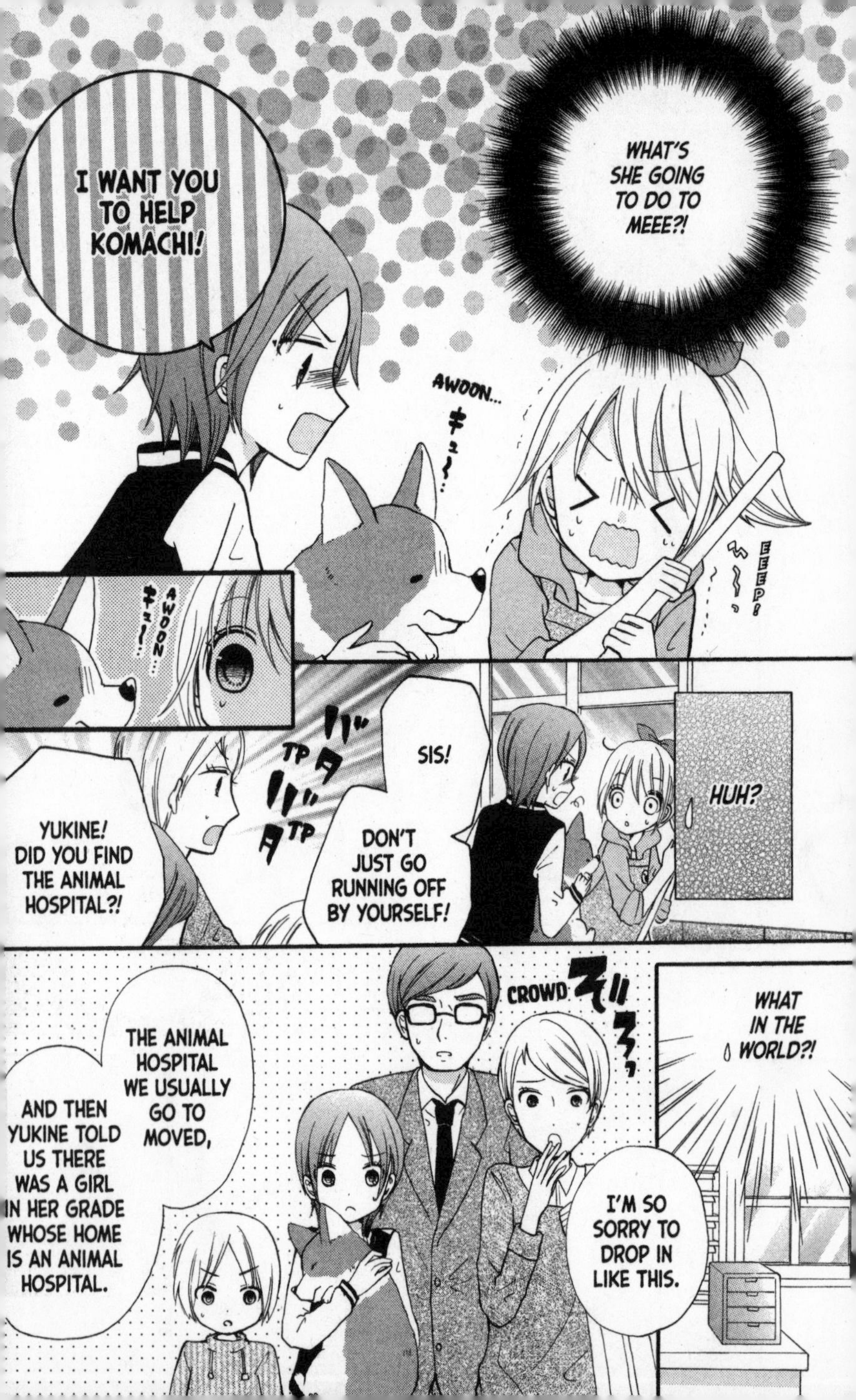
WHAT'S SHE GOING TO DO TO MEEE?!
I WANT YOU TO HELP KOMACHI!
EEEP!
AWOON...
AWOON...
HUH?
SIS!
DON'T JUST GO RUNNING OFF BY YOURSELF!
TP
TP
YUKINE! DID YOU FIND THE ANIMAL HOSPITAL?!
WHAT IN THE WORLD?!
CROWD
I'M SO SORRY TO DROP IN LIKE THIS.
THE ANIMAL HOSPITAL WE USUALLY GO TO MOVED,
AND THEN YUKINE TOLD US THERE WAS A GIRL IN HER GRADE WHOSE HOME IS AN ANIMAL HOSPITAL.

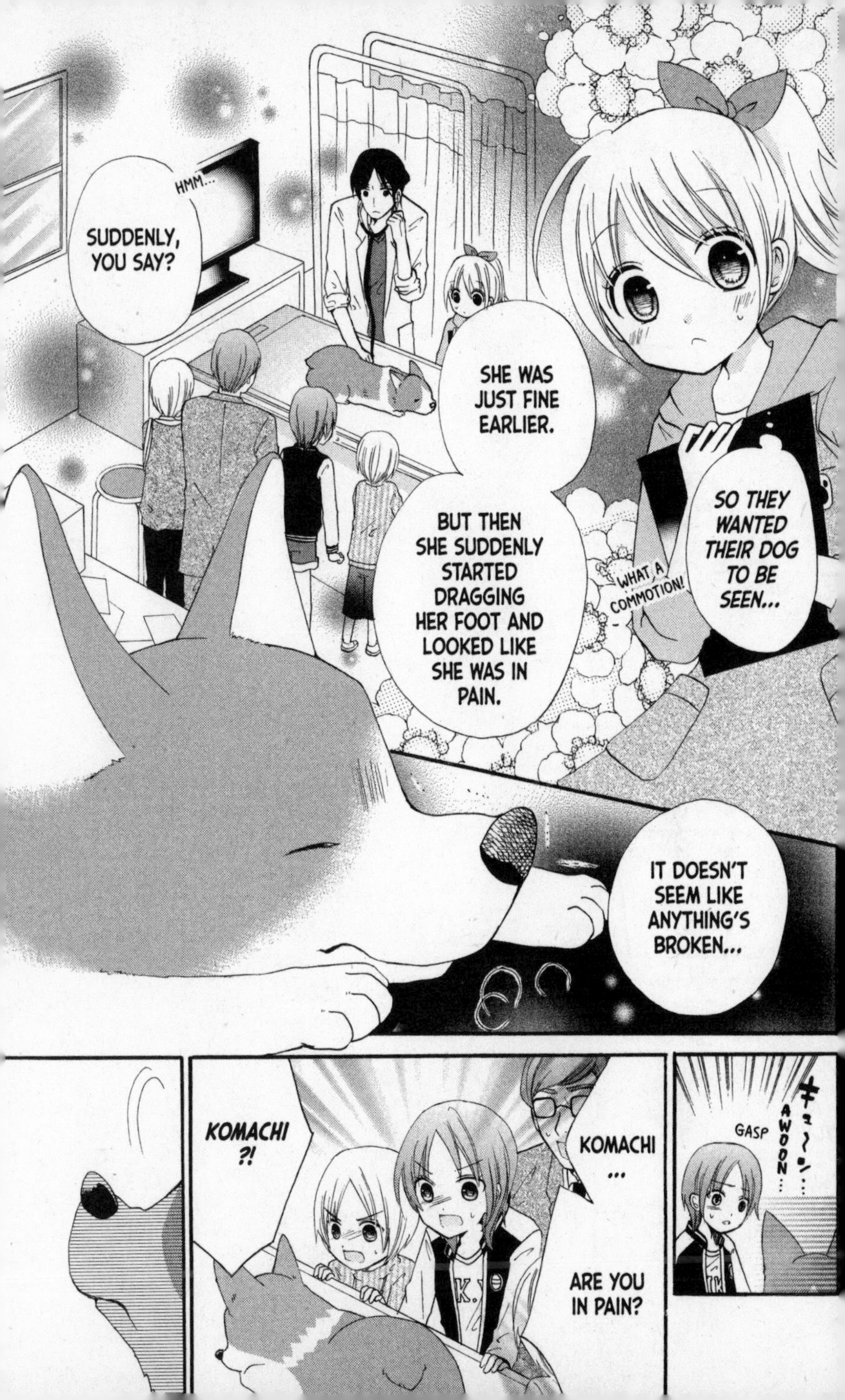
SO THEY WANTED THEIR DOG TO BE SEEN...
WHAT A COMMOTION!
SHE WAS JUST FINE EARLIER.
BUT THEN SHE SUDDENLY STARTED DRAGGING HER FOOT AND LOOKED LIKE SHE WAS IN PAIN.
HMM...
SUDDENLY, YOU SAY?
IT DOESN'T SEEM LIKE ANYTHING'S BROKEN...
GASP
AWOON...
KOMACHI ...
ARE YOU IN PAIN?
KOMACHI ?!

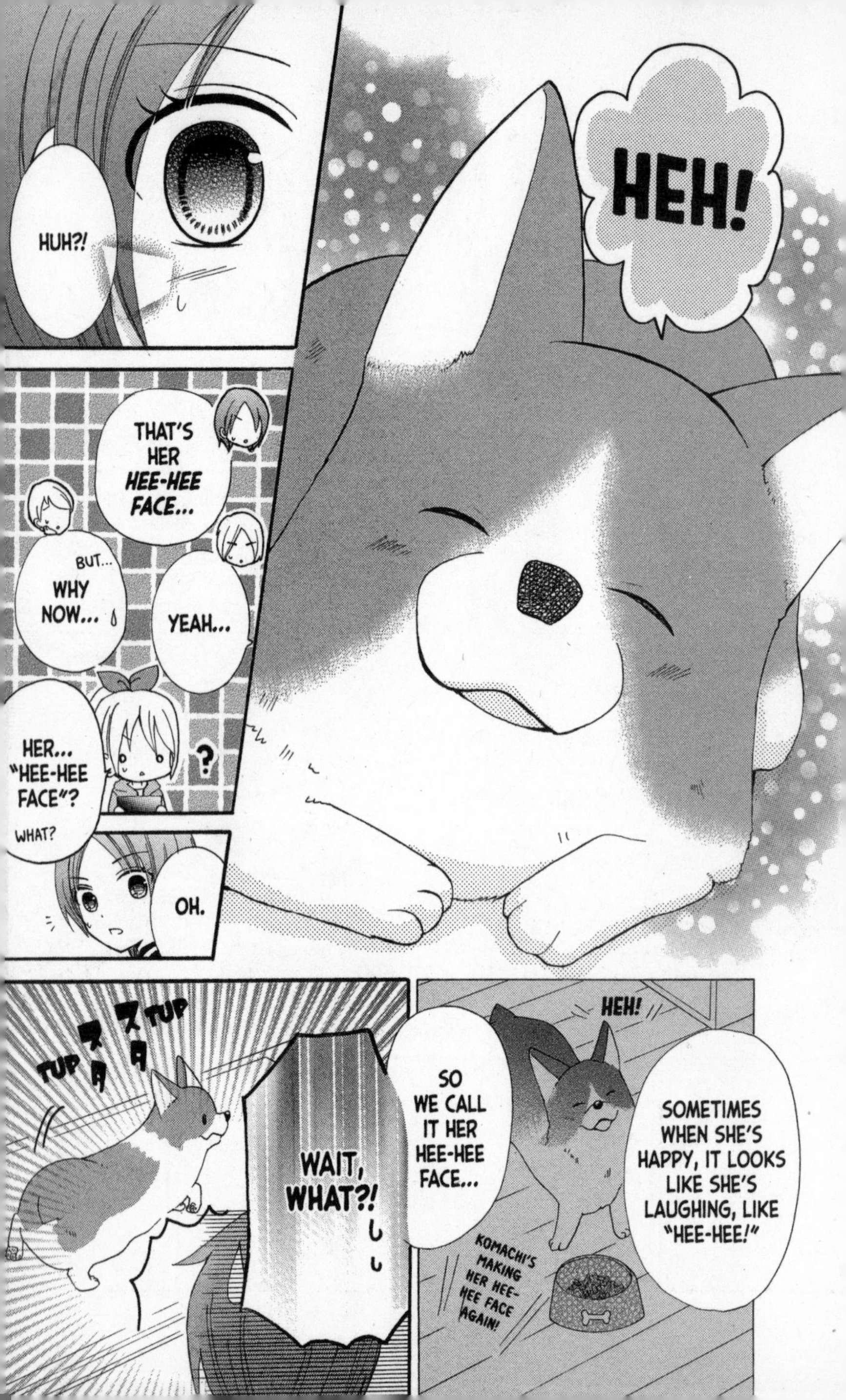

HEH!
HUH?!
THAT'S HER *HEE-HEE FACE*...
YEAH...
BUT... WHY NOW...
HER... "HEE-HEE FACE"? WHAT?
OH.
HEH!
SOMETIMES WHEN SHE'S HAPPY, IT LOOKS LIKE SHE'S LAUGHING, LIKE "HEE-HEE!"
SO WE CALL IT HER HEE-HEE FACE...
KOMACHI'S MAKING HER HEE-HEE FACE AGAIN!
WAIT, WHAT?!
スタ TUP
スタ TUP

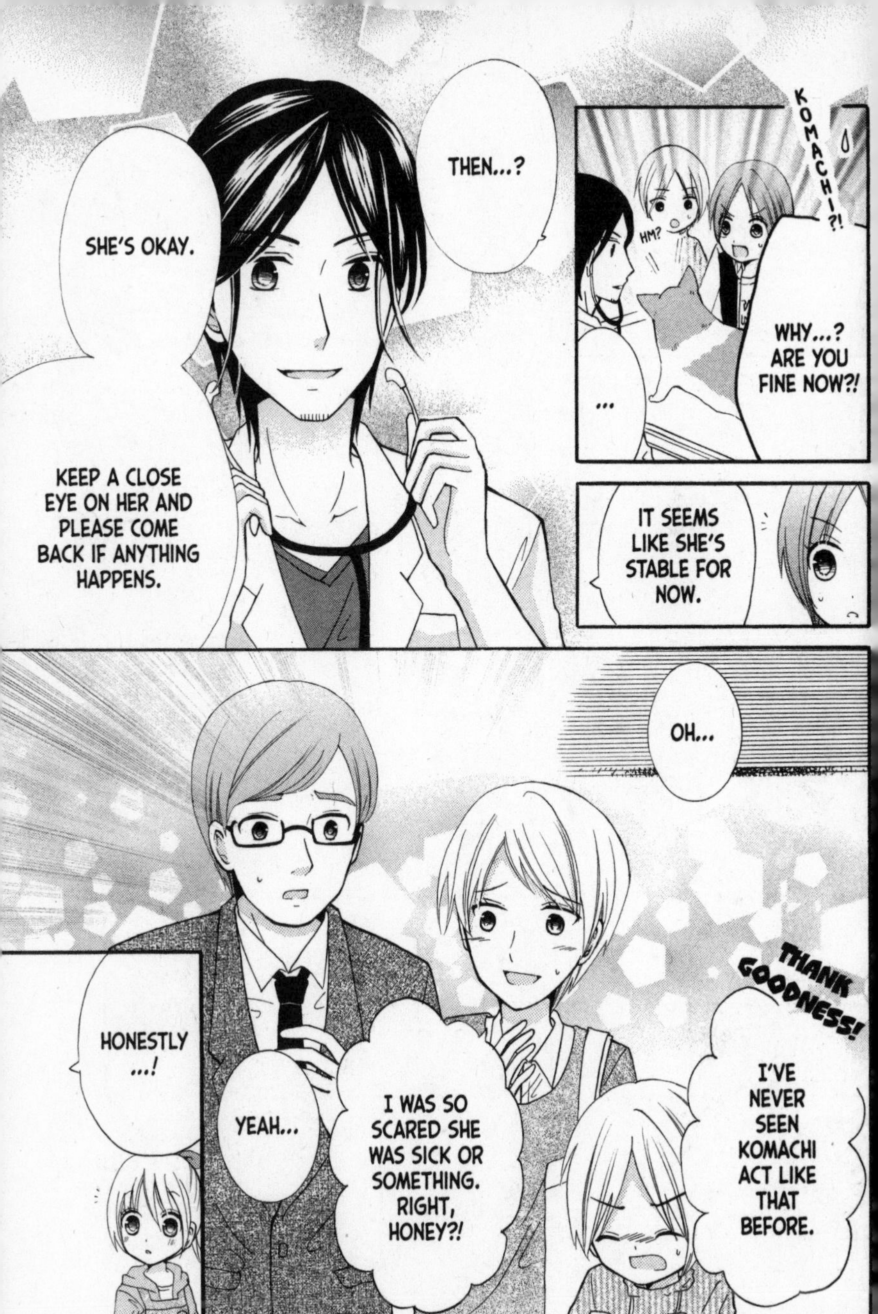
KOMACHI?!
HM?
WHY...? ARE YOU FINE NOW?!
...
IT SEEMS LIKE SHE'S STABLE FOR NOW.
THEN...?
SHE'S OKAY.
KEEP A CLOSE EYE ON HER AND PLEASE COME BACK IF ANYTHING HAPPENS.
OH...
THANK GOODNESS!
I'VE NEVER SEEN KOMACHI ACT LIKE THAT BEFORE.
I WAS SO SCARED SHE WAS SICK OR SOMETHING. RIGHT, HONEY?!
YEAH...
HONESTLY ...!

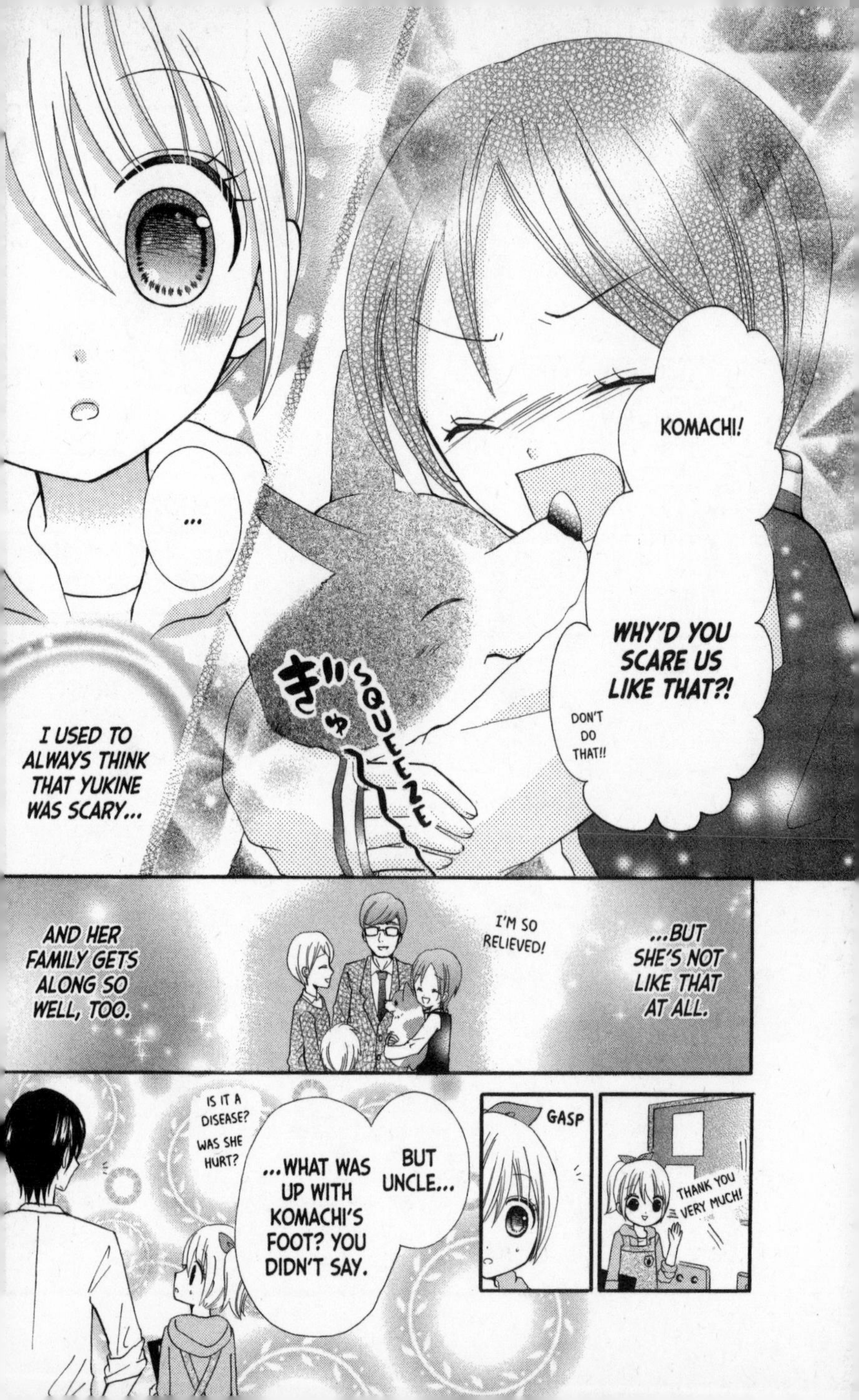
KOMACHI!
WHY'D YOU SCARE US LIKE THAT?!
DON'T DO THAT!!
ぎゅ
SQUEEZE
...
I USED TO ALWAYS THINK THAT YUKINE WAS SCARY...
...BUT SHE'S NOT LIKE THAT AT ALL.
I'M SO RELIEVED!
AND HER FAMILY GETS ALONG SO WELL, TOO.
THANK YOU VERY MUCH!
GASP
BUT UNCLE...
...WHAT WAS UP WITH KOMACHI'S FOOT? YOU DIDN'T SAY.
IS IT A DISEASE?
WAS SHE HURT?

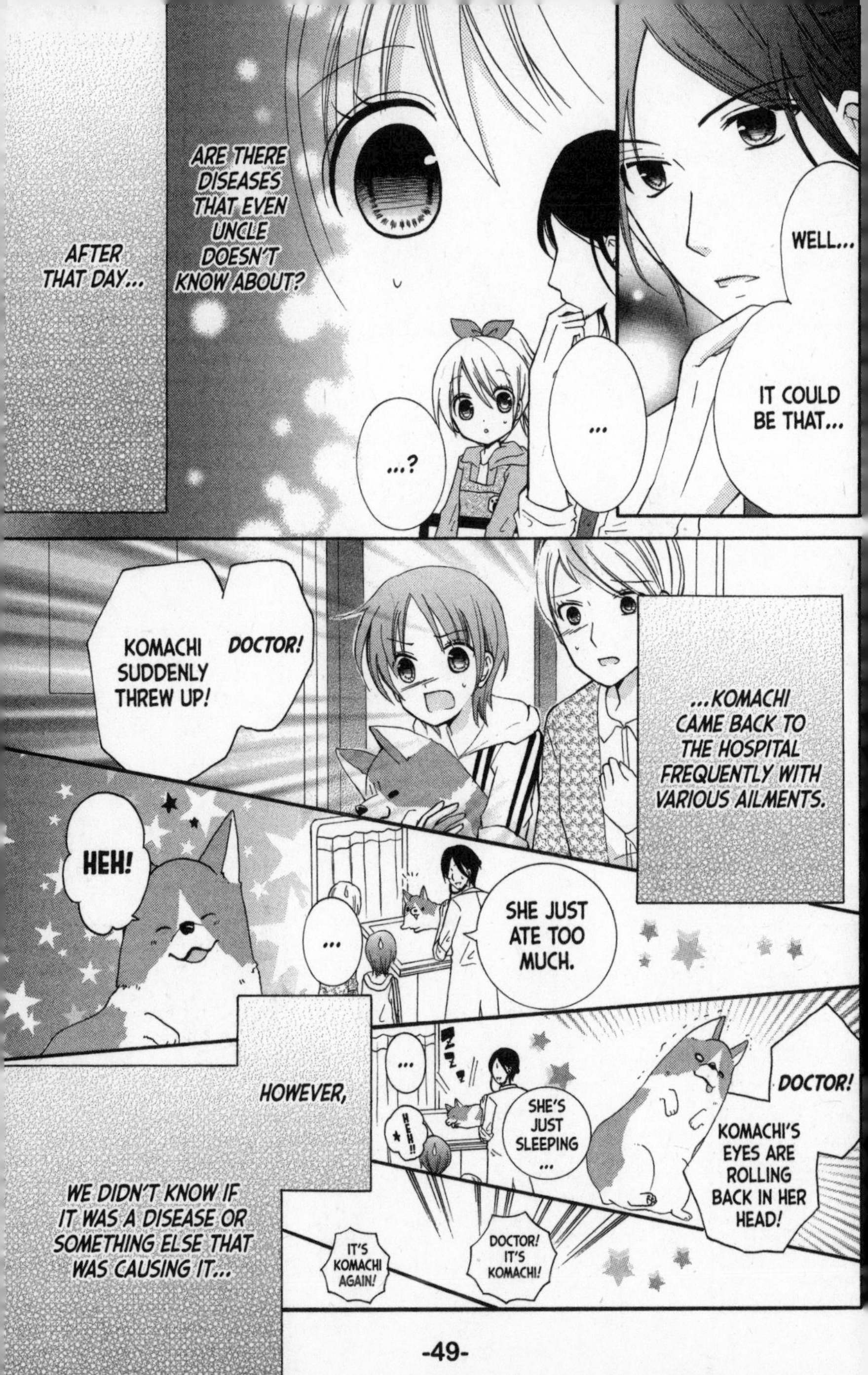
WELL...
IT COULD BE THAT...
...
...?
ARE THERE DISEASES THAT EVEN UNCLE DOESN'T KNOW ABOUT?
AFTER THAT DAY...
...KOMACHI CAME BACK TO THE HOSPITAL FREQUENTLY WITH VARIOUS AILMENTS.
DOCTOR!
KOMACHI SUDDENLY THREW UP!
SHE JUST ATE TOO MUCH.
...
HEH!
DOCTOR!
KOMACHI'S EYES ARE ROLLING BACK IN HER HEAD!
SHE'S JUST SLEEPING ...
HEH!!
...
HOWEVER,
DOCTOR! IT'S KOMACHI!
IT'S KOMACHI AGAIN!
WE DIDN'T KNOW IF IT WAS A DISEASE OR SOMETHING ELSE THAT WAS CAUSING IT...

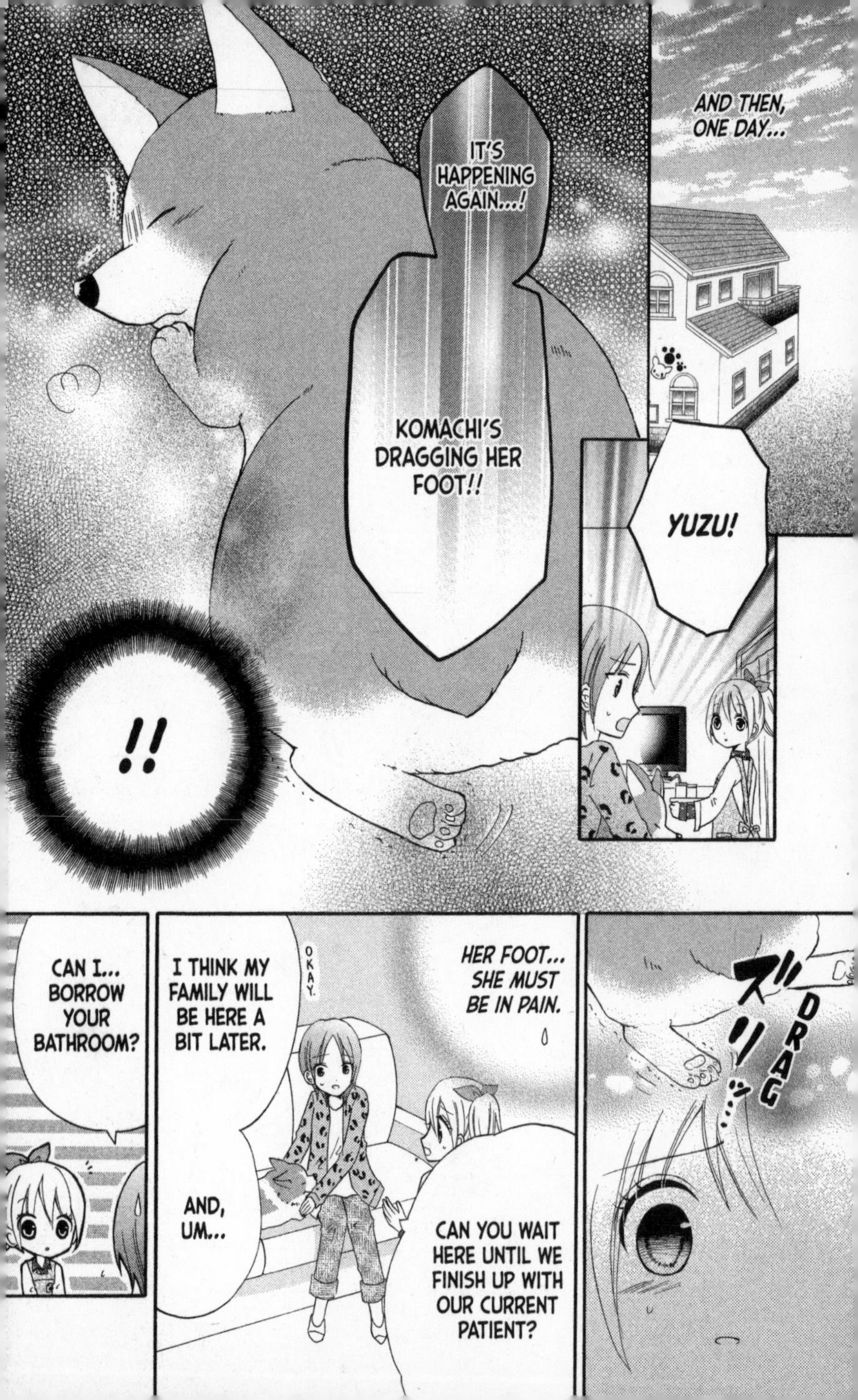
AND THEN, ONE DAY...
YUZU!
IT'S HAPPENING AGAIN...!
KOMACHI'S DRAGGING HER FOOT!!
!!
DRAG
HER FOOT... SHE MUST BE IN PAIN.
CAN YOU WAIT HERE UNTIL WE FINISH UP WITH OUR CURRENT PATIENT?
OKAY.
I THINK MY FAMILY WILL BE HERE A BIT LATER.
AND, UM...
CAN I... BORROW YOUR BATHROOM?

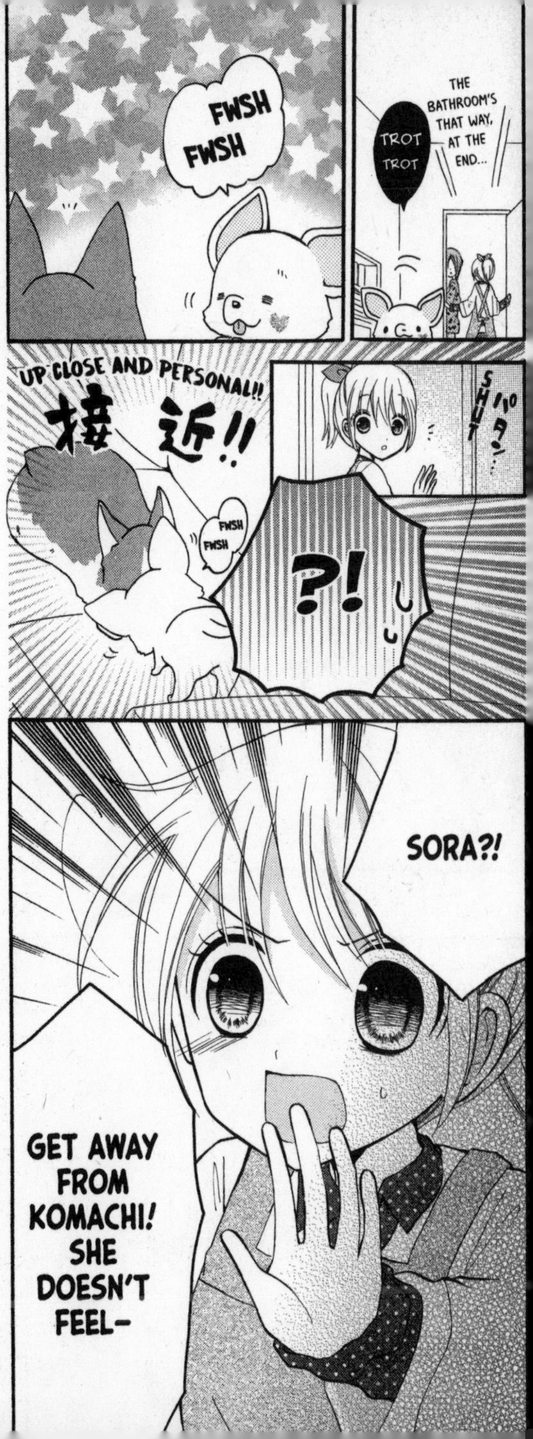
THE BATHROOM'S THAT WAY, AT THE END...
TROT TROT
FWSH FWSH
SHUT
パタッ...
?!
UP CLOSE AND PERSONAL!!
接近!!
FWSH FWSH
SORA?!
GET AWAY FROM KOMACHI! SHE DOESN'T FEEL-

• MEMORIES OF MY SCHOOL DAYS •

I TALKED ABOUT IT A LITTLE IN VOLUME 1, BUT WHEN I WORK ON *YUZU THE PET VET*, IT MAKES ME THINK BACK TO HOW I USED TO DRAW PICTURES OF ANIMALS ALL THE TIME WHEN I WAS STILL A STUDENT.

I DREW THEM SO MUCH THAT EVEN MY ART TEACHER ASKED ME, "WHY DO YOU DRAW SO MANY ANIMALS ALL THE TIME?" OF COURSE, I'VE ALWAYS BEEN AN ANIMAL LOVER, BUT I LOVED DRAWING THEM SO MUCH THAT EVEN I FOUND IT A BIT ODD.

EVEN THAT TIME WHEN I WAS SKETCHING BY MYSELF AT THE ZOO AND A KID POINTED AT ME IS A GOOD MEMORY... (HAHA)

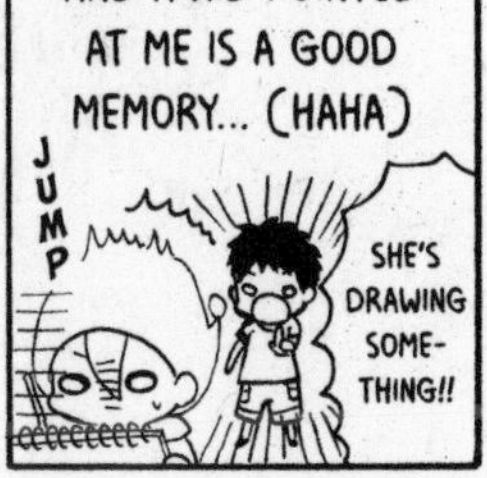
JUMP
SHE'S DRAWING SOME-THING!!

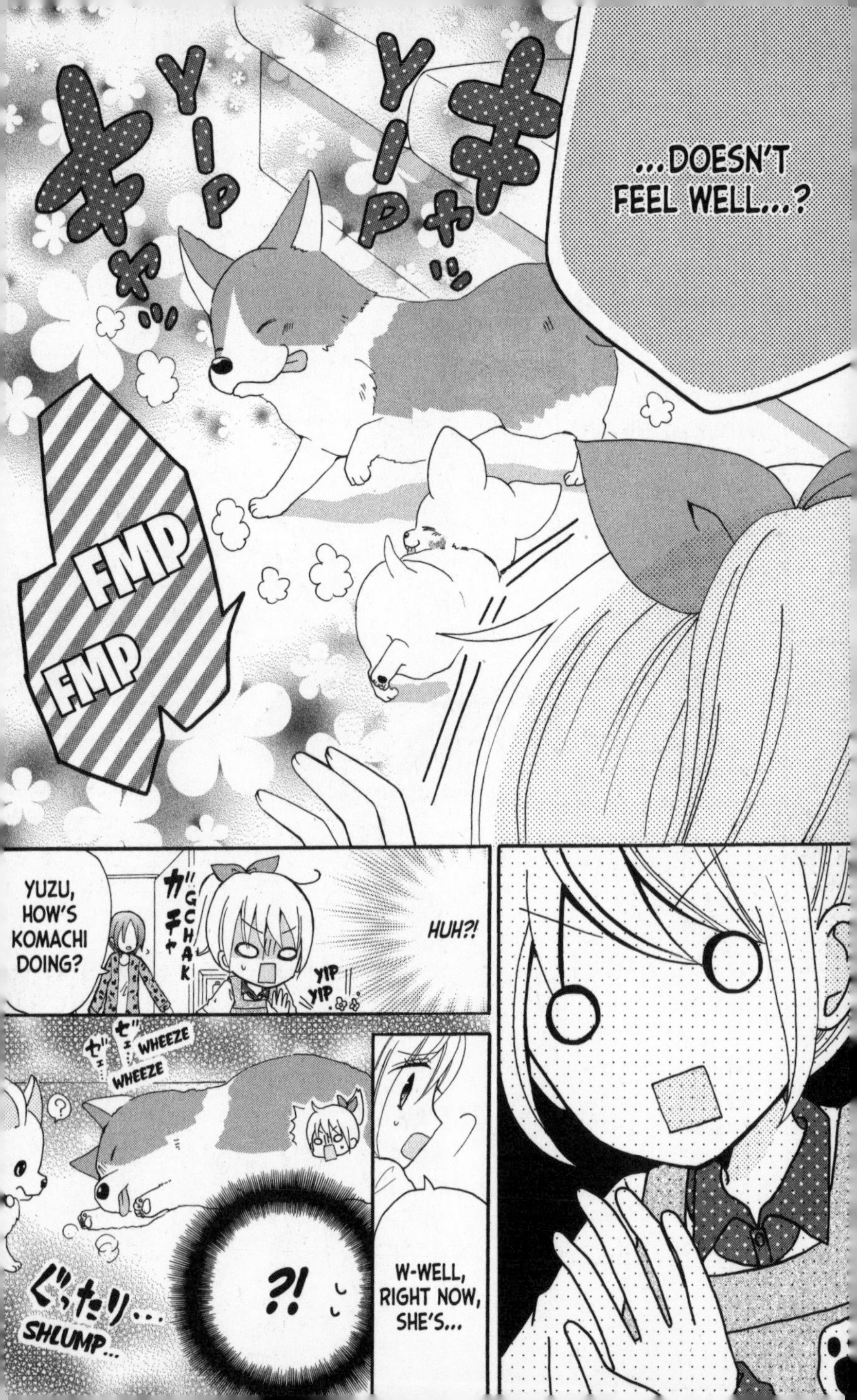
...DOESN'T FEEL WELL...?
YIP
YIP
FMP FMP
HUH?!
ガチャ GCHAK
YIP YIP
YUZU, HOW'S KOMACHI DOING?
W-WELL, RIGHT NOW, SHE'S...
ゼェ WHEEZE
ゼェ WHEEZE
?!
ぐったり... SHLUMP...

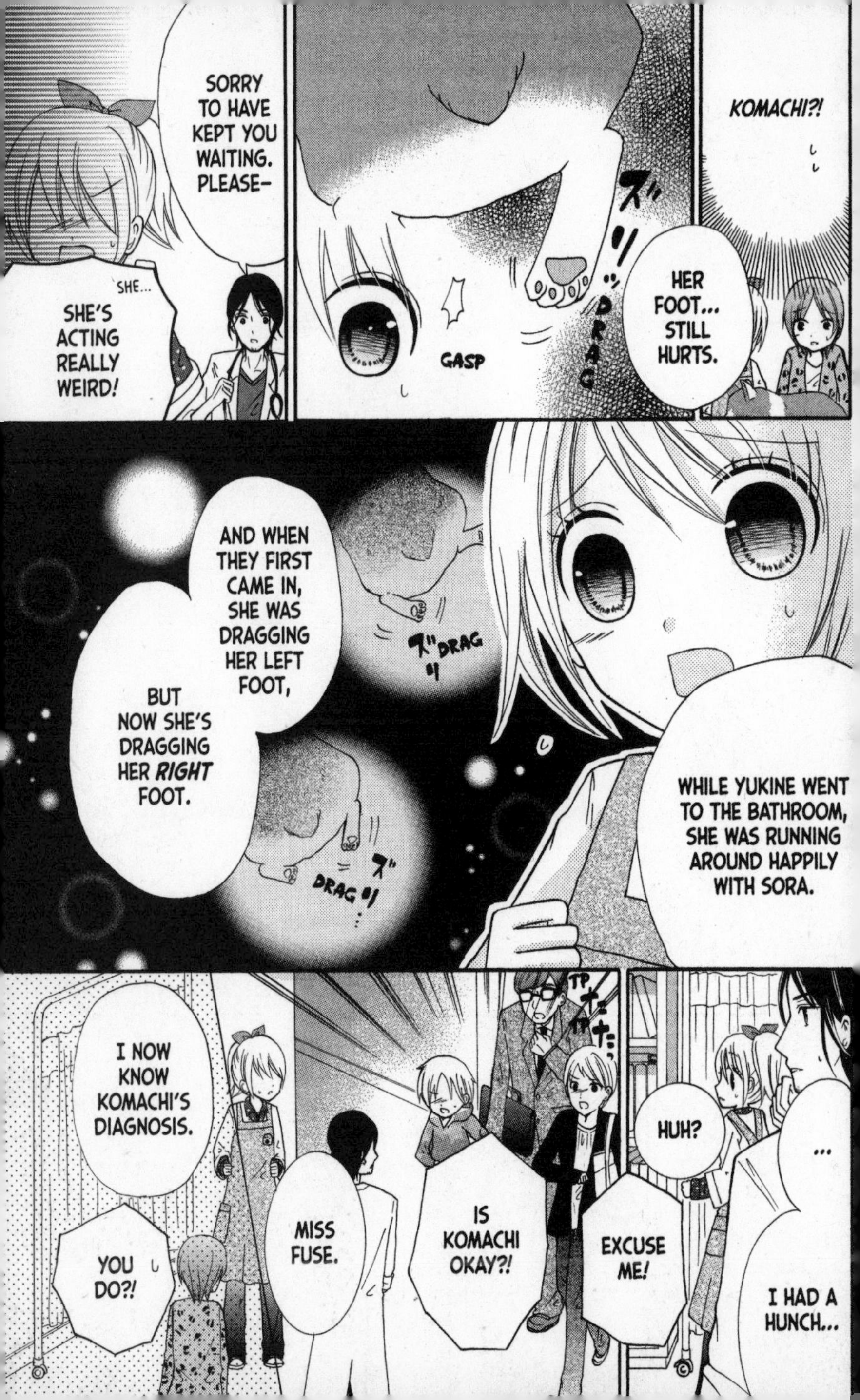
KOMACHI?!
HER FOOT... STILL HURTS.
DRAG
GASP
SORRY TO HAVE KEPT YOU WAITING. PLEASE—
SHE...
SHE'S ACTING REALLY WEIRD!
WHILE YUKINE WENT TO THE BATHROOM, SHE WAS RUNNING AROUND HAPPILY WITH SORA.
AND WHEN THEY FIRST CAME IN, SHE WAS DRAGGING HER LEFT FOOT,
DRAG
BUT NOW SHE'S DRAGGING HER *RIGHT* FOOT.
DRAG
...
I HAD A HUNCH...
HUH?
EXCUSE ME!
TP
IS KOMACHI OKAY?!
MISS FUSE.
I NOW KNOW KOMACHI'S DIAGNOSIS.
YOU DO?!

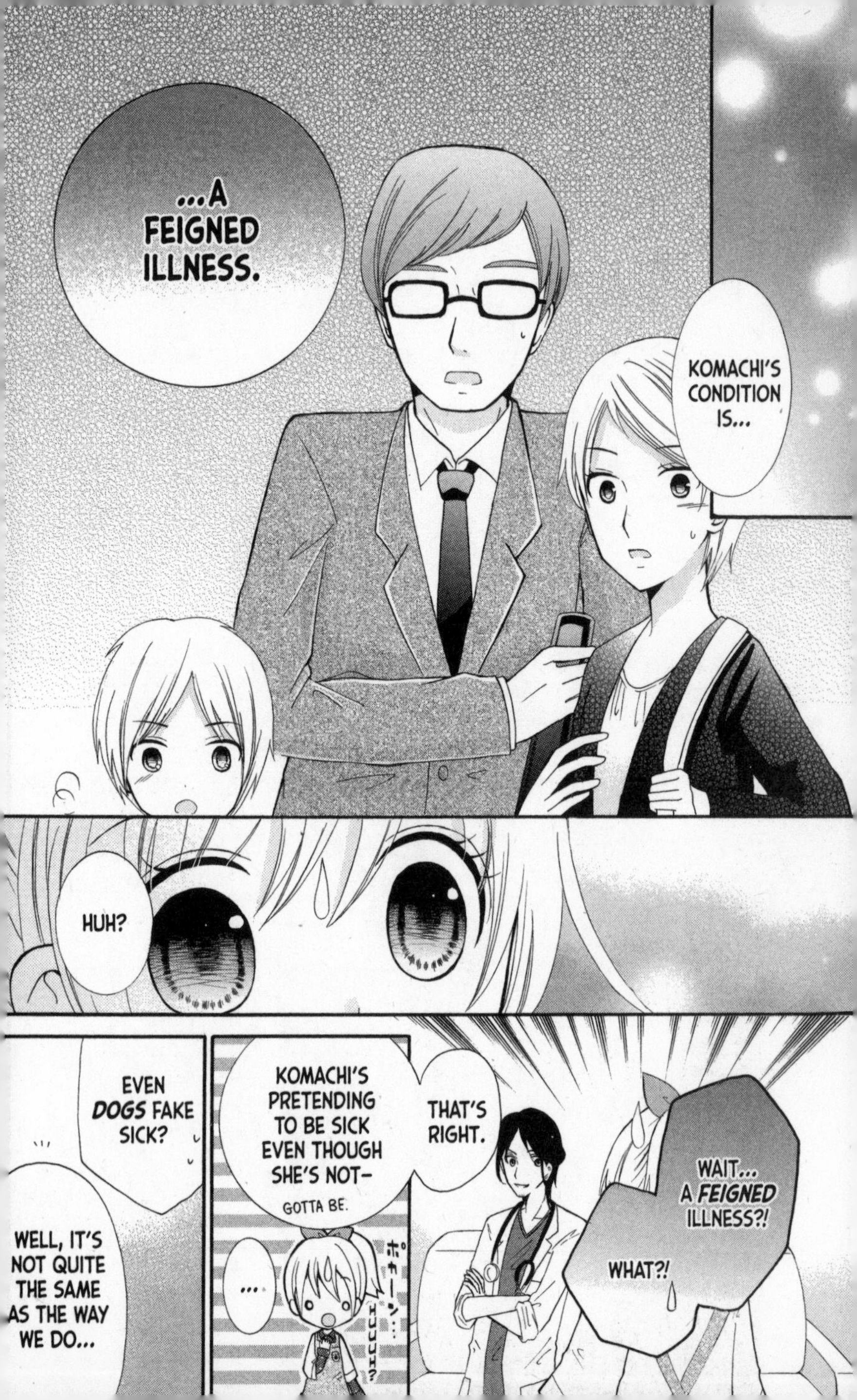
KOMACHI'S CONDITION IS...
...A FEIGNED ILLNESS.
HUH?
WAIT... A *FEIGNED* ILLNESS?!
WHAT?!
THAT'S RIGHT.
KOMACHI'S PRETENDING TO BE SICK EVEN THOUGH SHE'S NOT–
GOTTA BE.
...
ポカーン…
HUUUUUH?
EVEN *DOGS* FAKE SICK?
WELL, IT'S NOT QUITE THE SAME AS THE WAY WE DO...

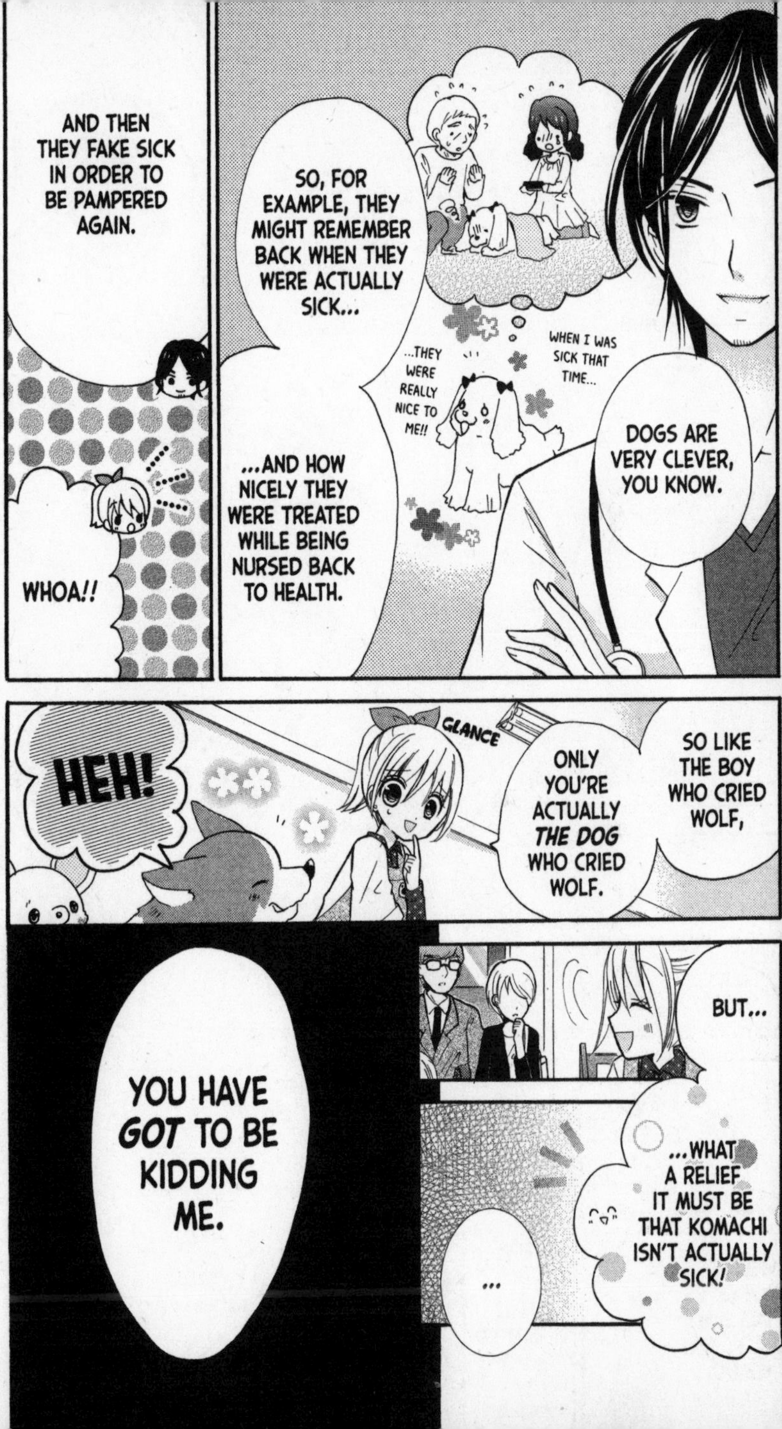
DOGS ARE VERY CLEVER, YOU KNOW.
WHEN I WAS SICK THAT TIME...
...THEY WERE REALLY NICE TO ME!!
SO, FOR EXAMPLE, THEY MIGHT REMEMBER BACK WHEN THEY WERE ACTUALLY SICK...
...AND HOW NICELY THEY WERE TREATED WHILE BEING NURSED BACK TO HEALTH.
AND THEN THEY FAKE SICK IN ORDER TO BE PAMPERED AGAIN.
WHOA!!
SO LIKE THE BOY WHO CRIED WOLF,
ONLY YOU'RE ACTUALLY *THE DOG* WHO CRIED WOLF.
GLANCE
HEH!
BUT...
...WHAT A RELIEF IT MUST BE THAT KOMACHI ISN'T ACTUALLY SICK!
...
YOU HAVE *GOT* TO BE KIDDING ME.

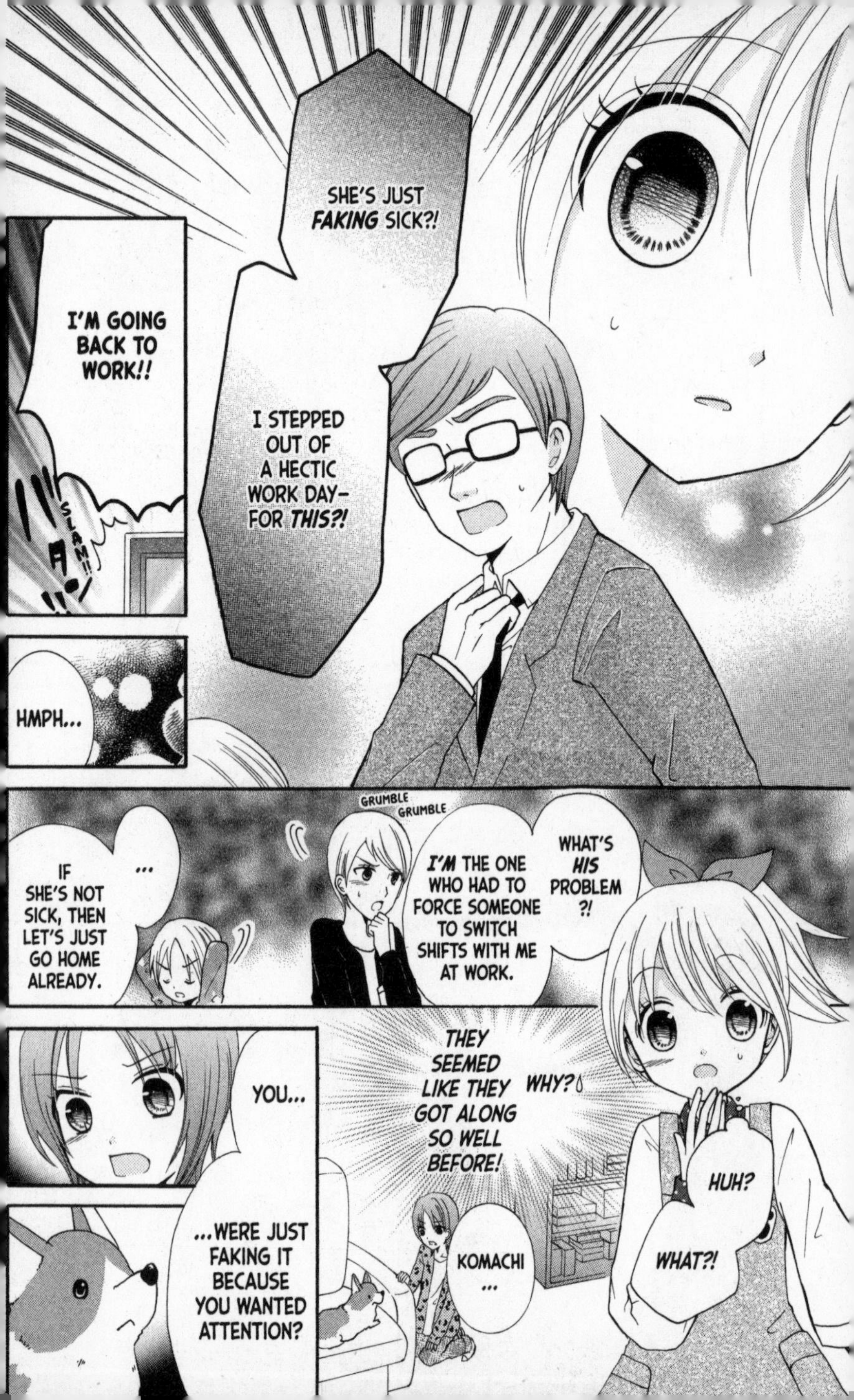
SHE'S JUST *FAKING* SICK?!
I STEPPED OUT OF A HECTIC WORK DAY— FOR *THIS?!*
I'M GOING BACK TO WORK!!
SLAM!!
HMPH...
WHAT'S *HIS* PROBLEM ?!
I'M THE ONE WHO HAD TO FORCE SOMEONE TO SWITCH SHIFTS WITH ME AT WORK.
GRUMBLE GRUMBLE
...
IF SHE'S NOT SICK, THEN LET'S JUST GO HOME ALREADY.
THEY SEEMED LIKE THEY GOT ALONG SO WELL BEFORE!
WHY?
HUH?
WHAT?!
KOMACHI ...
YOU...
...WERE JUST FAKING IT BECAUSE YOU WANTED ATTENTION?

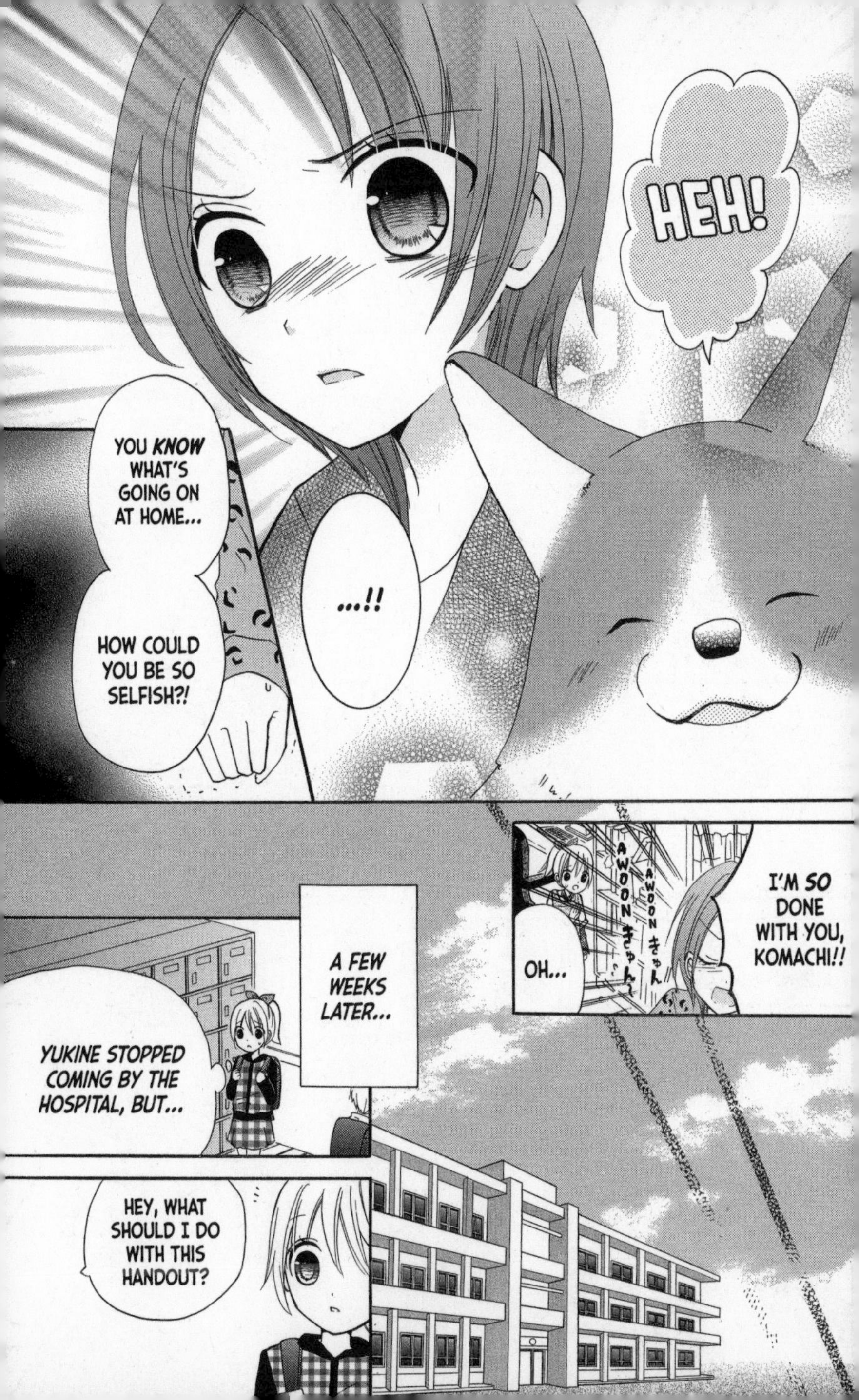
HEH!
YOU KNOW WHAT'S GOING ON AT HOME...
HOW COULD YOU BE SO SELFISH?!
...!!
I'M SO DONE WITH YOU, KOMACHI!!
AWOON きゅん
AWOON きゅん
OH...
A FEW WEEKS LATER...
YUKINE STOPPED COMING BY THE HOSPITAL, BUT...
HEY, WHAT SHOULD I DO WITH THIS HANDOUT?

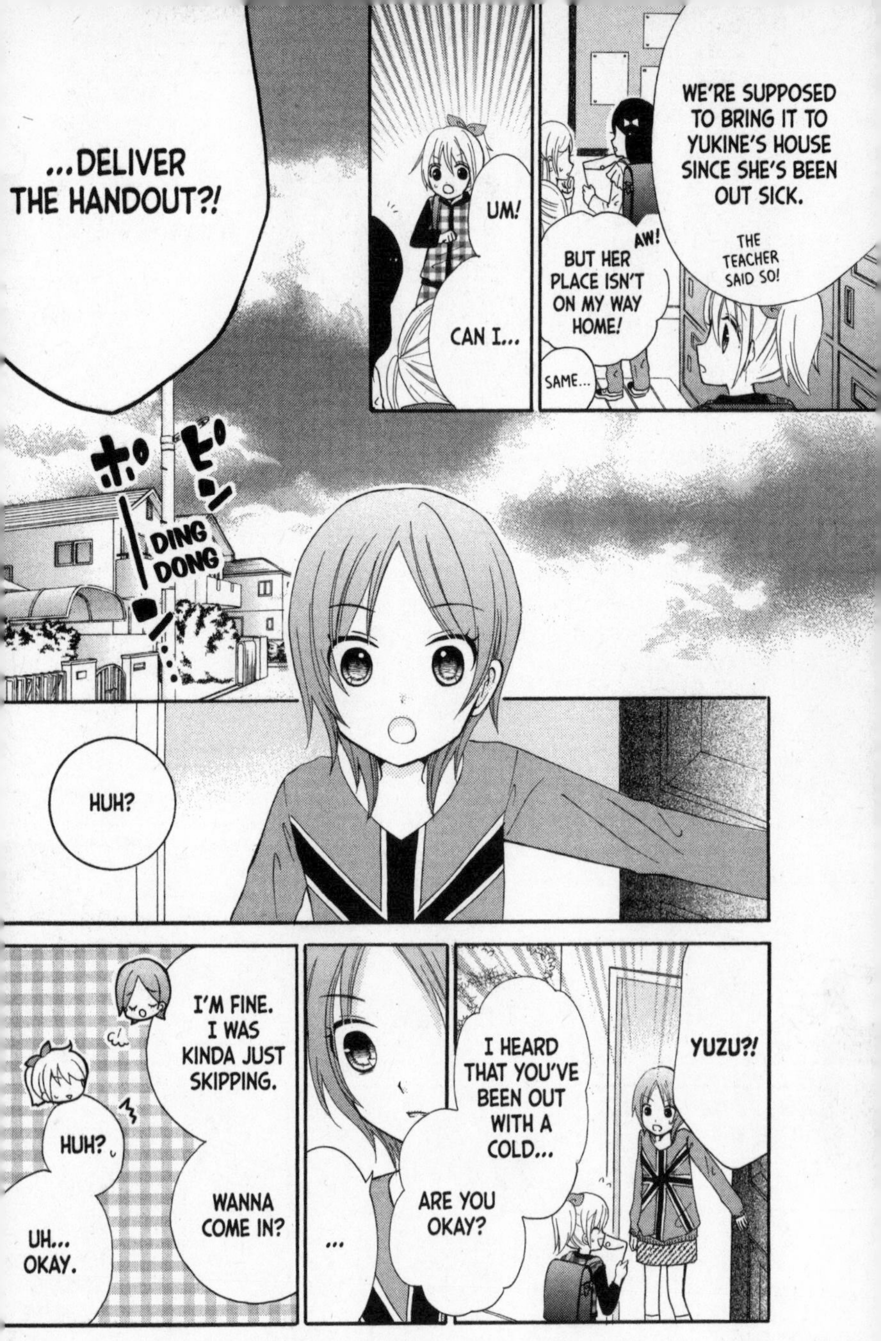
WE'RE SUPPOSED TO BRING IT TO YUKINE'S HOUSE SINCE SHE'S BEEN OUT SICK.
THE TEACHER SAID SO!
AW!
BUT HER PLACE ISN'T ON MY WAY HOME!
SAME...
UM!
CAN I...
...DELIVER THE HANDOUT?!
ピンポーン
DING DONG
HUH?
YUZU?!
I HEARD THAT YOU'VE BEEN OUT WITH A COLD...
ARE YOU OKAY?
...
I'M FINE. I WAS KINDA JUST SKIPPING.
HUH?
WANNA COME IN?
UH... OKAY.

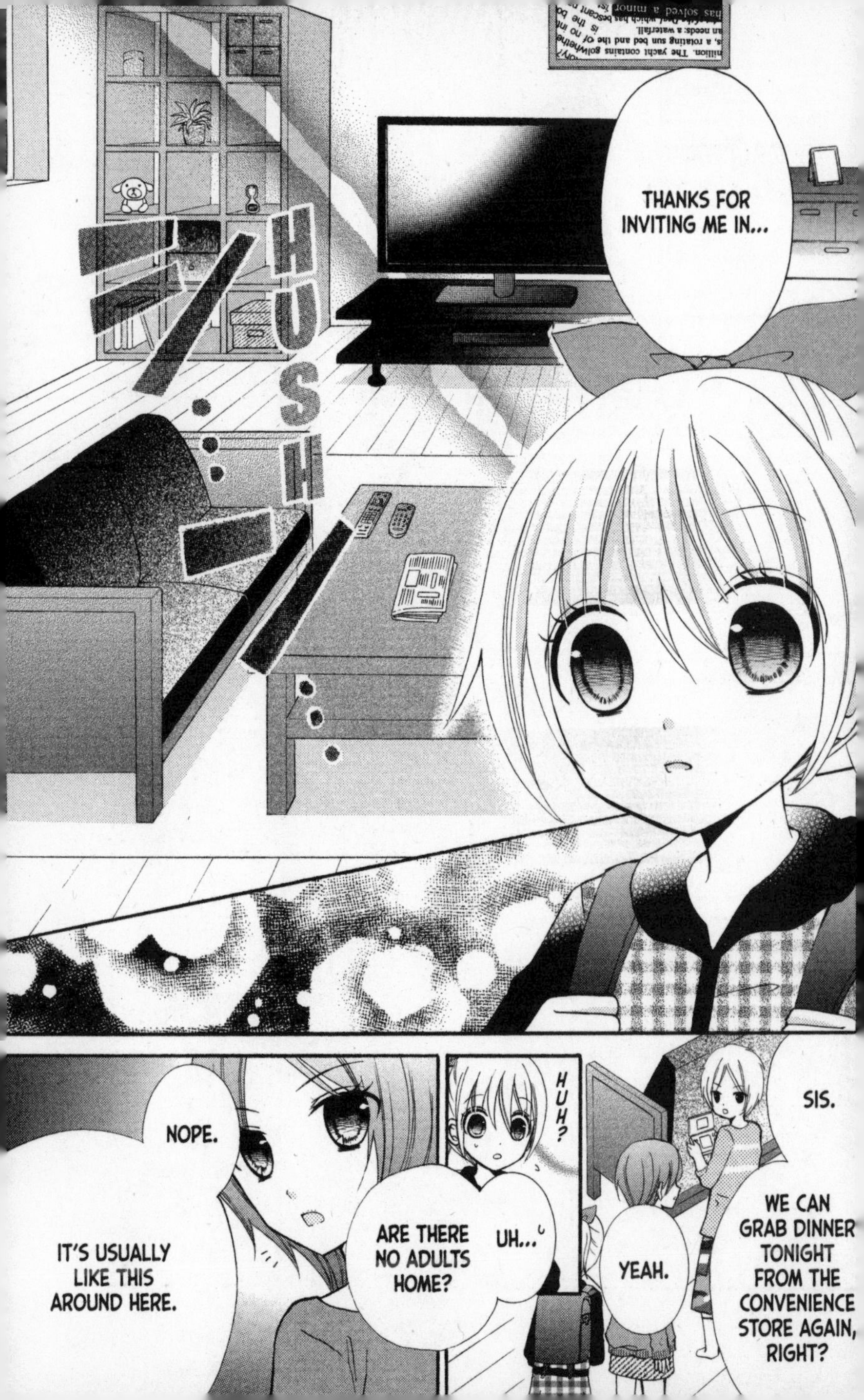
THANKS FOR INVITING ME IN...
HUSH
SIS.
WE CAN GRAB DINNER TONIGHT FROM THE CONVENIENCE STORE AGAIN, RIGHT?
YEAH.
HUH?
UH...
ARE THERE NO ADULTS HOME?
NOPE.
IT'S USUALLY LIKE THIS AROUND HERE.

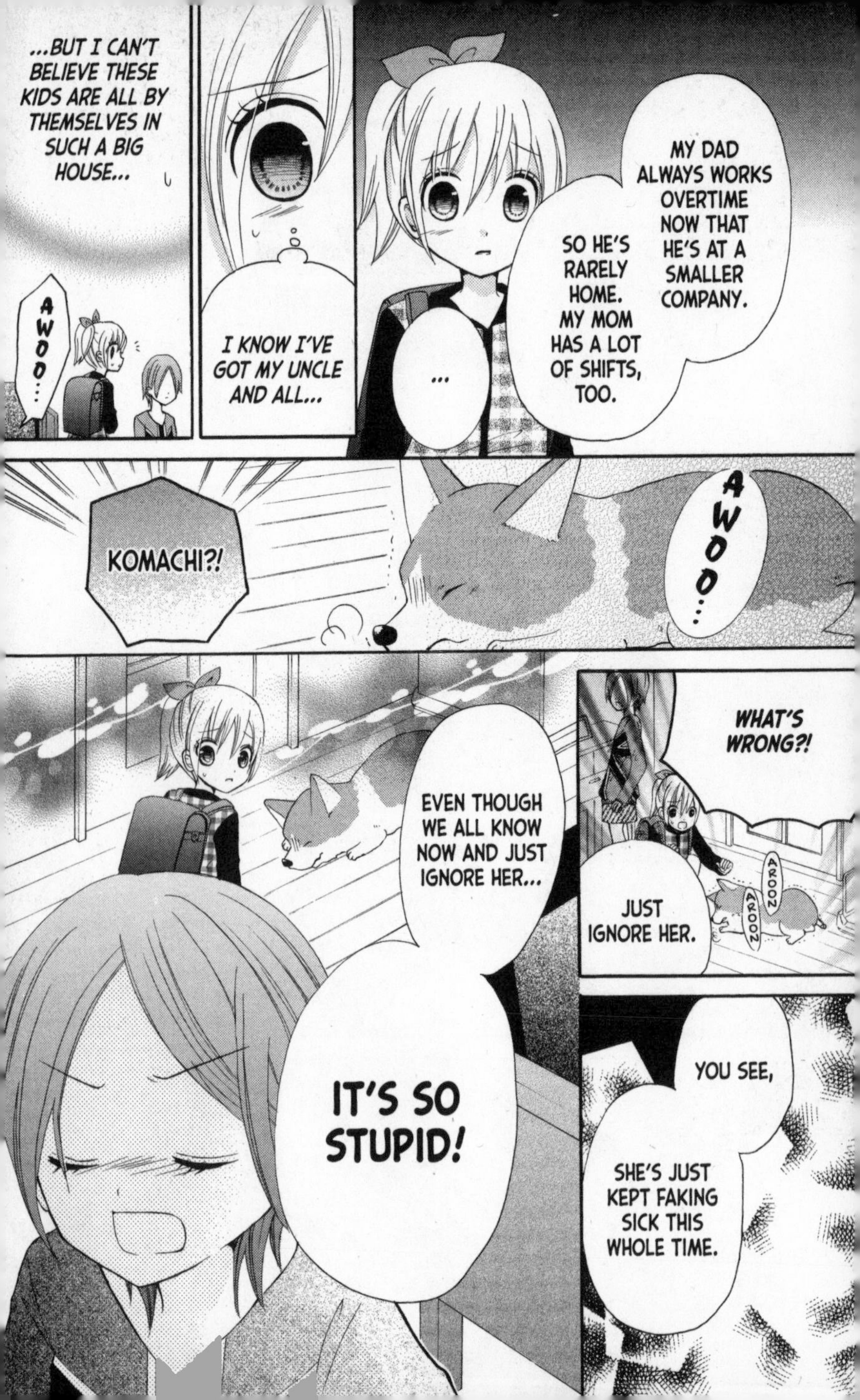
MY DAD ALWAYS WORKS OVERTIME NOW THAT HE'S AT A SMALLER COMPANY.
SO HE'S RARELY HOME. MY MOM HAS A LOT OF SHIFTS, TOO.
...
I KNOW I'VE GOT MY UNCLE AND ALL...
...BUT I CAN'T BELIEVE THESE KIDS ARE ALL BY THEMSELVES IN SUCH A BIG HOUSE...
AWOO...
AWOO...
KOMACHI?!
WHAT'S WRONG?!
AROON
AROON
JUST IGNORE HER.
YOU SEE,
SHE'S JUST KEPT FAKING SICK THIS WHOLE TIME.
EVEN THOUGH WE ALL KNOW NOW AND JUST IGNORE HER...
IT'S SO STUPID!

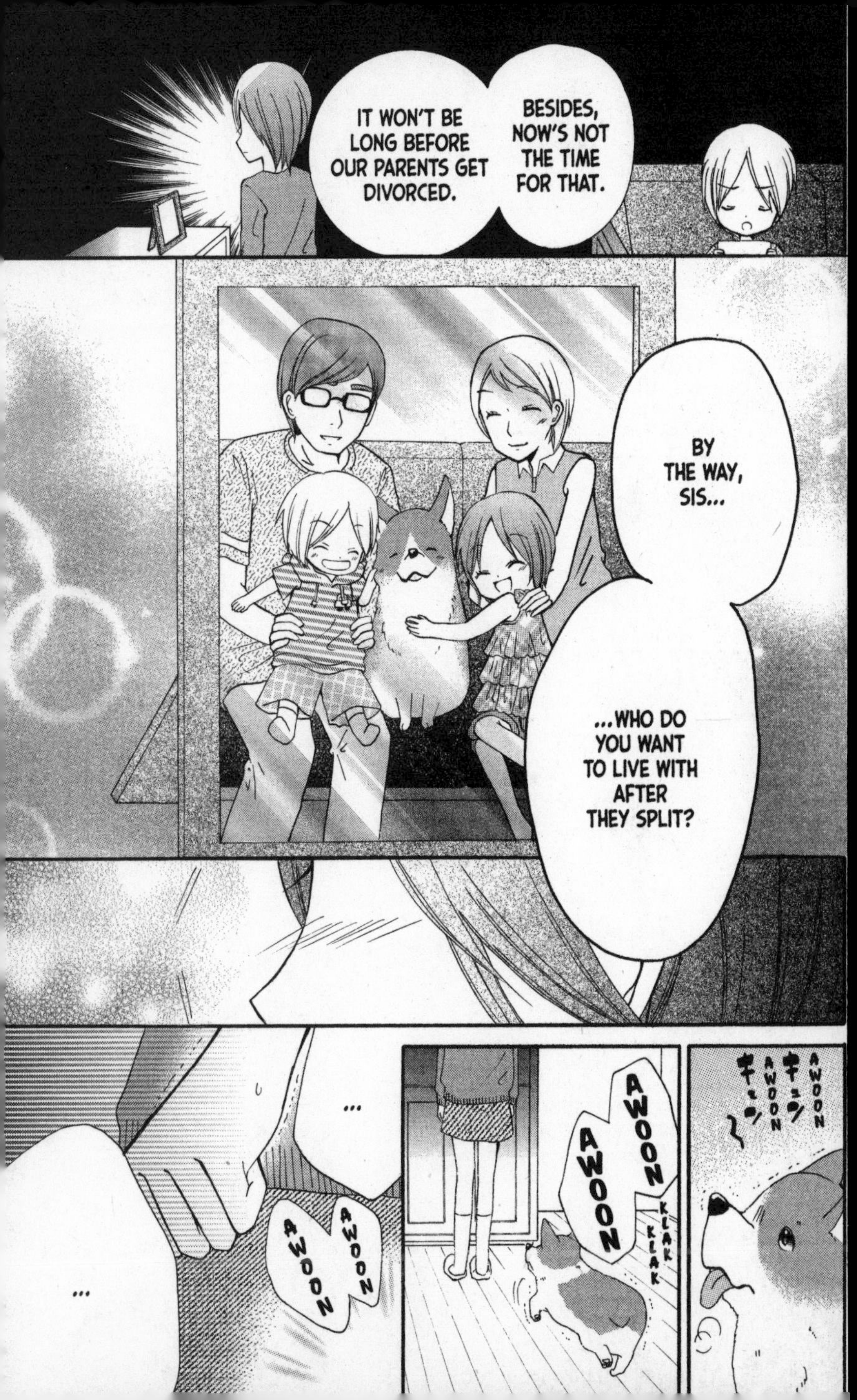
BESIDES, NOW'S NOT THE TIME FOR THAT.
IT WON'T BE LONG BEFORE OUR PARENTS GET DIVORCED.
BY THE WAY, SIS...
...WHO DO YOU WANT TO LIVE WITH AFTER THEY SPLIT?
AWOON
AWOON
AWOON
AWOON
KLAK
KLAK
...
AWOON
AWOON
...

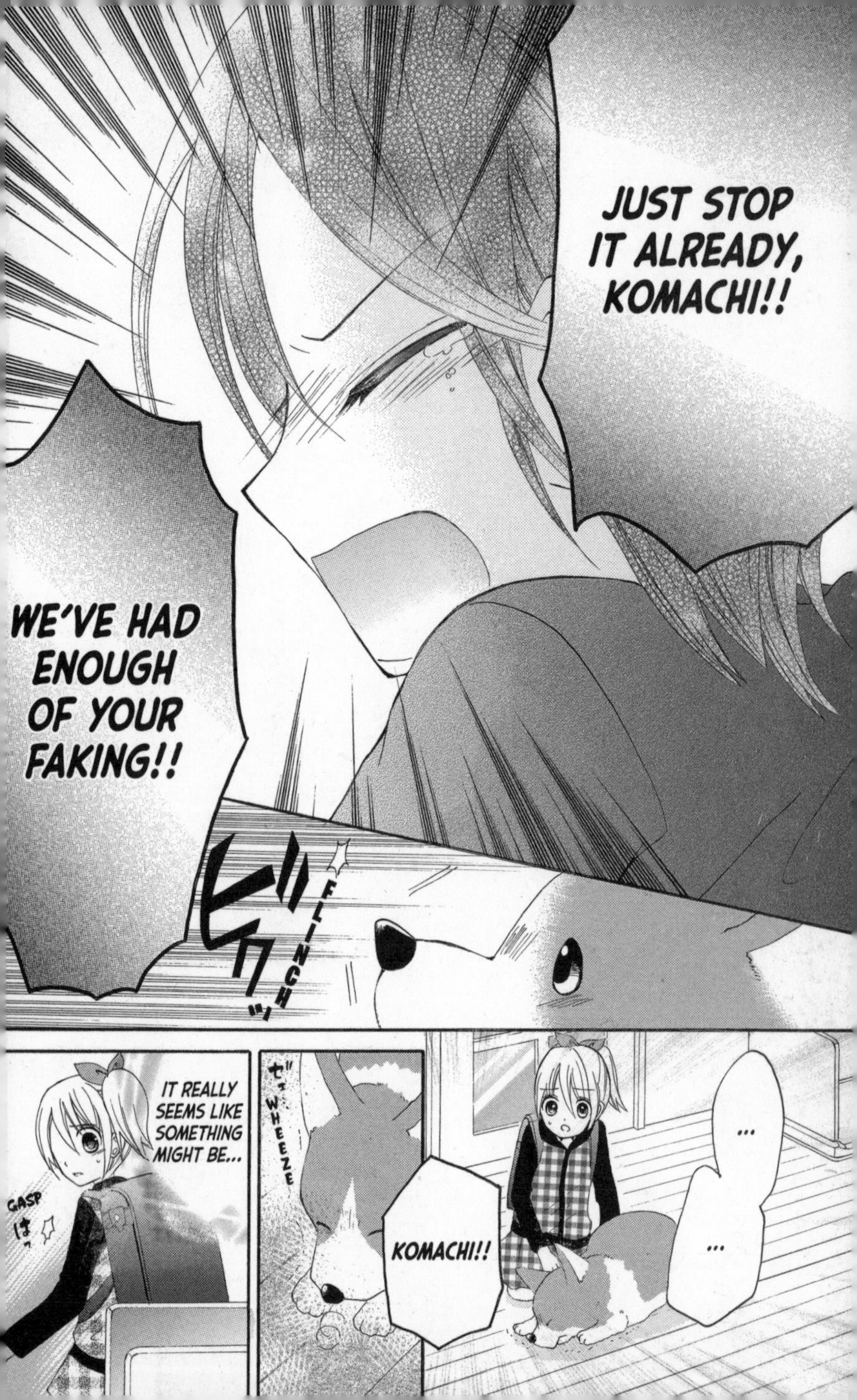
JUST STOP IT ALREADY, KOMACHI!!
WE'VE HAD ENOUGH OF YOUR FAKING!!
ビクッ
FLINCH
...
...
KOMACHI!!
ぜー
WHEEZE
IT REALLY SEEMS LIKE SOMETHING MIGHT BE...
GASP
はっ

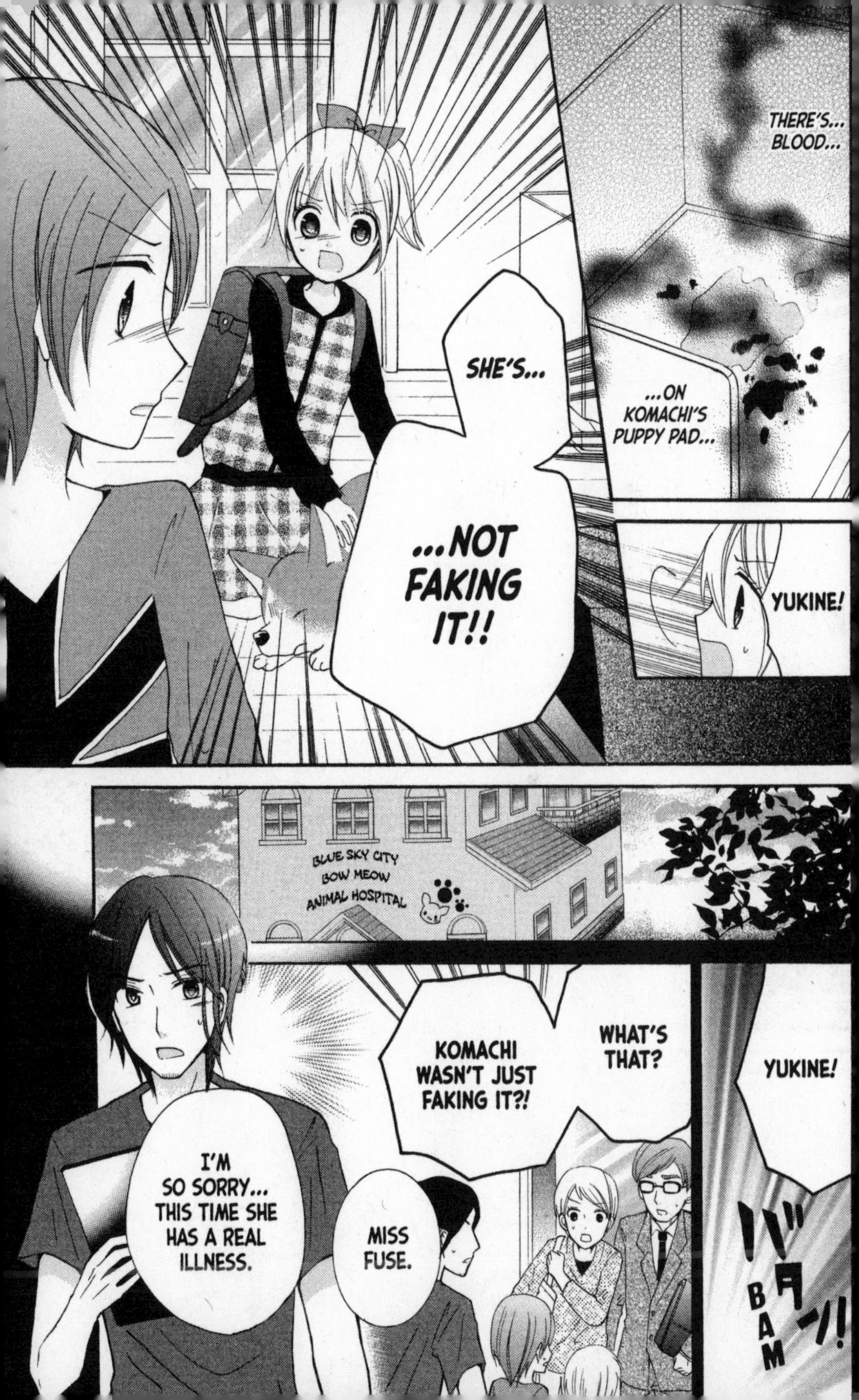
THERE'S... BLOOD...
...ON KOMACHI'S PUPPY PAD...
YUKINE!
SHE'S...
...NOT FAKING IT!!
BLUE SKY CITY BOW MEOW ANIMAL HOSPITAL
YUKINE!
BAM
WHAT'S THAT?
KOMACHI WASN'T JUST FAKING IT?!
MISS FUSE.
I'M SO SORRY... THIS TIME SHE HAS A REAL ILLNESS.

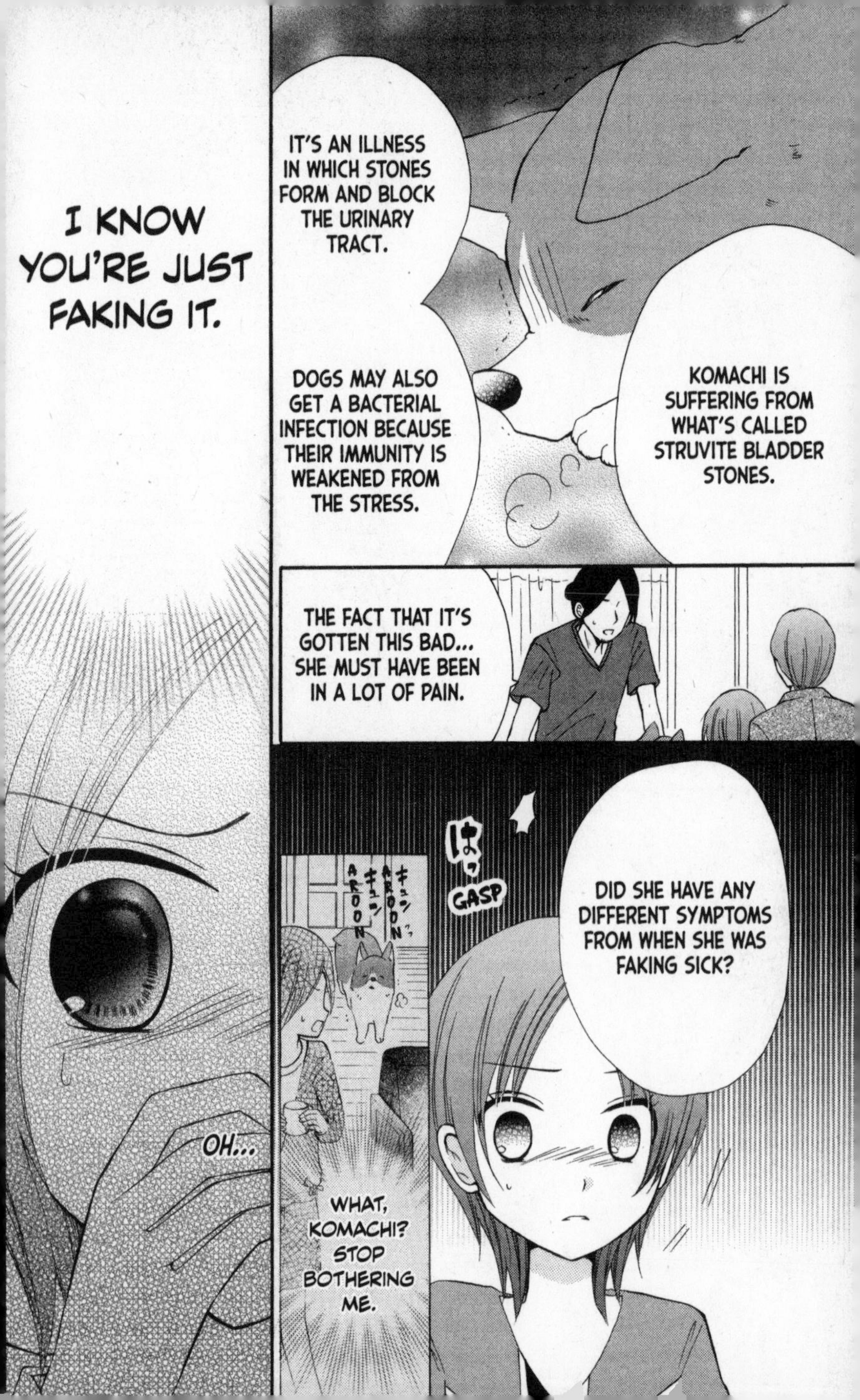
KOMACHI IS SUFFERING FROM WHAT'S CALLED STRUVITE BLADDER STONES.
IT'S AN ILLNESS IN WHICH STONES FORM AND BLOCK THE URINARY TRACT.
DOGS MAY ALSO GET A BACTERIAL INFECTION BECAUSE THEIR IMMUNITY IS WEAKENED FROM THE STRESS.
THE FACT THAT IT'S GOTTEN THIS BAD... SHE MUST HAVE BEEN IN A LOT OF PAIN.
DID SHE HAVE ANY DIFFERENT SYMPTOMS FROM WHEN SHE WAS FAKING SICK?
はっ
GASP
キュン
AROOON
キュン
AROOON
WHAT, KOMACHI? STOP BOTHERING ME.
I KNOW YOU'RE JUST FAKING IT.
OH...

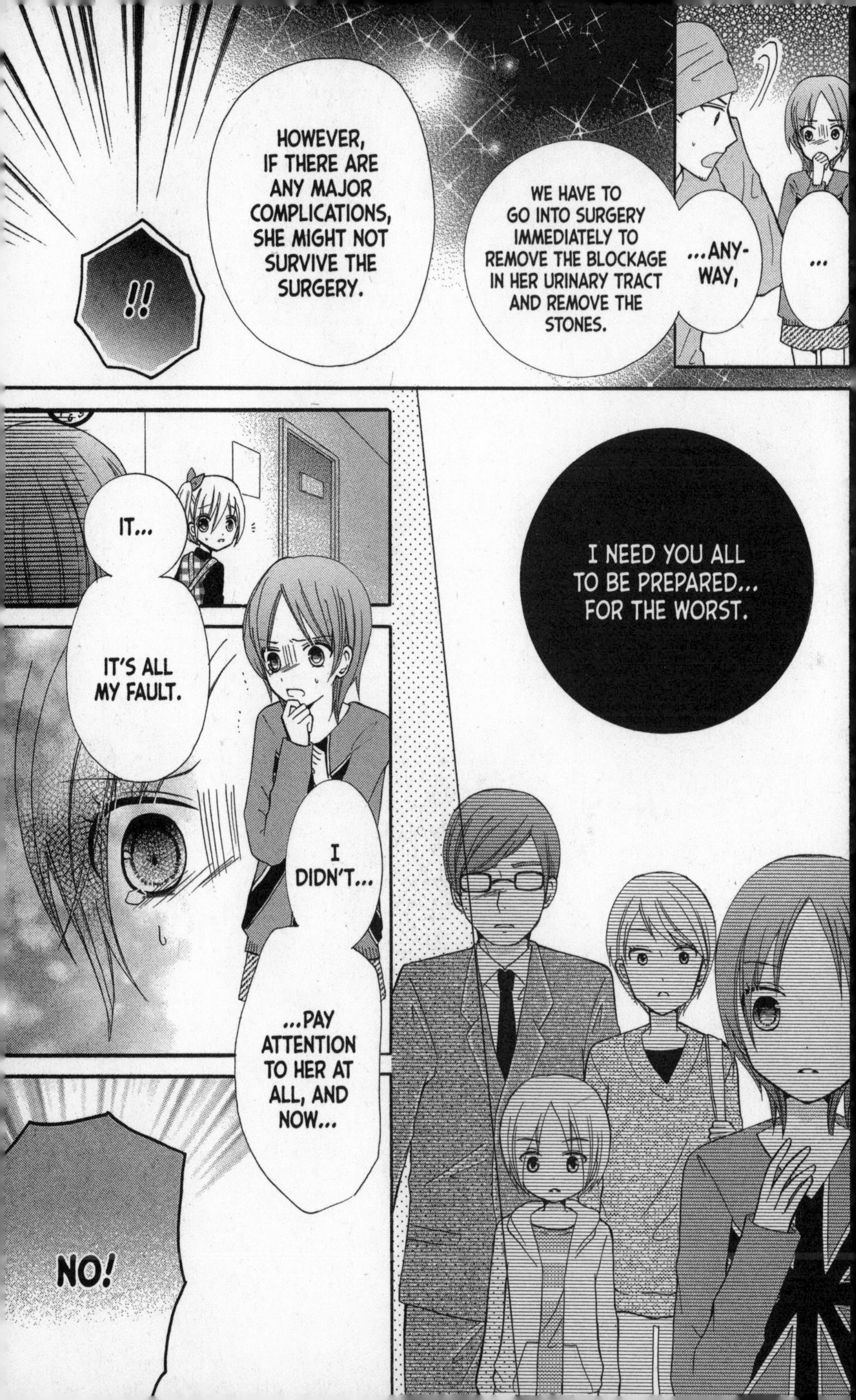
...
...ANY-WAY,
WE HAVE TO GO INTO SURGERY IMMEDIATELY TO REMOVE THE BLOCKAGE IN HER URINARY TRACT AND REMOVE THE STONES.
HOWEVER, IF THERE ARE ANY MAJOR COMPLICATIONS, SHE MIGHT NOT SURVIVE THE SURGERY.
!!
I NEED YOU ALL TO BE PREPARED... FOR THE WORST.
IT...
IT'S ALL MY FAULT.
I DIDN'T...
...PAY ATTENTION TO HER AT ALL, AND NOW...
NO!

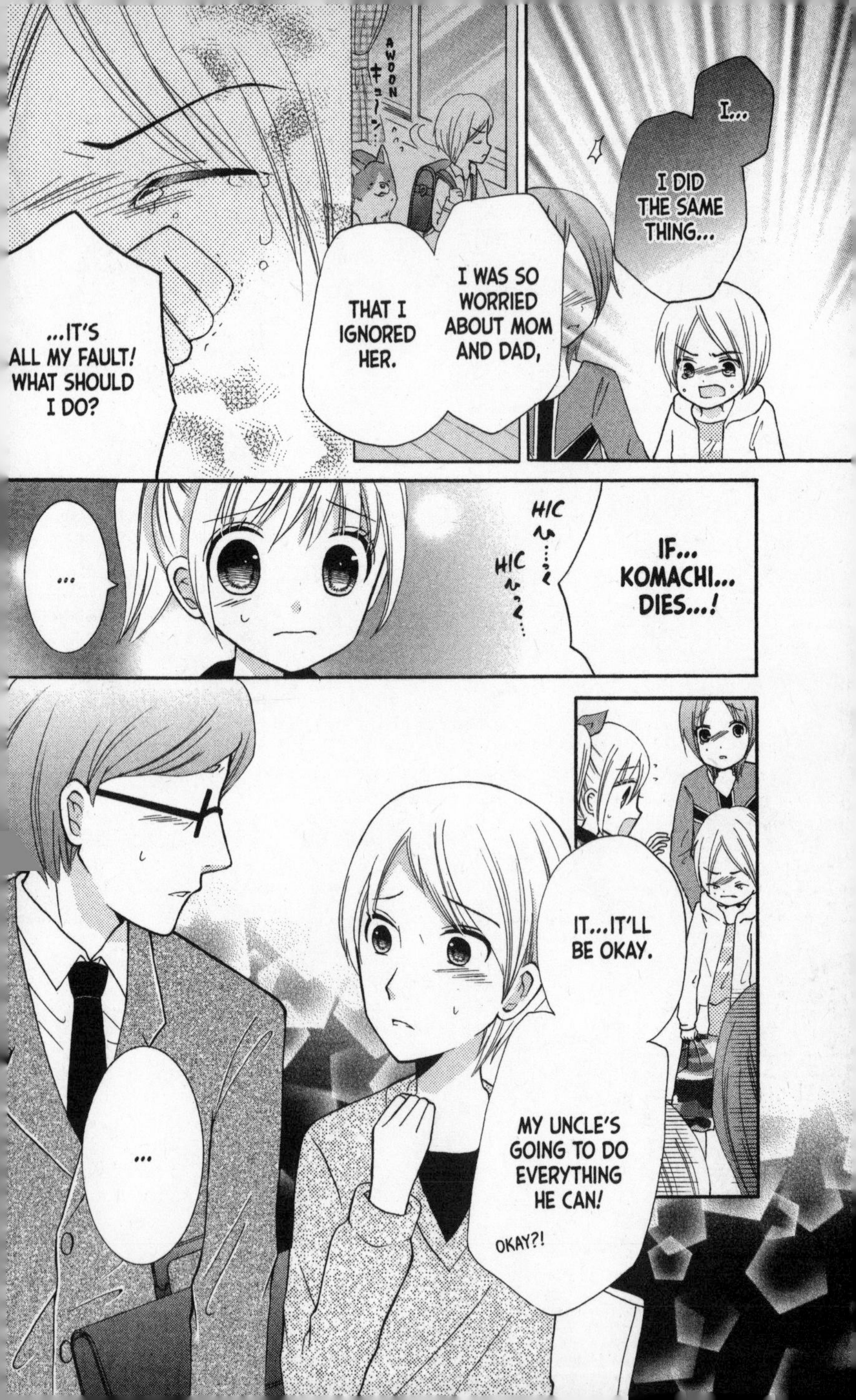
I...
I DID THE SAME THING...
AWOON
I WAS SO WORRIED ABOUT MOM AND DAD,
THAT I IGNORED HER.
...IT'S ALL MY FAULT! WHAT SHOULD I DO?
HIC
HIC
IF... KOMACHI... DIES...!
...
IT...IT'LL BE OKAY.
MY UNCLE'S GOING TO DO EVERYTHING HE CAN!
OKAY?!
...

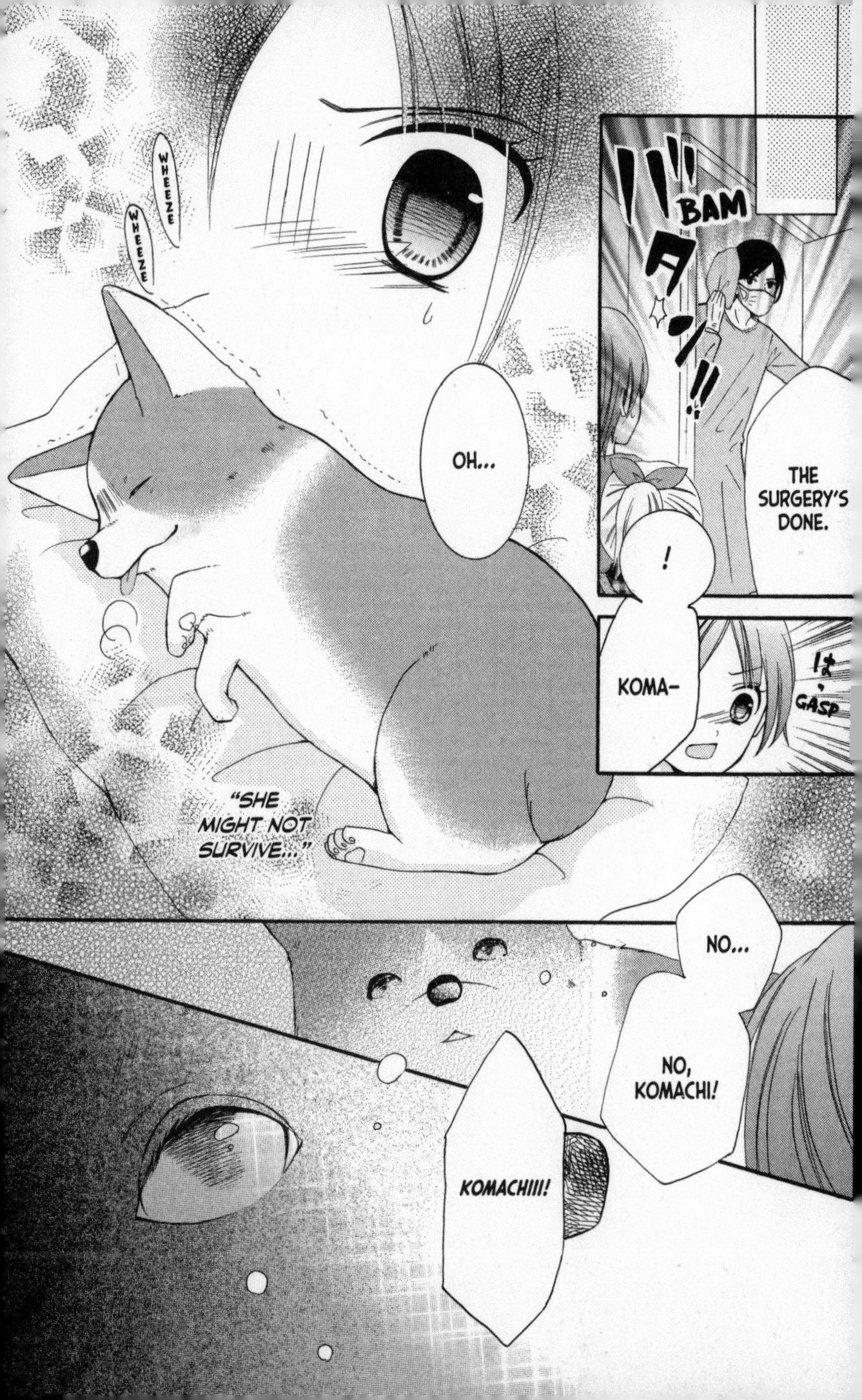
BAM
THE SURGERY'S DONE.
!
GASP
KOMA-
OH...
WHEEZE
WHEEZE
"SHE MIGHT NOT SURVIVE..."
NO...
NO, KOMACHI!
KOMACHIII!

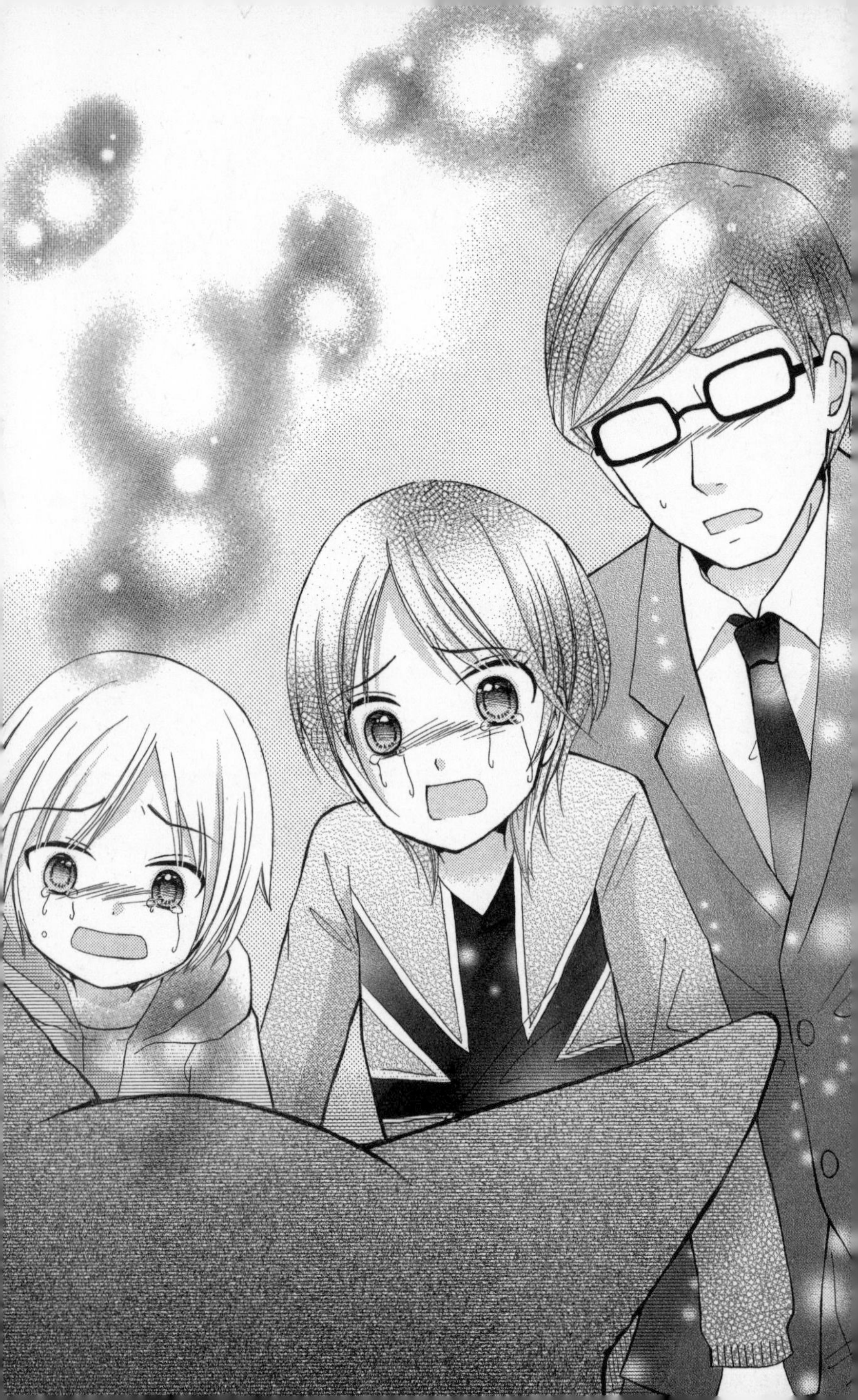

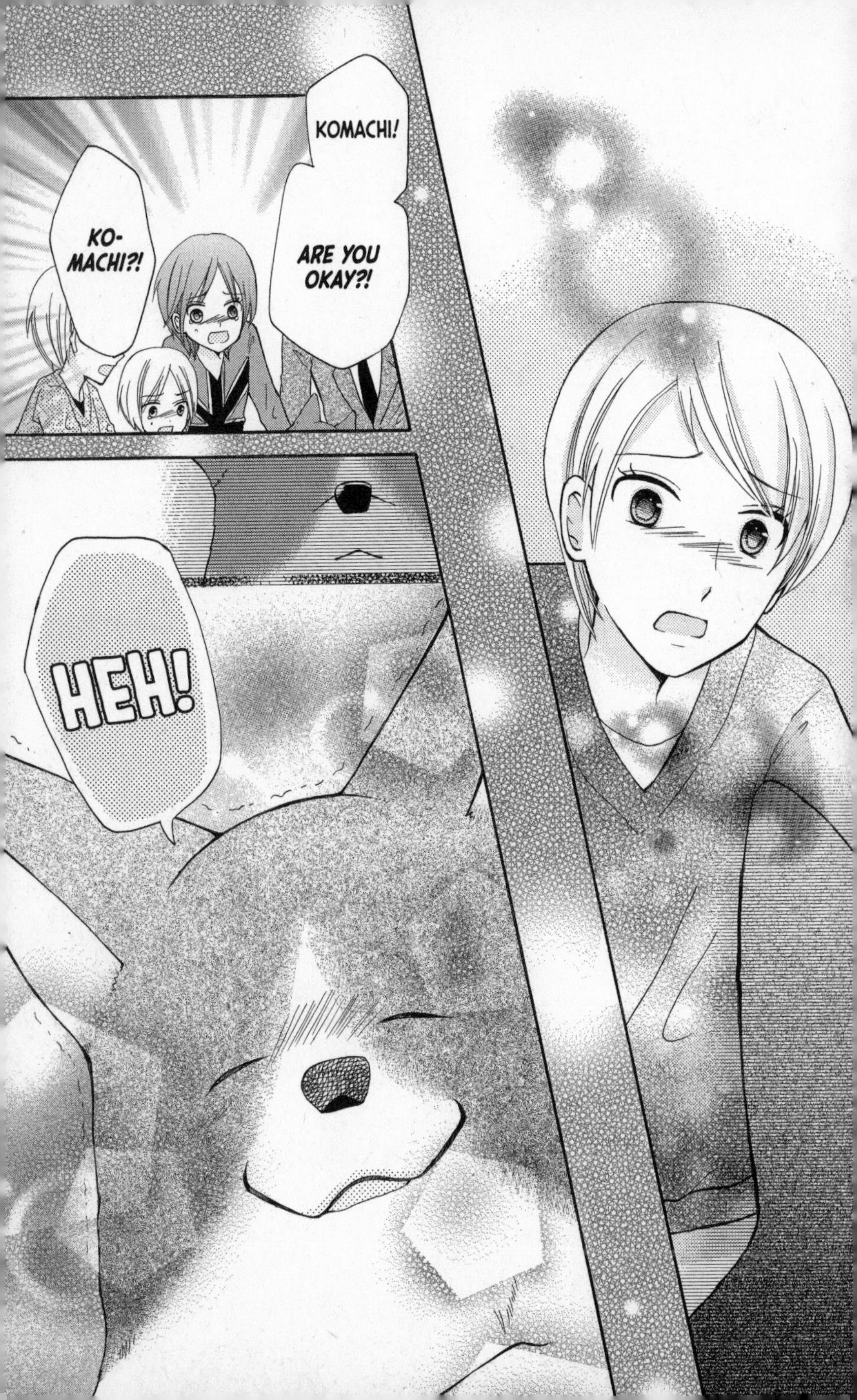
KOMACHI!
ARE YOU OKAY?!
KO-MACHI?!
HEH!

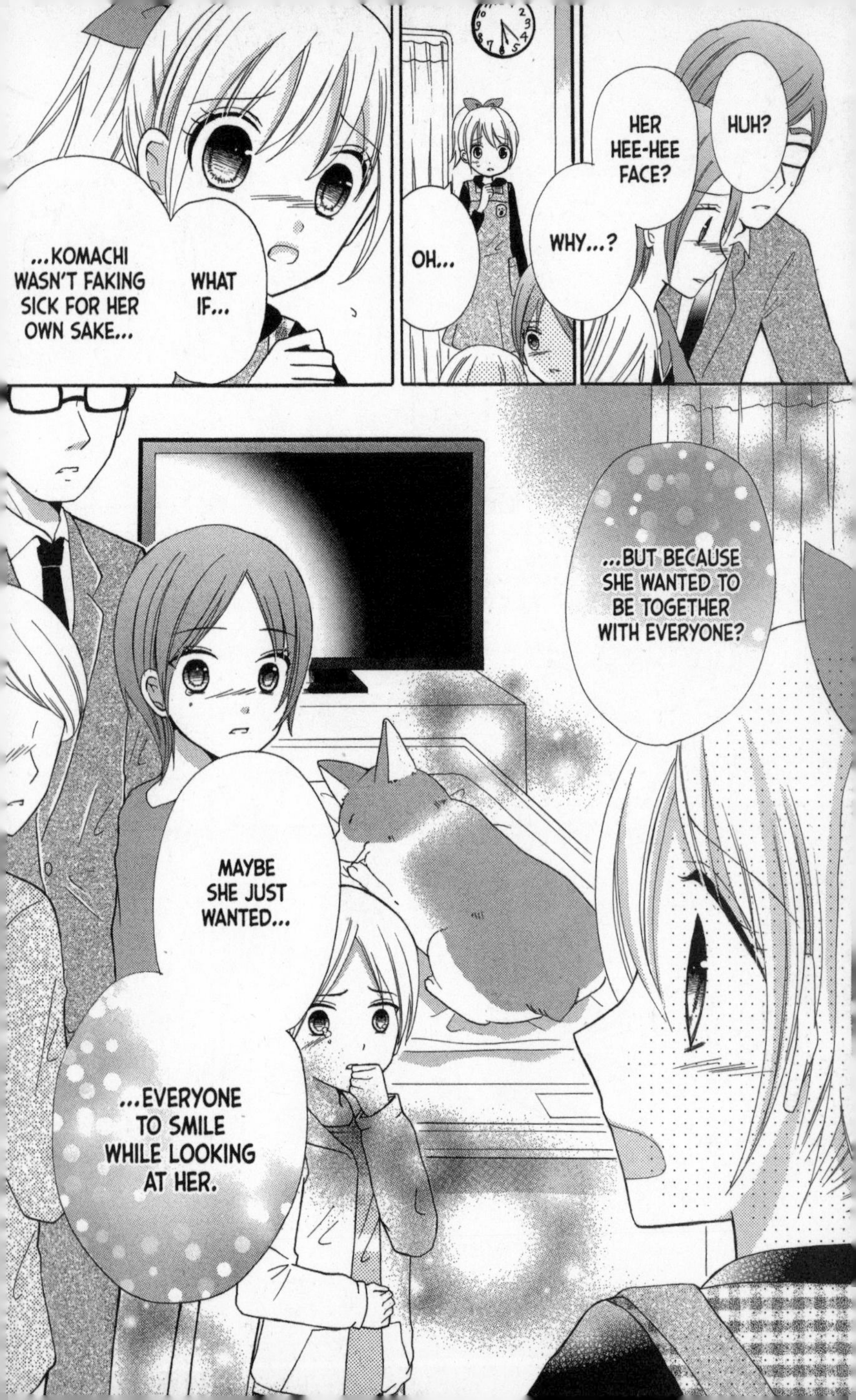
HUH?
HER HEE-HEE FACE?
WHY...?
OH...
WHAT IF...
...KOMACHI WASN'T FAKING SICK FOR HER OWN SAKE...
...BUT BECAUSE SHE WANTED TO BE TOGETHER WITH EVERYONE?
MAYBE SHE JUST WANTED...
...EVERYONE TO SMILE WHILE LOOKING AT HER.

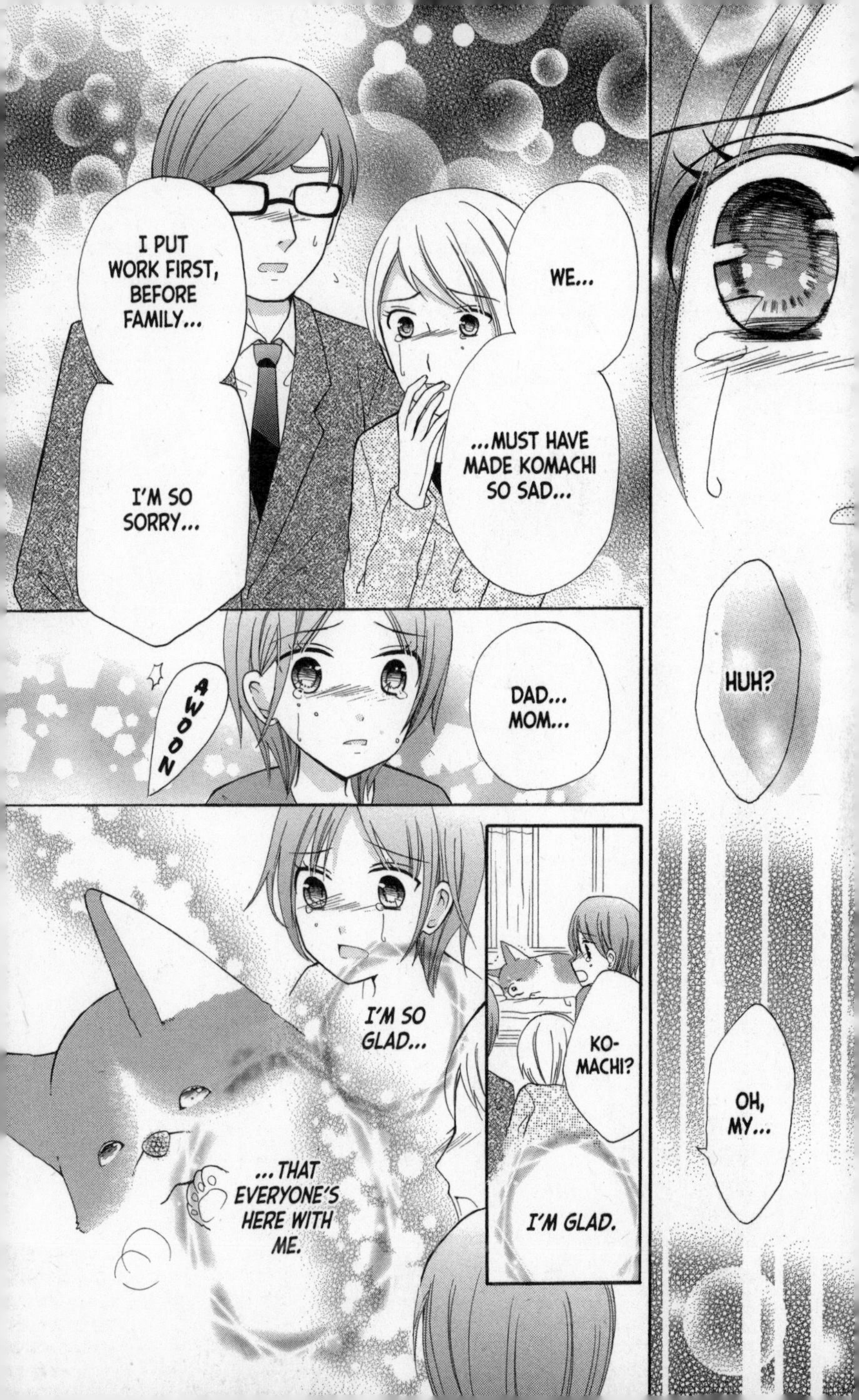
HUH?
OH, MY...
WE...
...MUST HAVE MADE KOMACHI SO SAD...
I PUT WORK FIRST, BEFORE FAMILY...
I'M SO SORRY...
DAD... MOM...
AWOOON
KO-MACHI?
I'M GLAD.
I'M SO GLAD...
...THAT EVERYONE'S HERE WITH ME.

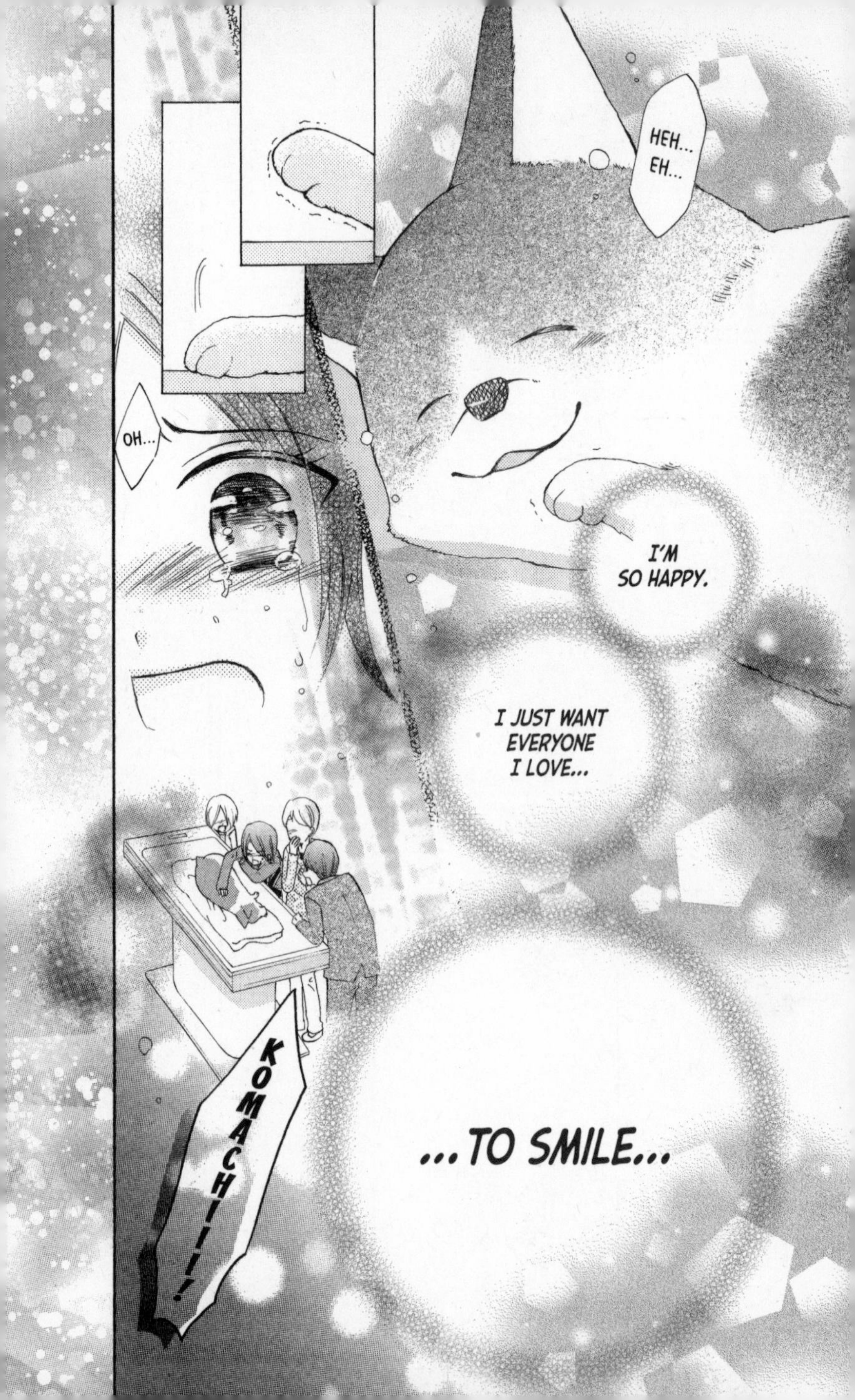
HEH... EH...
I'M SO HAPPY.
I JUST WANT EVERYONE I LOVE...
...TO SMILE...
OH...
KOMACHIIIII!

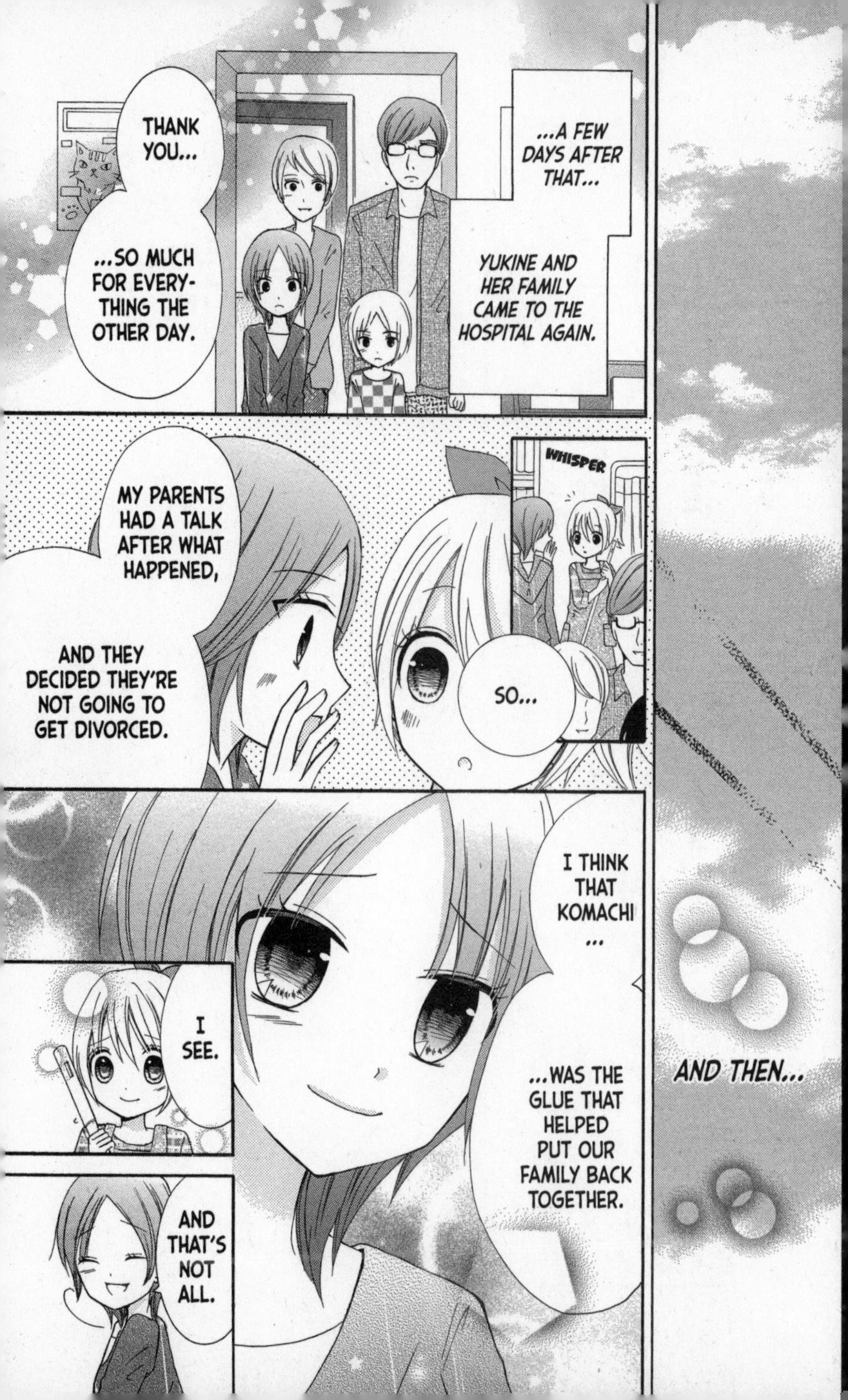
AND THEN...
...A FEW DAYS AFTER THAT...
YUKINE AND HER FAMILY CAME TO THE HOSPITAL AGAIN.
THANK YOU...
...SO MUCH FOR EVERY-THING THE OTHER DAY.
WHISPER
MY PARENTS HAD A TALK AFTER WHAT HAPPENED,
AND THEY DECIDED THEY'RE NOT GOING TO GET DIVORCED.
SO...
I THINK THAT KOMACHI ...
...WAS THE GLUE THAT HELPED PUT OUR FAMILY BACK TOGETHER.
I SEE.
AND THAT'S NOT ALL.

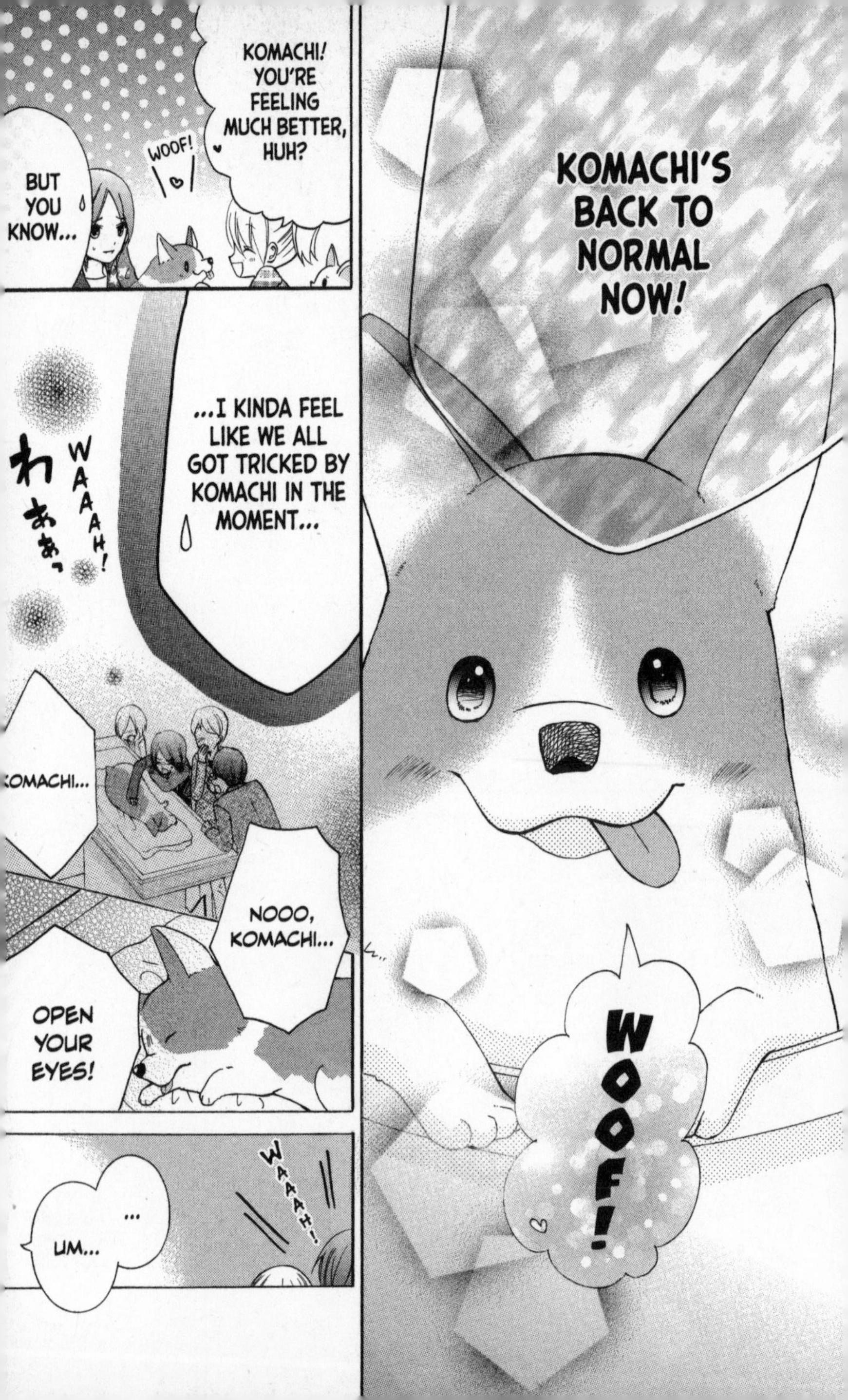
KOMACHI'S BACK TO NORMAL NOW!
WOOF!
KOMACHI! YOU'RE FEELING MUCH BETTER, HUH?
WOOF!
BUT YOU KNOW...
...I KINDA FEEL LIKE WE ALL GOT TRICKED BY KOMACHI IN THE MOMENT...
わぁあ
WAAAAH!
KOMACHI...
NOOO, KOMACHI...
OPEN YOUR EYES!
WAAAH!
...
UM...

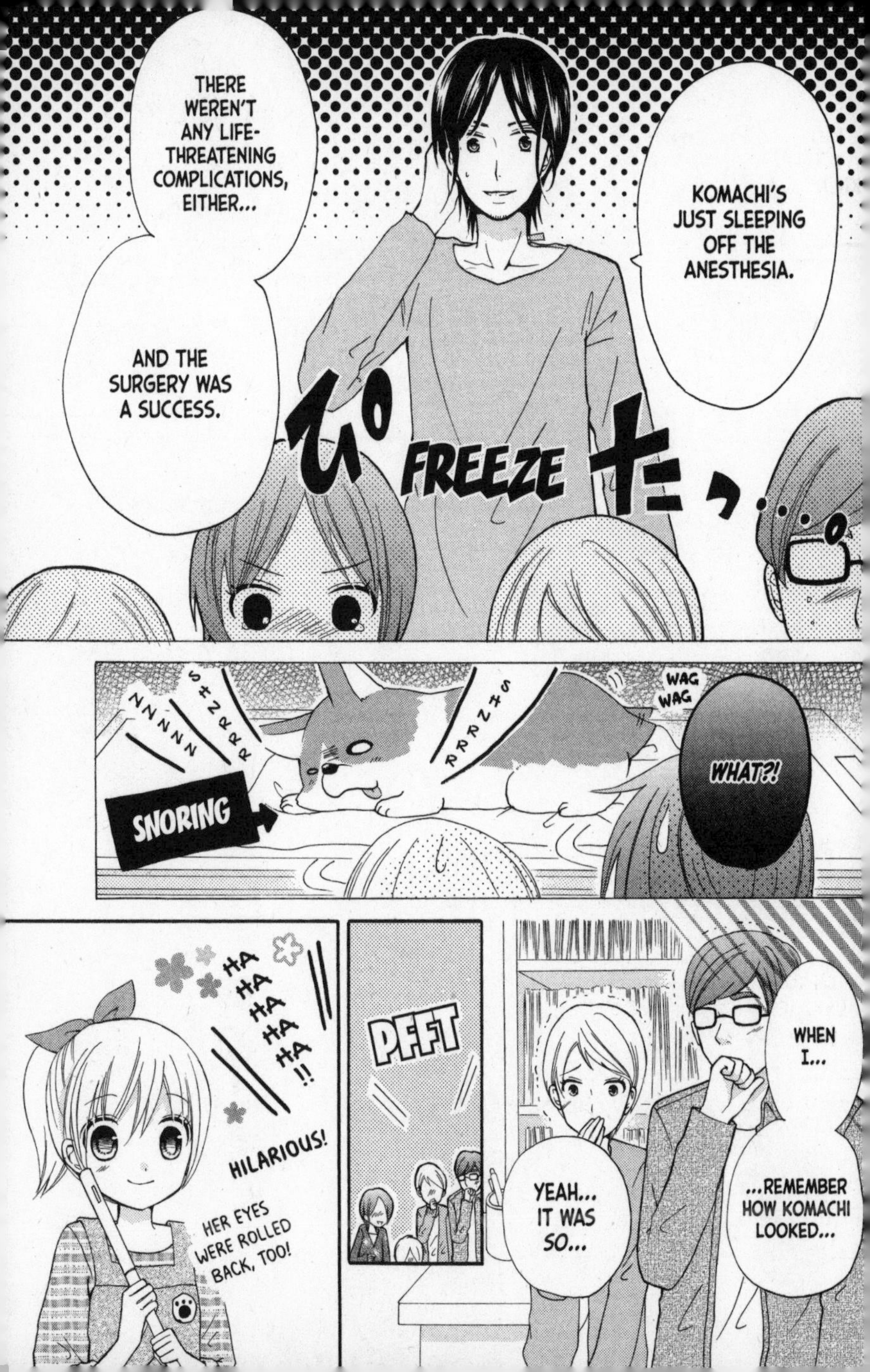
KOMACHI'S JUST SLEEPING OFF THE ANESTHESIA.
THERE WEREN'T ANY LIFE-THREATENING COMPLICATIONS, EITHER...
AND THE SURGERY WAS A SUCCESS.
FREEZE
WAG WAG
WHAT?!
NNNNN
SNORING
WHEN I...
...REMEMBER HOW KOMACHI LOOKED...
YEAH... IT WAS SO...
PFFT
HA HA HA HA HA!!
HILARIOUS!
HER EYES WERE ROLLED BACK, TOO!

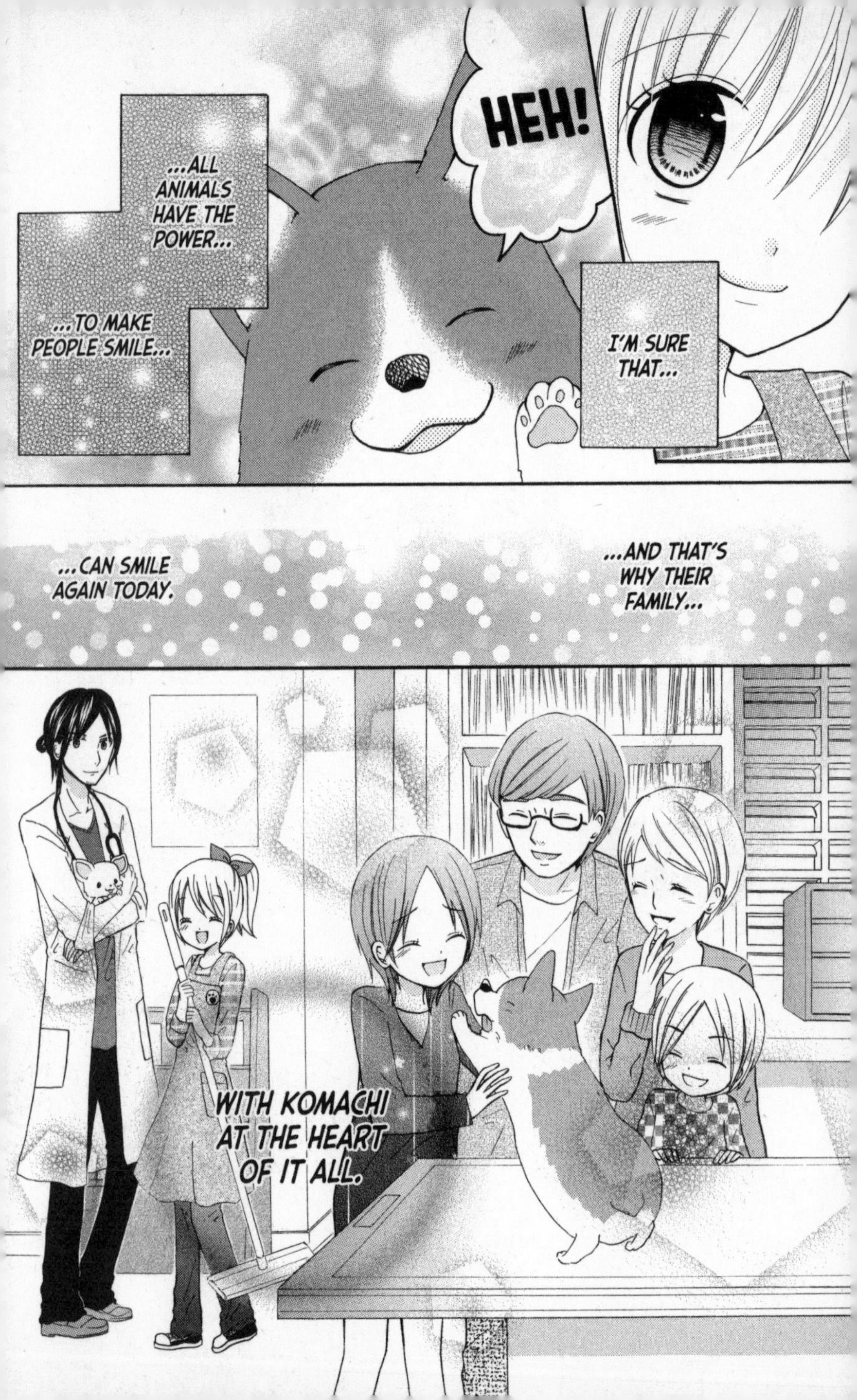
HEH!
I'M SURE THAT...
...ALL ANIMALS HAVE THE POWER...
...TO MAKE PEOPLE SMILE...
...AND THAT'S WHY THEIR FAMILY...
...CAN SMILE AGAIN TODAY.
WITH KOMACHI AT THE HEART OF IT ALL.

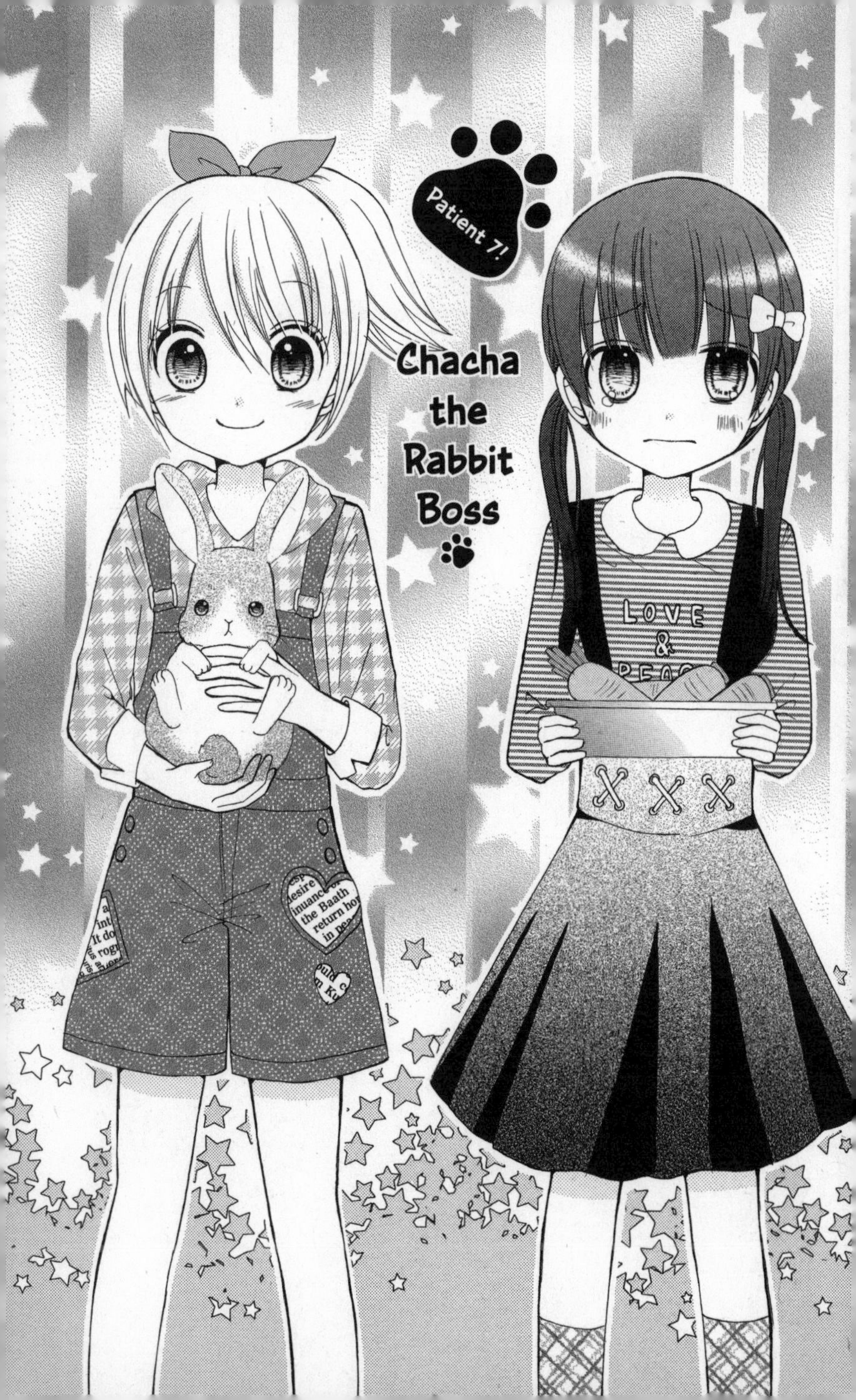
Patient 7!
Chacha the Rabbit Boss
LOVE &

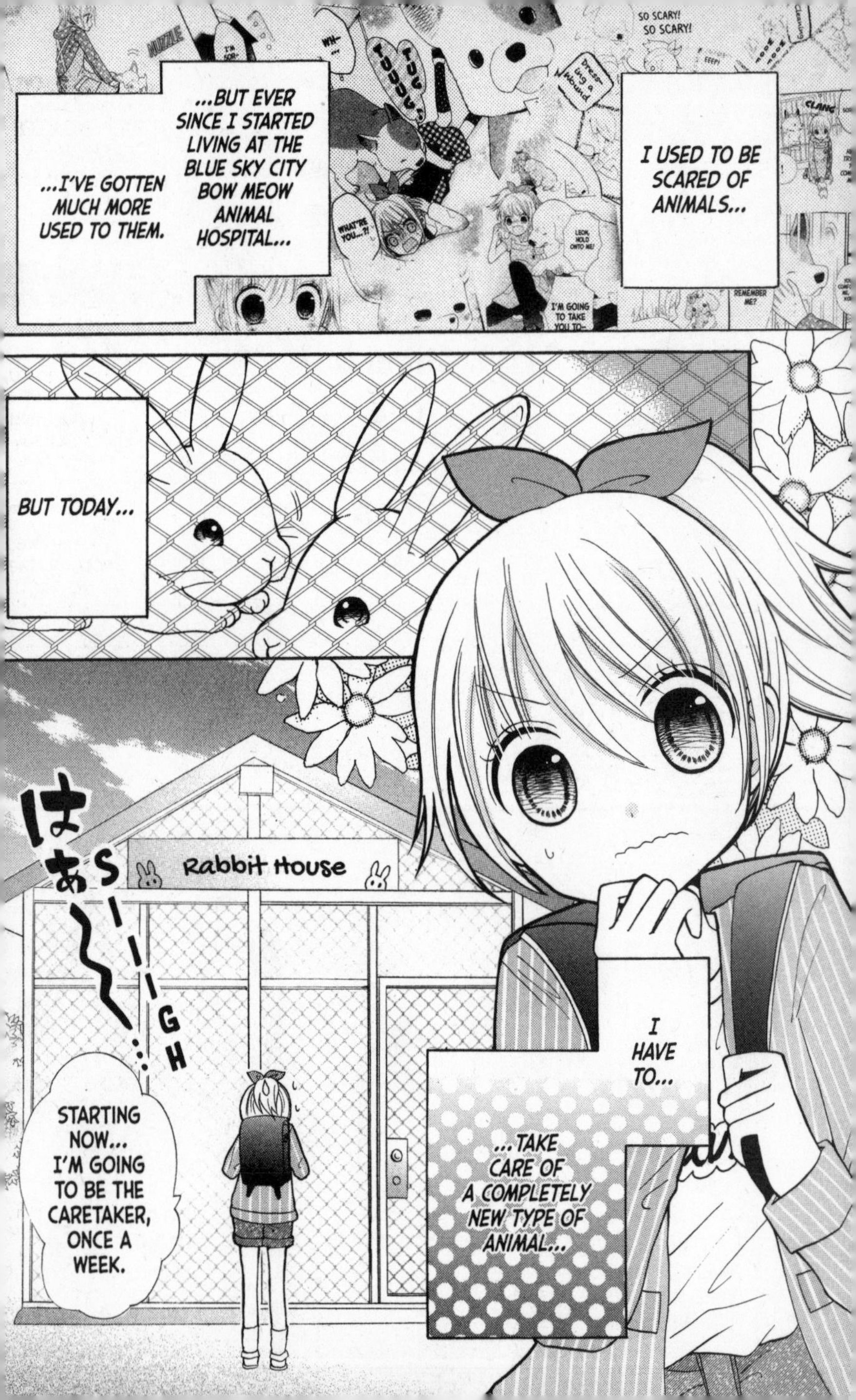
SO SCARY! SO SCARY!
I USED TO BE SCARED OF ANIMALS...
REMEMBER ME?
LEON, HOLD ONTO ME!
I'M GOING TO TAKE YOU TO-
WHAT'RE YOU...?!
...BUT EVER SINCE I STARTED LIVING AT THE BLUE SKY CITY BOW MEOW ANIMAL HOSPITAL...
NUZZLE
...I'VE GOTTEN MUCH MORE USED TO THEM.
BUT TODAY...
I HAVE TO...
...TAKE CARE OF A COMPLETELY NEW TYPE OF ANIMAL...
Rabbit House
はあ〜〜〜…
S-I-I-IGH
STARTING NOW... I'M GOING TO BE THE CARETAKER, ONCE A WEEK.

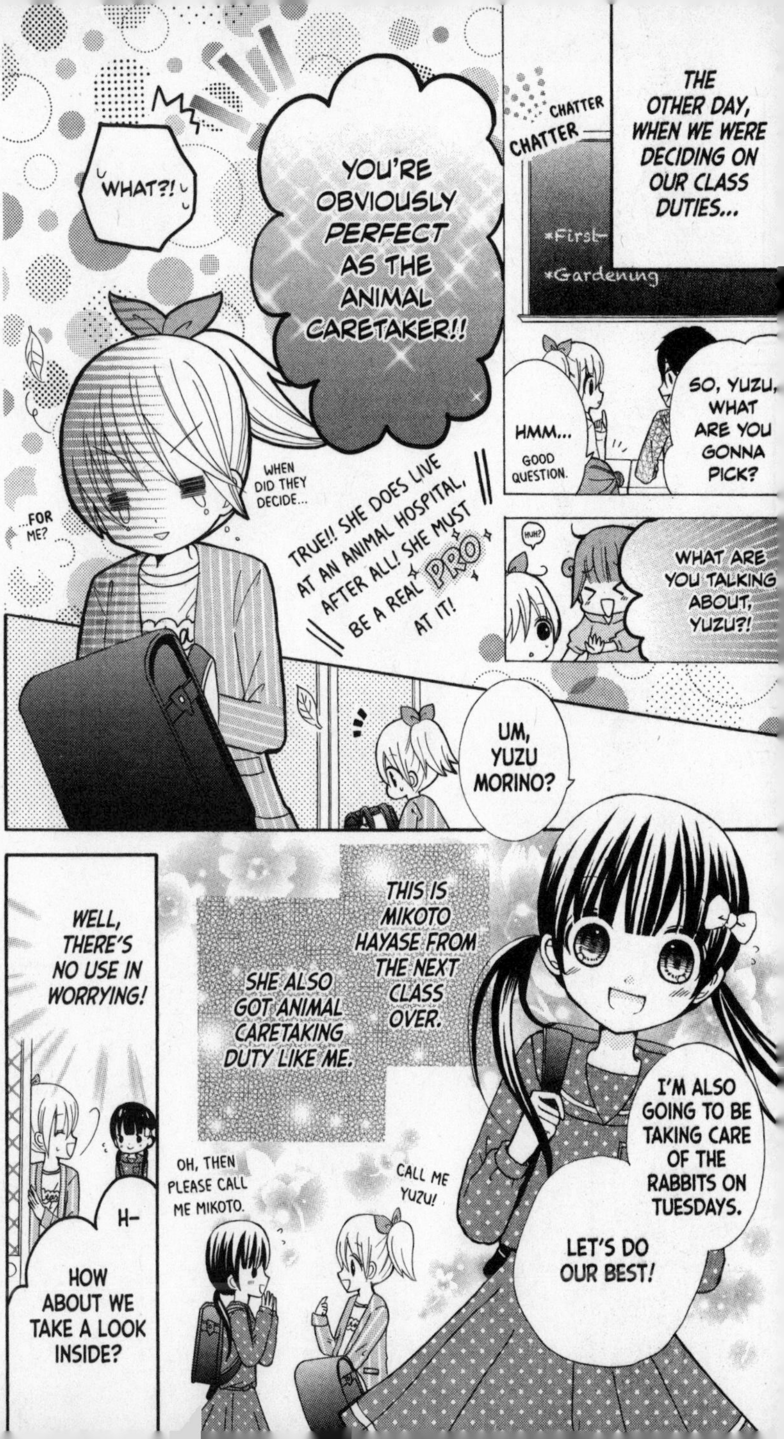
THE OTHER DAY, WHEN WE WERE DECIDING ON OUR CLASS DUTIES...
CHATTER CHATTER
*First
*Gardening
SO, YUZU, WHAT ARE YOU GONNA PICK?
HMM...
GOOD QUESTION.
WHAT ARE YOU TALKING ABOUT, YUZU?!
HUH?
YOU'RE OBVIOUSLY PERFECT AS THE ANIMAL CARETAKER!!
WHAT?!
TRUE!! SHE DOES LIVE AT AN ANIMAL HOSPITAL, AFTER ALL! SHE MUST BE A REAL PRO AT IT!
WHEN DID THEY DECIDE...
...FOR ME?
UM, YUZU MORINO?
I'M ALSO GOING TO BE TAKING CARE OF THE RABBITS ON TUESDAYS.
LET'S DO OUR BEST!
THIS IS MIKOTO HAYASE FROM THE NEXT CLASS OVER.
SHE ALSO GOT ANIMAL CARETAKING DUTY LIKE ME.
CALL ME YUZU!
OH, THEN PLEASE CALL ME MIKOTO.
WELL, THERE'S NO USE IN WORRYING!
H-
HOW ABOUT WE TAKE A LOOK INSIDE?

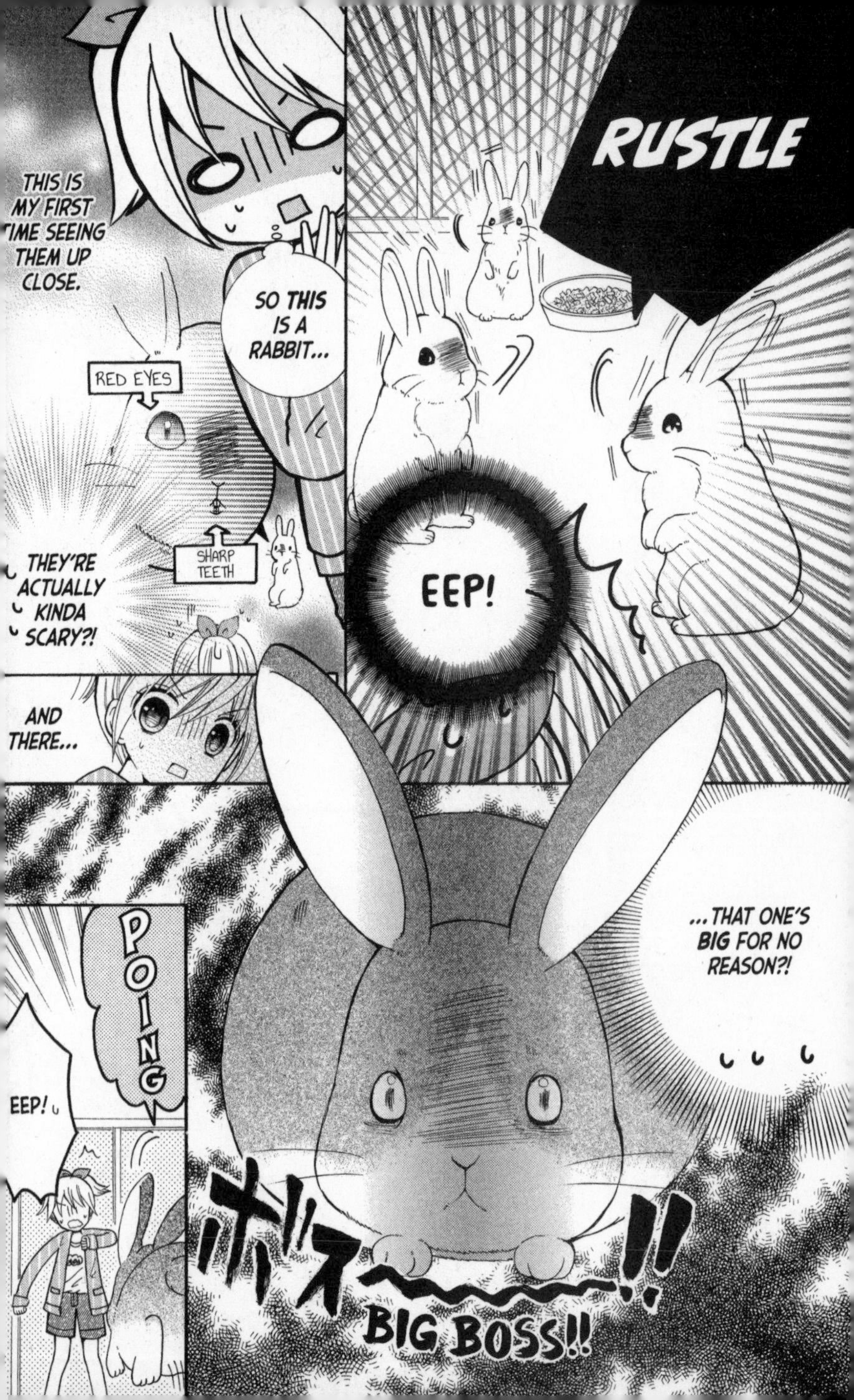
RUSTLE
EEP!
SO THIS IS A RABBIT...
THIS IS MY FIRST TIME SEEING THEM UP CLOSE.
RED EYES
SHARP TEETH
THEY'RE ACTUALLY KINDA SCARY?!
AND THERE...
...THAT ONE'S BIG FOR NO REASON?!
ボス〜〜!!
BIG BOSS!!
POING
EEP!

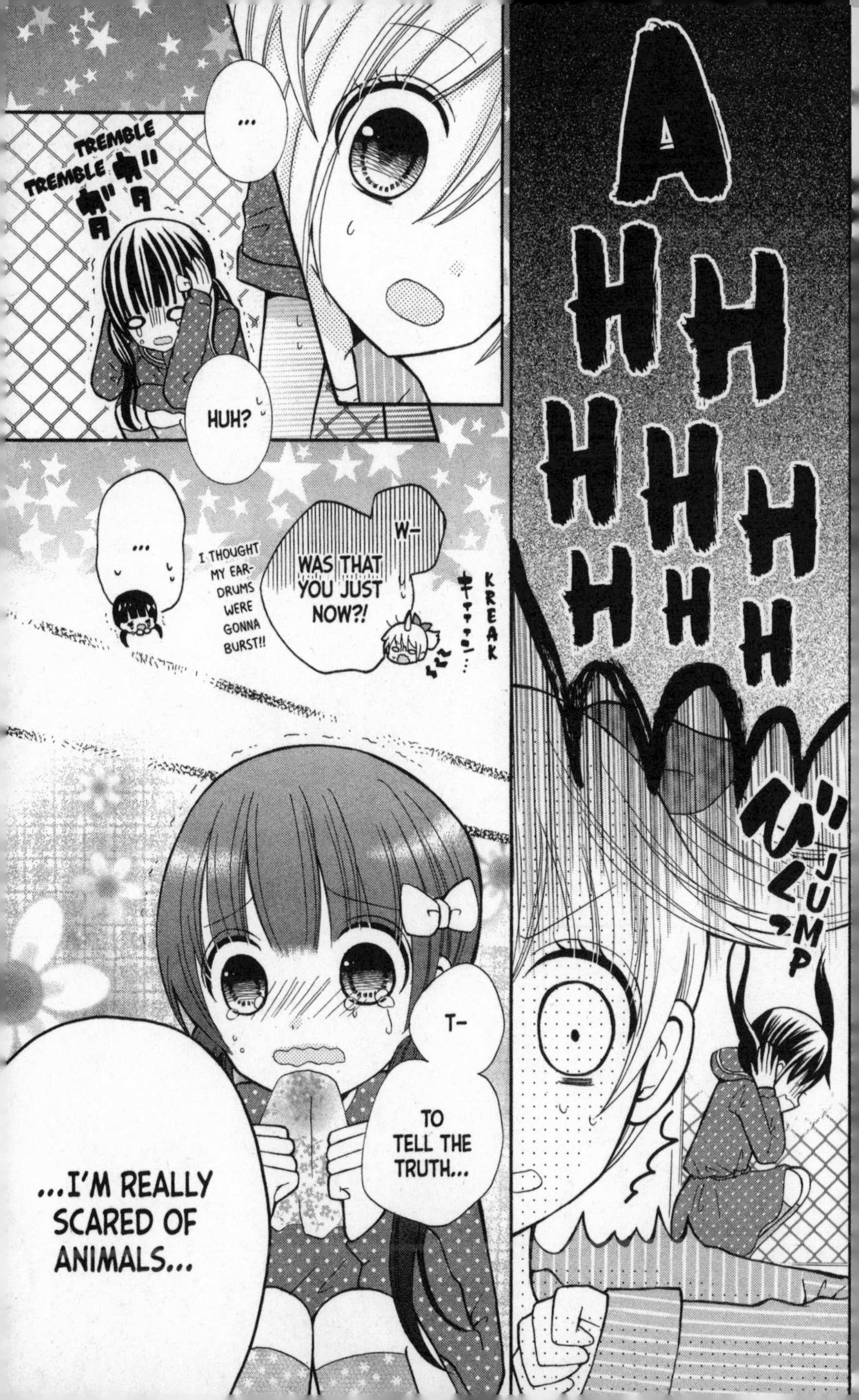
AHHHHHHHHHH
JUMP
...
TREMBLE TREMBLE
HUH?
W–
WAS THAT YOU JUST NOW?!
KREAK
...
I THOUGHT MY EAR-DRUMS WERE GONNA BURST!!
T–
TO TELL THE TRUTH...
...I'M REALLY SCARED OF ANIMALS...

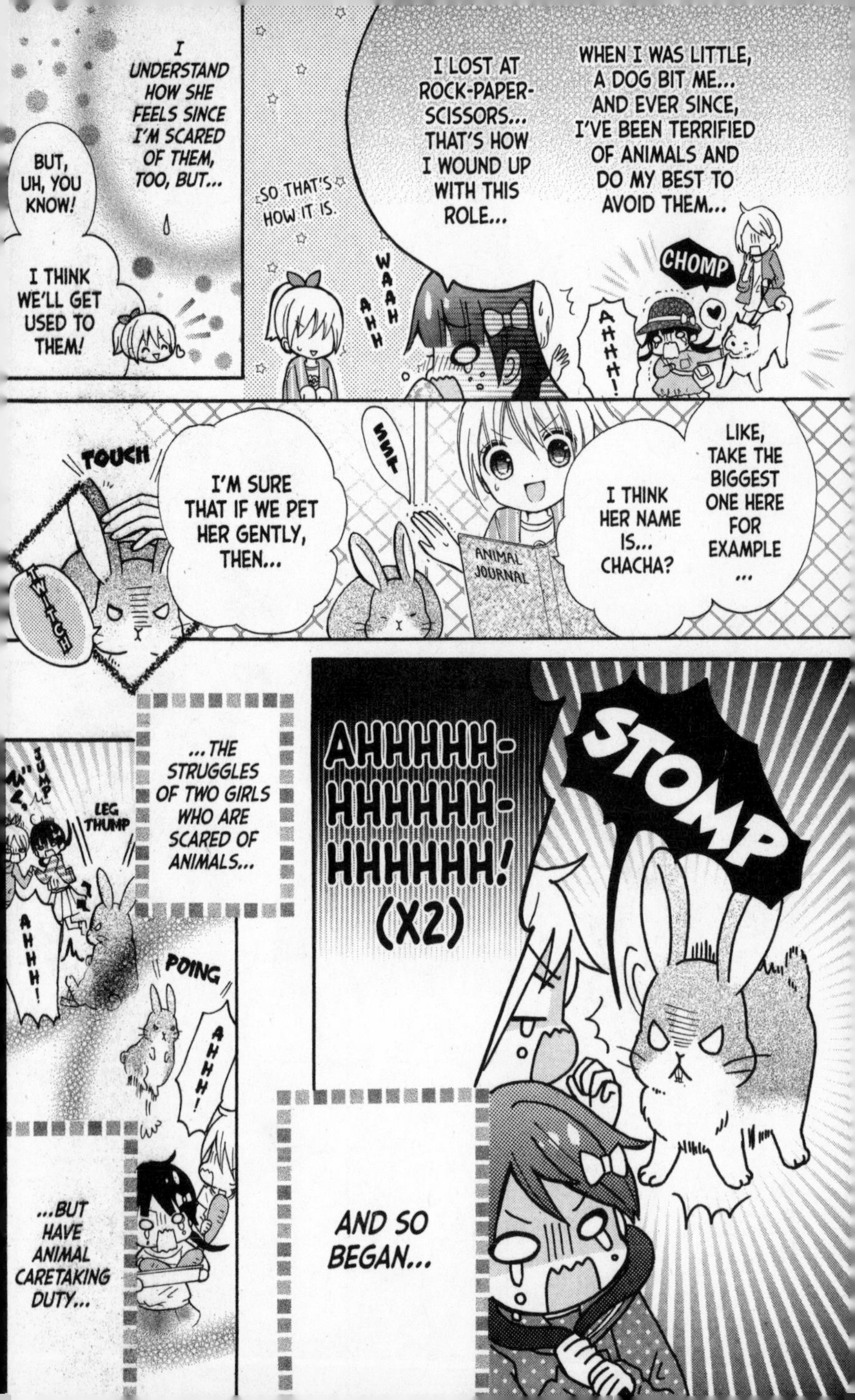
WHEN I WAS LITTLE, A DOG BIT ME... AND EVER SINCE, I'VE BEEN TERRIFIED OF ANIMALS AND DO MY BEST TO AVOID THEM...
CHOMP
AHHH!
I LOST AT ROCK-PAPER-SCISSORS... THAT'S HOW I WOUND UP WITH THIS ROLE...
WAAAH
AHH
SO THAT'S HOW IT IS.
I UNDERSTAND HOW SHE FEELS SINCE I'M SCARED OF THEM, TOO, BUT...
BUT, UH, YOU KNOW!
I THINK WE'LL GET USED TO THEM!
LIKE, TAKE THE BIGGEST ONE HERE FOR EXAMPLE ...
I THINK HER NAME IS... CHACHA?
SSST
I'M SURE THAT IF WE PET HER GENTLY, THEN...
TOUCH
TWITCH
STOMP
AHHHHH-HHHHHH-HHHHHH! (X2)
AND SO BEGAN...
...THE STRUGGLES OF TWO GIRLS WHO ARE SCARED OF ANIMALS...
JUMP
LEG THUMP
AHHH!
POING
AHHH!
...BUT HAVE ANIMAL CARETAKING DUTY...

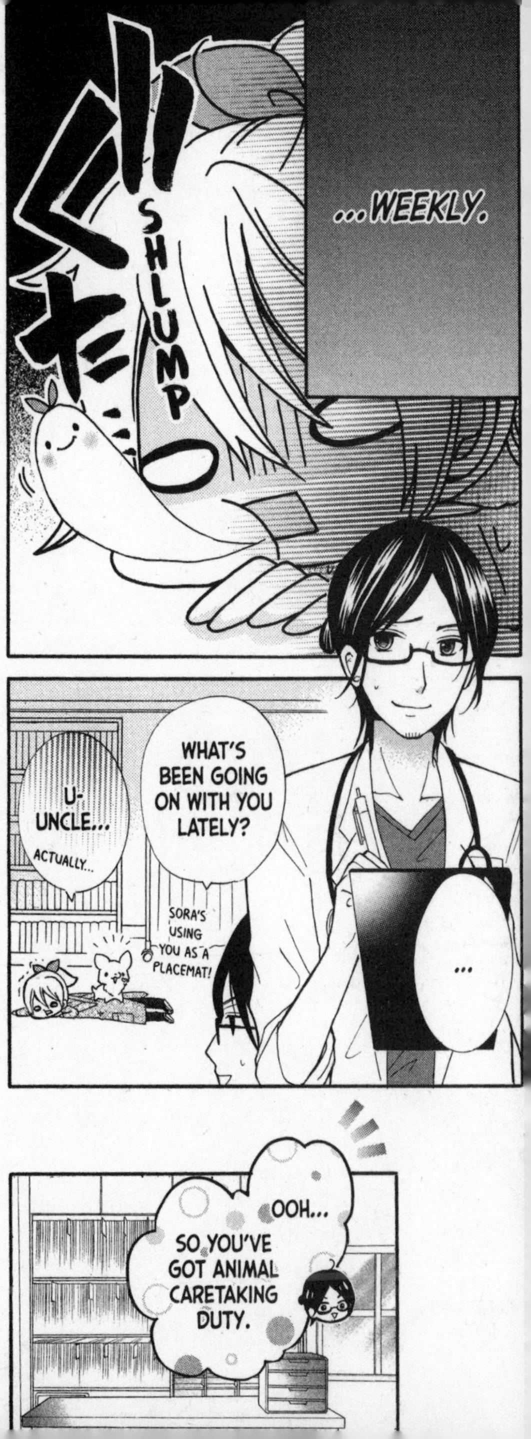
...WEEKLY.
SHLUMP
WHAT'S BEEN GOING ON WITH YOU LATELY?
U- UNCLE...
ACTUALLY...
SORA'S USING YOU AS A PLACEMAT!
...
OOH...
SO YOU'VE GOT ANIMAL CARETAKING DUTY.

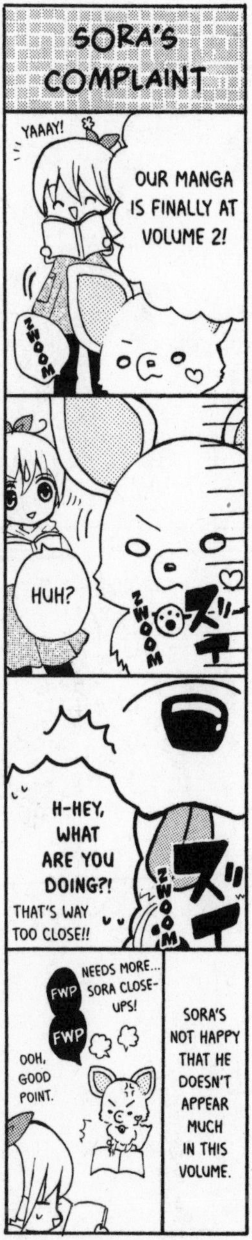
SORA'S COMPLAINT
YAAAY!
OUR MANGA IS FINALLY AT VOLUME 2!
ZWOOM
HUH?
ZWOOM
H-HEY, WHAT ARE YOU DOING?!
THAT'S WAY TOO CLOSE!!
ZWOOM
SORA'S NOT HAPPY THAT HE DOESN'T APPEAR MUCH IN THIS VOLUME.
NEEDS MORE... SORA CLOSE-UPS!
FWP
FWP
OOH, GOOD POINT.

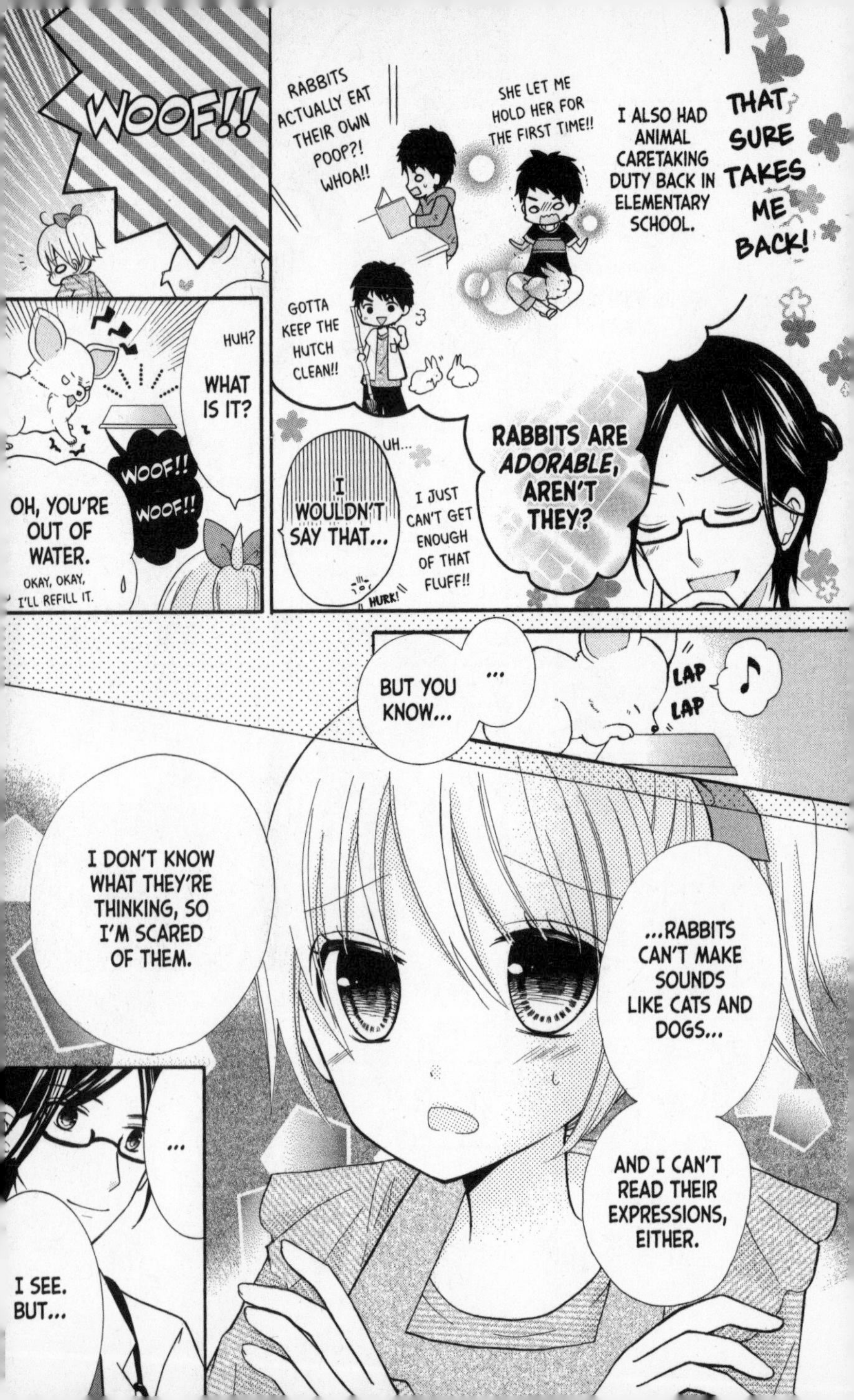
THAT SURE TAKES ME BACK!
I ALSO HAD ANIMAL CARETAKING DUTY BACK IN ELEMENTARY SCHOOL.
SHE LET ME HOLD HER FOR THE FIRST TIME!!
RABBITS ACTUALLY EAT THEIR OWN POOP?! WHOA!!
GOTTA KEEP THE HUTCH CLEAN!!
RABBITS ARE *ADORABLE*, AREN'T THEY?
UH...
I JUST CAN'T GET ENOUGH OF THAT FLUFF!!
I WOULDN'T SAY THAT...
HURK!
WOOF!!
HUH?
WHAT IS IT?
WOOF!!
WOOF!!
OH, YOU'RE OUT OF WATER.
OKAY, OKAY, I'LL REFILL IT.
...
BUT YOU KNOW...
LAP LAP
♪
...RABBITS CAN'T MAKE SOUNDS LIKE CATS AND DOGS...
AND I CAN'T READ THEIR EXPRESSIONS, EITHER.
I DON'T KNOW WHAT THEY'RE THINKING, SO I'M SCARED OF THEM.
...
I SEE. BUT...

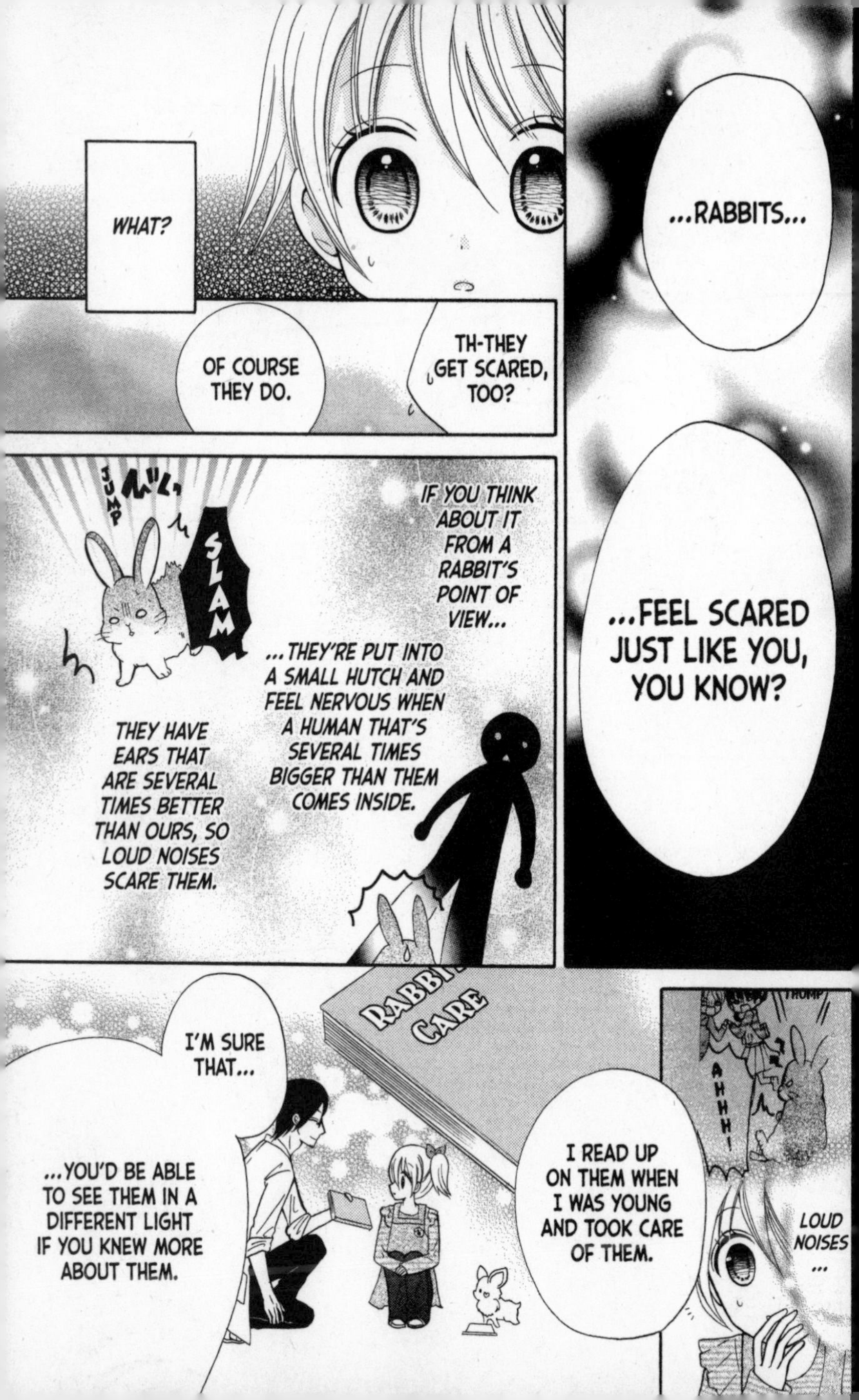
...RABBITS...
...FEEL SCARED JUST LIKE YOU, YOU KNOW?
WHAT?
TH-THEY GET SCARED, TOO?
OF COURSE THEY DO.
IF YOU THINK ABOUT IT FROM A RABBIT'S POINT OF VIEW...
...THEY'RE PUT INTO A SMALL HUTCH AND FEEL NERVOUS WHEN A HUMAN THAT'S SEVERAL TIMES BIGGER THAN THEM COMES INSIDE.
JUMP
SLAM
THEY HAVE EARS THAT ARE SEVERAL TIMES BETTER THAN OURS, SO LOUD NOISES SCARE THEM.
THUMP
AHHH!
LOUD NOISES...
I READ UP ON THEM WHEN I WAS YOUNG AND TOOK CARE OF THEM.
RABBIT CARE
I'M SURE THAT...
...YOU'D BE ABLE TO SEE THEM IN A DIFFERENT LIGHT IF YOU KNEW MORE ABOUT THEM.

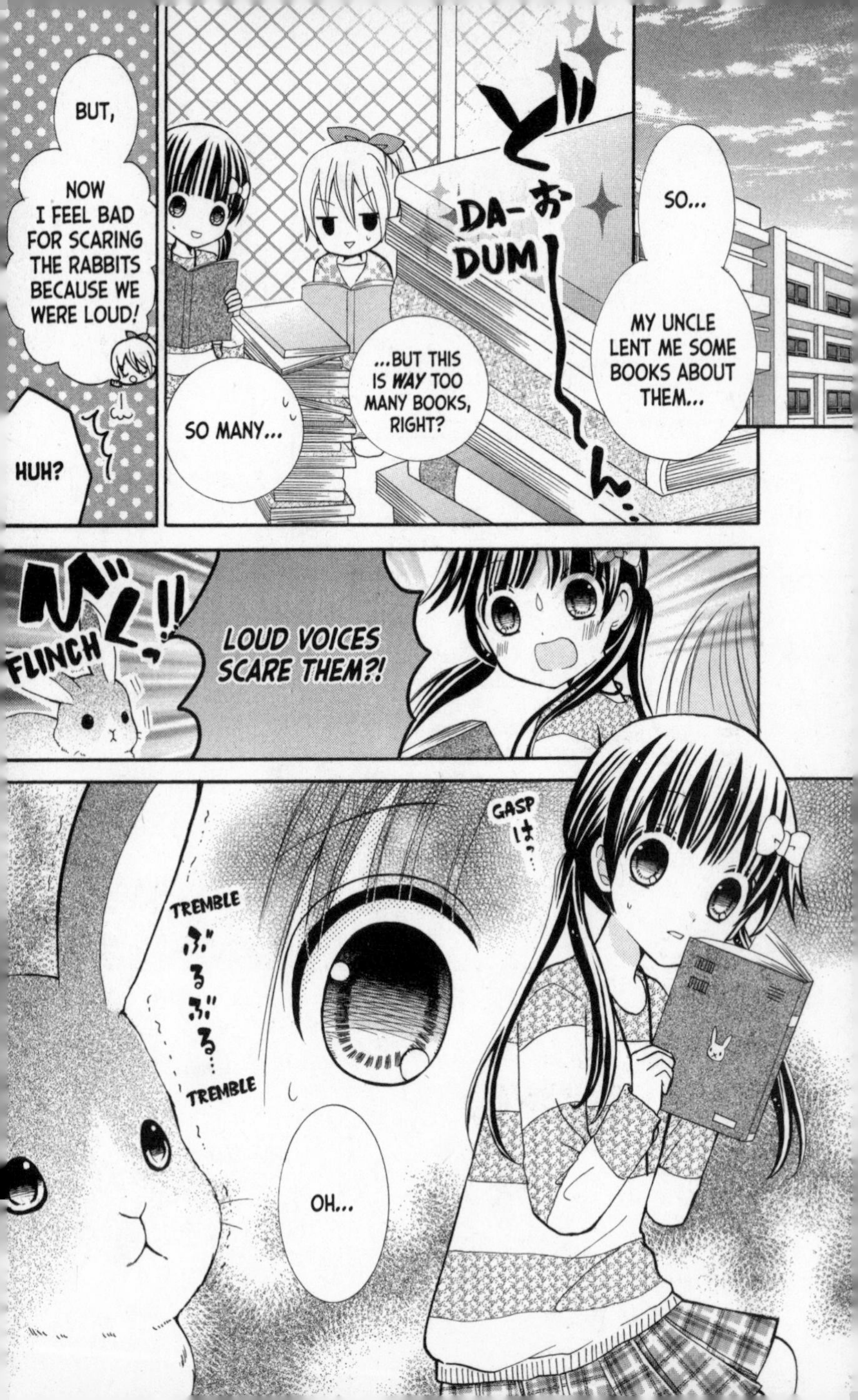
SO...
MY UNCLE LENT ME SOME BOOKS ABOUT THEM...
どーん…
DA-DUM
...BUT THIS IS WAY TOO MANY BOOKS, RIGHT?
SO MANY...
BUT,
NOW I FEEL BAD FOR SCARING THE RABBITS BECAUSE WE WERE LOUD!
HUH?
LOUD VOICES SCARE THEM?!
びくっ!!
FLINCH
GASP
はっ…
TREMBLE
ぶるぶる…
TREMBLE
OH...

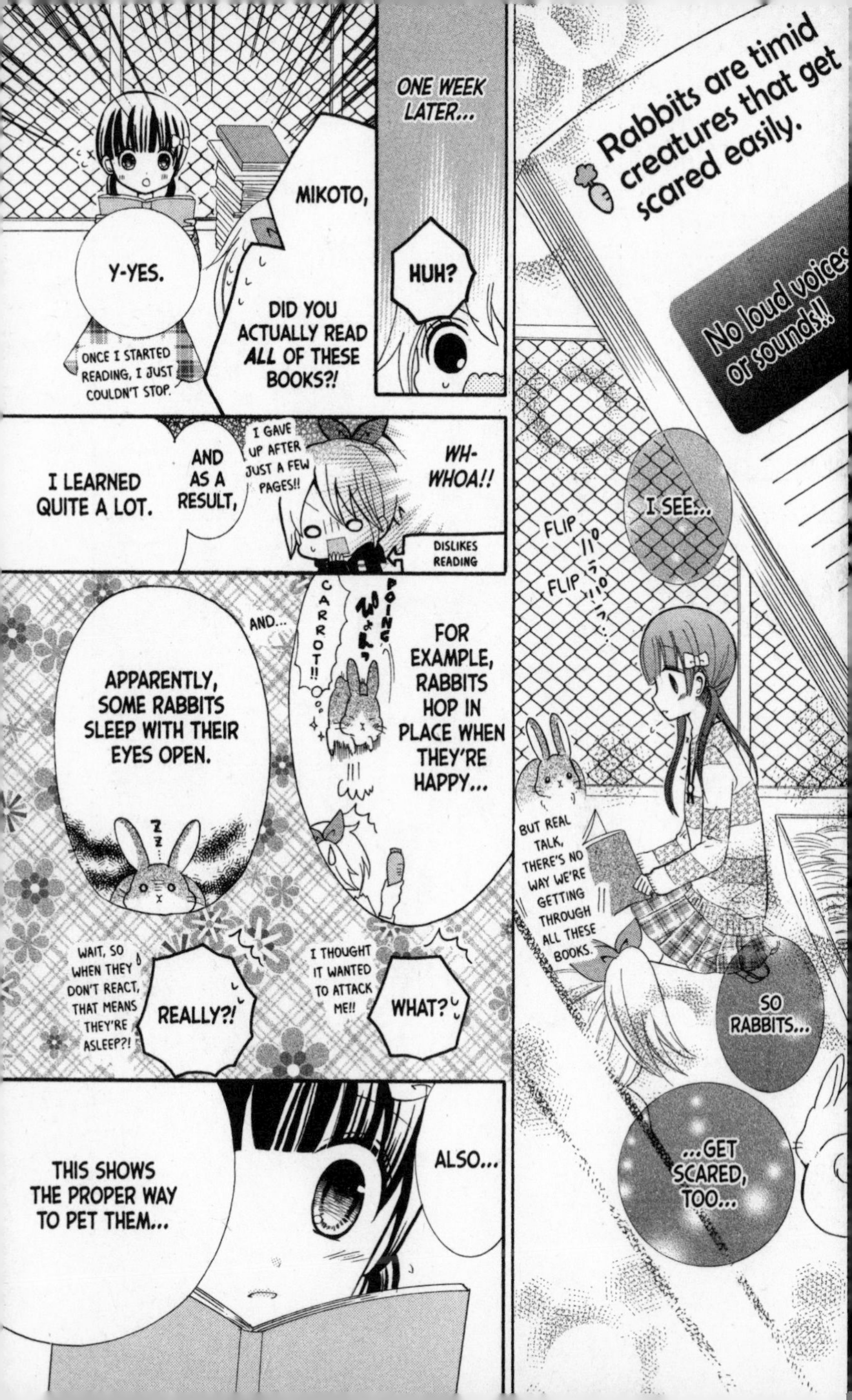
Rabbits are timid creatures that get scared easily.
No loud voices or sounds!!
I SEE...
FLIP
FLIP
BUT REAL TALK, THERE'S NO WAY WE'RE GETTING THROUGH ALL THESE BOOKS.
SO RABBITS...
...GET SCARED, TOO...
ONE WEEK LATER...
HUH?
MIKOTO,
DID YOU ACTUALLY READ ALL OF THESE BOOKS?!
Y-YES.
ONCE I STARTED READING, I JUST COULDN'T STOP.
WH-WHOA!!
DISLIKES READING
I GAVE UP AFTER JUST A FEW PAGES!!
AND AS A RESULT,
I LEARNED QUITE A LOT.
FOR EXAMPLE, RABBITS HOP IN PLACE WHEN THEY'RE HAPPY...
POING
CARROT!!
WHAT?
I THOUGHT IT WANTED TO ATTACK ME!!
AND...
APPARENTLY, SOME RABBITS SLEEP WITH THEIR EYES OPEN.
REALLY?!
WAIT, SO WHEN THEY DON'T REACT, THAT MEANS THEY'RE ASLEEP?!
ALSO...
THIS SHOWS THE PROPER WAY TO PET THEM...

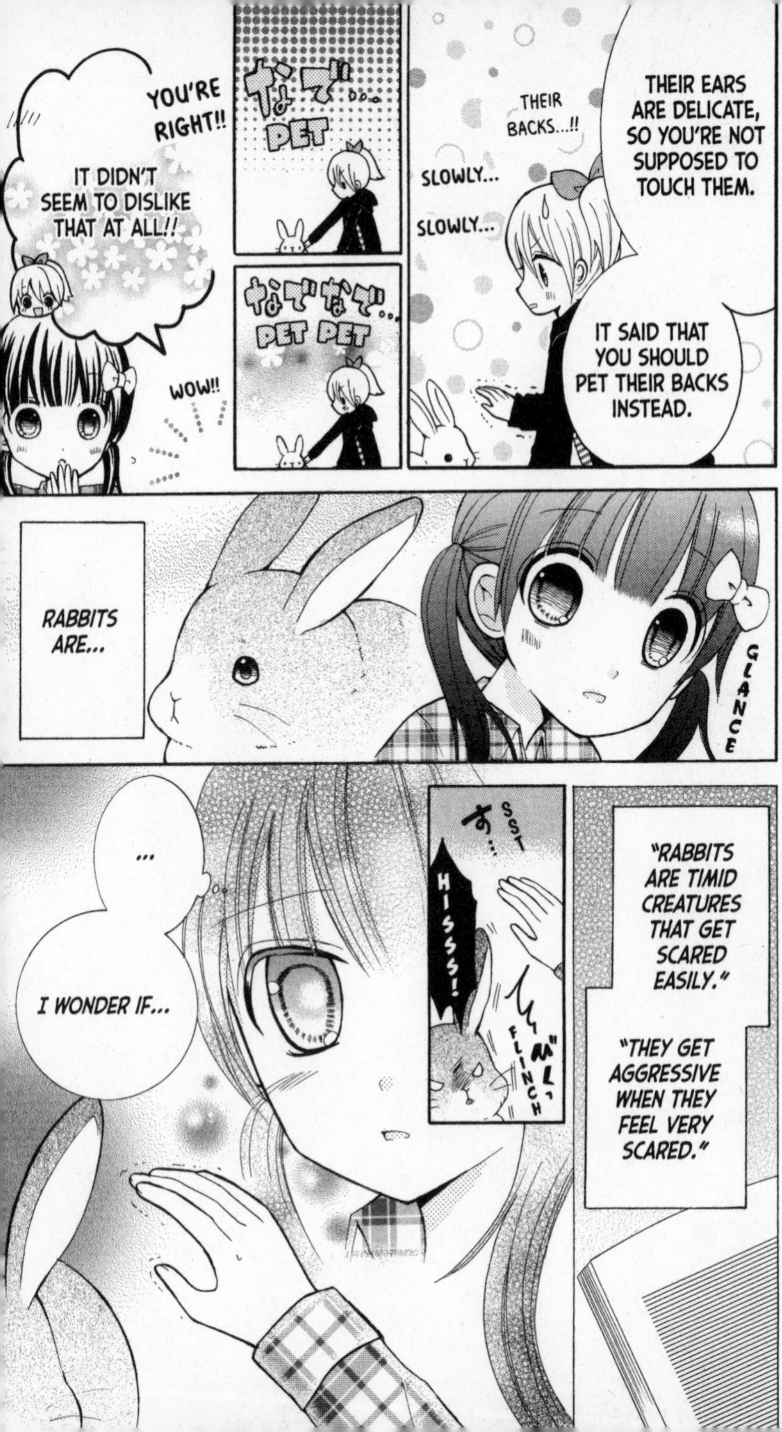
THEIR EARS ARE DELICATE, SO YOU'RE NOT SUPPOSED TO TOUCH THEM.
IT SAID THAT YOU SHOULD PET THEIR BACKS INSTEAD.
THEIR BACKS...!!
SLOWLY...
SLOWLY...
なで... PET
なでなで... PET PET
YOU'RE RIGHT!!
IT DIDN'T SEEM TO DISLIKE THAT AT ALL!!
WOW!!
GLANCE
RABBITS ARE...
"RABBITS ARE TIMID CREATURES THAT GET SCARED EASILY."
"THEY GET AGGRESSIVE WHEN THEY FEEL VERY SCARED."
す... SST
HISSS!
FLINCH
...
I WONDER IF...

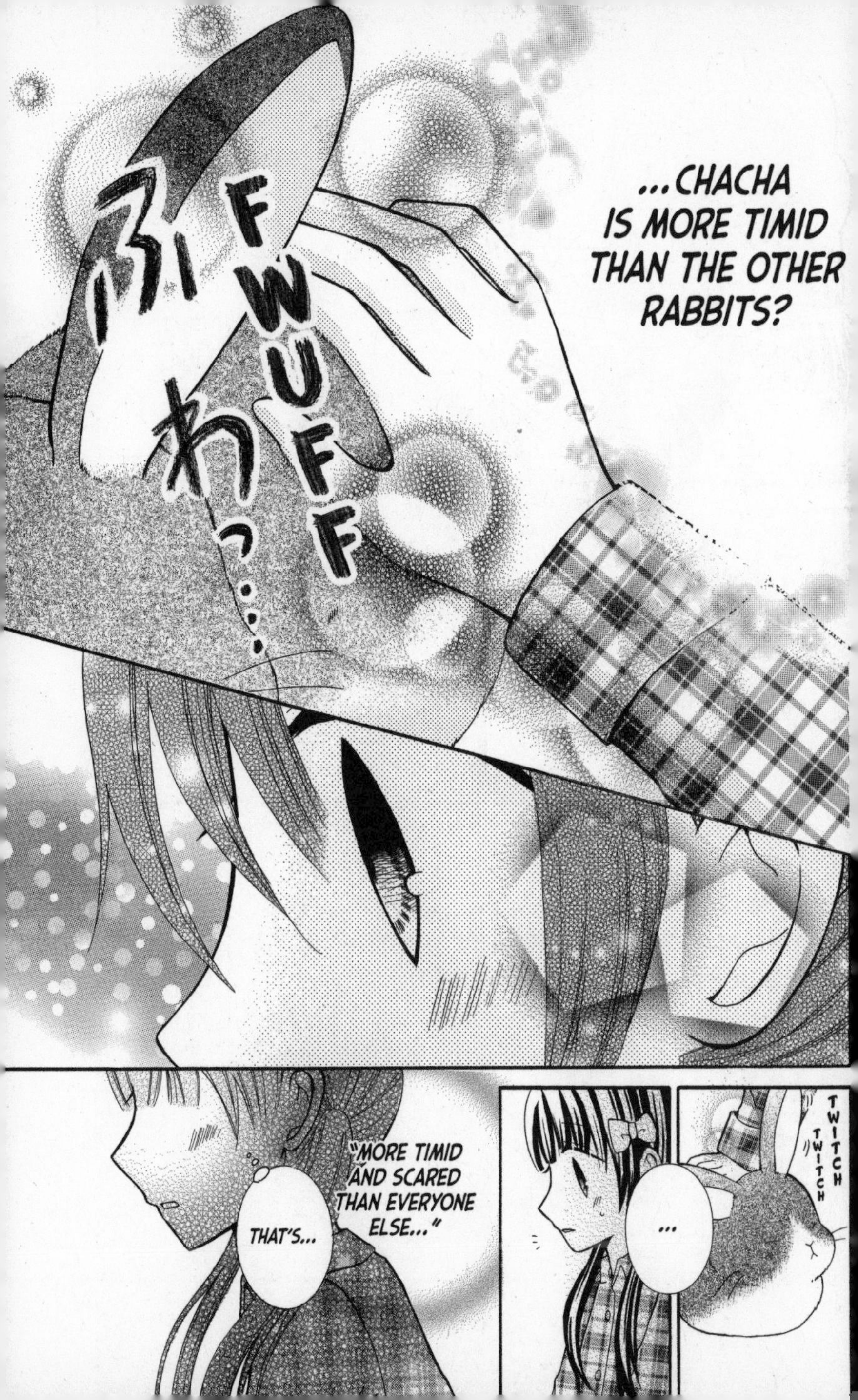
...CHACHA IS MORE TIMID THAN THE OTHER RABBITS?
FWUFF
ふわっ...
TWITCH TWITCH
...
"MORE TIMID AND SCARED THAN EVERYONE ELSE..."
THAT'S...

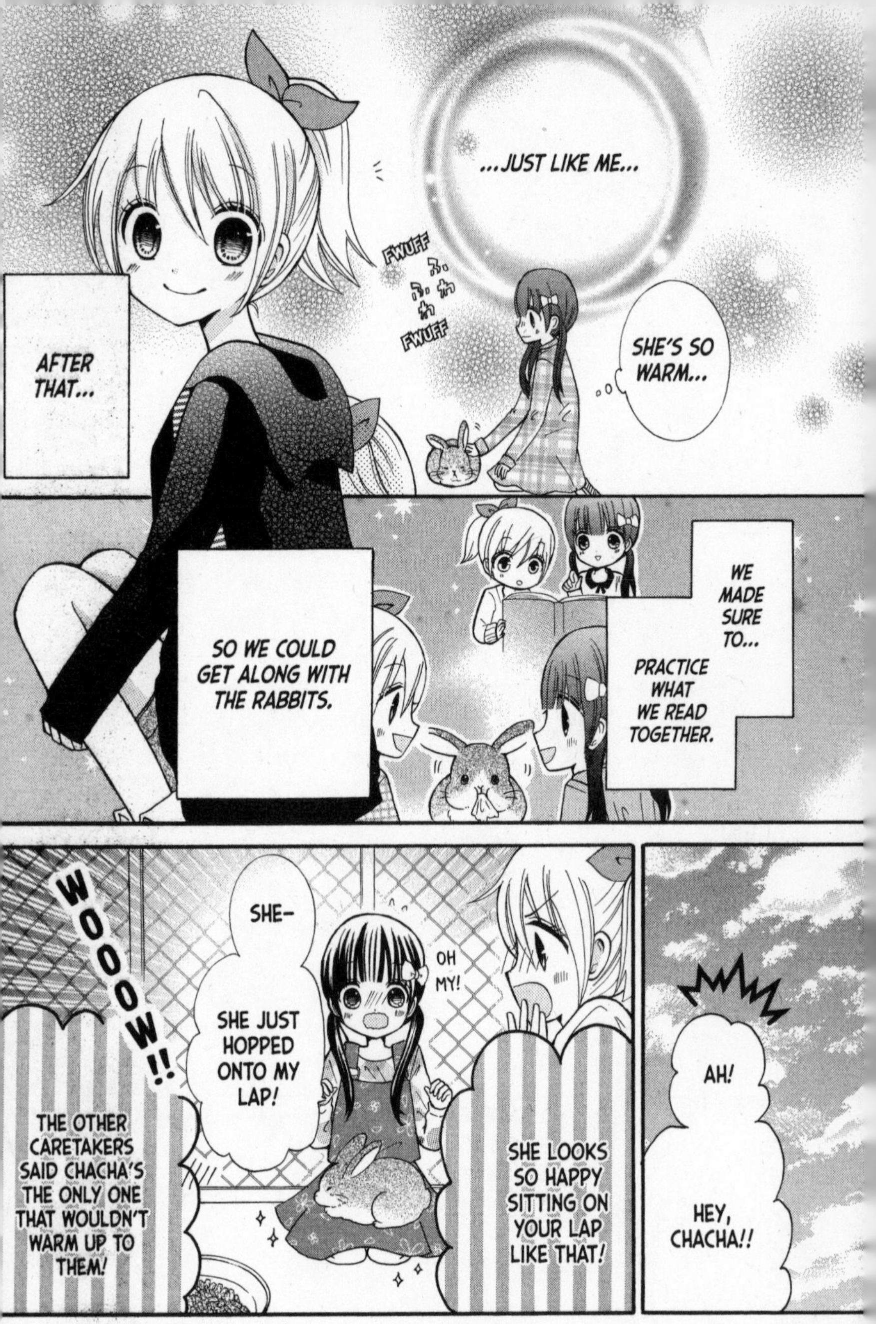
...JUST LIKE ME...
SHE'S SO WARM...
FWUFF
FWUFF
AFTER THAT...
WE MADE SURE TO... PRACTICE WHAT WE READ TOGETHER.
SO WE COULD GET ALONG WITH THE RABBITS.
AH!
HEY, CHACHA!!
SHE LOOKS SO HAPPY SITTING ON YOUR LAP LIKE THAT!
OH MY!
SHE-
SHE JUST HOPPED ONTO MY LAP!
WOOOOW!!
THE OTHER CARETAKERS SAID CHACHA'S THE ONLY ONE THAT WOULDN'T WARM UP TO THEM!

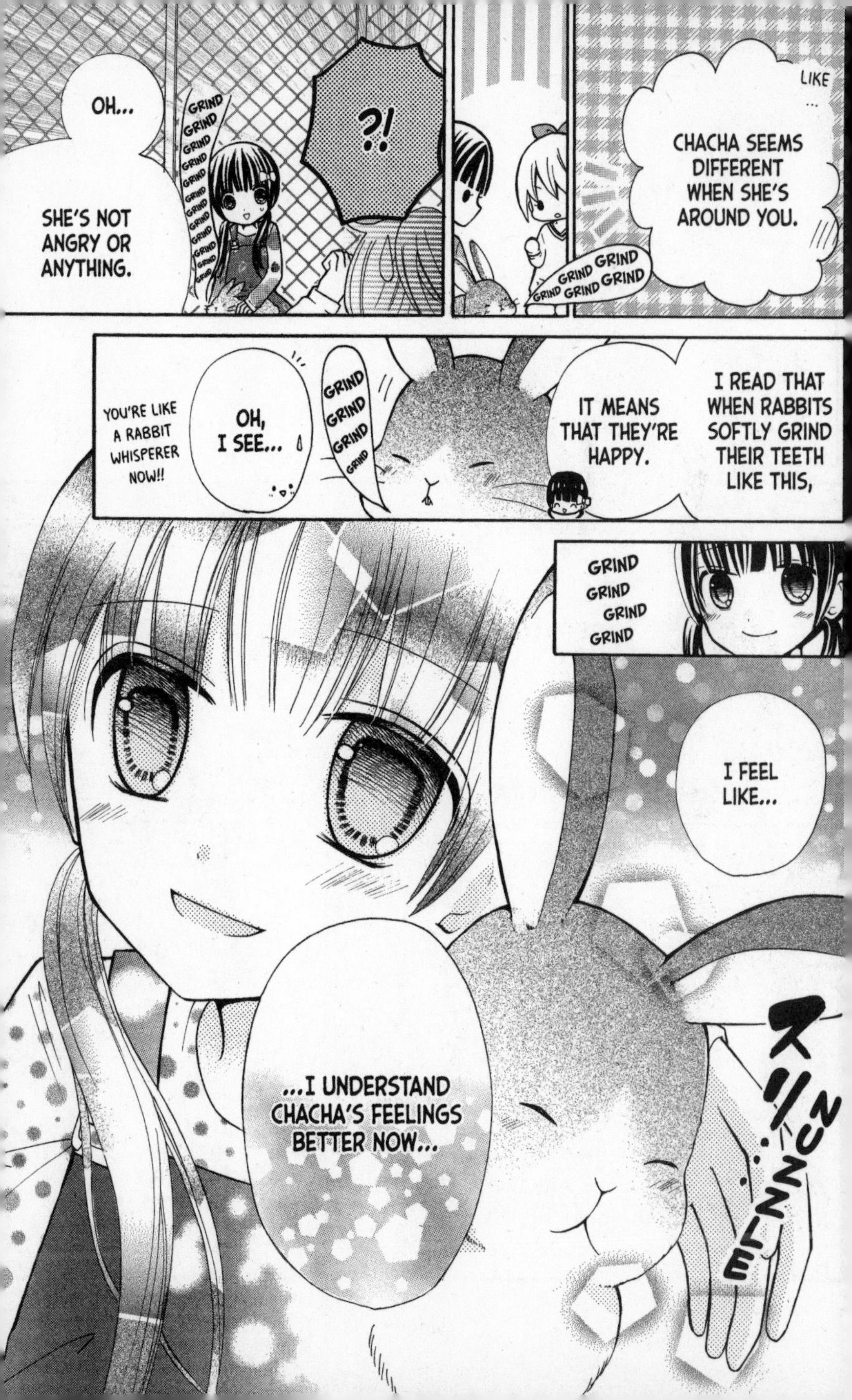
LIKE...
CHACHA SEEMS DIFFERENT WHEN SHE'S AROUND YOU.
GRIND GRIND GRIND GRIND GRIND
?!
OH...
SHE'S NOT ANGRY OR ANYTHING.
GRIND GRIND GRIND GRIND GRIND GRIND GRIND GRIND GRIND GRIND GRIND GRIND
I READ THAT WHEN RABBITS SOFTLY GRIND THEIR TEETH LIKE THIS,
IT MEANS THAT THEY'RE HAPPY.
GRIND GRIND GRIND GRIND
OH, I SEE...
YOU'RE LIKE A RABBIT WHISPERER NOW!!
GRIND GRIND GRIND GRIND
I FEEL LIKE...
...I UNDERSTAND CHACHA'S FEELINGS BETTER NOW...
NUZZLE

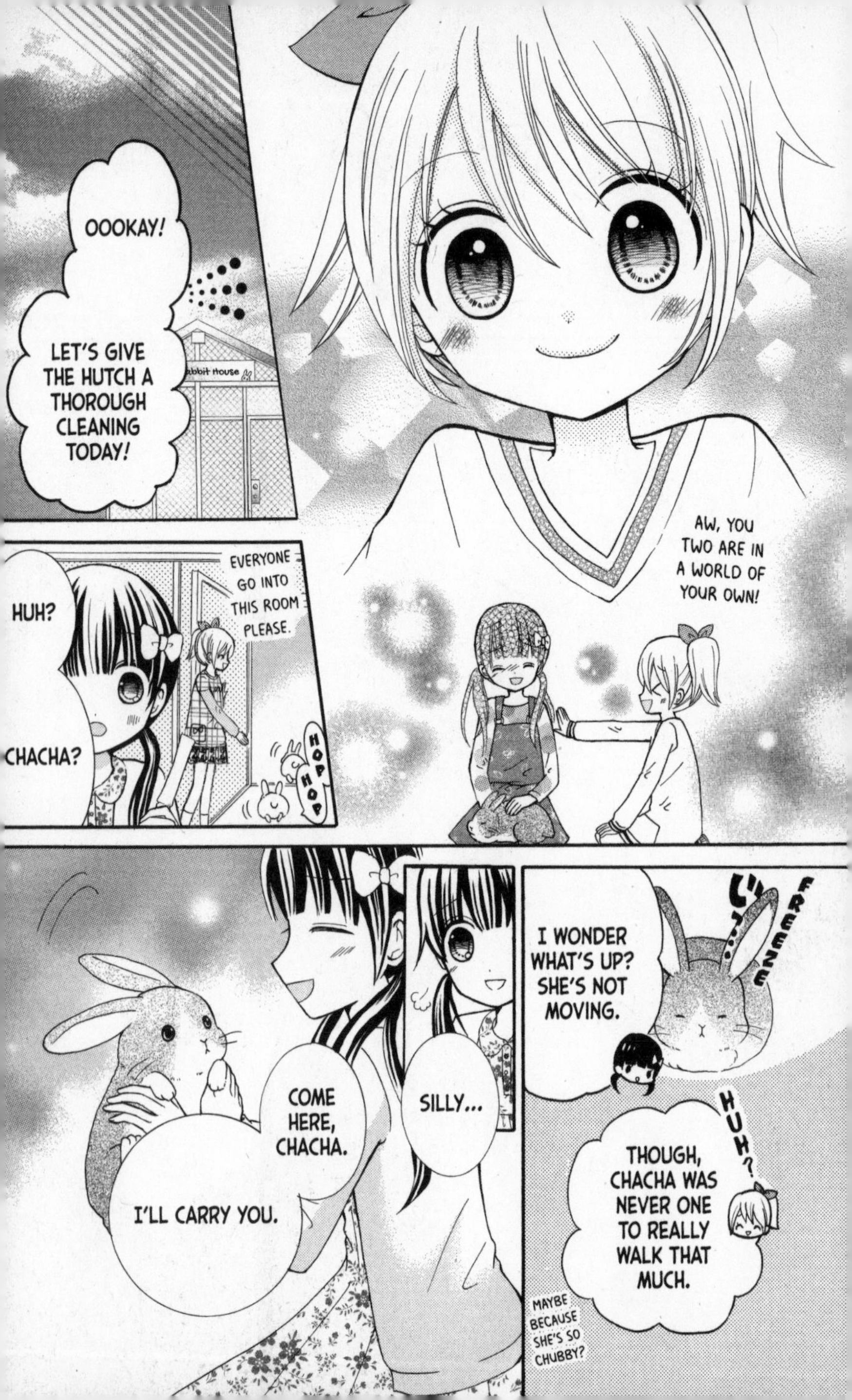
AW, YOU TWO ARE IN A WORLD OF YOUR OWN!
OOOKAY!
LET'S GIVE THE HUTCH A THOROUGH CLEANING TODAY!
EVERYONE GO INTO THIS ROOM PLEASE.
HUH?
CHACHA?
HOP HOP
I WONDER WHAT'S UP? SHE'S NOT MOVING.
FREEZE
HUH?
THOUGH, CHACHA WAS NEVER ONE TO REALLY WALK THAT MUCH.
MAYBE BECAUSE SHE'S SO CHUBBY?
SILLY...
COME HERE, CHACHA.
I'LL CARRY YOU.

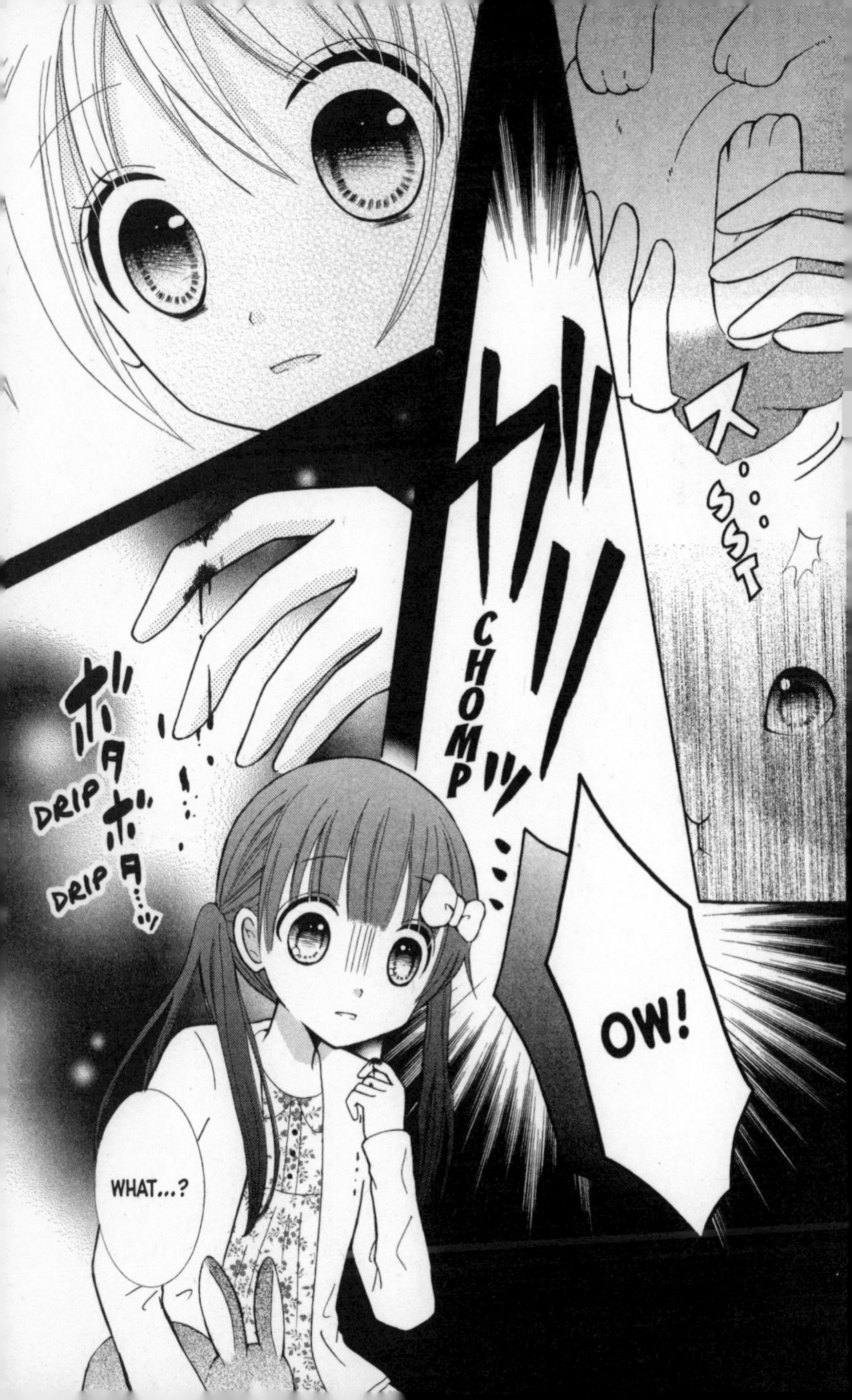
KSST
ガリッ
CHOMP
OW!
ボタボタ…ッ
DRIP
DRIP
WHAT...?

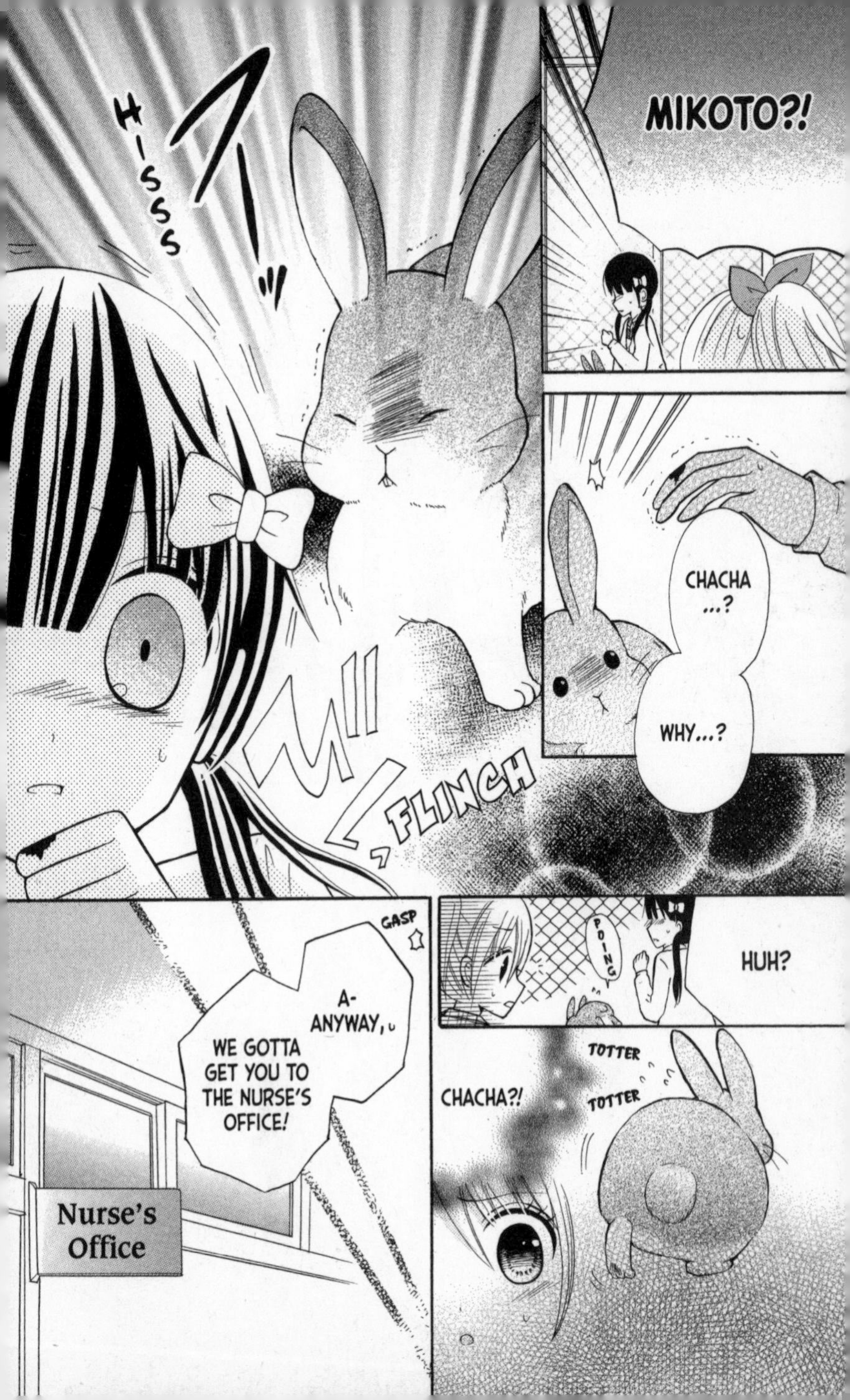
MIKOTO?!
CHACHA ...?
WHY...?
HISSS
FLINCH
POING
HUH?
CHACHA?!
TOTTER
TOTTER
GASP
A- ANYWAY,
WE GOTTA GET YOU TO THE NURSE'S OFFICE!
Nurse's Office

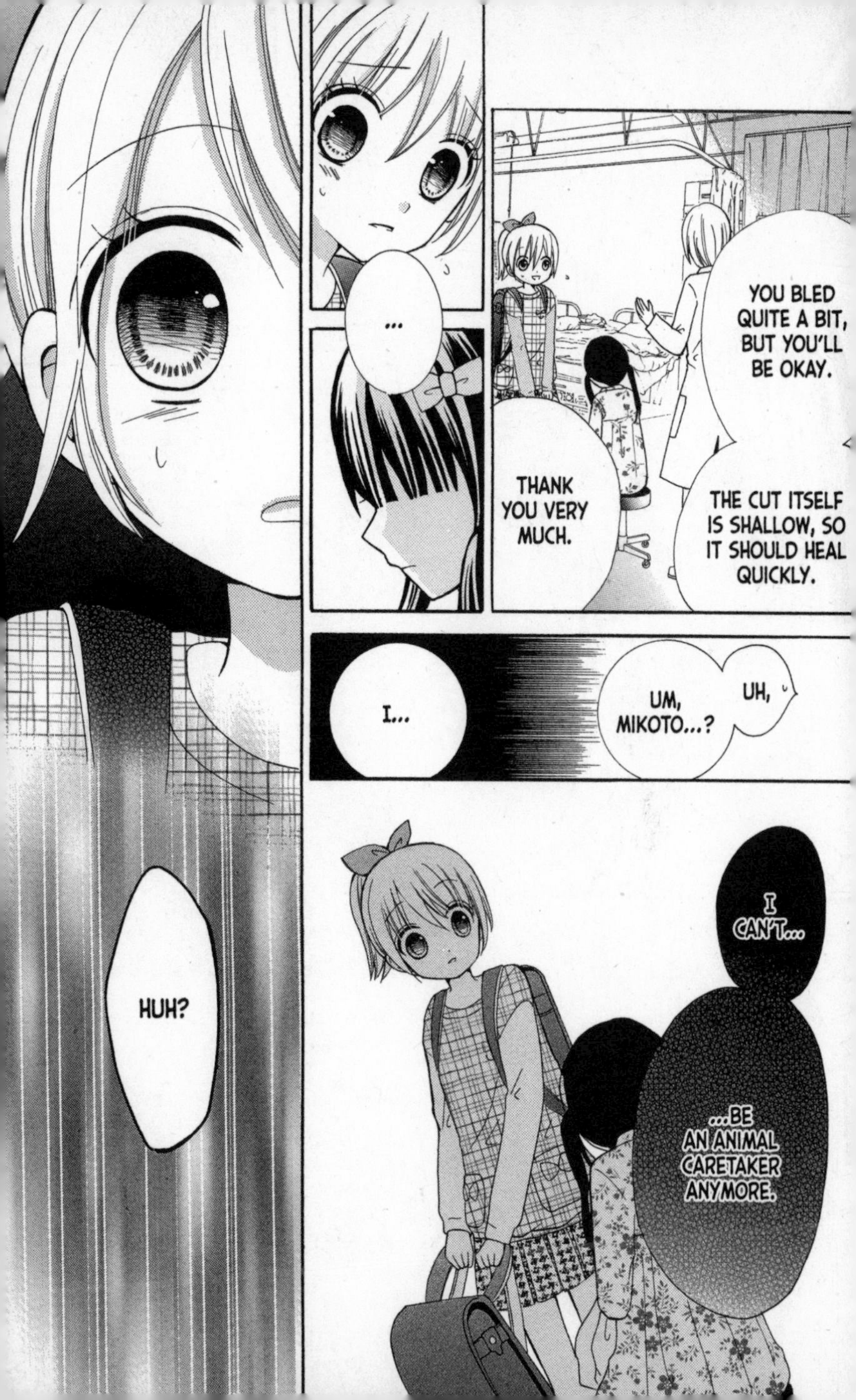
YOU BLED QUITE A BIT, BUT YOU'LL BE OKAY.
THE CUT ITSELF IS SHALLOW, SO IT SHOULD HEAL QUICKLY.
THANK YOU VERY MUCH.
...
UH,
UM, MIKOTO...?
I...
I CAN'T...
...BE AN ANIMAL CARETAKER ANYMORE.
HUH?

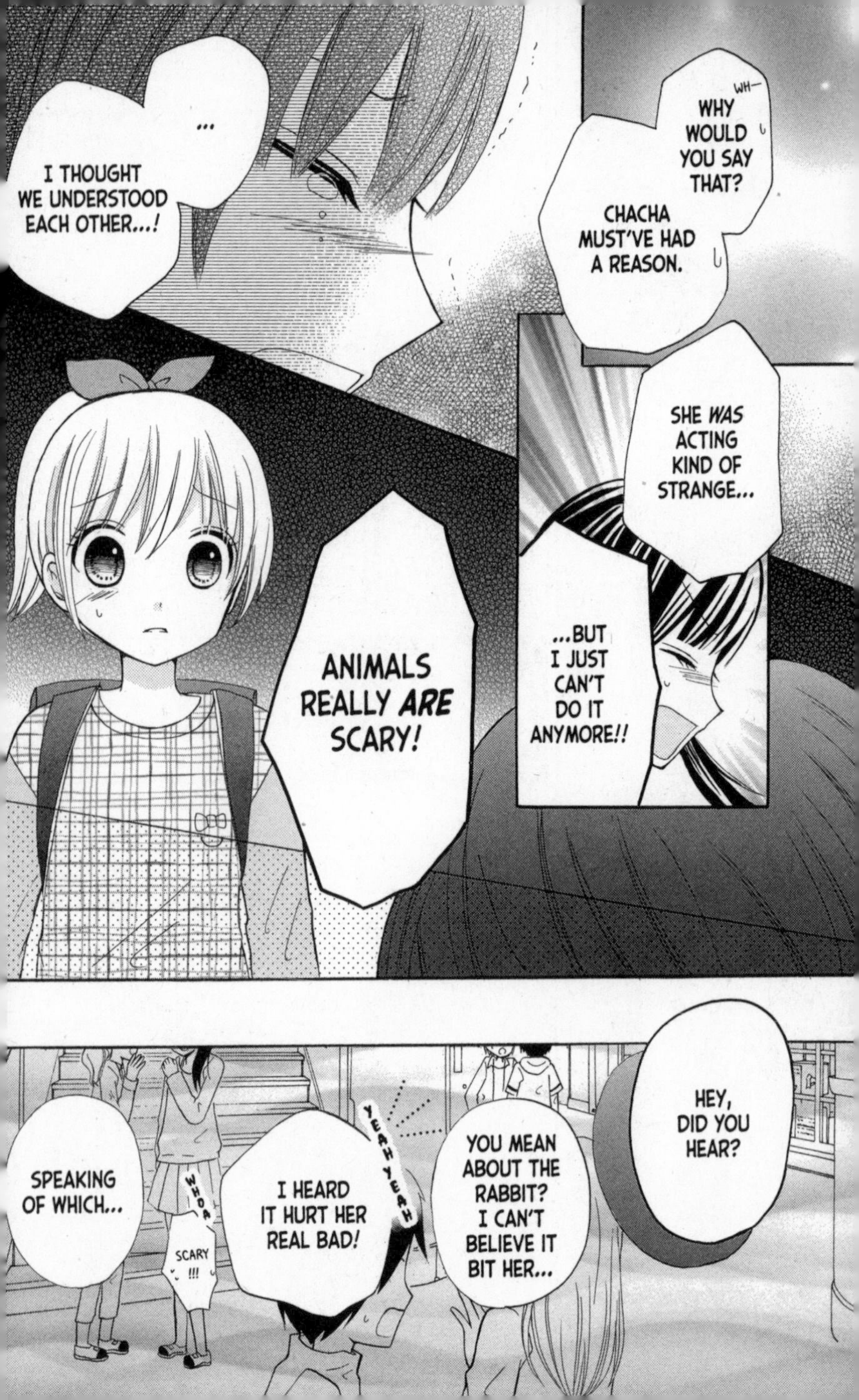
WH—
WHY WOULD YOU SAY THAT?
CHACHA MUST'VE HAD A REASON.
...
I THOUGHT WE UNDERSTOOD EACH OTHER...!
SHE *WAS* ACTING KIND OF STRANGE...
...BUT I JUST CAN'T DO IT ANYMORE!!
ANIMALS REALLY *ARE* SCARY!
HEY, DID YOU HEAR?
YOU MEAN ABOUT THE RABBIT? I CAN'T BELIEVE IT BIT HER...
YEAH YEAH
I HEARD IT HURT HER REAL BAD!
WHOA
SCARY !!!
SPEAKING OF WHICH...

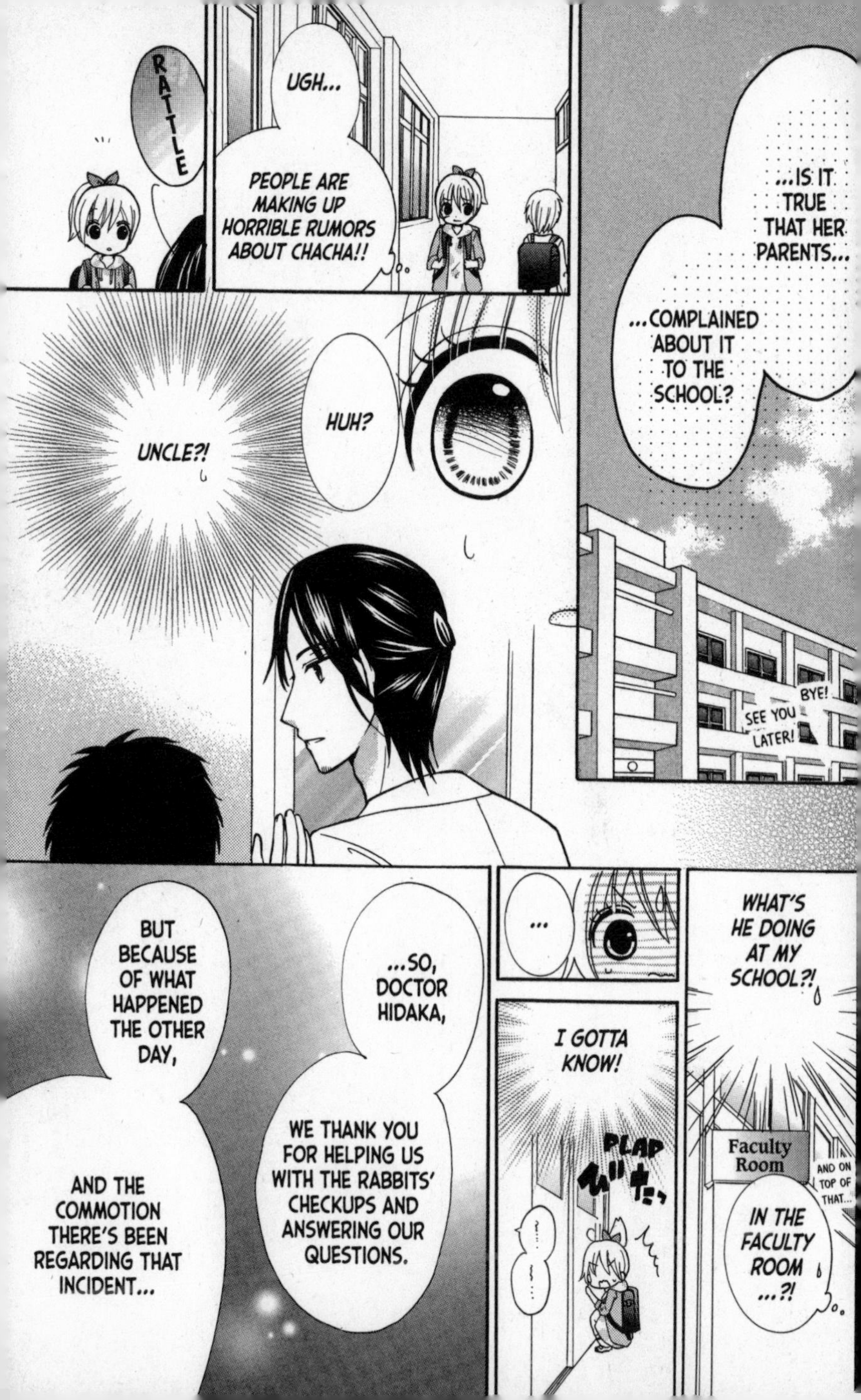
...IS IT TRUE THAT HER PARENTS...
...COMPLAINED ABOUT IT TO THE SCHOOL?
BYE!
SEE YOU LATER!
UGH...
PEOPLE ARE MAKING UP HORRIBLE RUMORS ABOUT CHACHA!!
RATTLE
HUH?
UNCLE?!
WHAT'S HE DOING AT MY SCHOOL?!
Faculty Room
AND ON TOP OF THAT...
IN THE FACULTY ROOM...?!
...
I GOTTA KNOW!
PLAP
...SO, DOCTOR HIDAKA,
WE THANK YOU FOR HELPING US WITH THE RABBITS' CHECKUPS AND ANSWERING OUR QUESTIONS.
BUT BECAUSE OF WHAT HAPPENED THE OTHER DAY,
AND THE COMMOTION THERE'S BEEN REGARDING THAT INCIDENT...

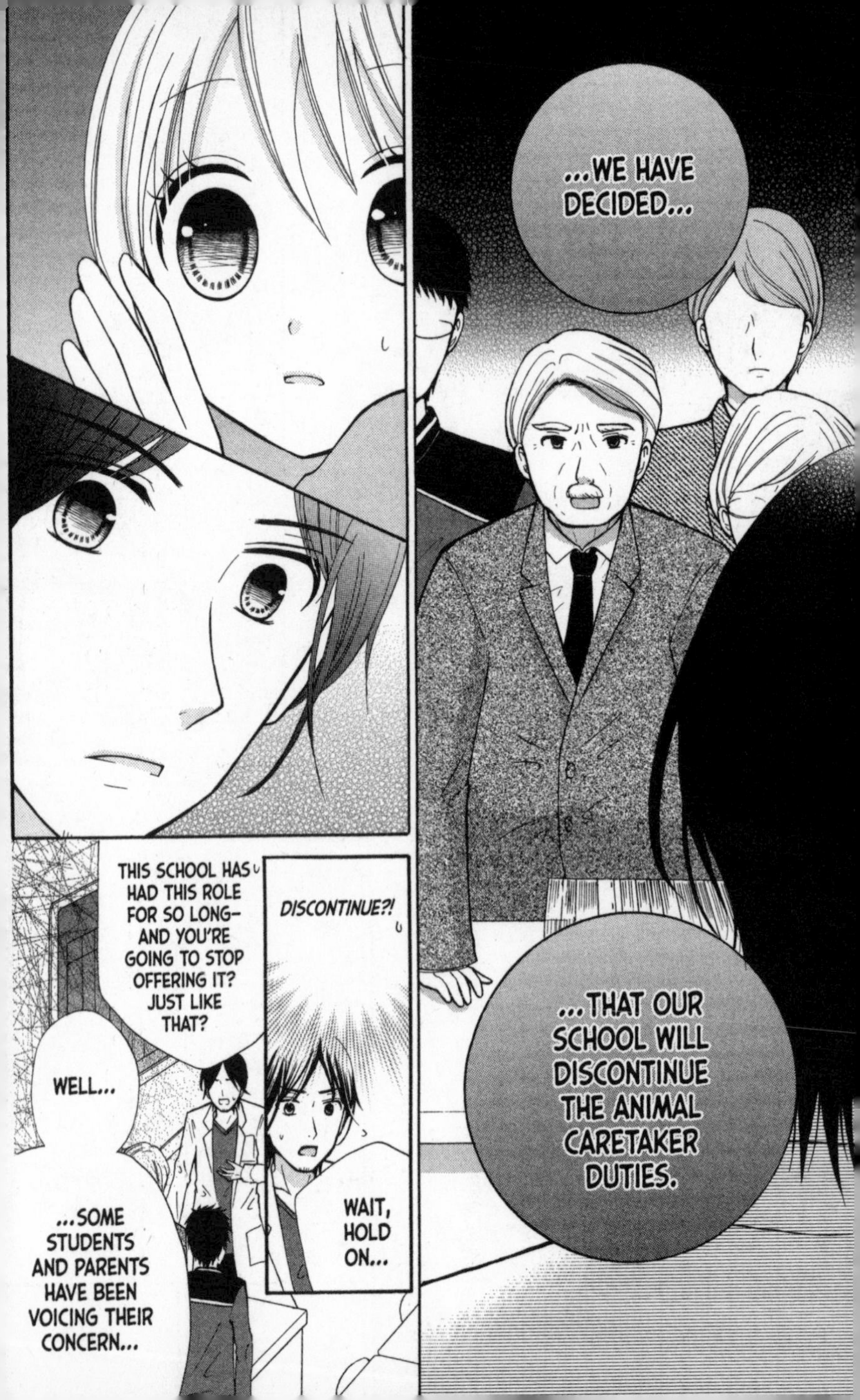
...WE HAVE DECIDED...
...THAT OUR SCHOOL WILL DISCONTINUE THE ANIMAL CARETAKER DUTIES.
DISCONTINUE?!
THIS SCHOOL HAS HAD THIS ROLE FOR SO LONG—AND YOU'RE GOING TO STOP OFFERING IT? JUST LIKE THAT?
WAIT, HOLD ON...
WELL...
...SOME STUDENTS AND PARENTS HAVE BEEN VOICING THEIR CONCERN...

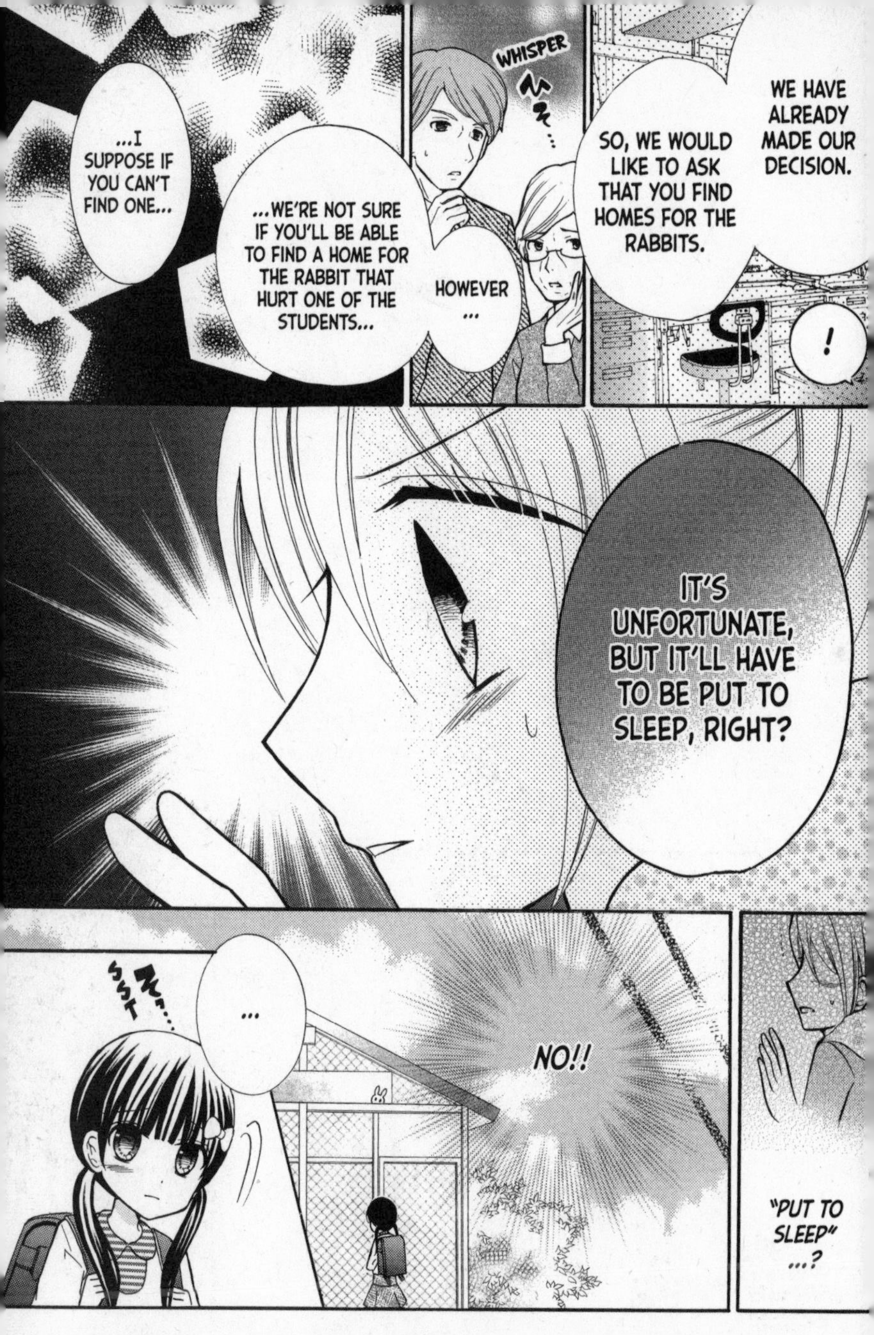
WE HAVE ALREADY MADE OUR DECISION.
!
SO, WE WOULD LIKE TO ASK THAT YOU FIND HOMES FOR THE RABBITS.
WHISPER
HOWEVER ...
...WE'RE NOT SURE IF YOU'LL BE ABLE TO FIND A HOME FOR THE RABBIT THAT HURT ONE OF THE STUDENTS...
...I SUPPOSE IF YOU CAN'T FIND ONE...
IT'S UNFORTUNATE, BUT IT'LL HAVE TO BE PUT TO SLEEP, RIGHT?
"PUT TO SLEEP" ...?
NO!!
...
SST

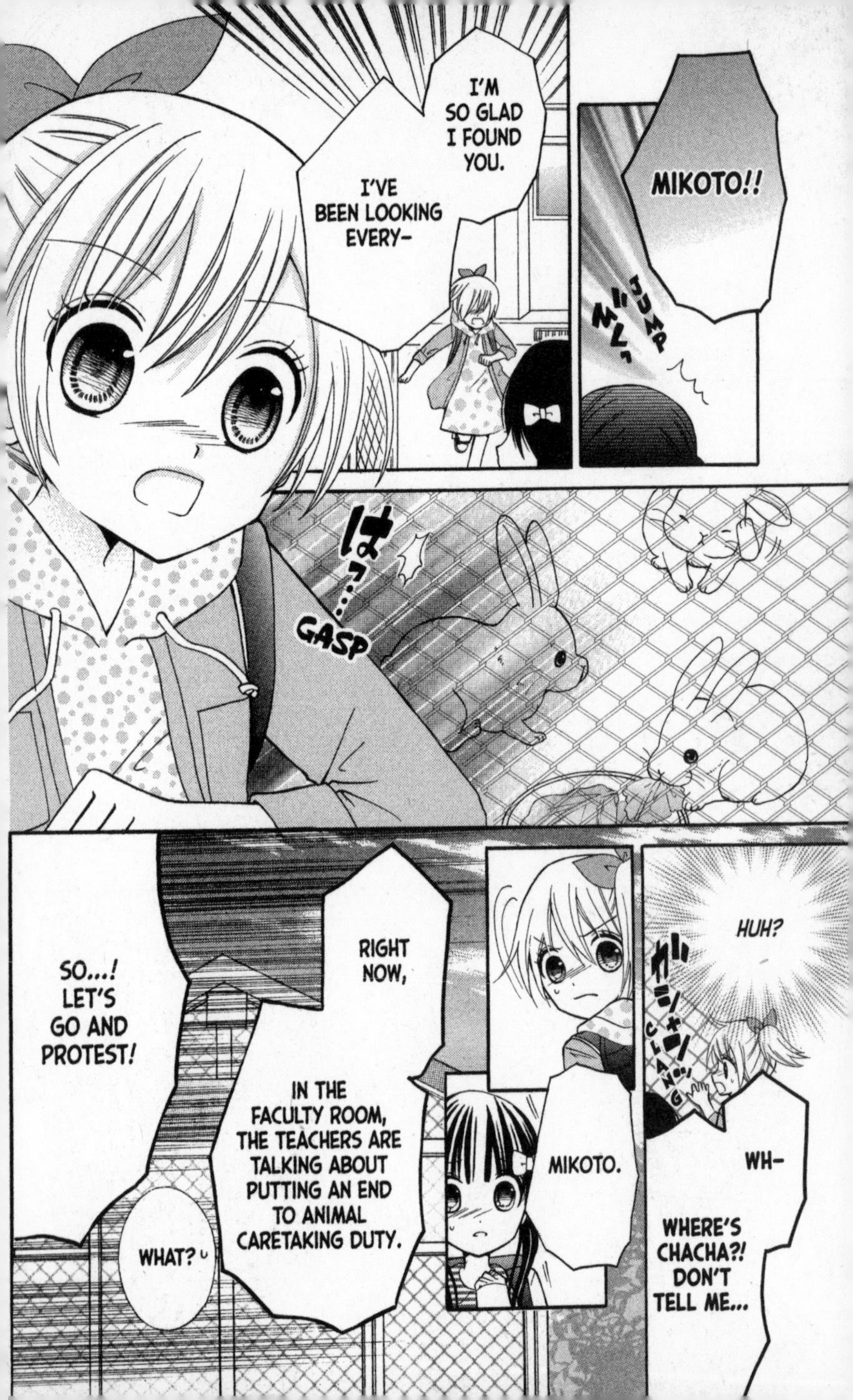
MIKOTO!!
JUMP
I'M SO GLAD I FOUND YOU.
I'VE BEEN LOOKING EVERY-
はっ…
GASP
HUH?
CLANG
WH-
WHERE'S CHACHA?! DON'T TELL ME...
MIKOTO.
RIGHT NOW,
IN THE FACULTY ROOM, THE TEACHERS ARE TALKING ABOUT PUTTING AN END TO ANIMAL CARETAKING DUTY.
WHAT?
SO...! LET'S GO AND PROTEST!

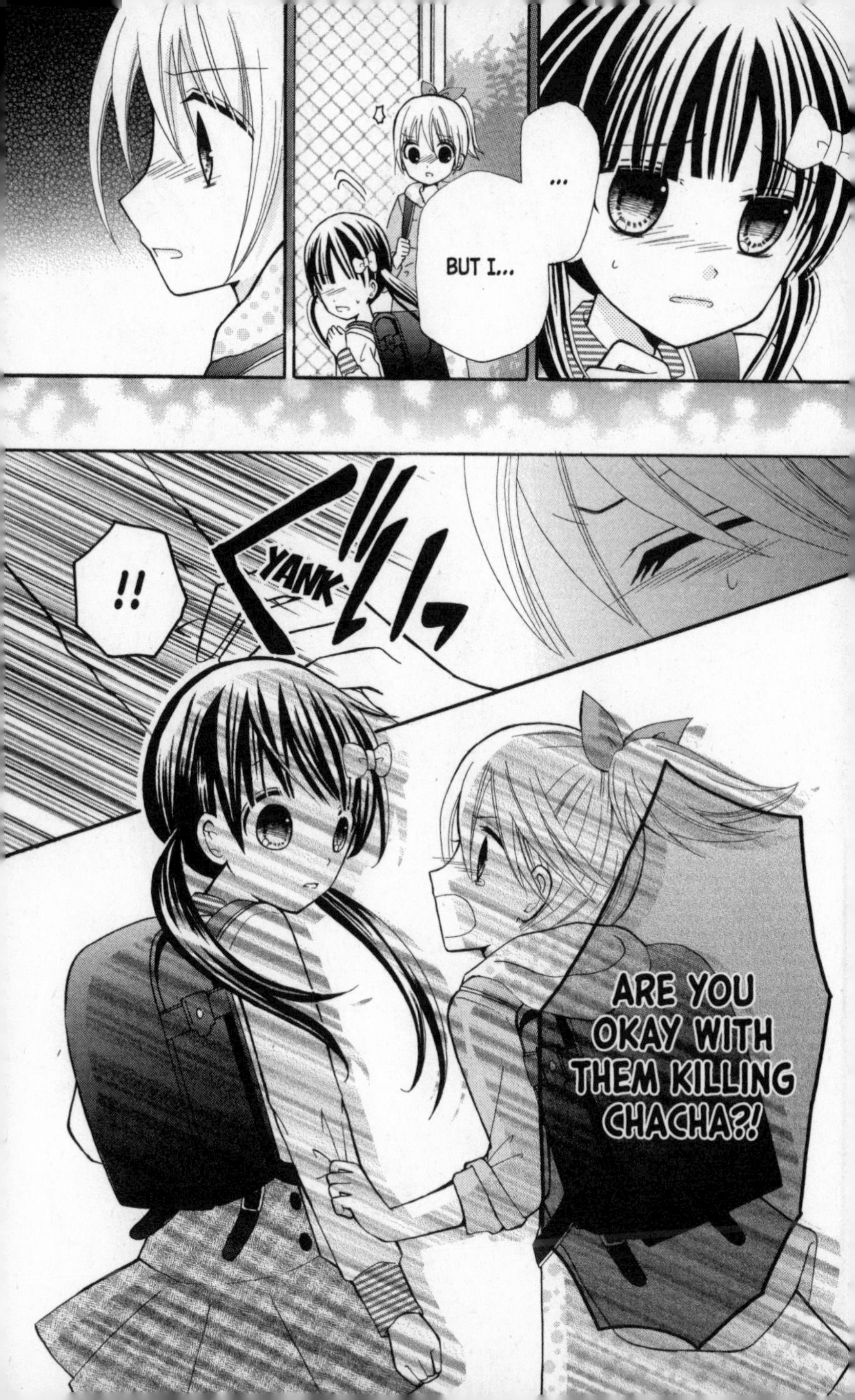
...
BUT I...
!!
YANK
ARE YOU OKAY WITH THEM KILLING CHACHA?!

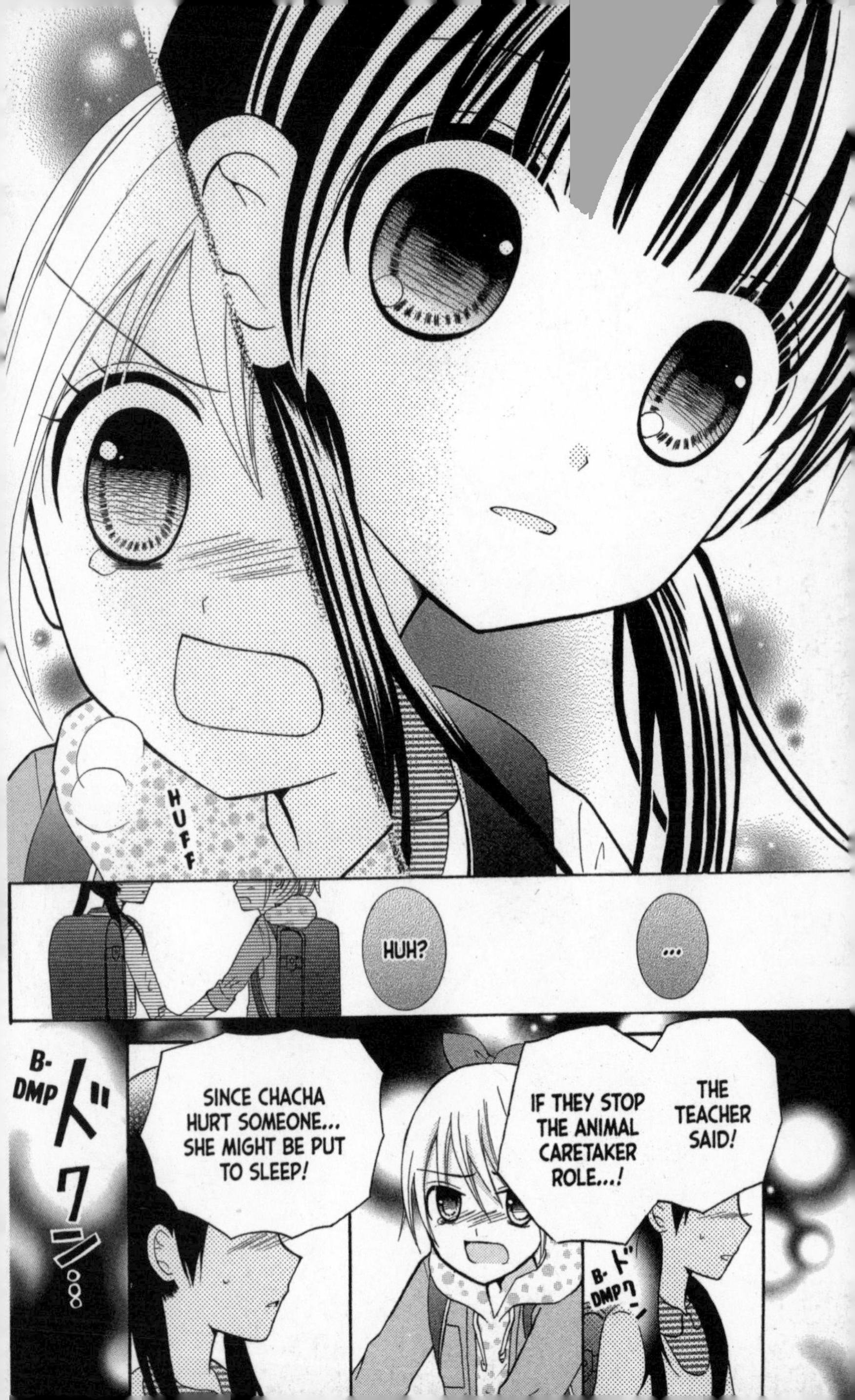
HUFF
...
HUH?
THE TEACHER SAID!
B-DMP ドクン
IF THEY STOP THE ANIMAL CARETAKER ROLE...!
SINCE CHACHA HURT SOMEONE... SHE MIGHT BE PUT TO SLEEP!
B-DMP ドクン…

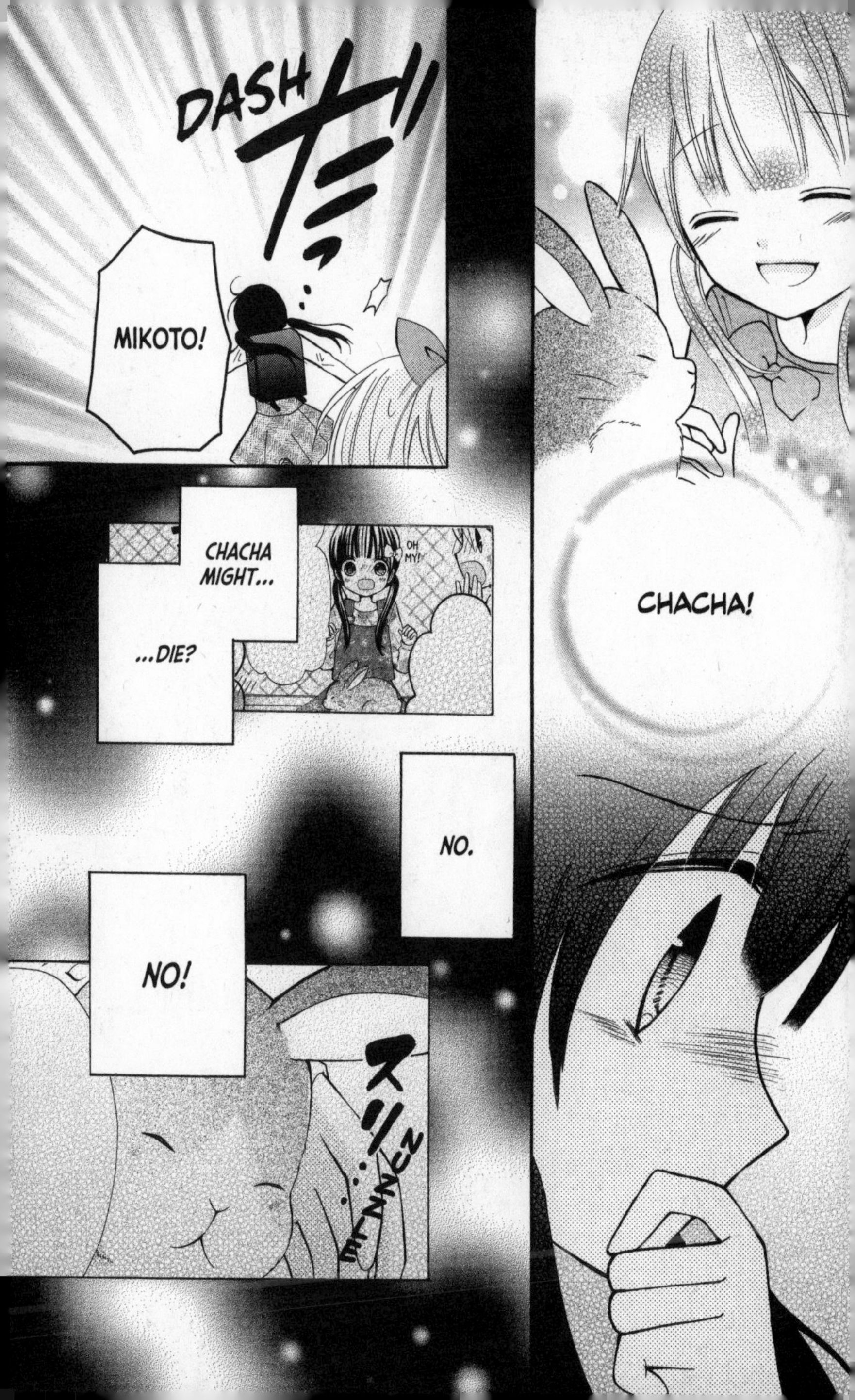
CHACHA!
DASH
MIKOTO!
CHACHA MIGHT...
...DIE?
OH MY!
NO.
NO!
NUZZLE

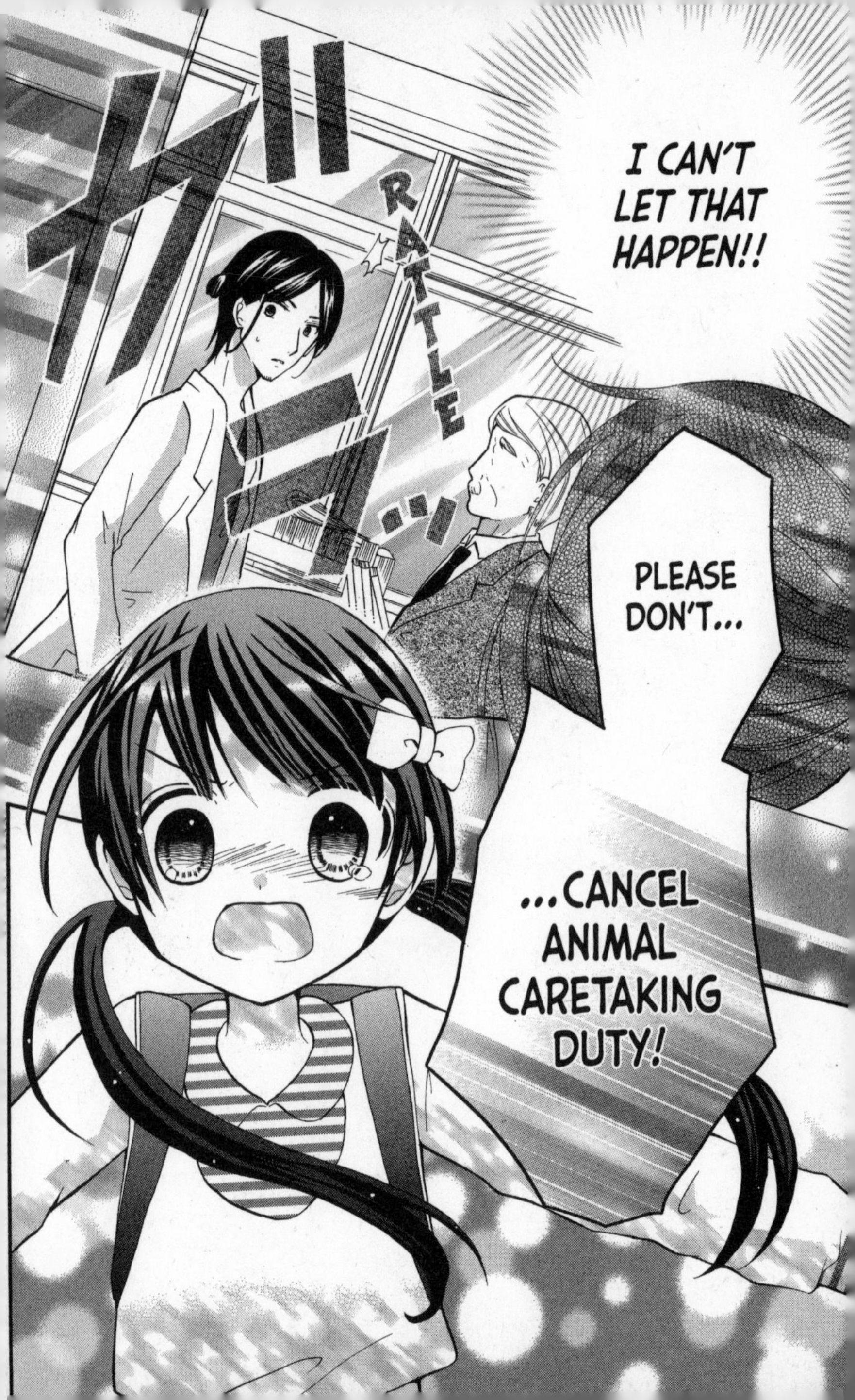
I CAN'T LET THAT HAPPEN!!
RATTLE
PLEASE DON'T...
...CANCEL ANIMAL CARETAKING DUTY!

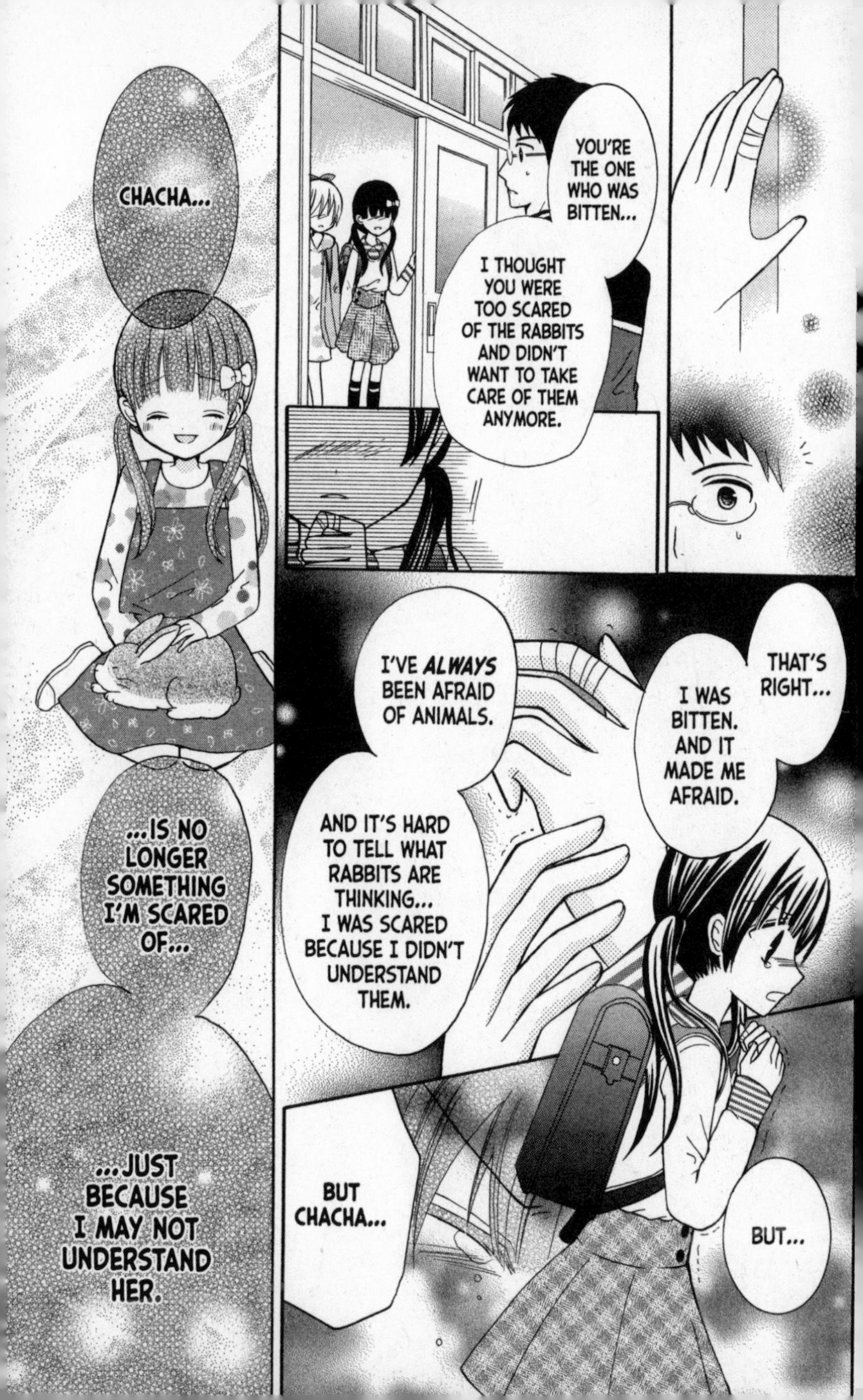
YOU'RE THE ONE WHO WAS BITTEN...
I THOUGHT YOU WERE TOO SCARED OF THE RABBITS AND DIDN'T WANT TO TAKE CARE OF THEM ANYMORE.
THAT'S RIGHT...
I WAS BITTEN. AND IT MADE ME AFRAID.
I'VE *ALWAYS* BEEN AFRAID OF ANIMALS.
AND IT'S HARD TO TELL WHAT RABBITS ARE THINKING... I WAS SCARED BECAUSE I DIDN'T UNDERSTAND THEM.
BUT...
BUT CHACHA...
CHACHA...
...IS NO LONGER SOMETHING I'M SCARED OF...
...JUST BECAUSE I MAY NOT UNDERSTAND HER.

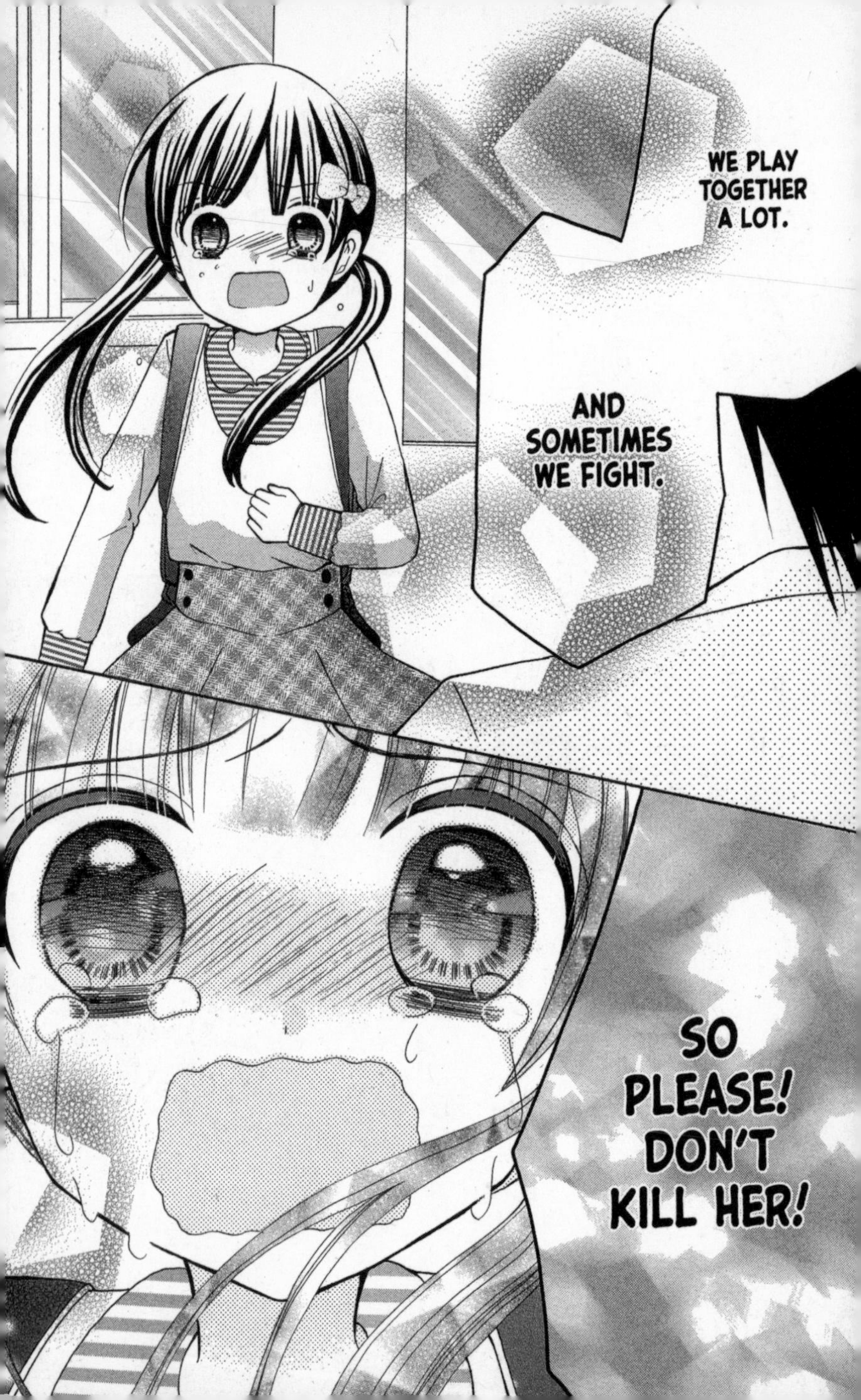
WE PLAY TOGETHER A LOT.
AND SOMETIMES WE FIGHT.
SO PLEASE! DON'T KILL HER!

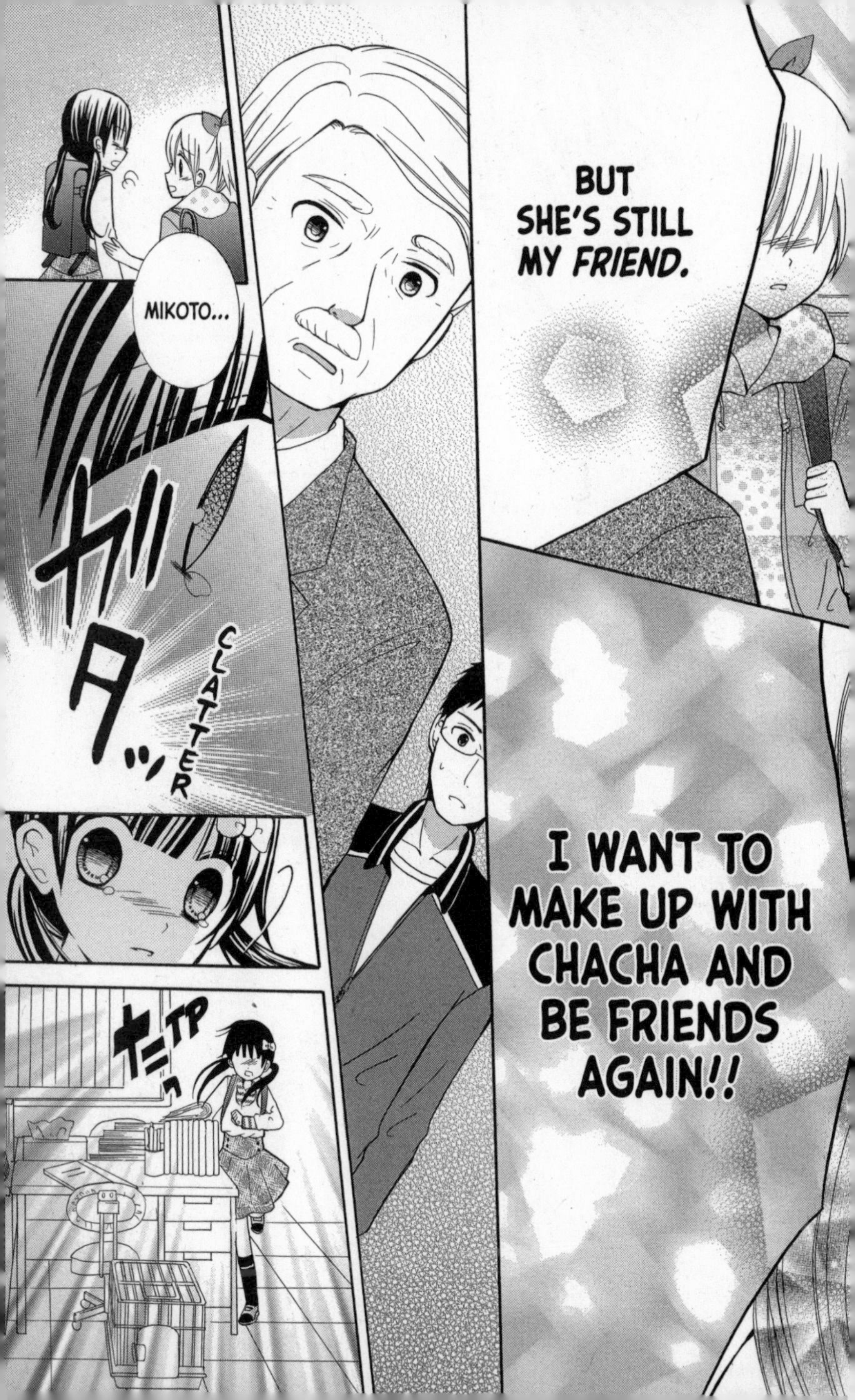
BUT SHE'S STILL MY FRIEND.
I WANT TO MAKE UP WITH CHACHA AND BE FRIENDS AGAIN!!
MIKOTO...
CLATTER
TP

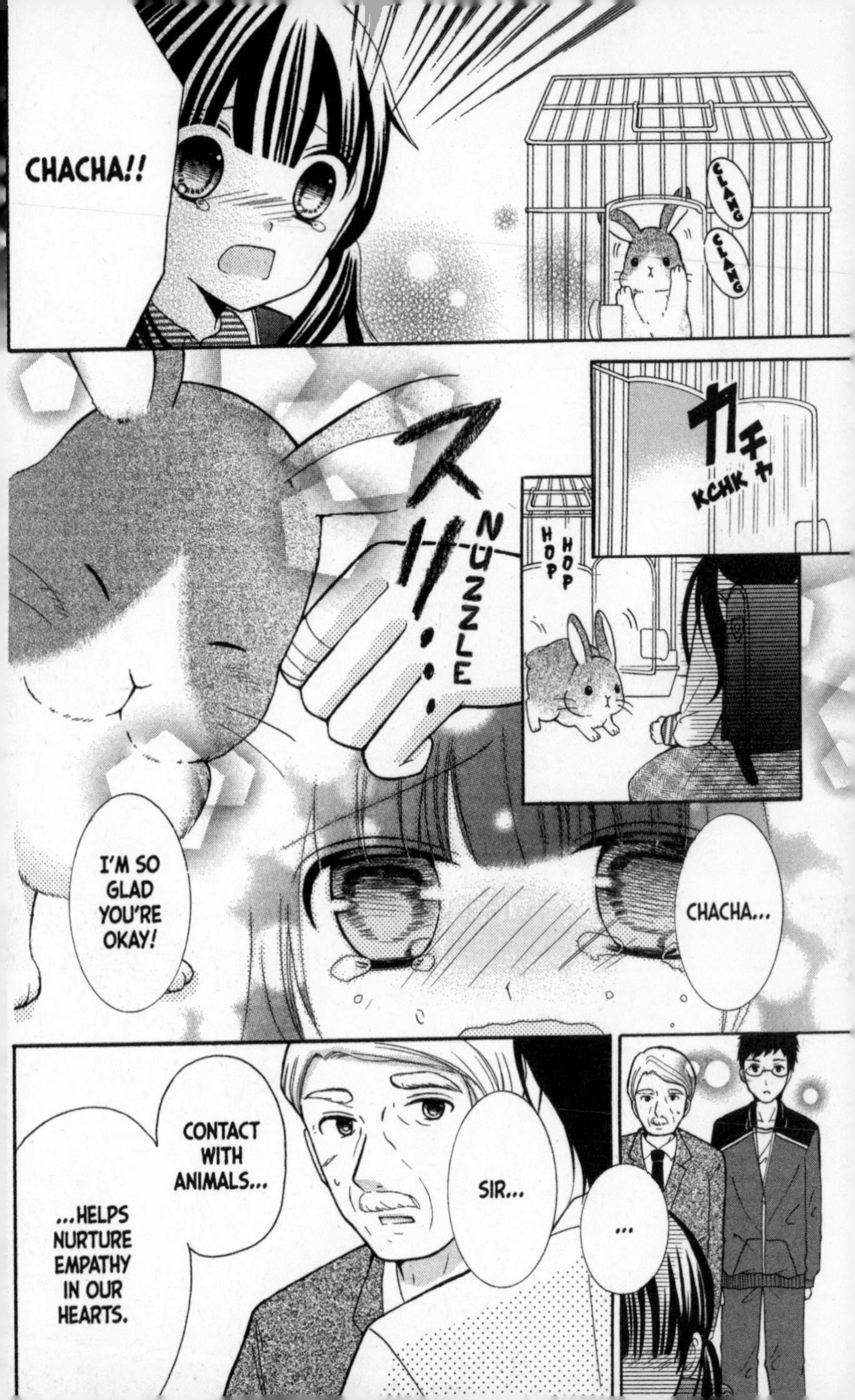
CLANG
CLANG
CHACHA!!
カチャ
KCHK
HOP HOP
ス
NUZZLE
CHACHA...
I'M SO GLAD YOU'RE OKAY!
...
SIR...
CONTACT WITH ANIMALS...
...HELPS NURTURE EMPATHY IN OUR HEARTS.

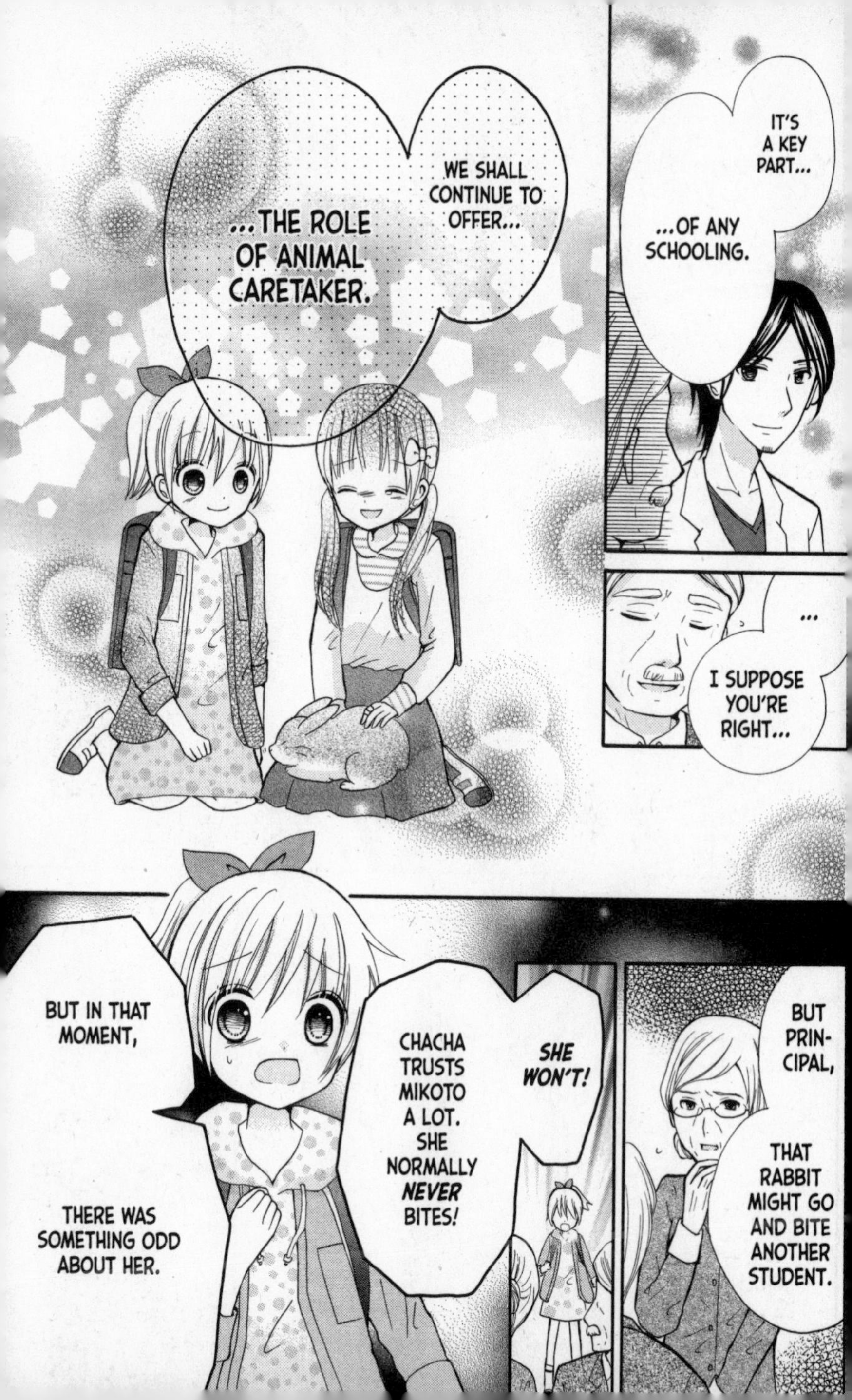
IT'S A KEY PART...
...OF ANY SCHOOLING.
...
I SUPPOSE YOU'RE RIGHT...
WE SHALL CONTINUE TO OFFER...
...THE ROLE OF ANIMAL CARETAKER.
BUT PRINCIPAL,
THAT RABBIT MIGHT GO AND BITE ANOTHER STUDENT.
SHE WON'T!
CHACHA TRUSTS MIKOTO A LOT. SHE NORMALLY NEVER BITES!
BUT IN THAT MOMENT,
THERE WAS SOMETHING ODD ABOUT HER.

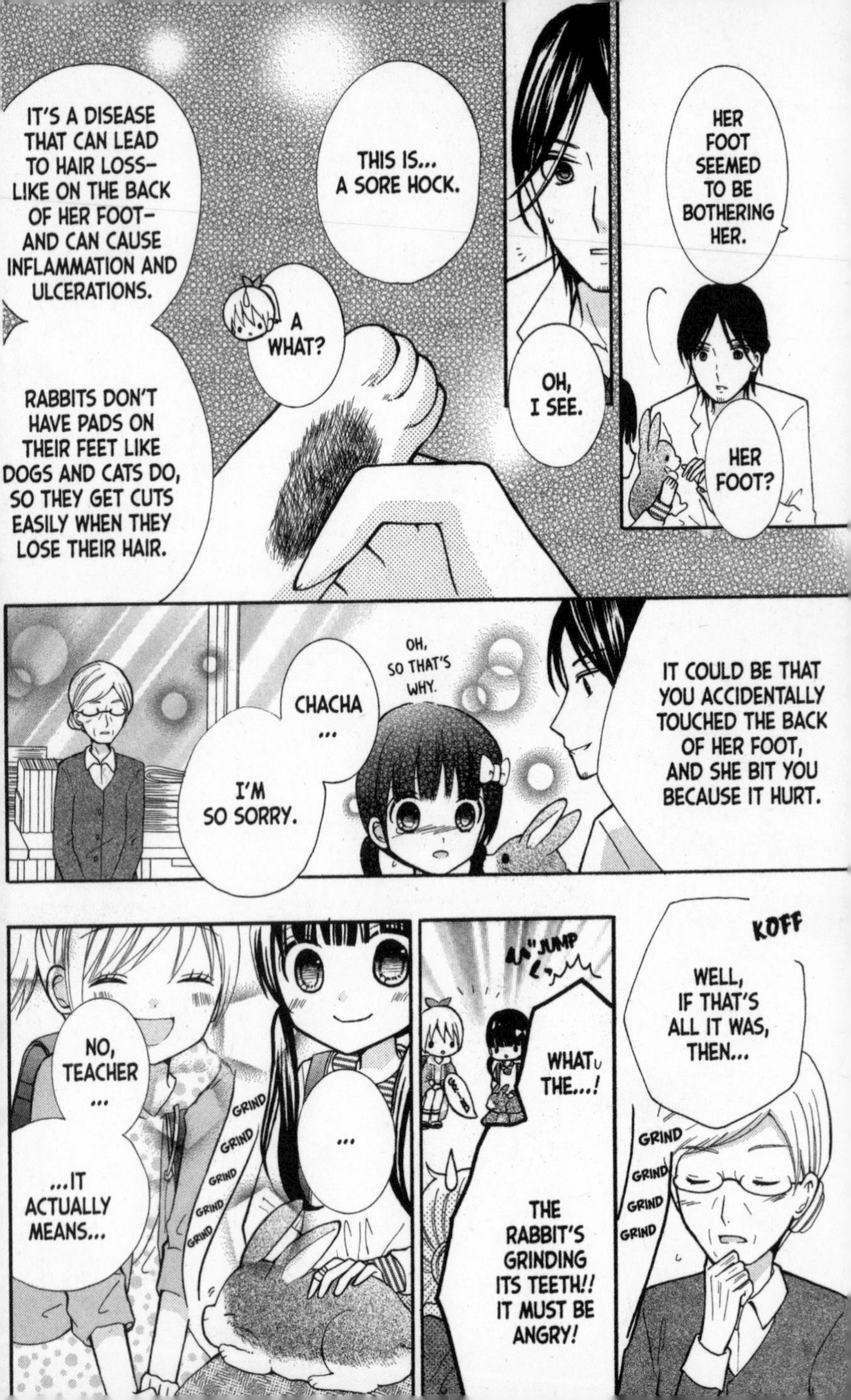
HER FOOT SEEMED TO BE BOTHERING HER.
HER FOOT?
OH, I SEE.
THIS IS... A SORE HOCK.
A WHAT?
IT'S A DISEASE THAT CAN LEAD TO HAIR LOSS—LIKE ON THE BACK OF HER FOOT—AND CAN CAUSE INFLAMMATION AND ULCERATIONS.
RABBITS DON'T HAVE PADS ON THEIR FEET LIKE DOGS AND CATS DO, SO THEY GET CUTS EASILY WHEN THEY LOSE THEIR HAIR.
IT COULD BE THAT YOU ACCIDENTALLY TOUCHED THE BACK OF HER FOOT, AND SHE BIT YOU BECAUSE IT HURT.
OH, SO THAT'S WHY.
CHACHA...
I'M SO SORRY.
KOFF
WELL, IF THAT'S ALL IT WAS, THEN...
GRIND
GRIND
GRIND
GRIND
JUMP
WHAT THE...!
THE RABBIT'S GRINDING ITS TEETH!! IT MUST BE ANGRY!
...
NO, TEACHER...
...IT ACTUALLY MEANS...
GRIND
GRIND
GRIND
GRIND
GRIND

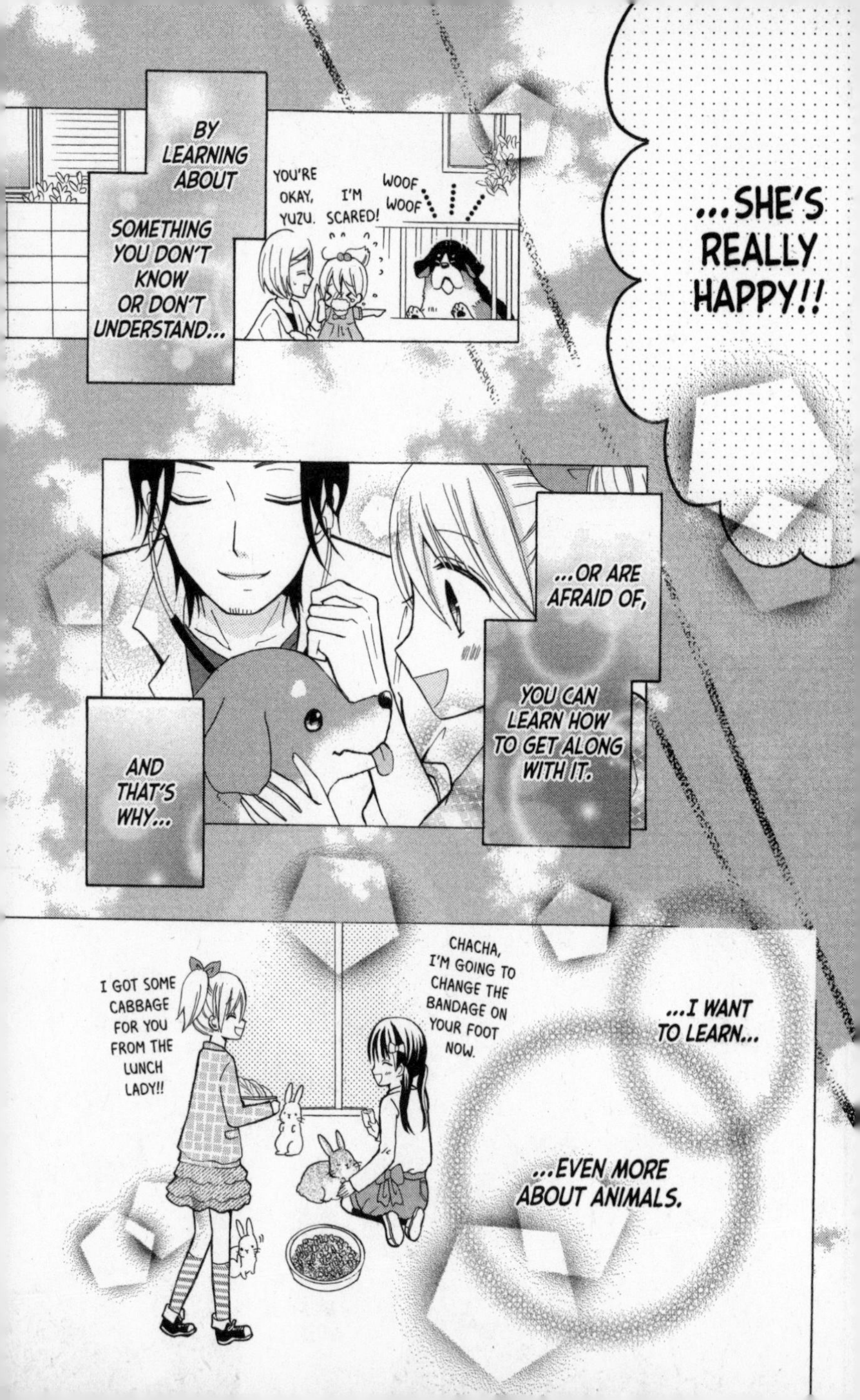
...SHE'S REALLY HAPPY!!
BY LEARNING ABOUT SOMETHING YOU DON'T KNOW OR DON'T UNDERSTAND...
WOOF WOOF
I'M SCARED!
YOU'RE OKAY, YUZU.
...OR ARE AFRAID OF,
YOU CAN LEARN HOW TO GET ALONG WITH IT.
AND THAT'S WHY...
...I WANT TO LEARN...
...EVEN MORE ABOUT ANIMALS.
CHACHA, I'M GOING TO CHANGE THE BANDAGE ON YOUR FOOT NOW.
I GOT SOME CABBAGE FOR YOU FROM THE LUNCH LADY!!

YUZU THE
PET VET

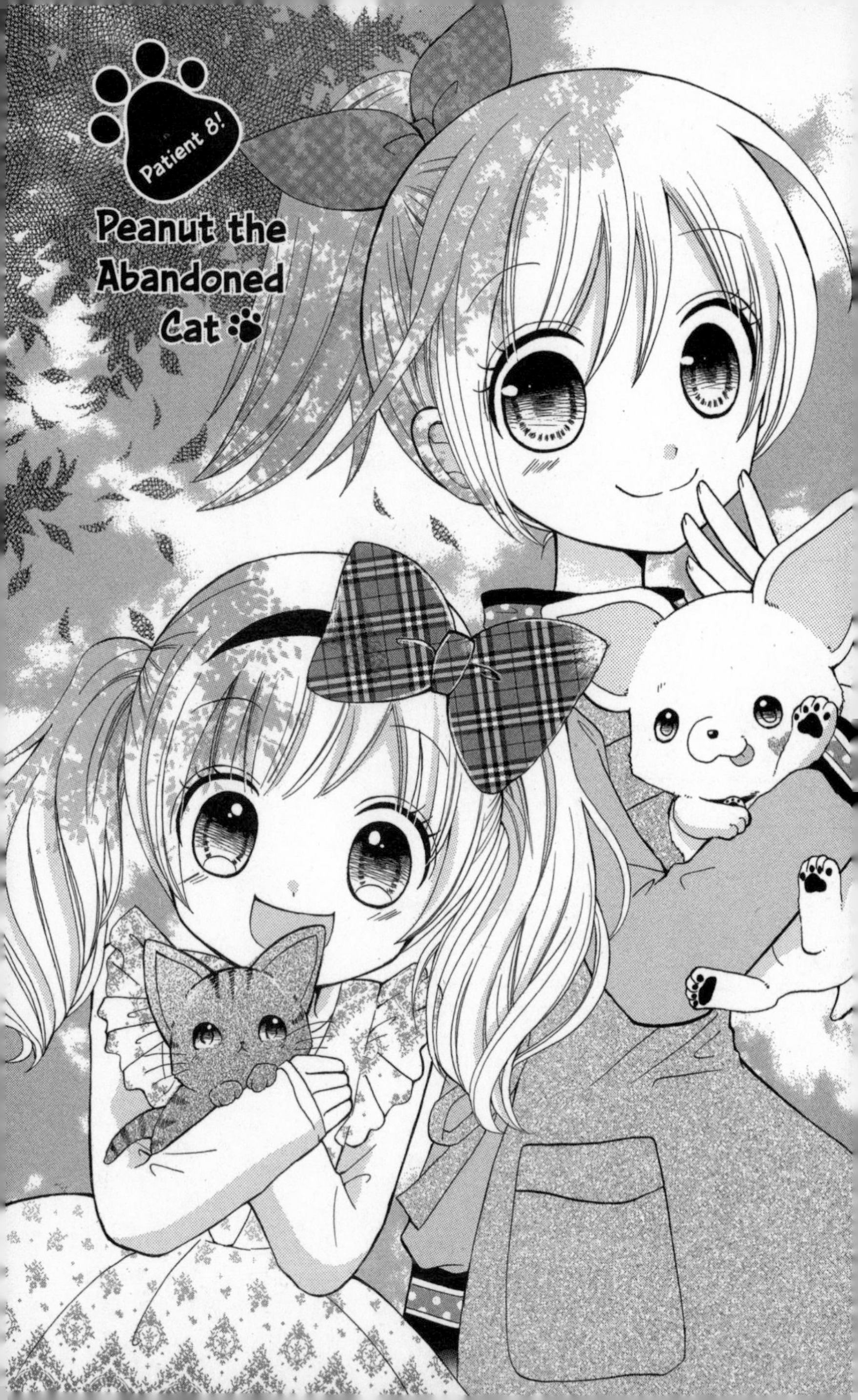
Patient 8!
Peanut the Abandoned Cat

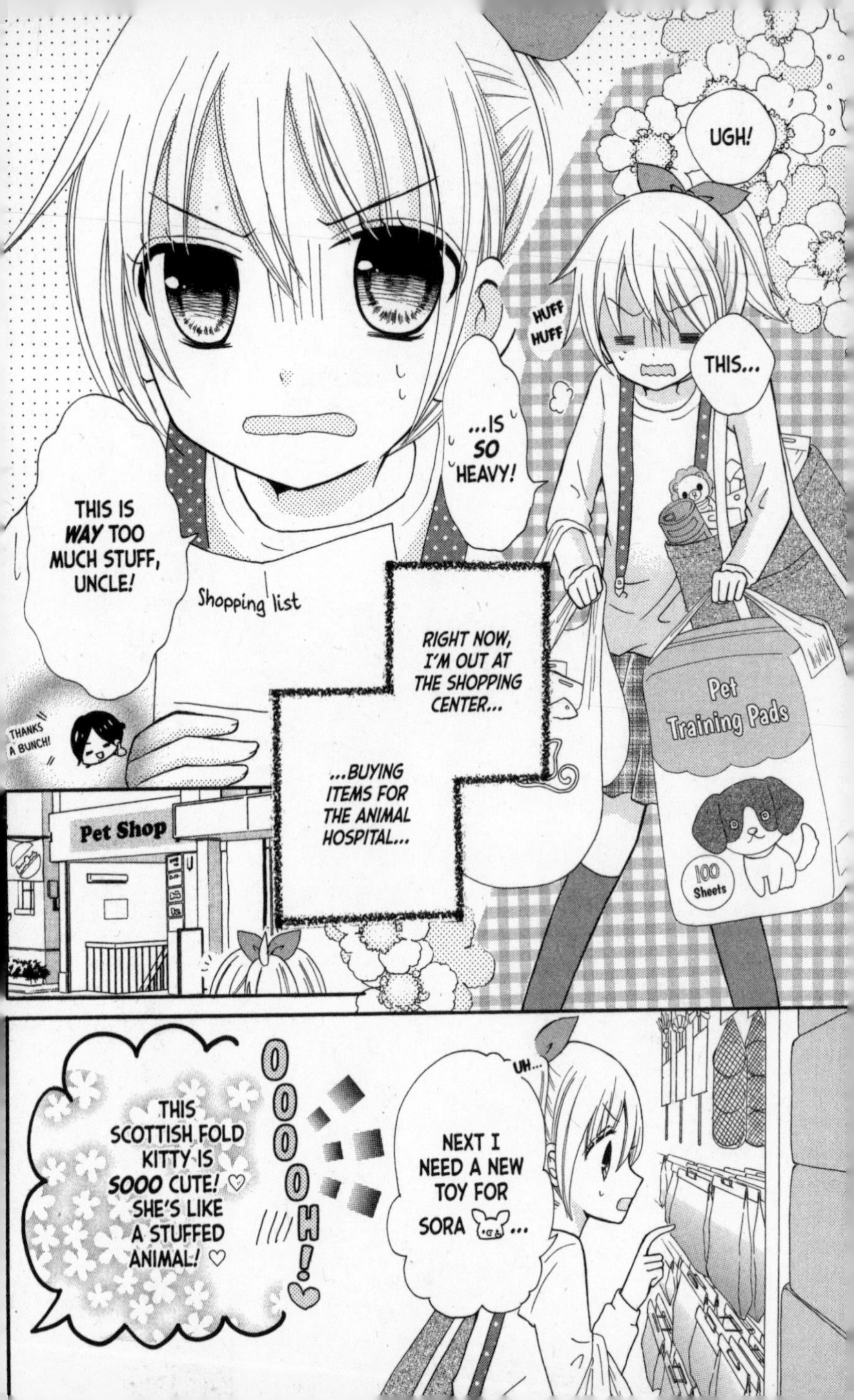
UGH!
HUFF HUFF
THIS...
...IS SO HEAVY!
Pet Training Pads
100 Sheets
THIS IS WAY TOO MUCH STUFF, UNCLE!
Shopping list
THANKS A BUNCH!
RIGHT NOW, I'M OUT AT THE SHOPPING CENTER...
...BUYING ITEMS FOR THE ANIMAL HOSPITAL...
Pet Shop
UH...
NEXT I NEED A NEW TOY FOR SORA ...
OOOOOH!
THIS SCOTTISH FOLD KITTY IS SOOO CUTE! ♡ SHE'S LIKE A STUFFED ANIMAL! ♡

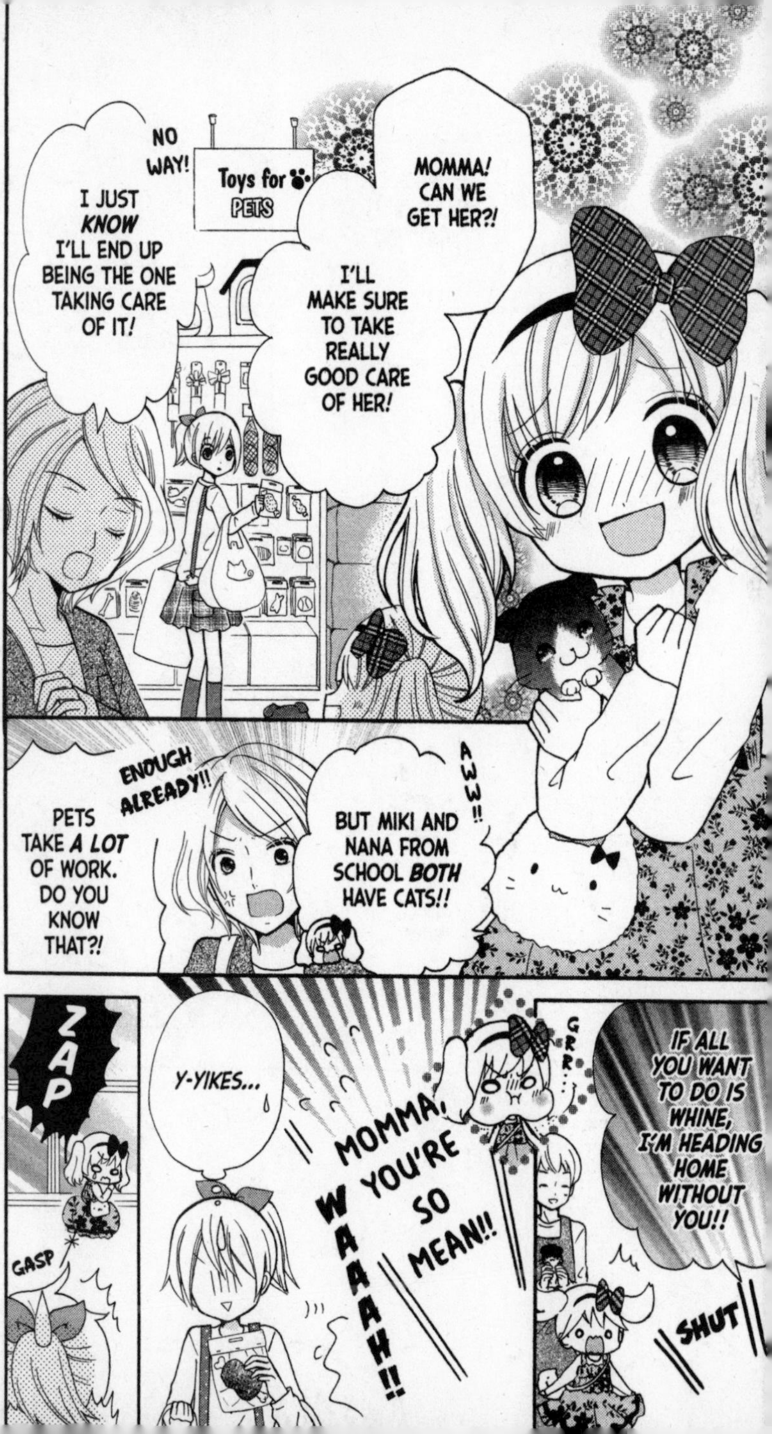
MOMMA! CAN WE GET HER?!
I'LL MAKE SURE TO TAKE REALLY GOOD CARE OF HER!
Toys for PETS
NO WAY!
I JUST *KNOW* I'LL END UP BEING THE ONE TAKING CARE OF IT!
AWW!!
BUT MIKI AND NANA FROM SCHOOL *BOTH* HAVE CATS!!
ENOUGH ALREADY!!
PETS TAKE *A LOT* OF WORK. DO YOU KNOW THAT?!
IF ALL YOU WANT TO DO IS WHINE, I'M HEADING HOME WITHOUT YOU!!
SHUT
GRR...
MOMMA, YOU'RE SO MEAN!!
WAAAAH!!
Y-YIKES...
ZAP
GASP

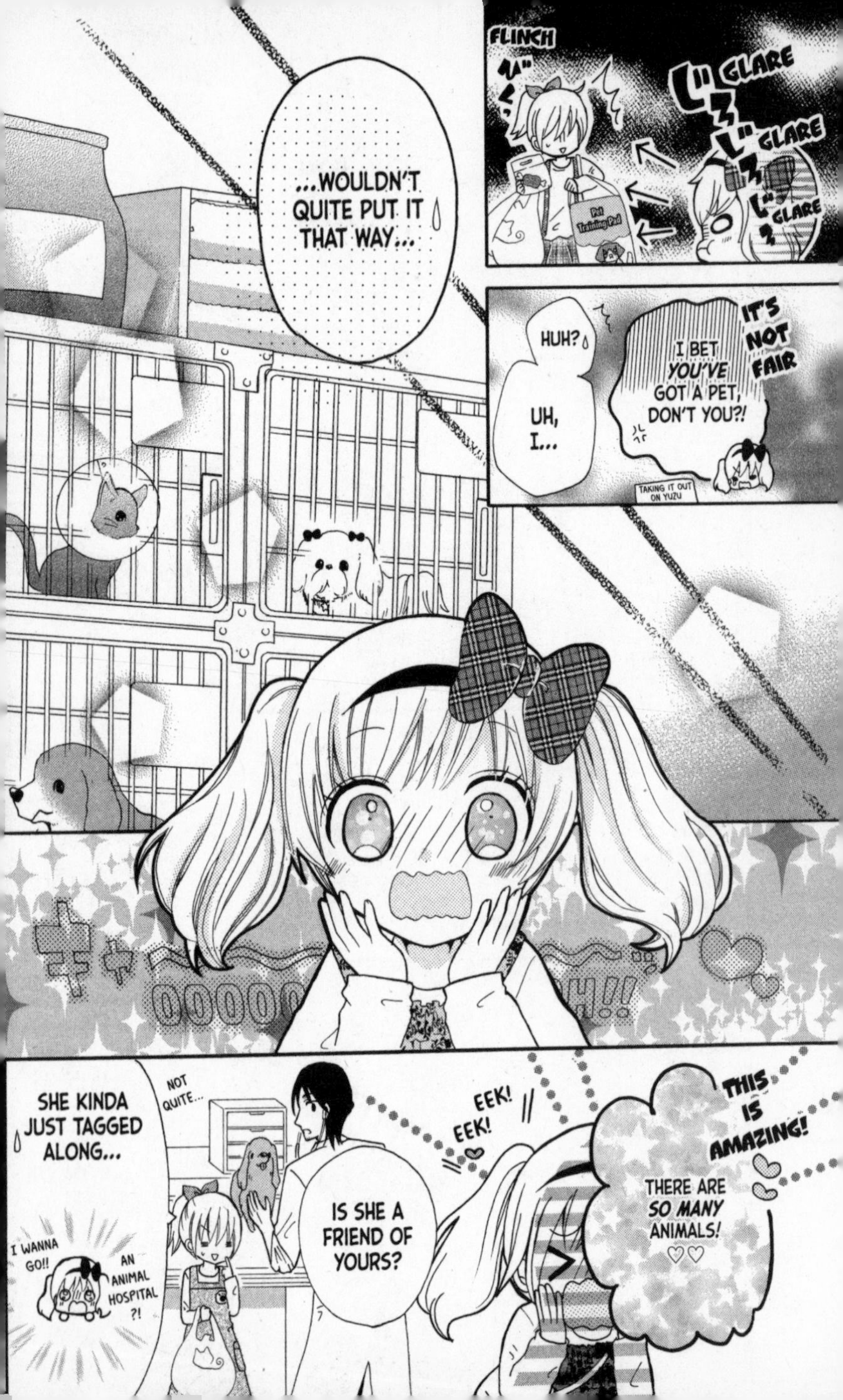
FLINCH
GLARE
GLARE
GLARE
Pet Training Pad
IT'S NOT FAIR
I BET YOU'VE GOT A PET, DON'T YOU?!
TAKING IT OUT ON YUZU
HUH?
UH, I...
...WOULDN'T QUITE PUT IT THAT WAY...
THIS IS AMAZING!
THERE ARE SO MANY ANIMALS! ♡♡
EEK! EEK!
IS SHE A FRIEND OF YOURS?
NOT QUITE...
SHE KINDA JUST TAGGED ALONG...
AN ANIMAL HOSPITAL ?!
I WANNA GO!!

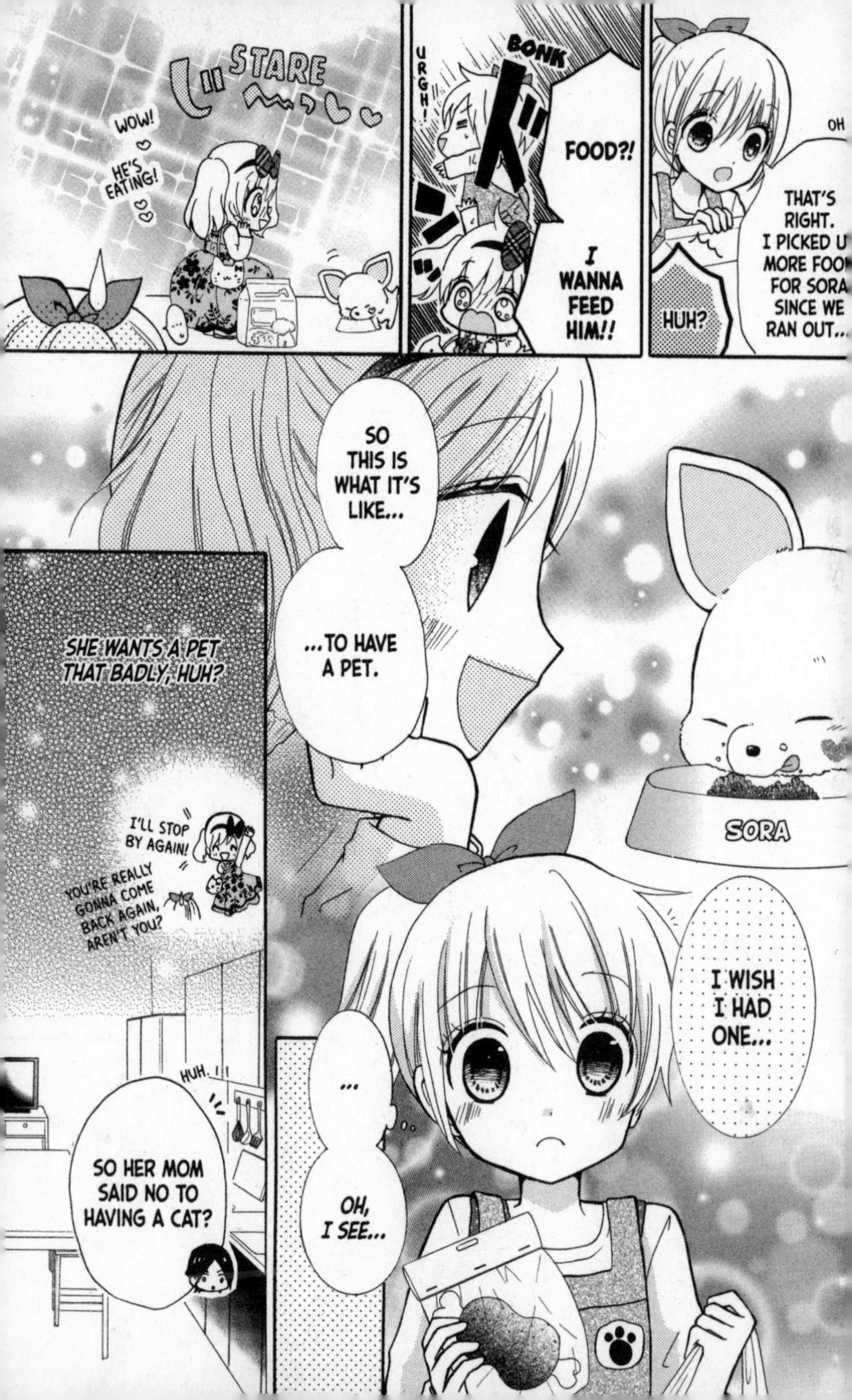
OH
THAT'S RIGHT. I PICKED U MORE FOO FOR SORA SINCE WE RAN OUT...
HUH?
BONK
URGH!
FOOD?!
I WANNA FEED HIM!!
STARE
WOW!
HE'S EATING!
...
SO THIS IS WHAT IT'S LIKE...
...TO HAVE A PET.
SORA
I WISH I HAD ONE...
...
OH, I SEE...
SHE WANTS A PET THAT BADLY, HUH?
I'LL STOP BY AGAIN!
YOU'RE REALLY GONNA COME BACK AGAIN, AREN'T YOU?
HUH.
SO HER MOM SAID NO TO HAVING A CAT?

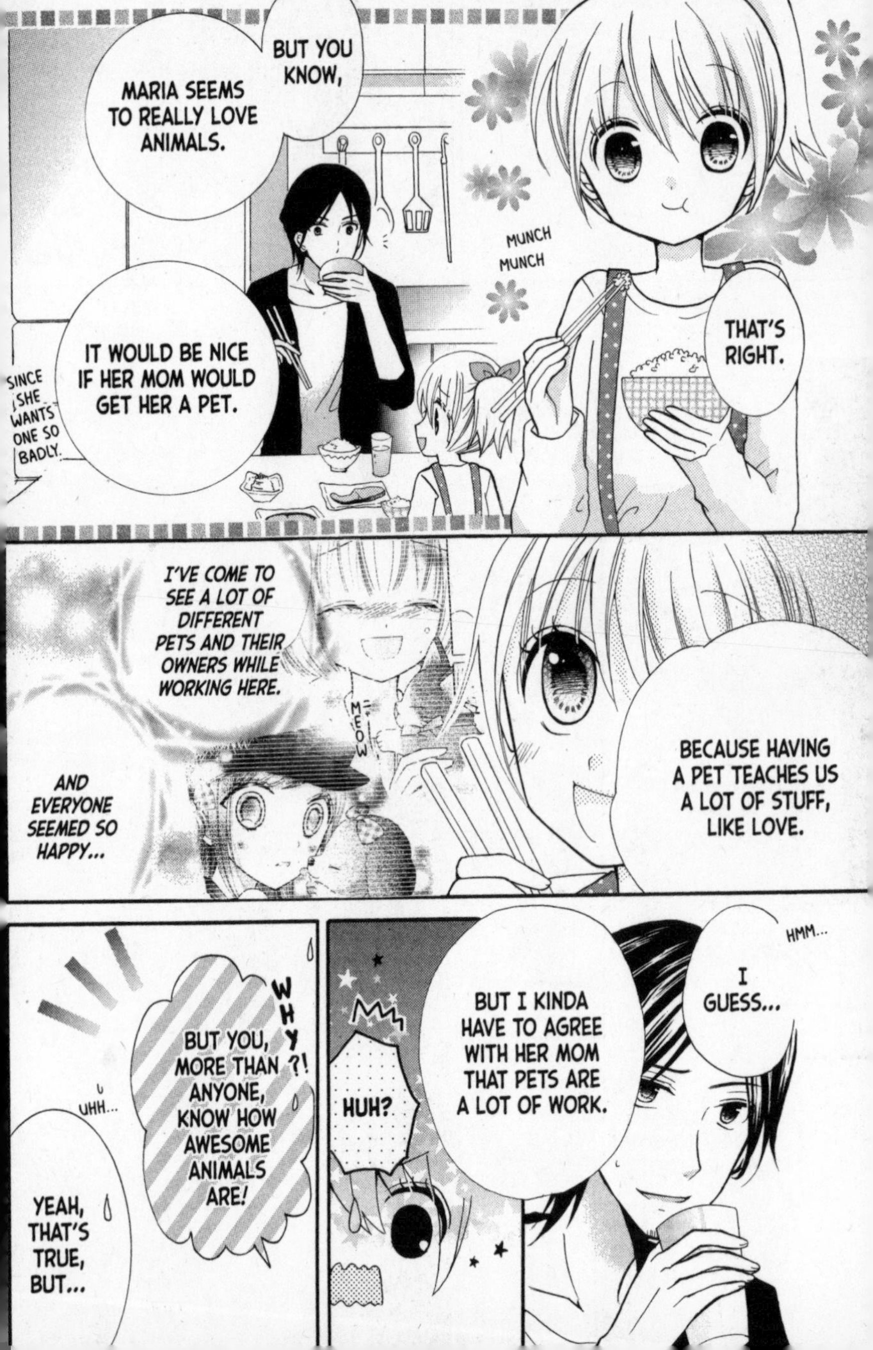
BUT YOU KNOW,
MARIA SEEMS TO REALLY LOVE ANIMALS.
MUNCH MUNCH
THAT'S RIGHT.
IT WOULD BE NICE IF HER MOM WOULD GET HER A PET.
SINCE SHE WANTS ONE SO BADLY.
BECAUSE HAVING A PET TEACHES US A LOT OF STUFF, LIKE LOVE.
I'VE COME TO SEE A LOT OF DIFFERENT PETS AND THEIR OWNERS WHILE WORKING HERE.
MEOW
AND EVERYONE SEEMED SO HAPPY...
HMM...
I GUESS...
BUT I KINDA HAVE TO AGREE WITH HER MOM THAT PETS ARE A LOT OF WORK.
HUH?
WHY?!
BUT YOU, MORE THAN ANYONE, KNOW HOW AWESOME ANIMALS ARE!
UHH...
YEAH, THAT'S TRUE, BUT...

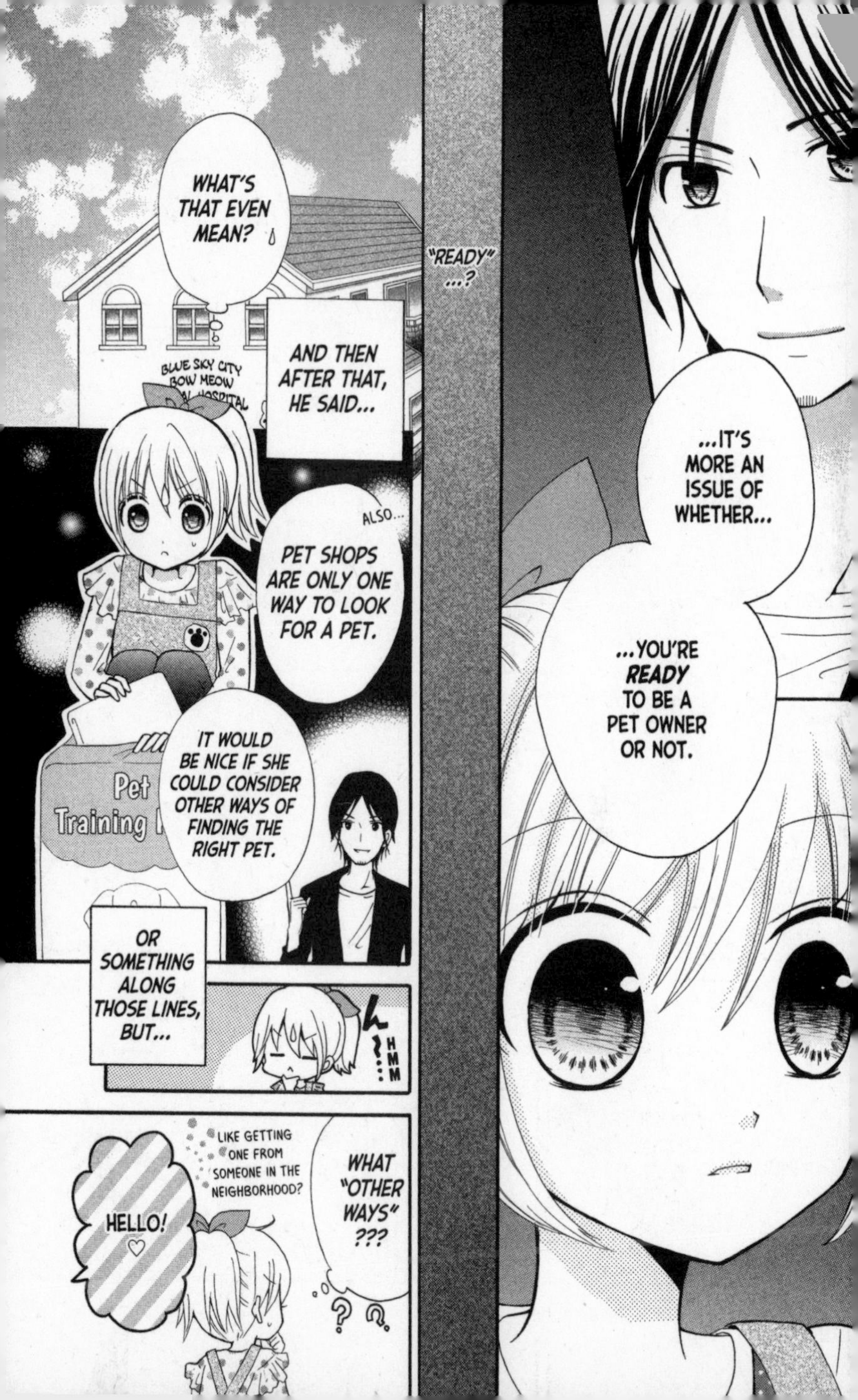
...IT'S MORE AN ISSUE OF WHETHER...
...YOU'RE *READY* TO BE A PET OWNER OR NOT.
"READY" ...?
WHAT'S THAT EVEN MEAN?
BLUE SKY CITY BOW MEOW
AND THEN AFTER THAT, HE SAID...
ALSO...
PET SHOPS ARE ONLY ONE WAY TO LOOK FOR A PET.
IT WOULD BE NICE IF SHE COULD CONSIDER OTHER WAYS OF FINDING THE RIGHT PET.
Pet
Training
OR SOMETHING ALONG THOSE LINES, BUT...
HMM...
WHAT "OTHER WAYS" ???
LIKE GETTING ONE FROM SOMEONE IN THE NEIGHBORHOOD?
HELLO! ♡

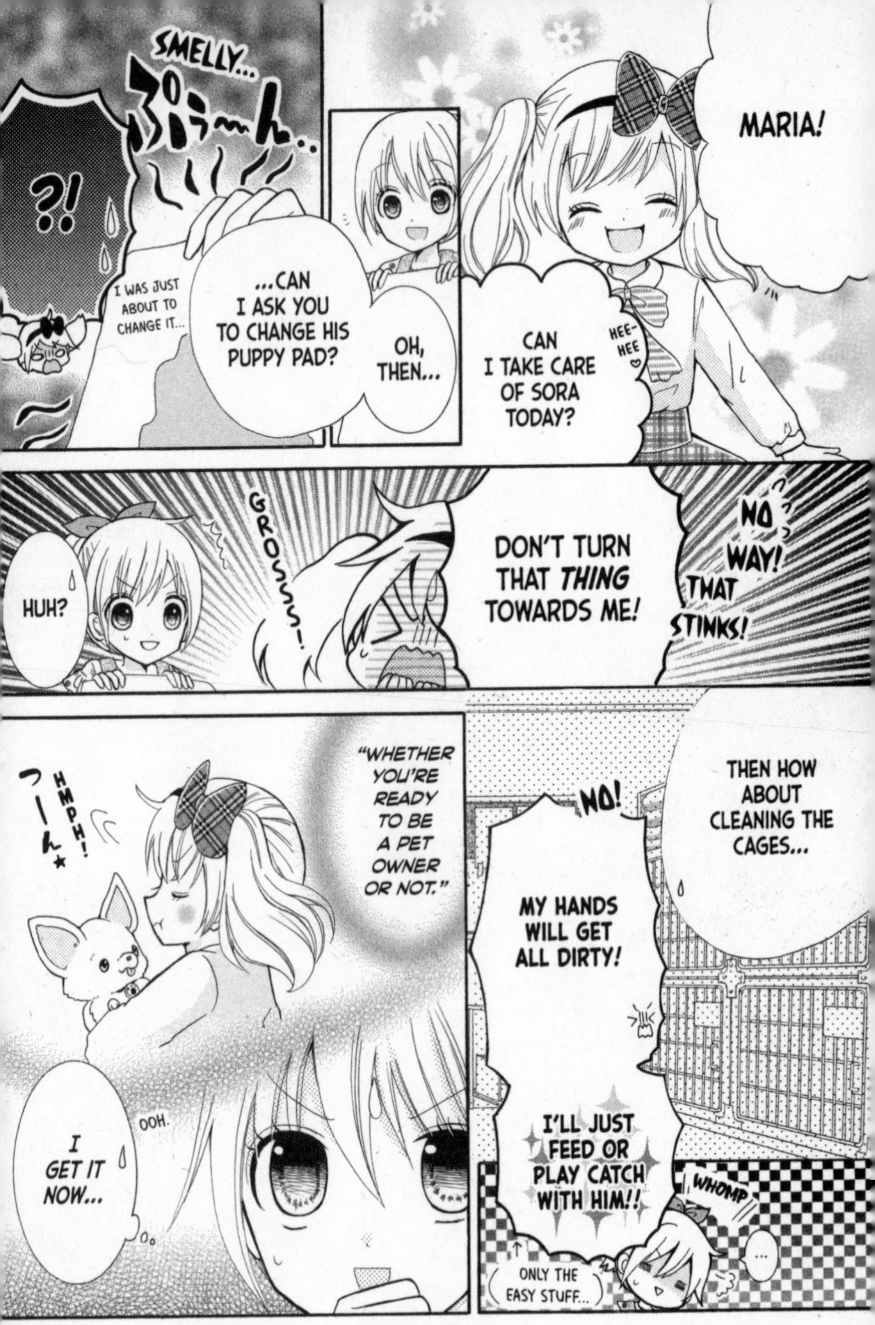
MARIA!
CAN I TAKE CARE OF SORA TODAY?
HEE-HEE ♡
OH, THEN...
...CAN I ASK YOU TO CHANGE HIS PUPPY PAD?
SMELLY...
?!
I WAS JUST ABOUT TO CHANGE IT...
NO WAY! THAT STINKS!
DON'T TURN THAT *THING* TOWARDS ME!
GROSSS!
HUH?
THEN HOW ABOUT CLEANING THE CAGES...
NO!
MY HANDS WILL GET ALL DIRTY!
I'LL JUST FEED OR PLAY CATCH WITH HIM!!
WHOMP
...
ONLY THE EASY STUFF...
"WHETHER YOU'RE READY TO BE A PET OWNER OR NOT."
HMPH!
OOH.
I GET IT NOW...

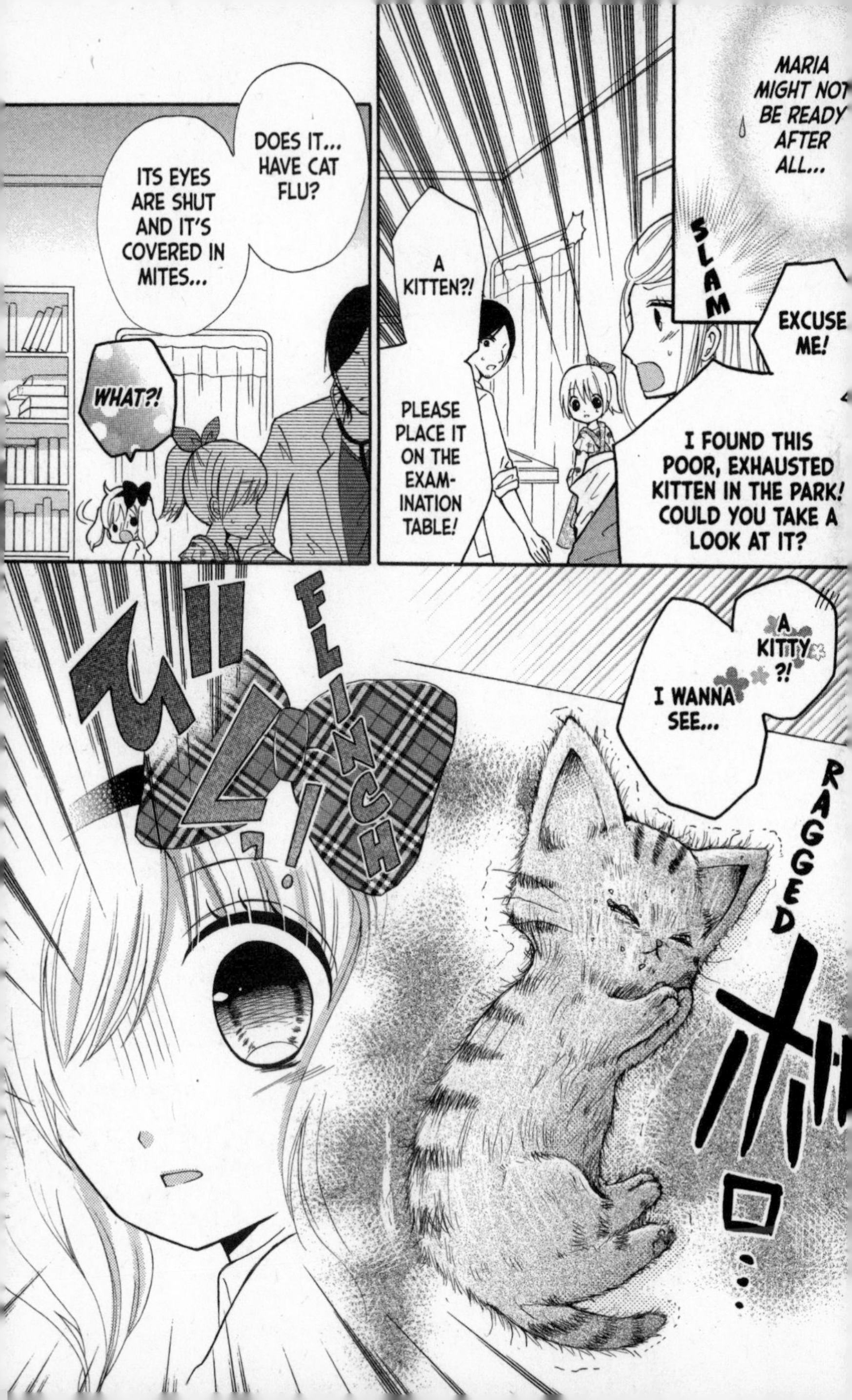
MARIA MIGHT NOT BE READY AFTER ALL...
SLAM
EXCUSE ME!
I FOUND THIS POOR, EXHAUSTED KITTEN IN THE PARK! COULD YOU TAKE A LOOK AT IT?
A KITTEN?!
PLEASE PLACE IT ON THE EXAMINATION TABLE!
DOES IT... HAVE CAT FLU?
ITS EYES ARE SHUT AND IT'S COVERED IN MITES...
WHAT?!
A KITTY?! I WANNA SEE...
RAGGED
FLINCH

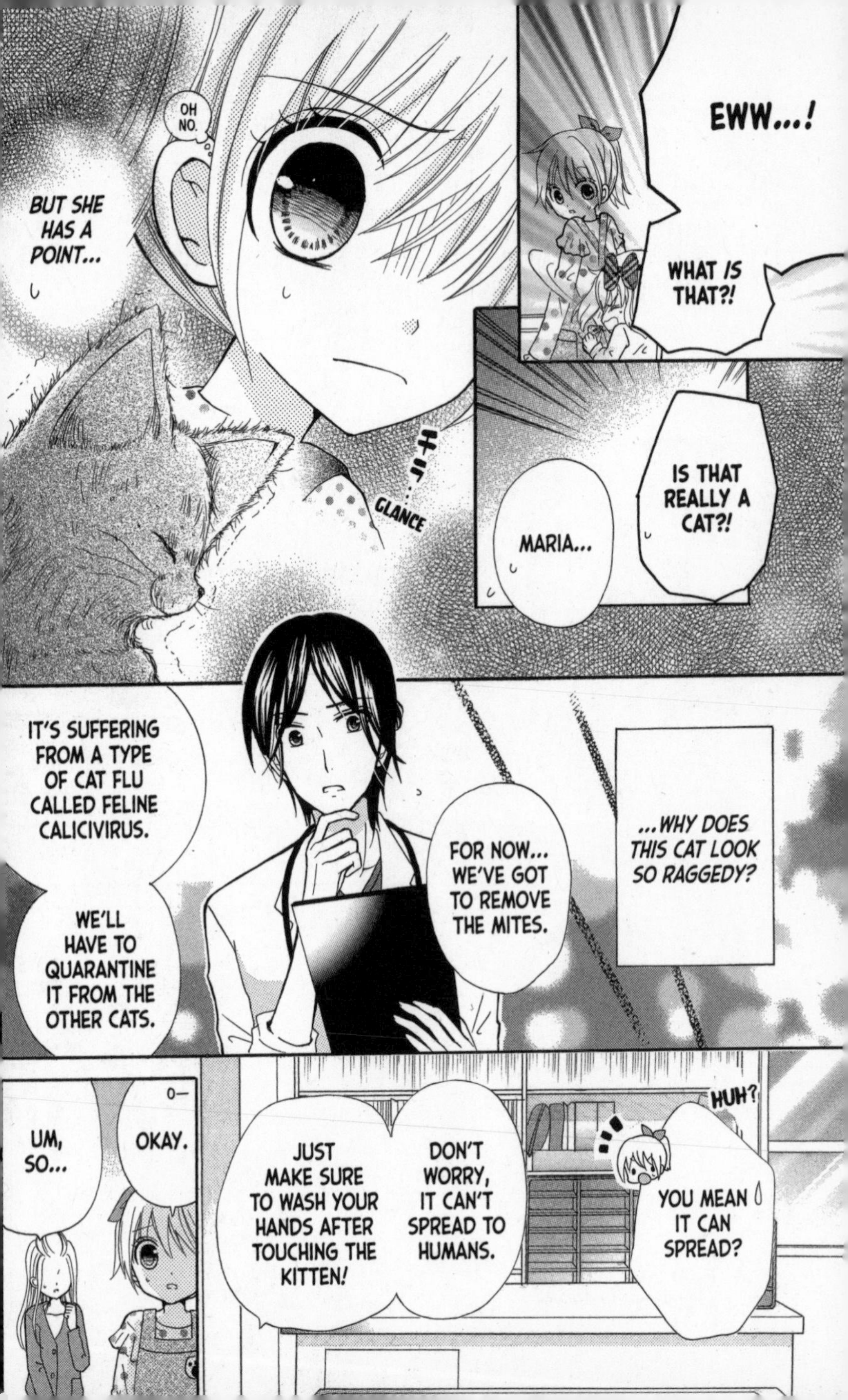
EWW...!
WHAT IS THAT?!
IS THAT REALLY A CAT?!
MARIA...
OH NO.
BUT SHE HAS A POINT...
チラ... GLANCE
...WHY DOES THIS CAT LOOK SO RAGGEDY?
FOR NOW... WE'VE GOT TO REMOVE THE MITES.
IT'S SUFFERING FROM A TYPE OF CAT FLU CALLED FELINE CALICIVIRUS.
WE'LL HAVE TO QUARANTINE IT FROM THE OTHER CATS.
HUH?
YOU MEAN IT CAN SPREAD?
DON'T WORRY, IT CAN'T SPREAD TO HUMANS.
JUST MAKE SURE TO WASH YOUR HANDS AFTER TOUCHING THE KITTEN!
OKAY.
UM, SO...

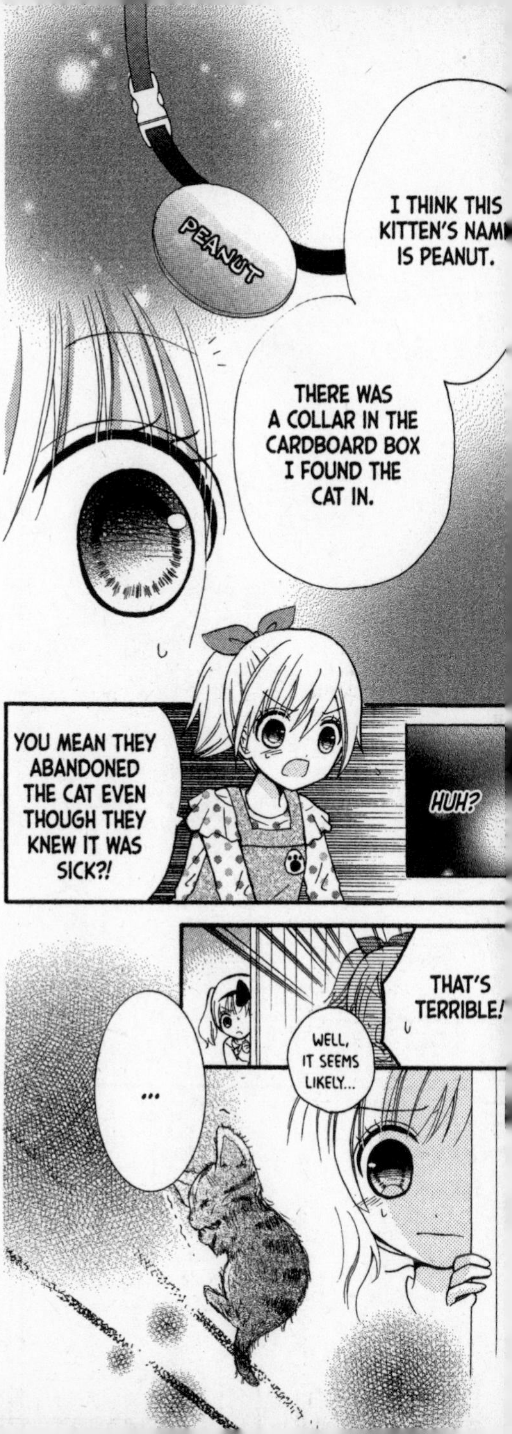
PEANUT
I THINK THIS KITTEN'S NAM IS PEANUT.
THERE WAS A COLLAR IN THE CARDBOARD BOX I FOUND THE CAT IN.
HUH?
YOU MEAN THEY ABANDONED THE CAT EVEN THOUGH THEY KNEW IT WAS SICK?!
THAT'S TERRIBLE!
WELL, IT SEEMS LIKELY...
...

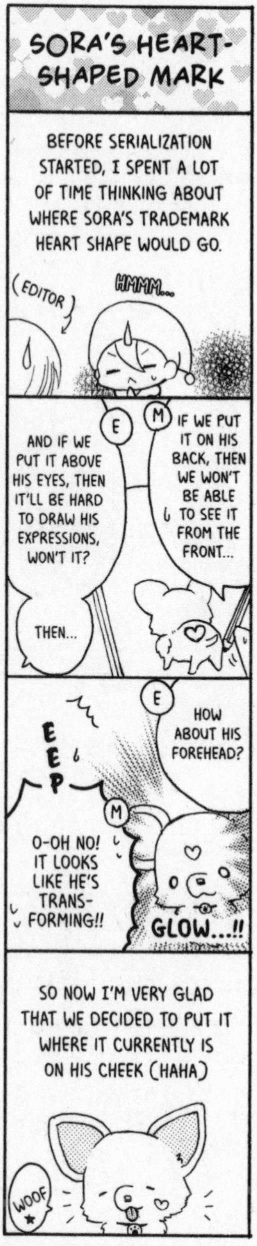
SORA'S HEART-SHAPED MARK
BEFORE SERIALIZATION STARTED, I SPENT A LOT OF TIME THINKING ABOUT WHERE SORA'S TRADEMARK HEART SHAPE WOULD GO.
HMMM...
(EDITOR)
M
IF WE PUT IT ON HIS BACK, THEN WE WON'T BE ABLE TO SEE IT FROM THE FRONT...
E
AND IF WE PUT IT ABOVE HIS EYES, THEN IT'LL BE HARD TO DRAW HIS EXPRESSIONS, WON'T IT?
THEN...
E
HOW ABOUT HIS FOREHEAD?
EEEP
M
O-OH NO! IT LOOKS LIKE HE'S TRANS-FORMING!!
GLOW...!!
SO NOW I'M VERY GLAD THAT WE DECIDED TO PUT IT WHERE IT CURRENTLY IS ON HIS CHEEK (HAHA)
WOOF ★

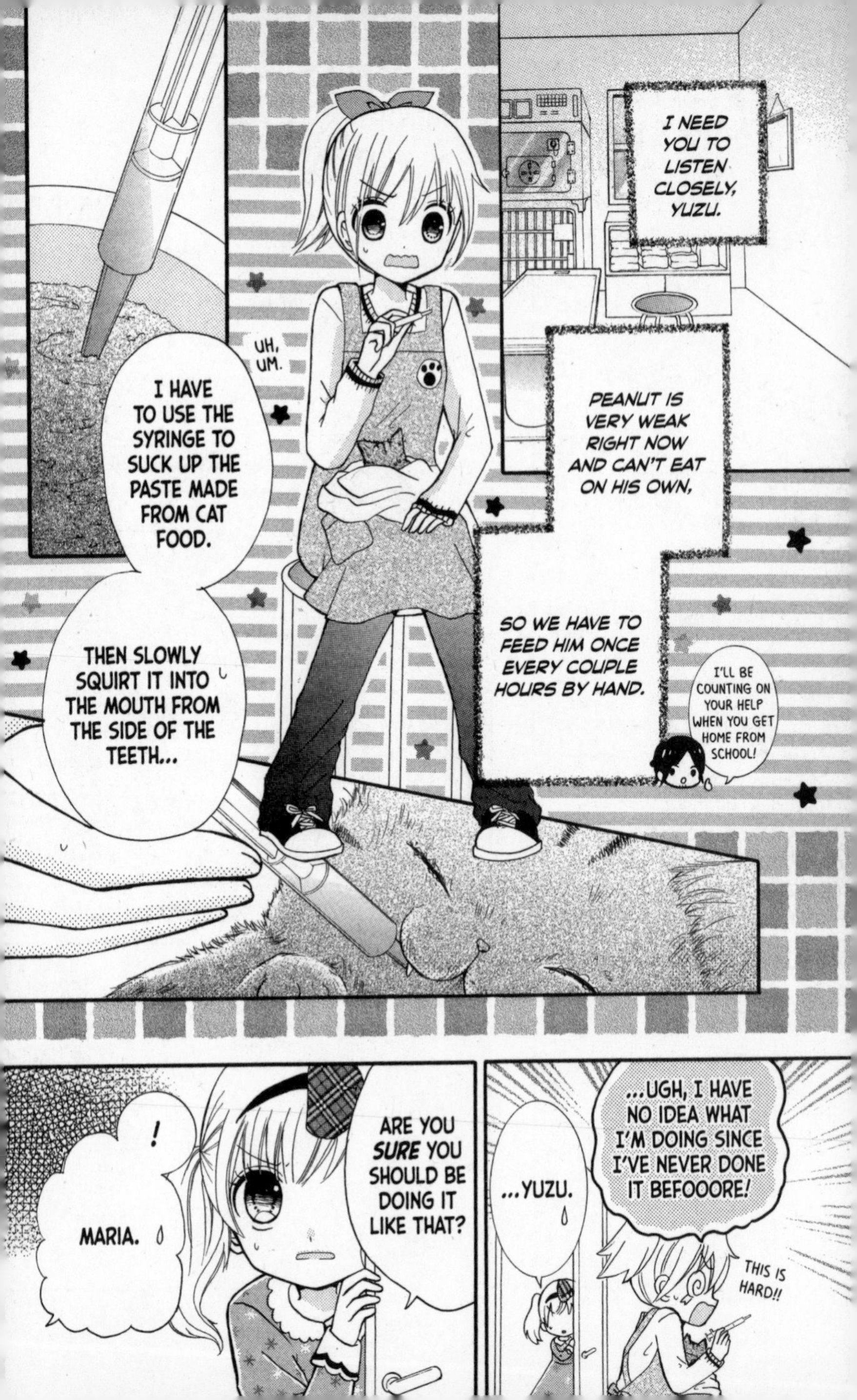
I NEED YOU TO LISTEN CLOSELY, YUZU.
PEANUT IS VERY WEAK RIGHT NOW AND CAN'T EAT ON HIS OWN,
SO WE HAVE TO FEED HIM ONCE EVERY COUPLE HOURS BY HAND.
I'LL BE COUNTING ON YOUR HELP WHEN YOU GET HOME FROM SCHOOL!
UH, UM.
I HAVE TO USE THE SYRINGE TO SUCK UP THE PASTE MADE FROM CAT FOOD.
THEN SLOWLY SQUIRT IT INTO THE MOUTH FROM THE SIDE OF THE TEETH...
...UGH, I HAVE NO IDEA WHAT I'M DOING SINCE I'VE NEVER DONE IT BEFOOORE!
THIS IS HARD!!
...YUZU.
ARE YOU SURE YOU SHOULD BE DOING IT LIKE THAT?
!
MARIA.

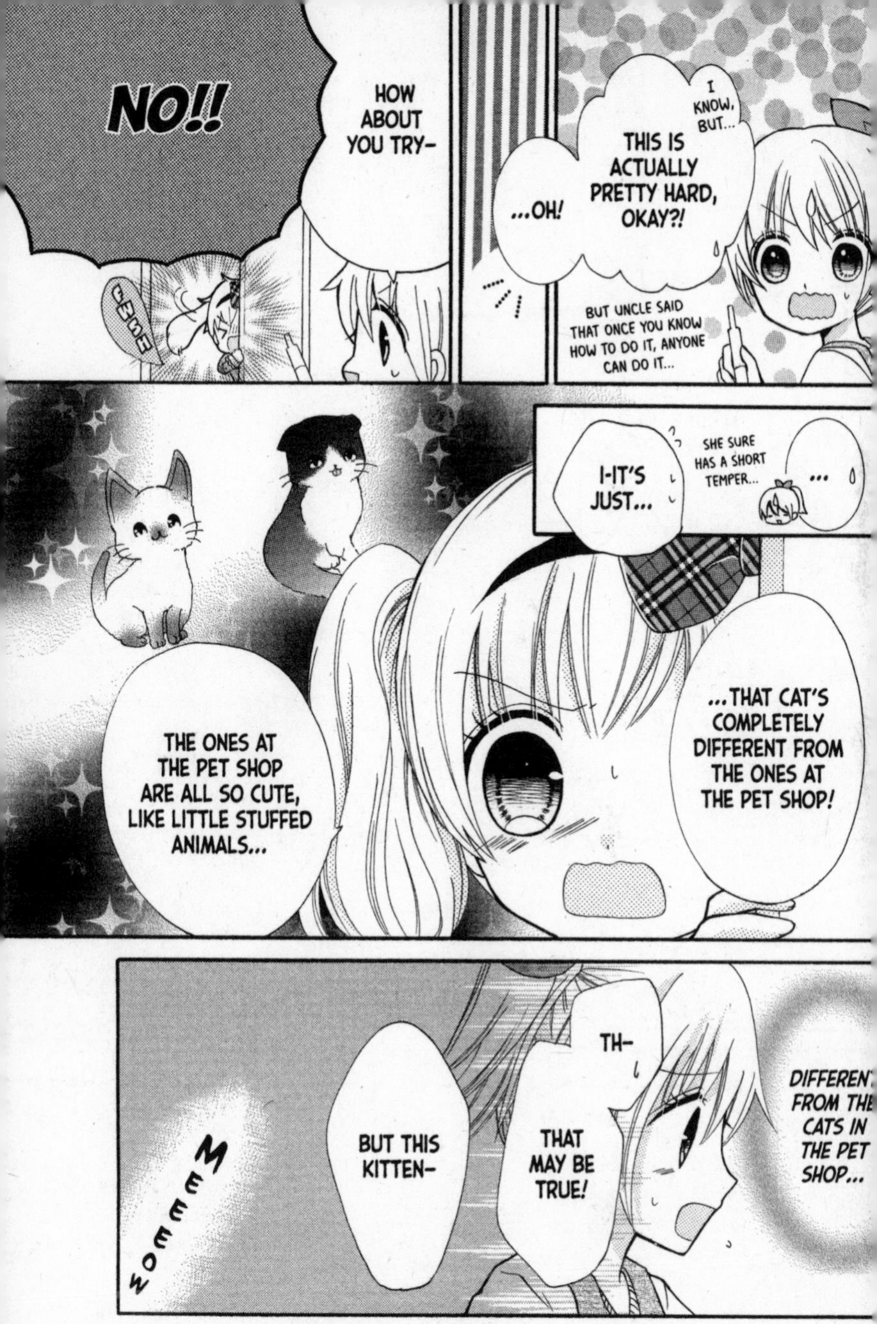
I KNOW, BUT...
THIS IS ACTUALLY PRETTY HARD, OKAY?!
...OH!
BUT UNCLE SAID THAT ONCE YOU KNOW HOW TO DO IT, ANYONE CAN DO IT...
HOW ABOUT YOU TRY-
NO!!
FWSH
...
SHE SURE HAS A SHORT TEMPER...
I-IT'S JUST...
...THAT CAT'S COMPLETELY DIFFERENT FROM THE ONES AT THE PET SHOP!
THE ONES AT THE PET SHOP ARE ALL SO CUTE, LIKE LITTLE STUFFED ANIMALS...
DIFFERENT FROM THE CATS IN THE PET SHOP...
TH-
THAT MAY BE TRUE!
BUT THIS KITTEN-
MEEEEOW

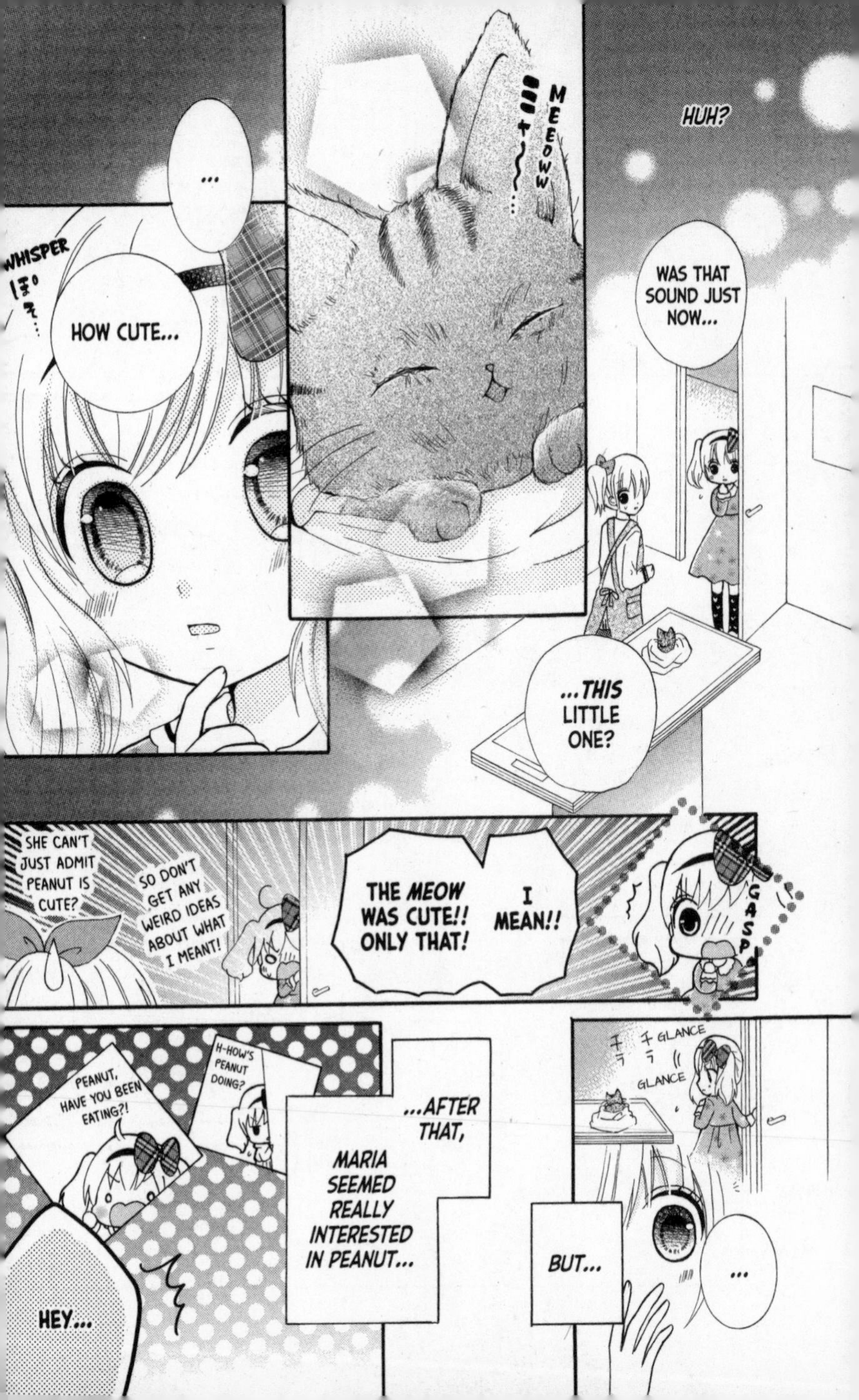
HUH?
WAS THAT SOUND JUST NOW...
...THIS LITTLE ONE?
MEEEOWW
...
WHISPER
HOW CUTE...
GASP
I MEAN!!
THE MEOW WAS CUTE!! ONLY THAT!
SO DON'T GET ANY WEIRD IDEAS ABOUT WHAT I MEANT!
SHE CAN'T JUST ADMIT PEANUT IS CUTE?
GLANCE
GLANCE
...
BUT...
...AFTER THAT,
MARIA SEEMED REALLY INTERESTED IN PEANUT...
H-HOW'S PEANUT DOING?
PEANUT, HAVE YOU BEEN EATING?!
HEY...

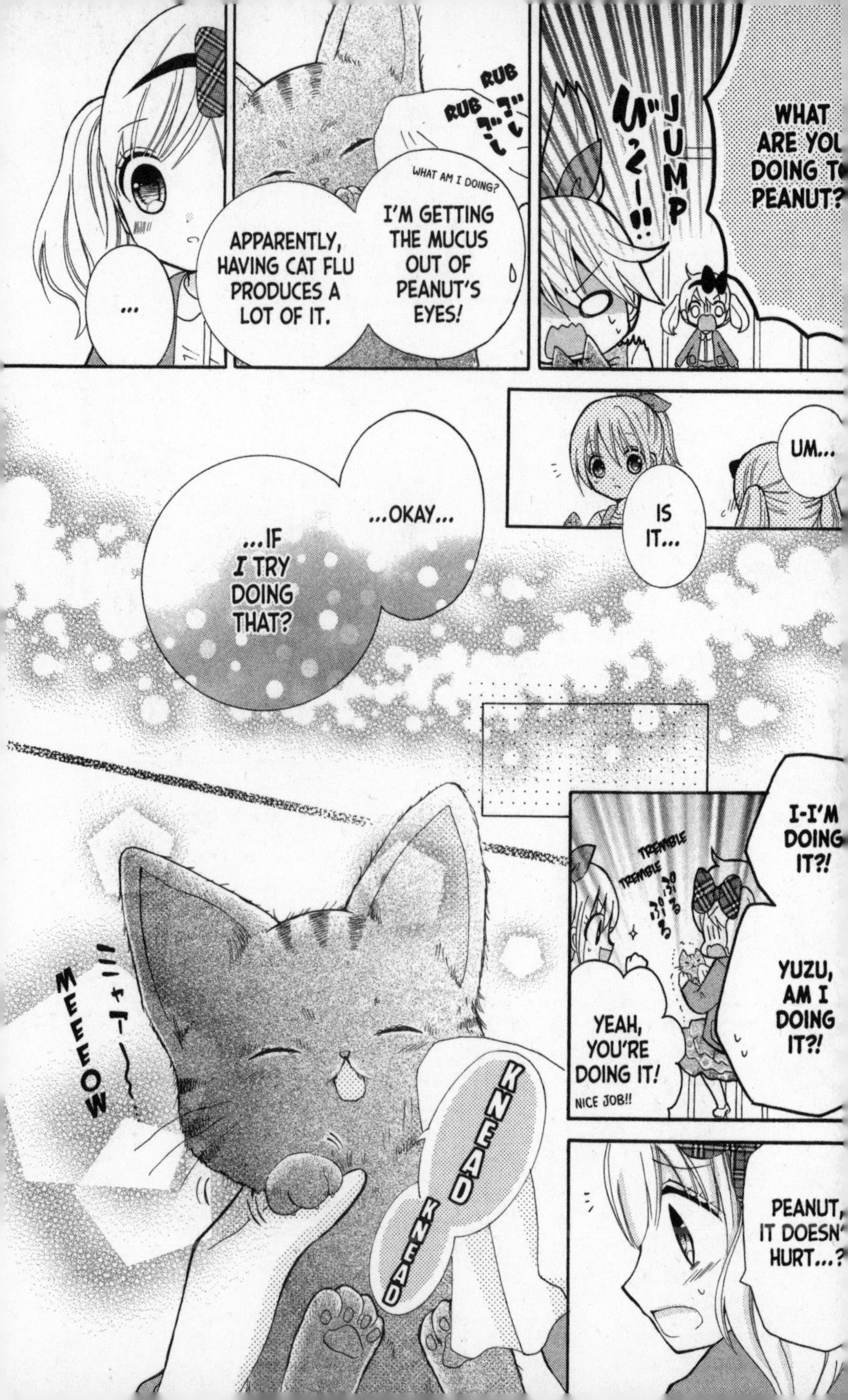
WHAT ARE YOU DOING TO PEANUT?
JUMP
RUB RUB
WHAT AM I DOING?
I'M GETTING THE MUCUS OUT OF PEANUT'S EYES!
APPARENTLY, HAVING CAT FLU PRODUCES A LOT OF IT.
...
UM...
IS IT...
...OKAY...
...IF I TRY DOING THAT?
I-I'M DOING IT?!
YUZU, AM I DOING IT?!
TREMBLE TREMBLE
YEAH, YOU'RE DOING IT!
NICE JOB!!
PEANUT, IT DOESN'T HURT...?
KNEAD KNEAD
MEEEOW

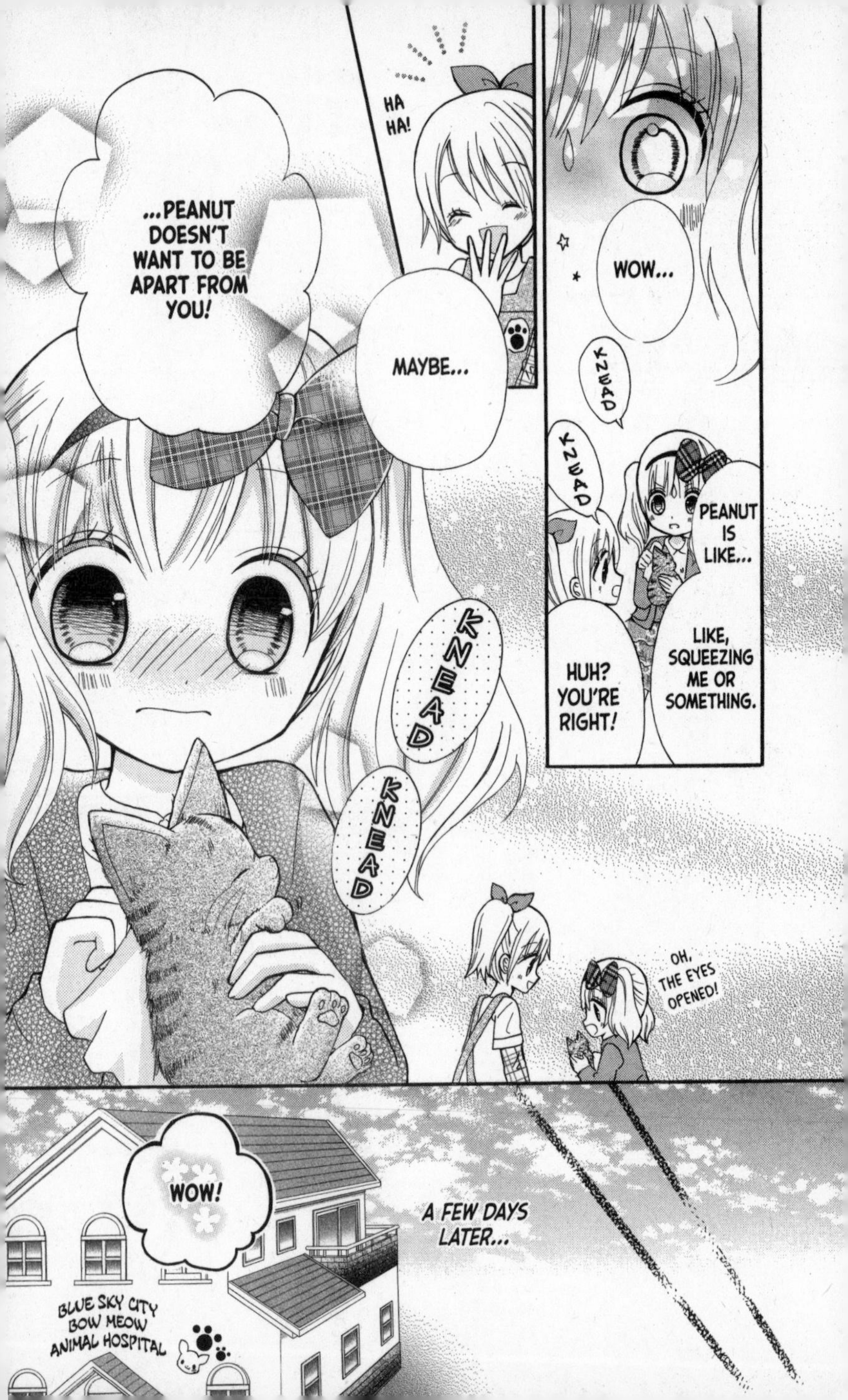
WOW...
KNEAD
KNEAD
PEANUT IS LIKE...
LIKE, SQUEEZING ME OR SOMETHING.
HUH? YOU'RE RIGHT!
HA HA!
MAYBE...
...PEANUT DOESN'T WANT TO BE APART FROM YOU!
KNEAD
KNEAD
OH, THE EYES OPENED!
A FEW DAYS LATER...
WOW!
BLUE SKY CITY BOW MEOW ANIMAL HOSPITAL

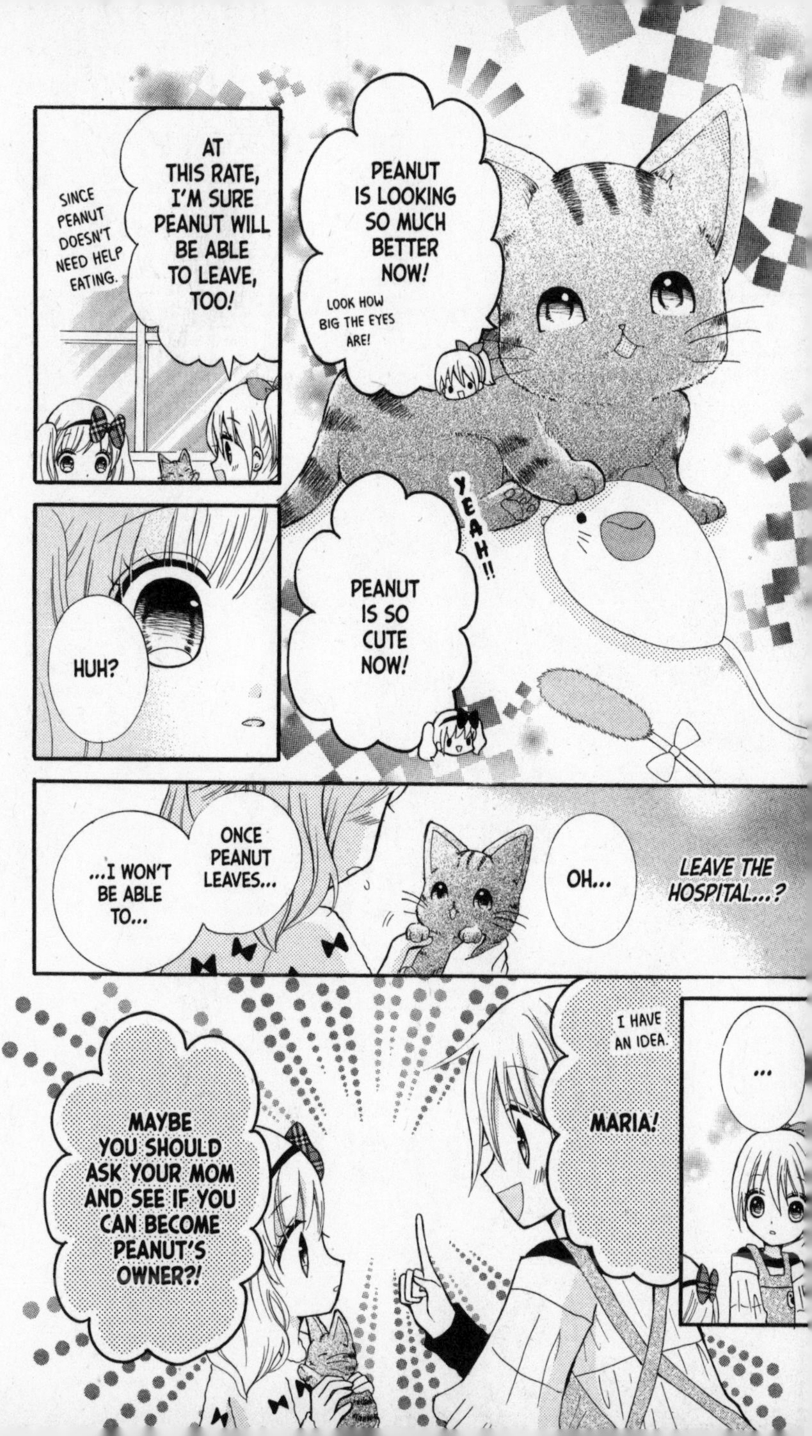
PEANUT IS LOOKING SO MUCH BETTER NOW!
LOOK HOW BIG THE EYES ARE!
YEAH!!
PEANUT IS SO CUTE NOW!
AT THIS RATE, I'M SURE PEANUT WILL BE ABLE TO LEAVE, TOO!
SINCE PEANUT DOESN'T NEED HELP EATING.
HUH?
LEAVE THE HOSPITAL...?
OH...
ONCE PEANUT LEAVES...
...I WON'T BE ABLE TO...
...
I HAVE AN IDEA.
MARIA!
MAYBE YOU SHOULD ASK YOUR MOM AND SEE IF YOU CAN BECOME PEANUT'S OWNER?!

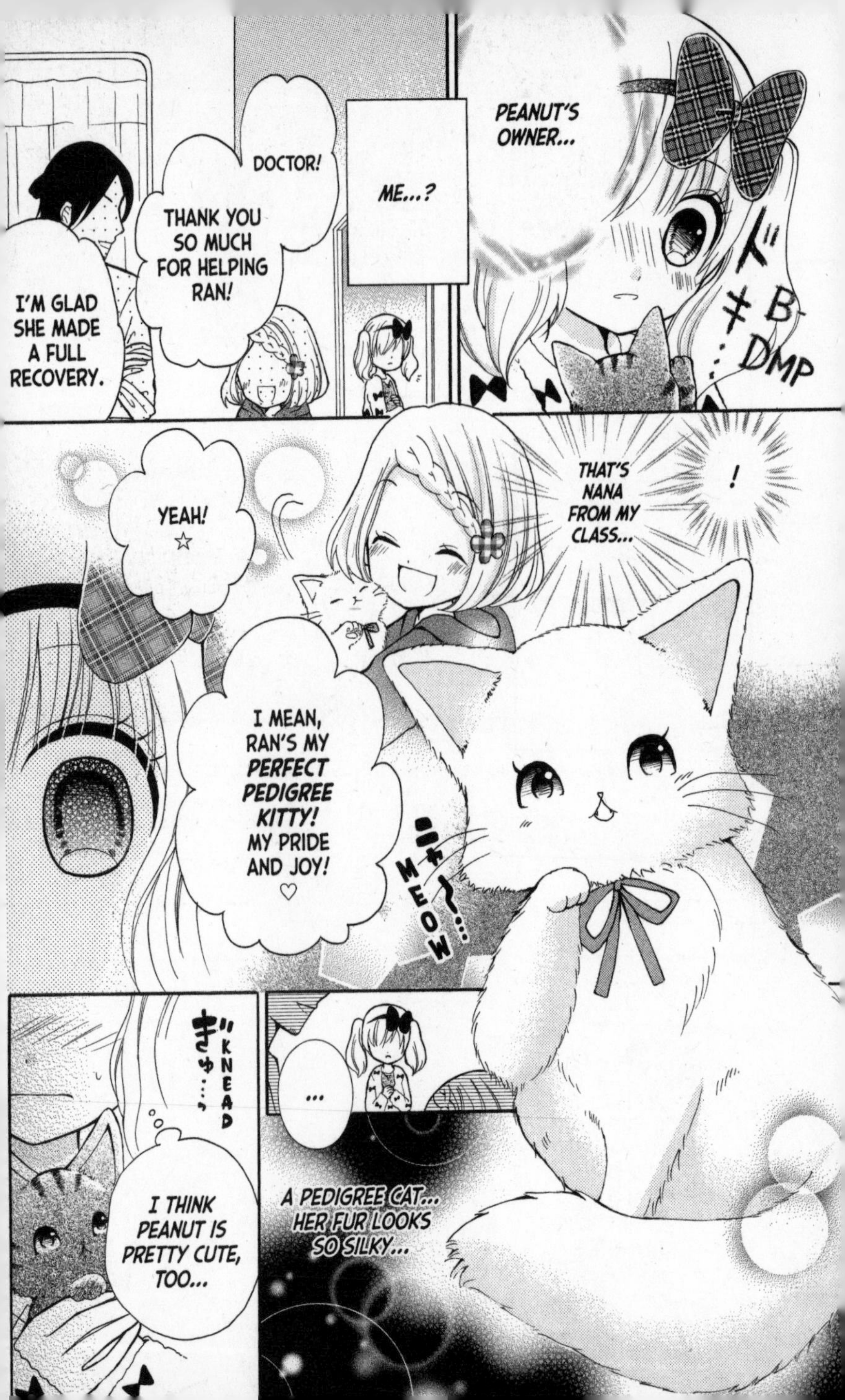
PEANUT'S OWNER...
ドキ
B-DMP
ME...?
DOCTOR!
THANK YOU SO MUCH FOR HELPING RAN!
I'M GLAD SHE MADE A FULL RECOVERY.
!
THAT'S NANA FROM MY CLASS...
YEAH! ☆
I MEAN, RAN'S MY *PERFECT PEDIGREE KITTY!* MY PRIDE AND JOY! ♡
ニャ〜…
MEOW
A PEDIGREE CAT... HER FUR LOOKS SO SILKY...
...
きゅ…
KNEAD
I THINK PEANUT IS PRETTY CUTE, TOO...

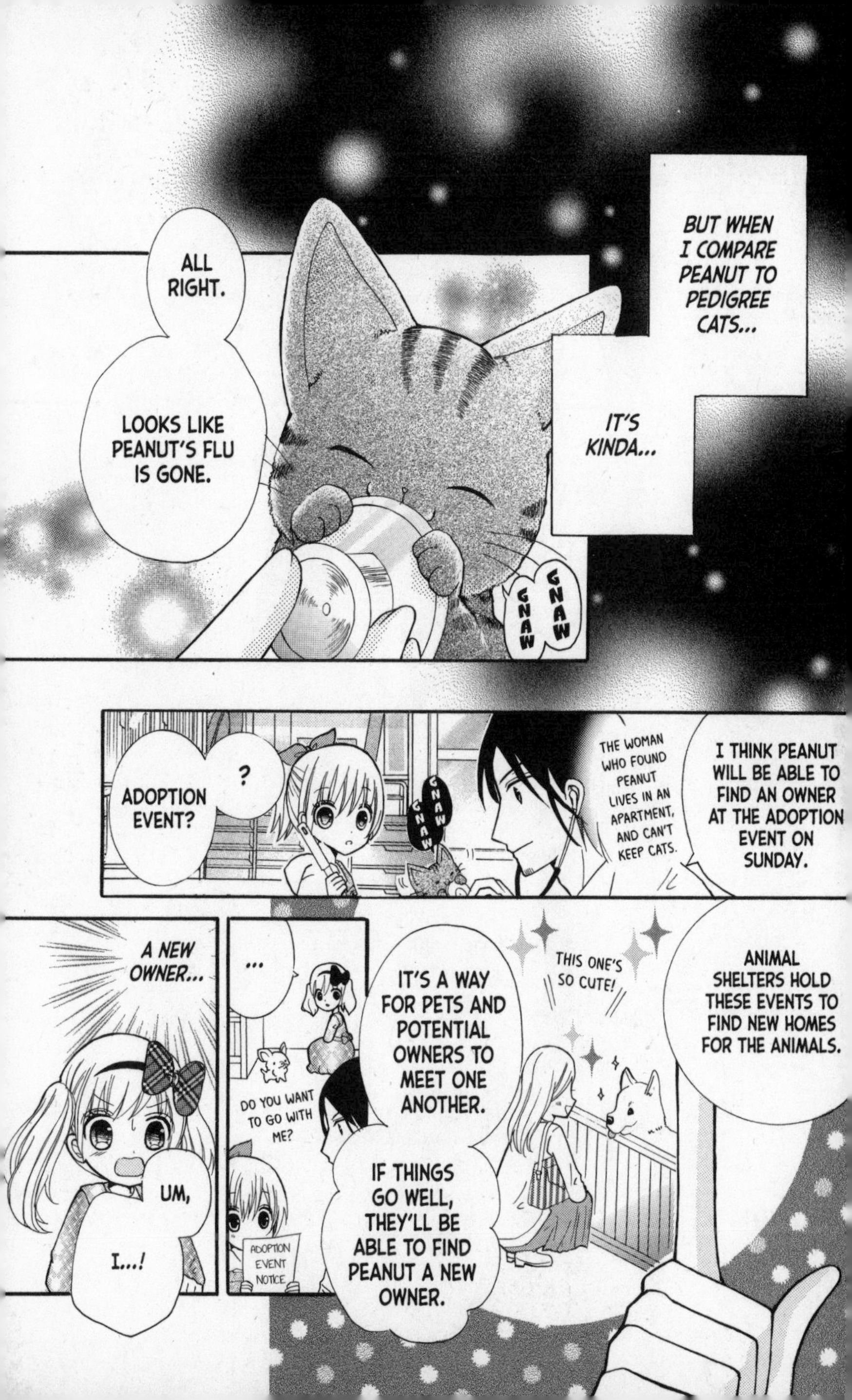
BUT WHEN I COMPARE PEANUT TO PEDIGREE CATS...
IT'S KINDA...
GNAW GNAW
ALL RIGHT.
LOOKS LIKE PEANUT'S FLU IS GONE.
I THINK PEANUT WILL BE ABLE TO FIND AN OWNER AT THE ADOPTION EVENT ON SUNDAY.
THE WOMAN WHO FOUND PEANUT LIVES IN AN APARTMENT, AND CAN'T KEEP CATS.
GNAW GNAW
?
ADOPTION EVENT?
ANIMAL SHELTERS HOLD THESE EVENTS TO FIND NEW HOMES FOR THE ANIMALS.
THIS ONE'S SO CUTE!
IT'S A WAY FOR PETS AND POTENTIAL OWNERS TO MEET ONE ANOTHER.
IF THINGS GO WELL, THEY'LL BE ABLE TO FIND PEANUT A NEW OWNER.
...
DO YOU WANT TO GO WITH ME?
ADOPTION EVENT NOTICE
A NEW OWNER...
UM,
I...!

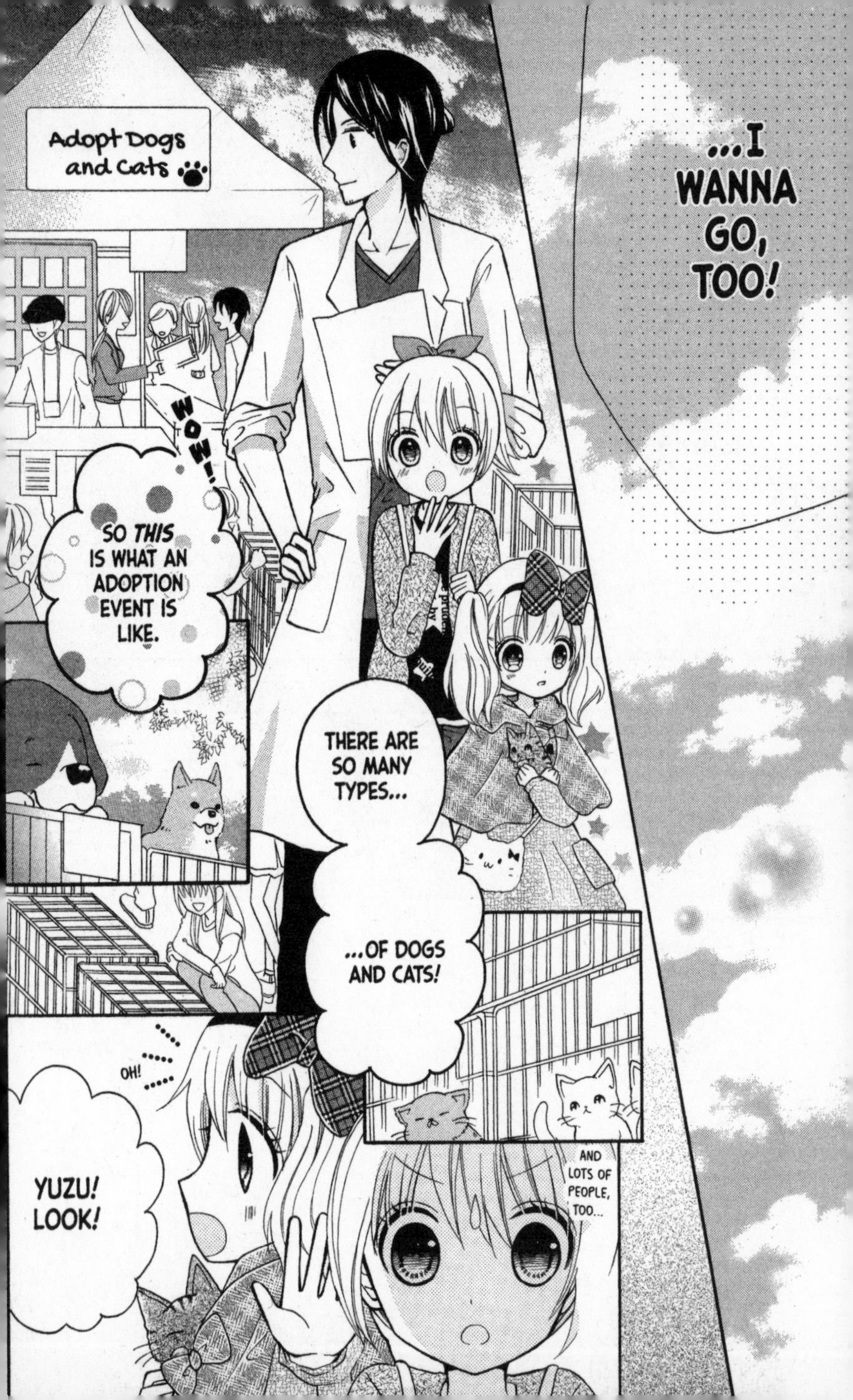
...I WANNA GO, TOO!
Adopt Dogs and Cats
WOW!
SO THIS IS WHAT AN ADOPTION EVENT IS LIKE.
THERE ARE SO MANY TYPES...
...OF DOGS AND CATS!
AND LOTS OF PEOPLE, TOO...
OH!
YUZU! LOOK!

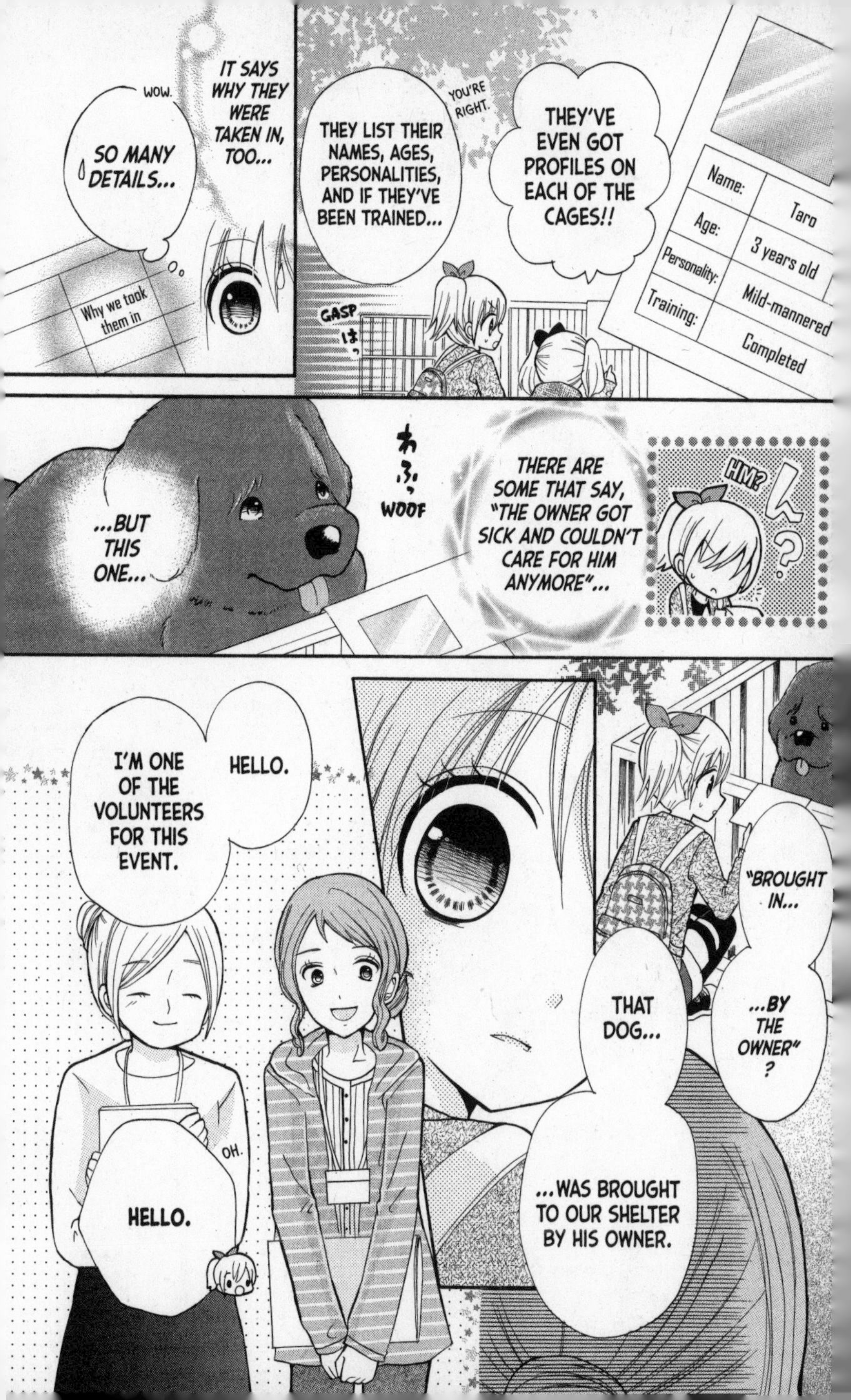
Name: Taro
Age: 3 years old
Personality: Mild-mannered
Training: Completed
THEY'VE EVEN GOT PROFILES ON EACH OF THE CAGES!!
YOU'RE RIGHT.
THEY LIST THEIR NAMES, AGES, PERSONALITIES, AND IF THEY'VE BEEN TRAINED...
GASP
はっ
IT SAYS WHY THEY WERE TAKEN IN, TOO...
WOW.
SO MANY DETAILS...
Why we took them in
HM?
ん?
THERE ARE SOME THAT SAY, "THE OWNER GOT SICK AND COULDN'T CARE FOR HIM ANYMORE"...
わふっ
WOOF
...BUT THIS ONE...
"BROUGHT IN...
...BY THE OWNER"?
THAT DOG...
...WAS BROUGHT TO OUR SHELTER BY HIS OWNER.
HELLO.
I'M ONE OF THE VOLUNTEERS FOR THIS EVENT.
OH.
HELLO.

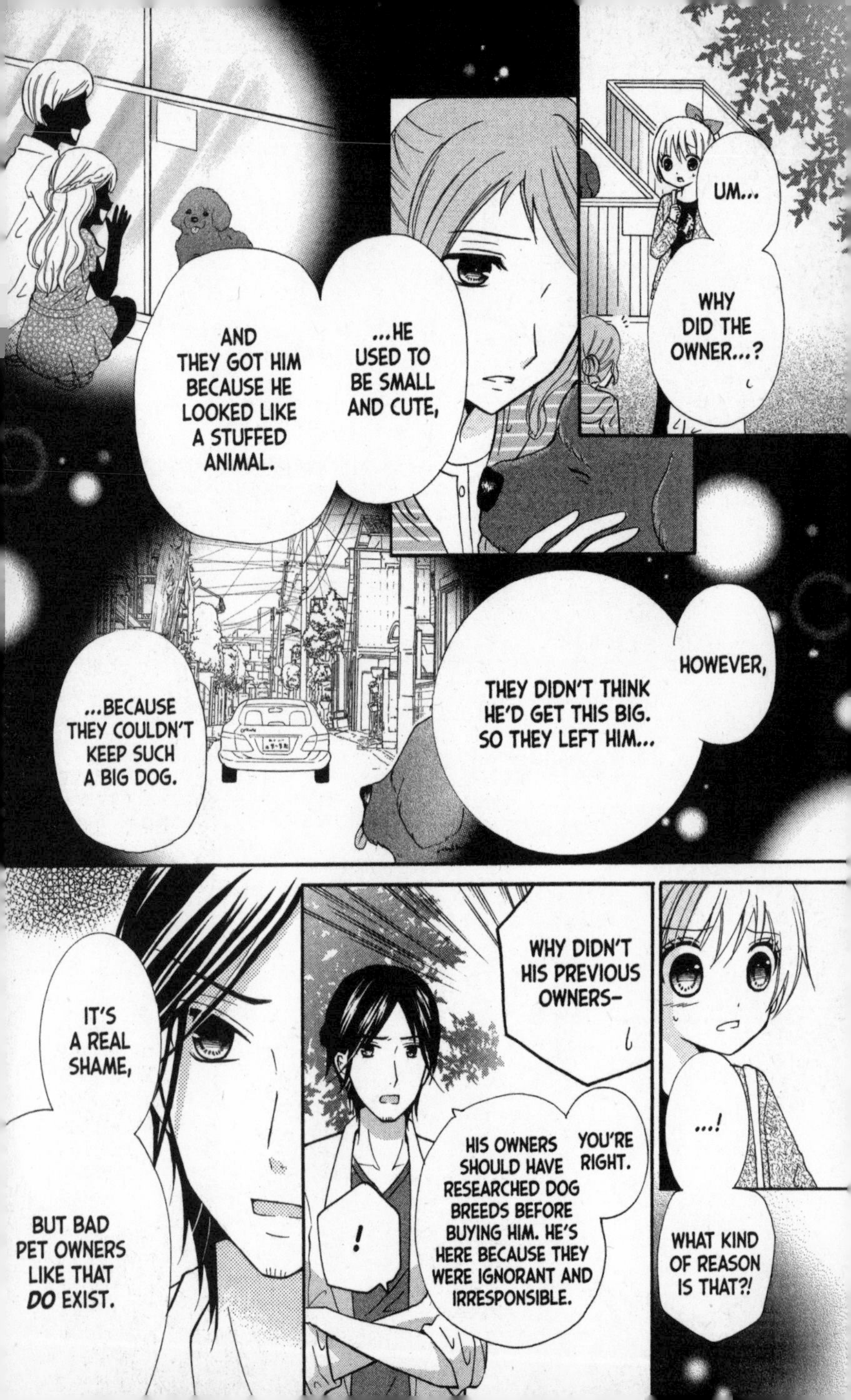
UM...
WHY DID THE OWNER...?
...HE USED TO BE SMALL AND CUTE,
AND THEY GOT HIM BECAUSE HE LOOKED LIKE A STUFFED ANIMAL.
HOWEVER,
THEY DIDN'T THINK HE'D GET THIS BIG. SO THEY LEFT HIM...
...BECAUSE THEY COULDN'T KEEP SUCH A BIG DOG.
...!
WHAT KIND OF REASON IS THAT?!
WHY DIDN'T HIS PREVIOUS OWNERS–
YOU'RE RIGHT.
HIS OWNERS SHOULD HAVE RESEARCHED DOG BREEDS BEFORE BUYING HIM. HE'S HERE BECAUSE THEY WERE IGNORANT AND IRRESPONSIBLE.
!
IT'S A REAL SHAME,
BUT BAD PET OWNERS LIKE THAT *DO* EXIST.

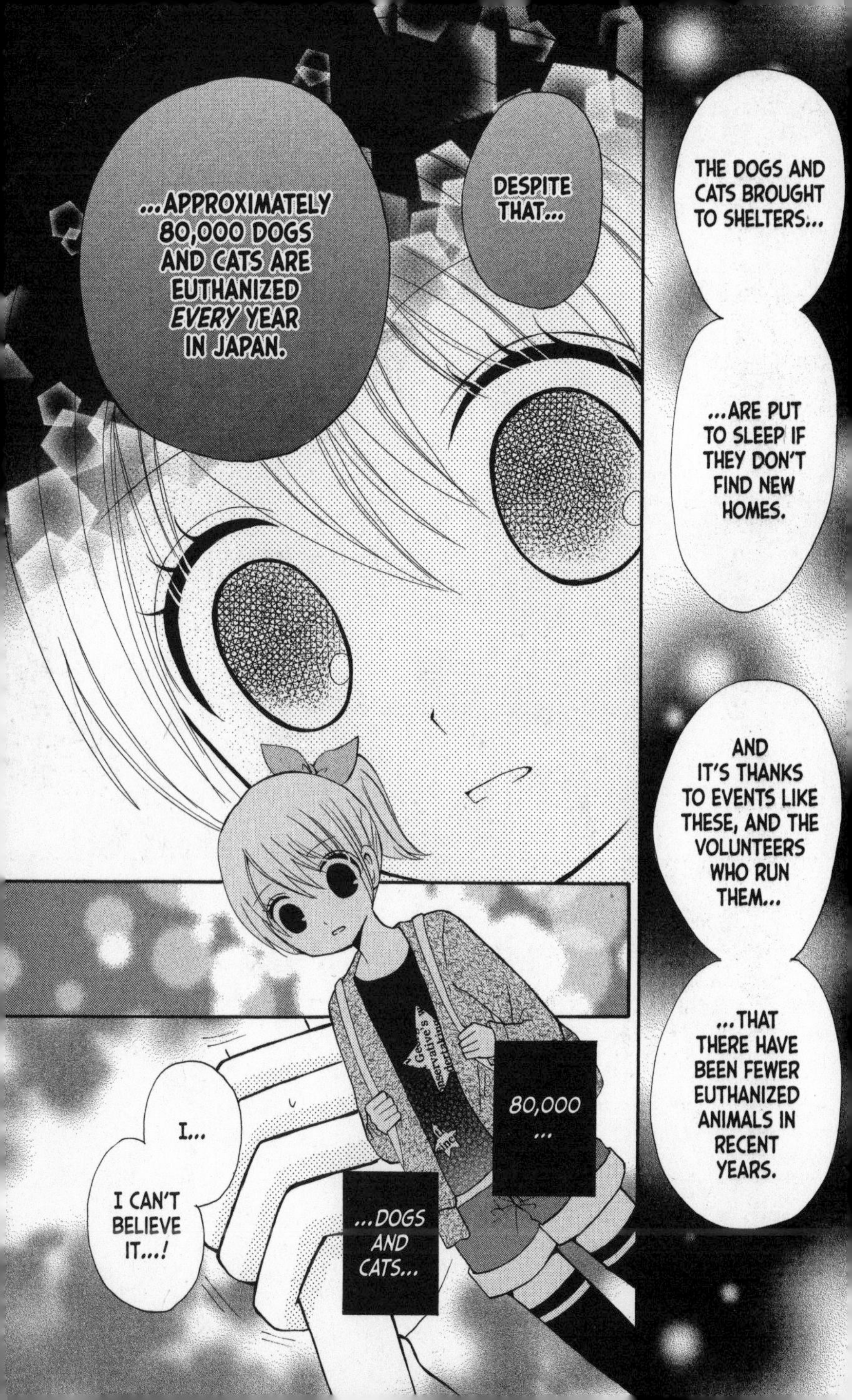
THE DOGS AND CATS BROUGHT TO SHELTERS...
...ARE PUT TO SLEEP IF THEY DON'T FIND NEW HOMES.
AND IT'S THANKS TO EVENTS LIKE THESE, AND THE VOLUNTEERS WHO RUN THEM...
...THAT THERE HAVE BEEN FEWER EUTHANIZED ANIMALS IN RECENT YEARS.
DESPITE THAT...
...APPROXIMATELY 80,000 DOGS AND CATS ARE EUTHANIZED *EVERY* YEAR IN JAPAN.
80,000 ...
...DOGS AND CATS...
I...
I CAN'T BELIEVE IT...!

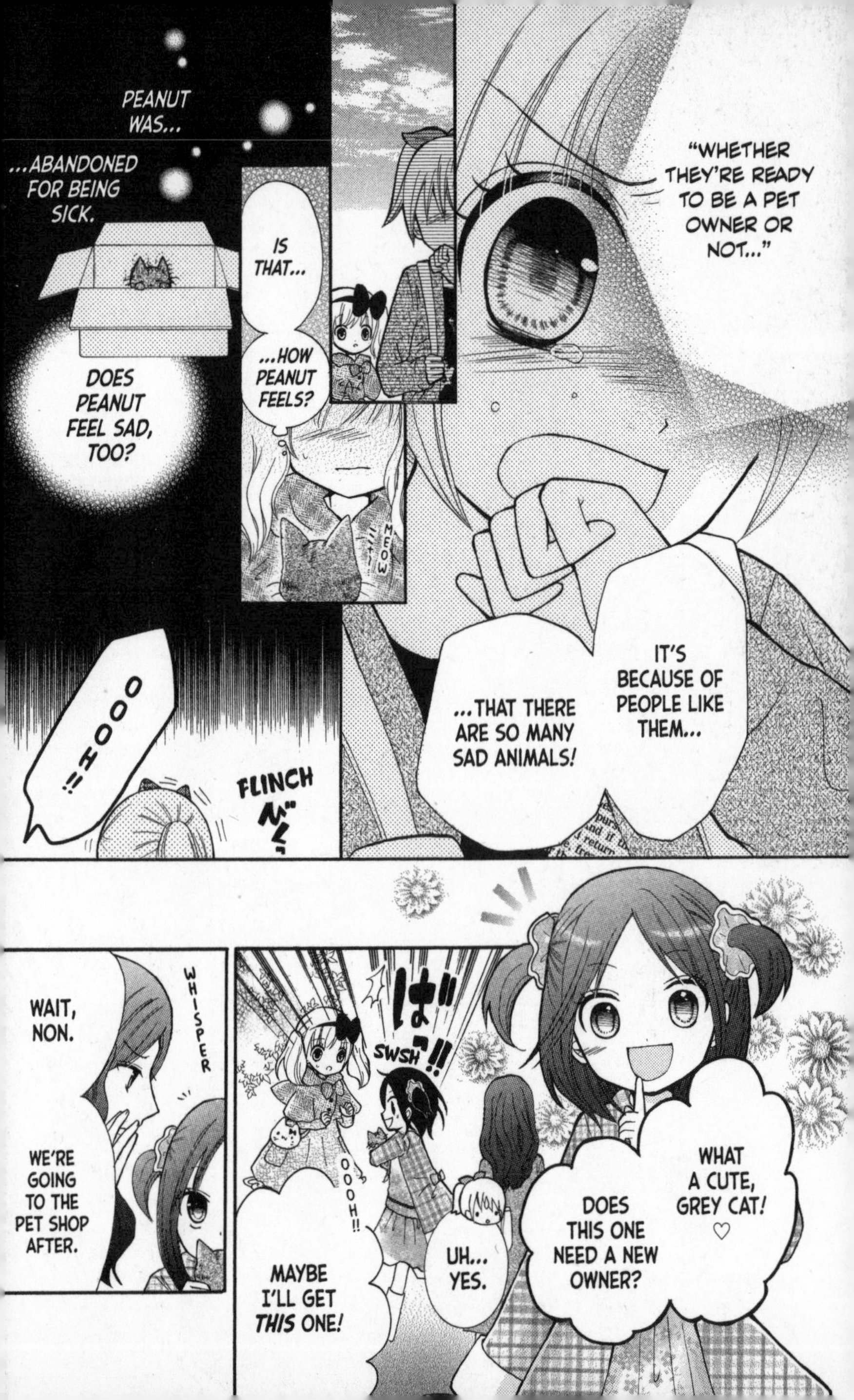
"WHETHER THEY'RE READY TO BE A PET OWNER OR NOT..."
IT'S BECAUSE OF PEOPLE LIKE THEM...
...THAT THERE ARE SO MANY SAD ANIMALS!
IS THAT...
...HOW PEANUT FEELS?
MEOW
PEANUT WAS...
...ABANDONED FOR BEING SICK.
DOES PEANUT FEEL SAD, TOO?
OOOOH!!
FLINCH
WHAT A CUTE, GREY CAT! ♡
DOES THIS ONE NEED A NEW OWNER?
UH... YES.
SWSH!!
OOOOH!!
MAYBE I'LL GET *THIS* ONE!
WAIT, NON.
WHISPER
WE'RE GOING TO THE PET SHOP AFTER.

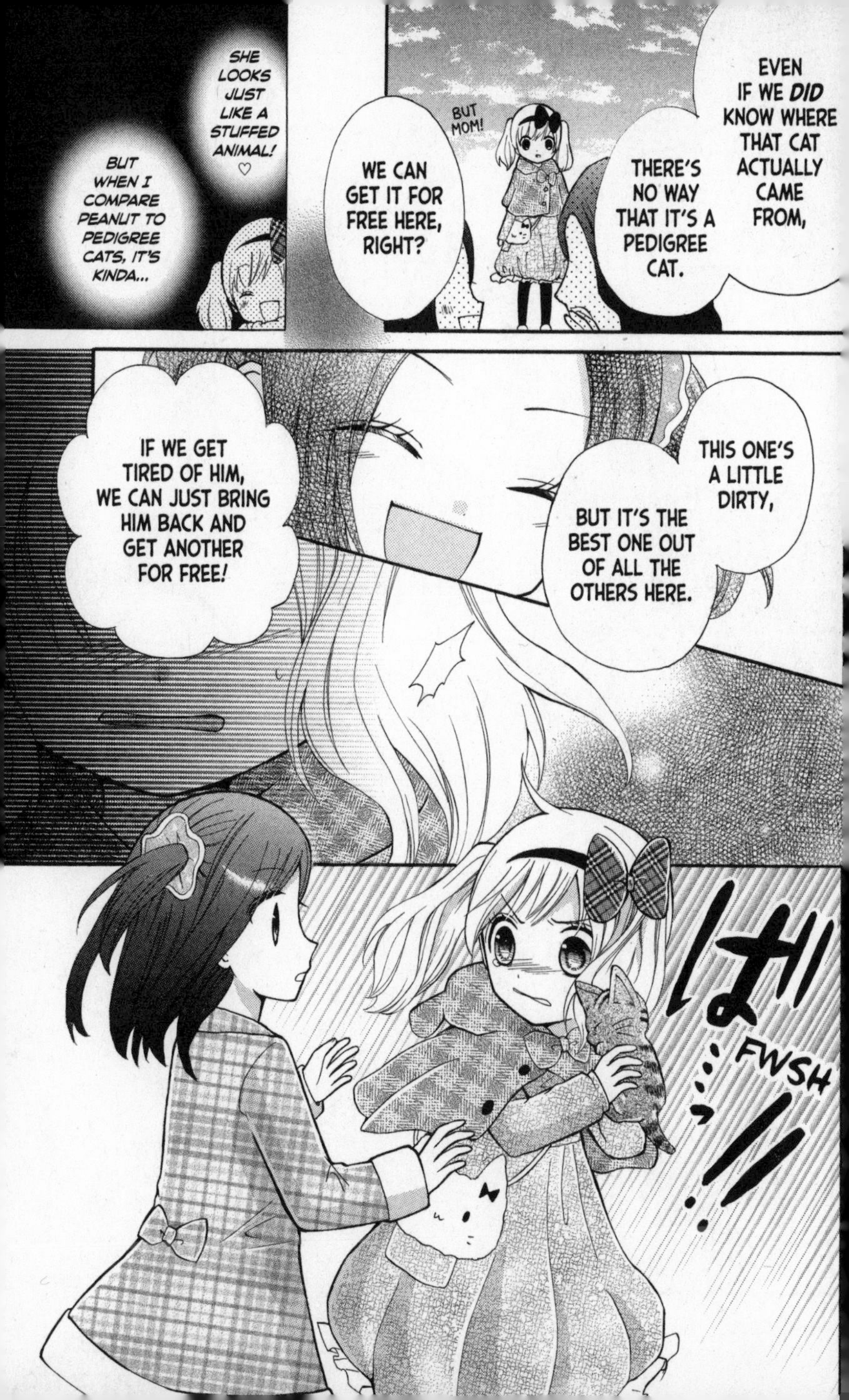
EVEN IF WE *DID* KNOW WHERE THAT CAT ACTUALLY CAME FROM,
THERE'S NO WAY THAT IT'S A PEDIGREE CAT.
BUT MOM!
WE CAN GET IT FOR FREE HERE, RIGHT?
SHE LOOKS JUST LIKE A STUFFED ANIMAL! ♡
BUT WHEN I COMPARE PEANUT TO PEDIGREE CATS, IT'S KINDA...
THIS ONE'S A LITTLE DIRTY,
BUT IT'S THE BEST ONE OUT OF ALL THE OTHERS HERE.
IF WE GET TIRED OF HIM, WE CAN JUST BRING HIM BACK AND GET ANOTHER FOR FREE!
FWSH

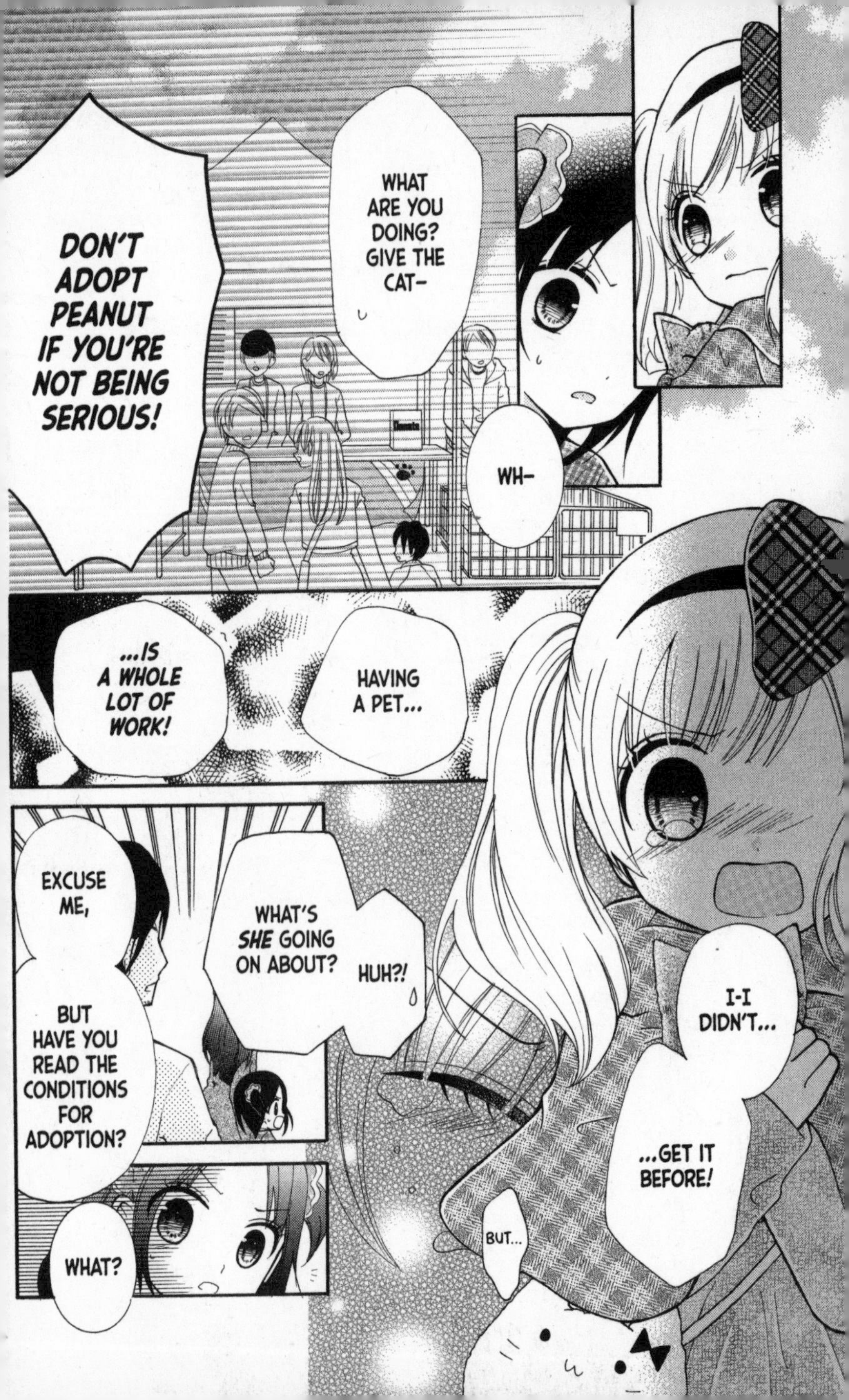
WH-
WHAT ARE YOU DOING? GIVE THE CAT–
DON'T ADOPT PEANUT IF YOU'RE NOT BEING SERIOUS!
I-I DIDN'T...
...GET IT BEFORE!
BUT...
HAVING A PET...
...IS A WHOLE LOT OF WORK!
HUH?!
WHAT'S *SHE* GOING ON ABOUT?
EXCUSE ME,
BUT HAVE YOU READ THE CONDITIONS FOR ADOPTION?
WHAT?

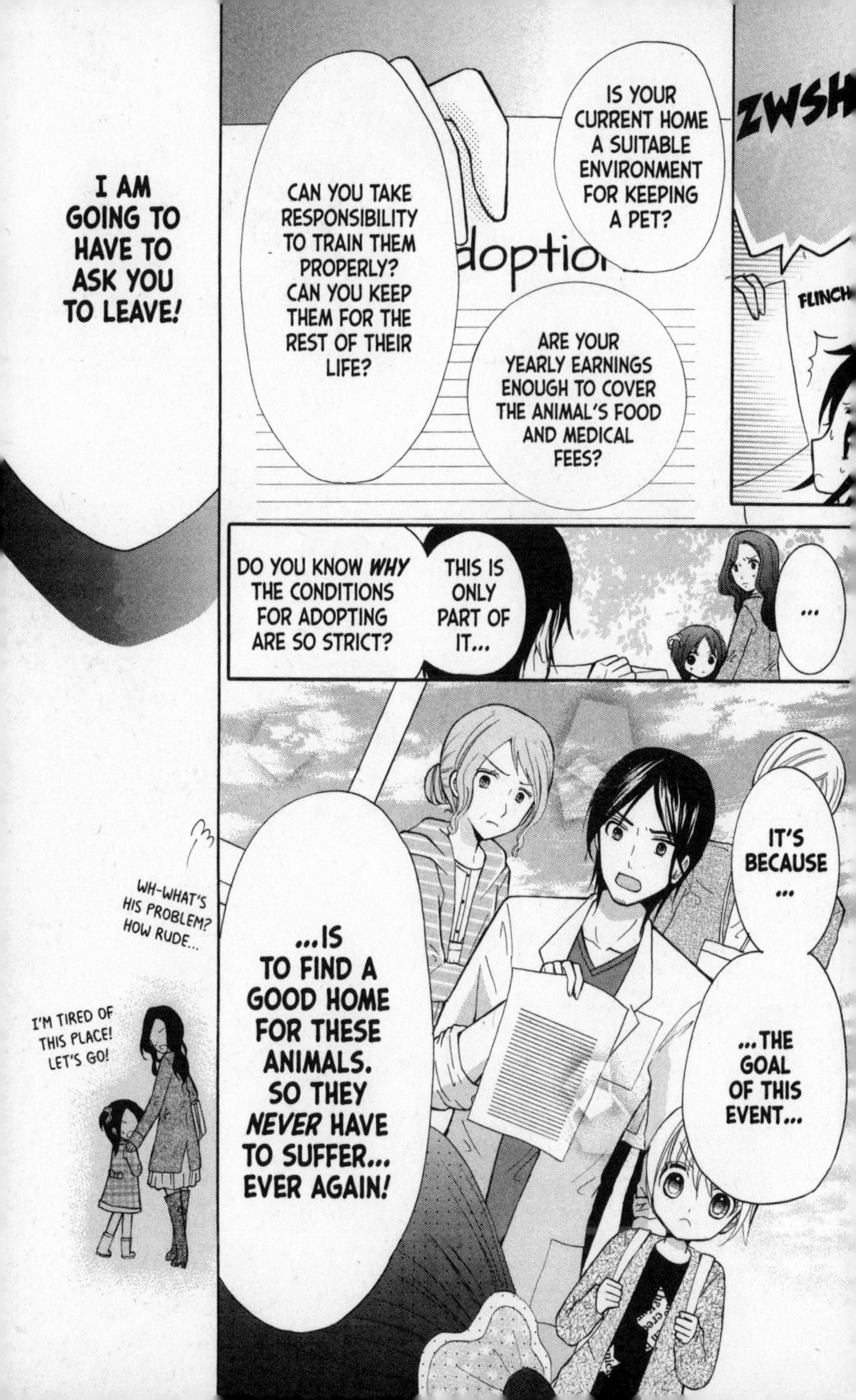
ZWSH
FLINCH
IS YOUR CURRENT HOME A SUITABLE ENVIRONMENT FOR KEEPING A PET?
ARE YOUR YEARLY EARNINGS ENOUGH TO COVER THE ANIMAL'S FOOD AND MEDICAL FEES?
CAN YOU TAKE RESPONSIBILITY TO TRAIN THEM PROPERLY? CAN YOU KEEP THEM FOR THE REST OF THEIR LIFE?
...
THIS IS ONLY PART OF IT...
DO YOU KNOW *WHY* THE CONDITIONS FOR ADOPTING ARE SO STRICT?
IT'S BECAUSE...
...THE GOAL OF THIS EVENT...
...IS TO FIND A GOOD HOME FOR THESE ANIMALS. SO THEY *NEVER* HAVE TO SUFFER... EVER AGAIN!
I AM GOING TO HAVE TO ASK YOU TO LEAVE!
WH-WHAT'S HIS PROBLEM? HOW RUDE...
I'M TIRED OF THIS PLACE! LET'S GO!

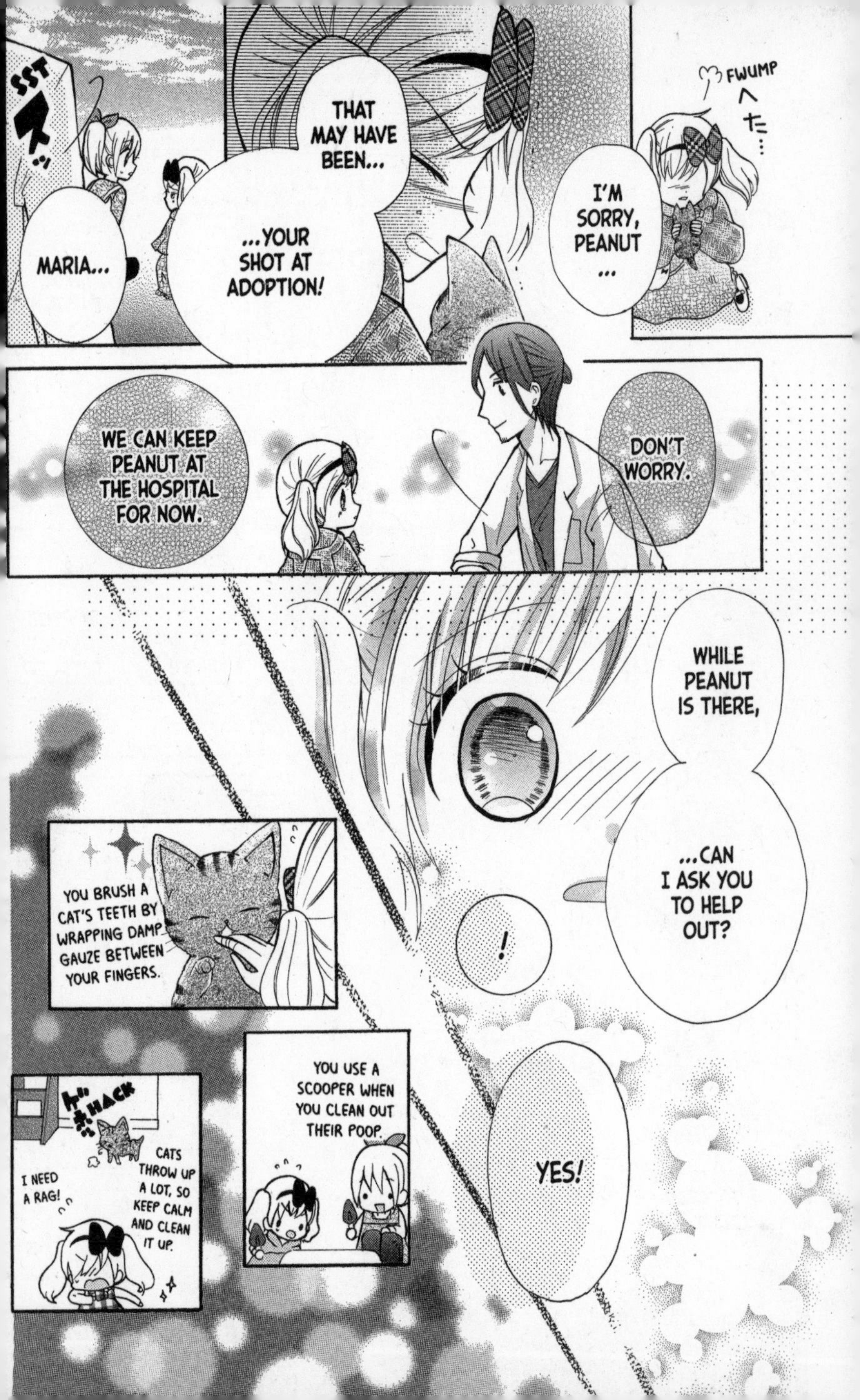
FWUMP
I'M SORRY, PEANUT ...
THAT MAY HAVE BEEN...
...YOUR SHOT AT ADOPTION!
SST
MARIA...
DON'T WORRY.
WE CAN KEEP PEANUT AT THE HOSPITAL FOR NOW.
WHILE PEANUT IS THERE,
...CAN I ASK YOU TO HELP OUT?
!
YES!
YOU BRUSH A CAT'S TEETH BY WRAPPING DAMP GAUZE BETWEEN YOUR FINGERS.
YOU USE A SCOOPER WHEN YOU CLEAN OUT THEIR POOP.
HACK
CATS THROW UP A LOT, SO KEEP CALM AND CLEAN IT UP.
I NEED A RAG!

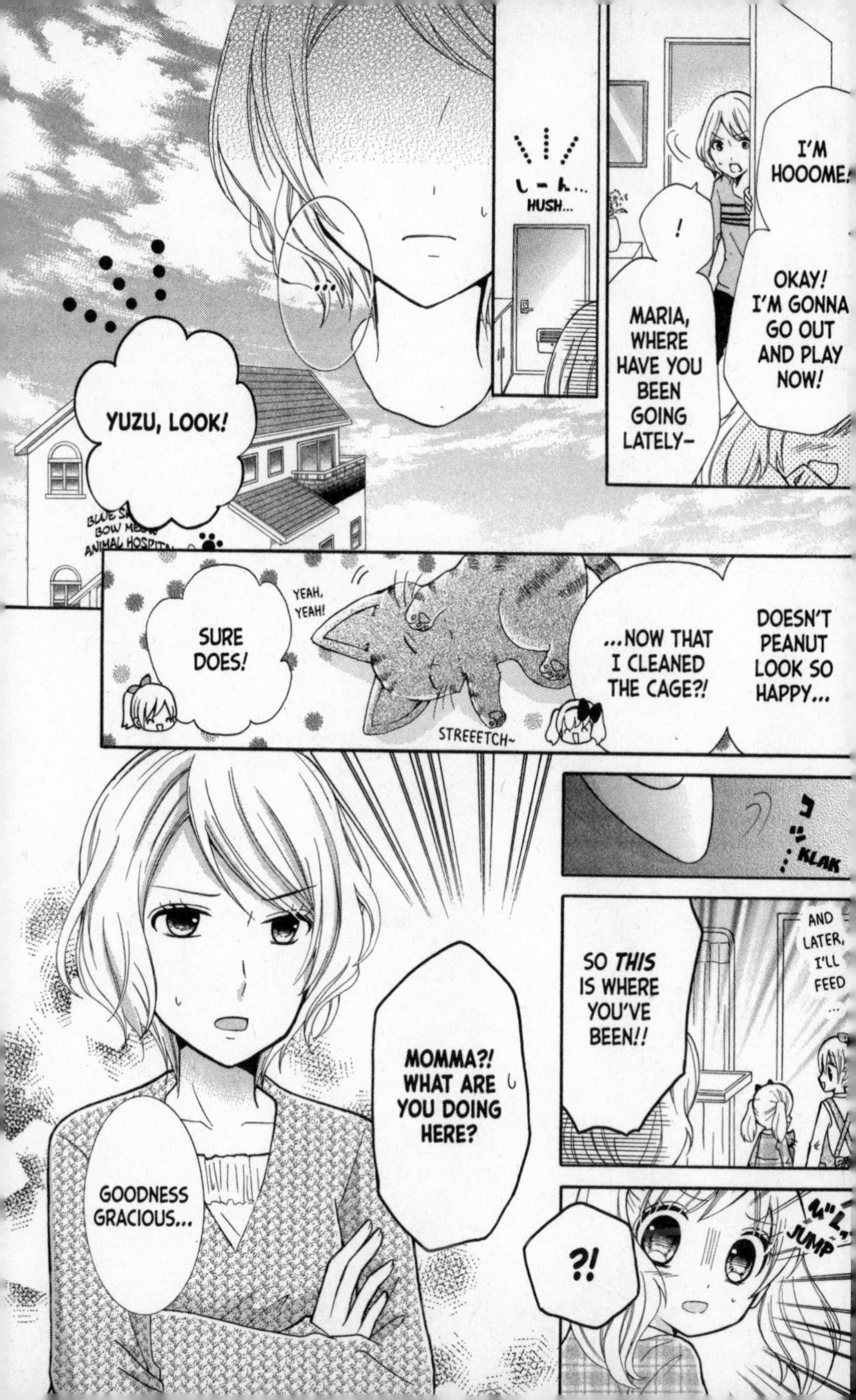
I'M HOOOME!
OKAY! I'M GONNA GO OUT AND PLAY NOW!
!
MARIA, WHERE HAVE YOU BEEN GOING LATELY–
しーん…
HUSH...
...
YUZU, LOOK!
BLUE SA
BOW MEOW
ANIMAL HOSPITA
DOESN'T PEANUT LOOK SO HAPPY...
...NOW THAT I CLEANED THE CAGE?!
STREEETCH~
YEAH, YEAH!
SURE DOES!
KLAK
AND LATER, I'LL FEED ...
SO THIS IS WHERE YOU'VE BEEN!!
JUMP
?!
MOMMA?! WHAT ARE YOU DOING HERE?
GOODNESS GRACIOUS...

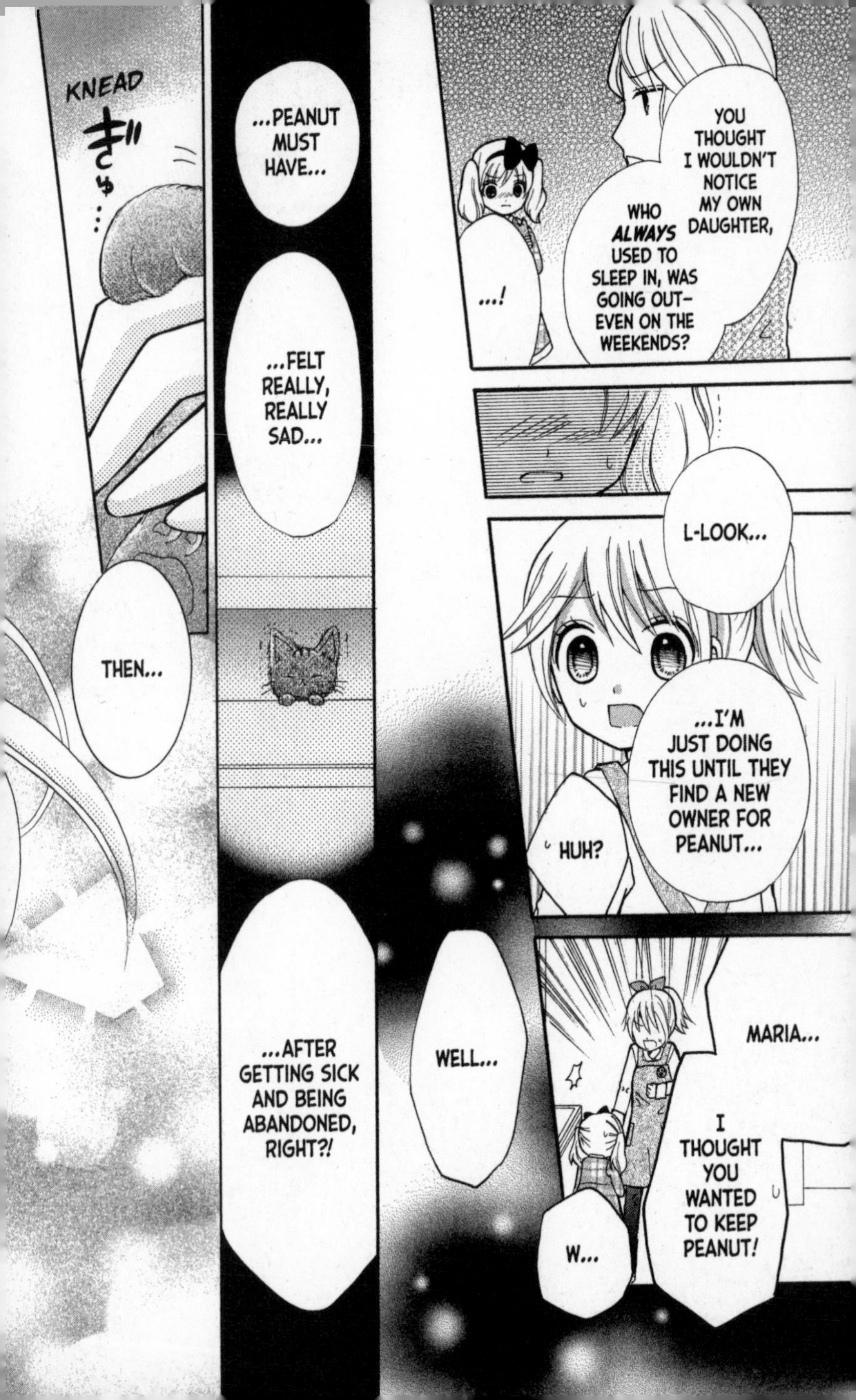
YOU THOUGHT I WOULDN'T NOTICE MY OWN DAUGHTER,
WHO *ALWAYS* USED TO SLEEP IN, WAS GOING OUT— EVEN ON THE WEEKENDS?
...!
L-LOOK...
...I'M JUST DOING THIS UNTIL THEY FIND A NEW OWNER FOR PEANUT...
HUH?
MARIA...
I THOUGHT YOU WANTED TO KEEP PEANUT!
W...
WELL...
...PEANUT MUST HAVE...
...FELT REALLY, REALLY SAD...
...AFTER GETTING SICK AND BEING ABANDONED, RIGHT?!
KNEAD
THEN...

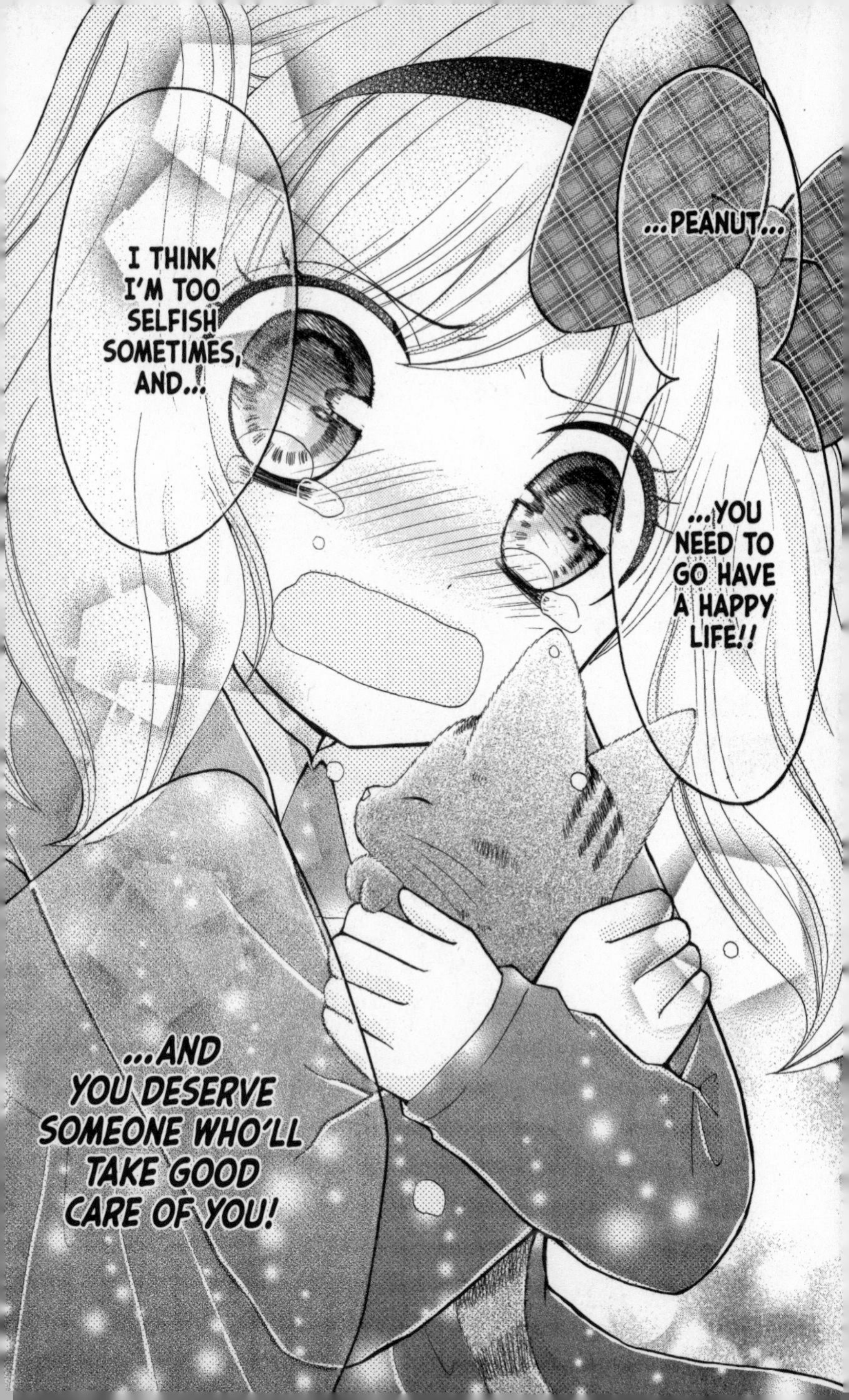
...PEANUT...
...YOU NEED TO GO HAVE A HAPPY LIFE!!
I THINK I'M TOO SELFISH SOMETIMES, AND...!
...AND YOU DESERVE SOMEONE WHO'LL TAKE GOOD CARE OF YOU!

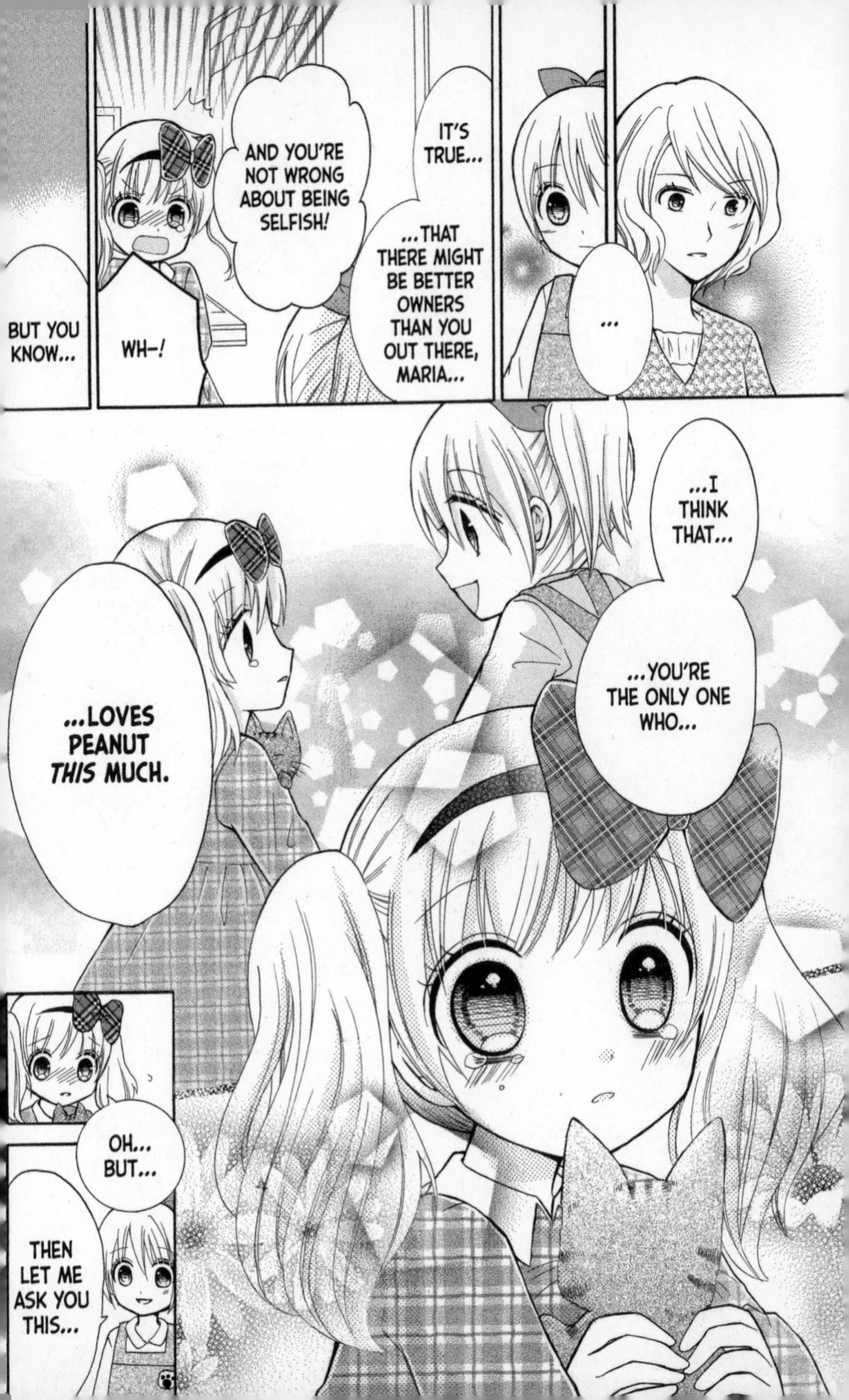
...
IT'S TRUE...
...THAT THERE MIGHT BE BETTER OWNERS THAN YOU OUT THERE, MARIA...
AND YOU'RE NOT WRONG ABOUT BEING SELFISH!
WH-!
BUT YOU KNOW...
...I THINK THAT...
...YOU'RE THE ONLY ONE WHO...
...LOVES PEANUT *THIS* MUCH.
OH... BUT...
THEN LET ME ASK YOU THIS...

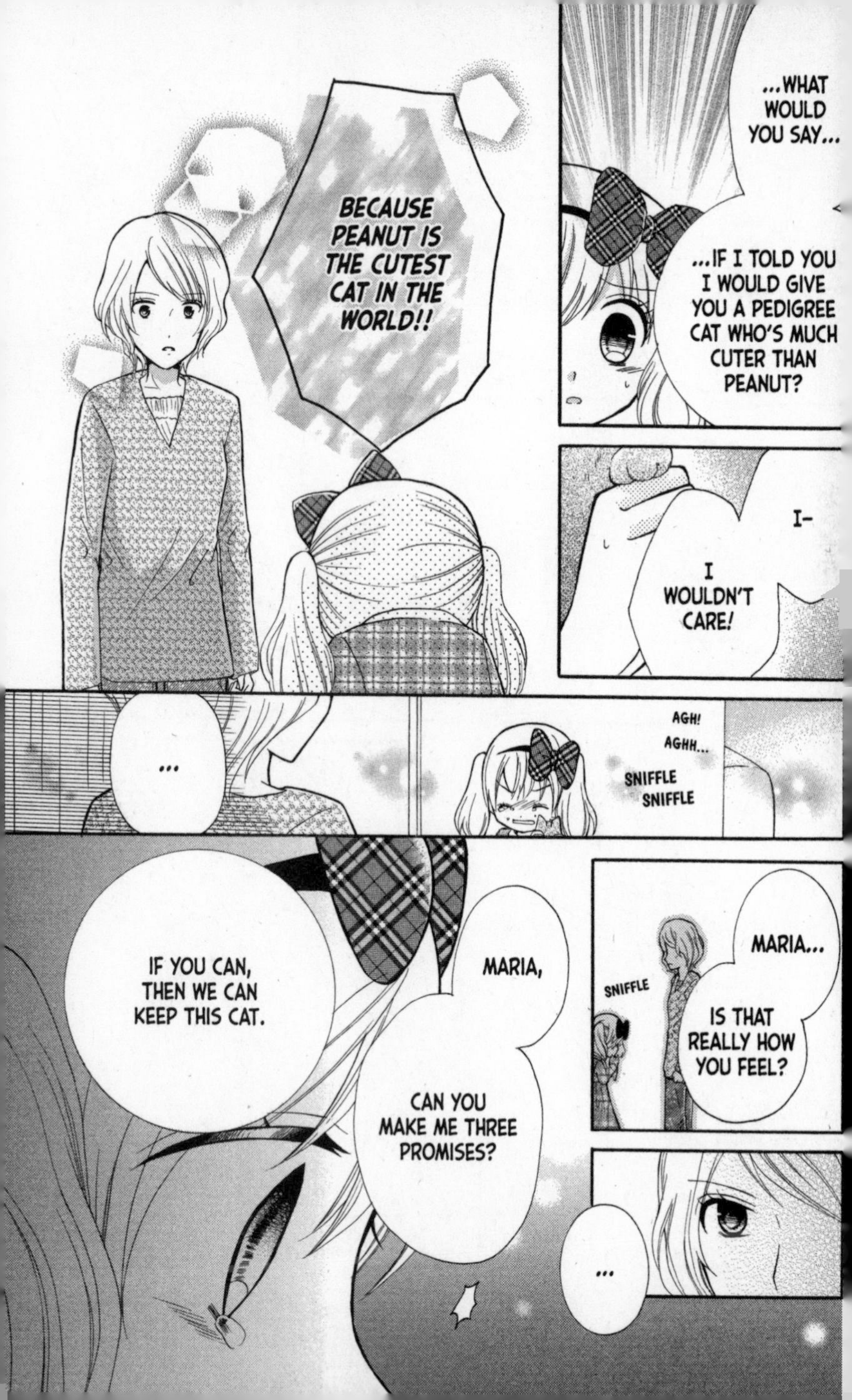
...WHAT WOULD YOU SAY...
...IF I TOLD YOU I WOULD GIVE YOU A PEDIGREE CAT WHO'S MUCH CUTER THAN PEANUT?
I-
I WOULDN'T CARE!
BECAUSE PEANUT IS THE CUTEST CAT IN THE WORLD!!
AGH!
AGHH...
SNIFFLE
SNIFFLE
...
MARIA...
IS THAT REALLY HOW YOU FEEL?
SNIFFLE
...
MARIA,
CAN YOU MAKE ME THREE PROMISES?
IF YOU CAN, THEN WE CAN KEEP THIS CAT.

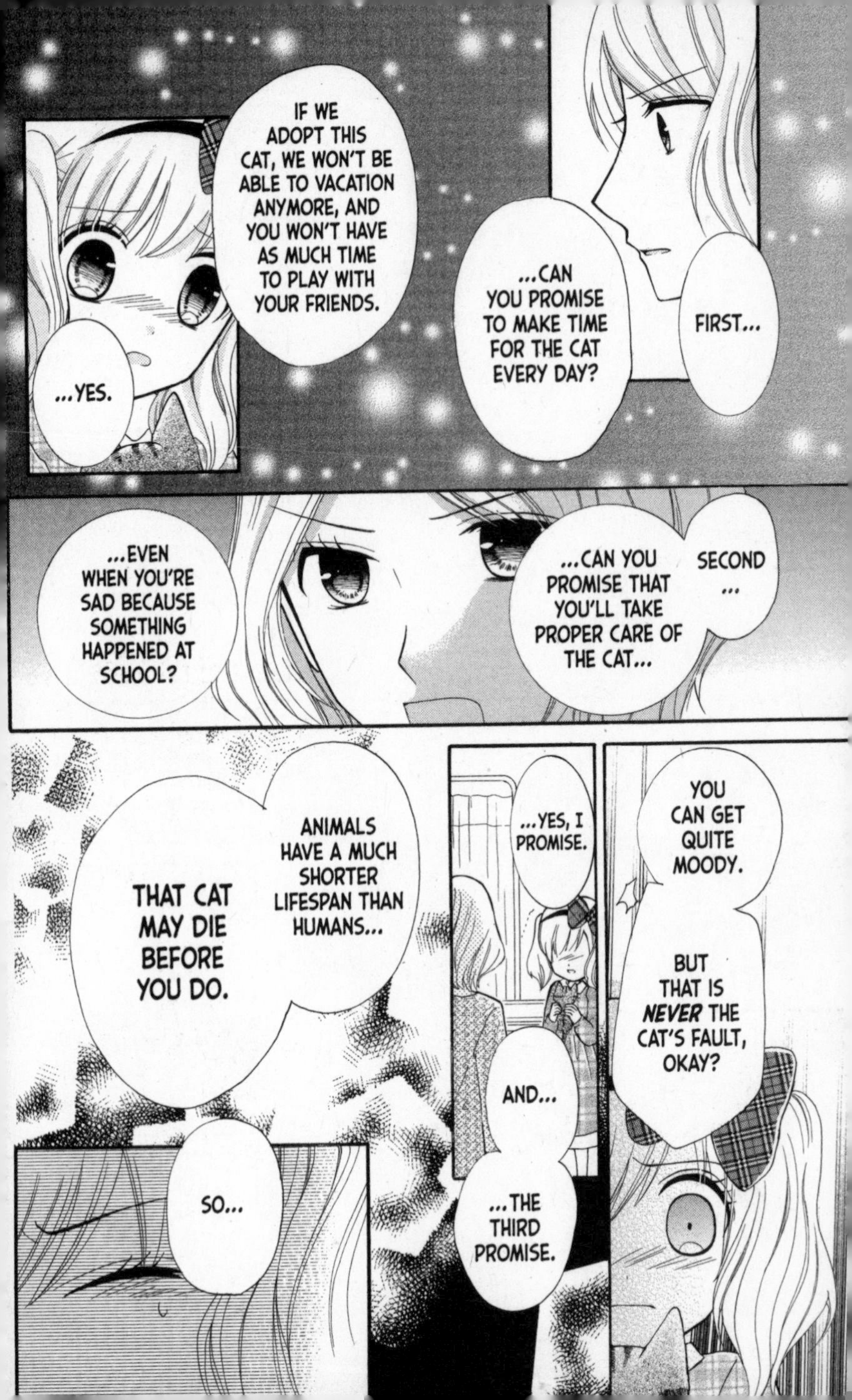
FIRST...
...CAN YOU PROMISE TO MAKE TIME FOR THE CAT EVERY DAY?
IF WE ADOPT THIS CAT, WE WON'T BE ABLE TO VACATION ANYMORE, AND YOU WON'T HAVE AS MUCH TIME TO PLAY WITH YOUR FRIENDS.
...YES.
SECOND ...
...CAN YOU PROMISE THAT YOU'LL TAKE PROPER CARE OF THE CAT...
...EVEN WHEN YOU'RE SAD BECAUSE SOMETHING HAPPENED AT SCHOOL?
YOU CAN GET QUITE MOODY.
BUT THAT IS *NEVER* THE CAT'S FAULT, OKAY?
...YES, I PROMISE.
AND...
...THE THIRD PROMISE.
ANIMALS HAVE A MUCH SHORTER LIFESPAN THAN HUMANS...
THAT CAT MAY DIE BEFORE YOU DO.
SO...

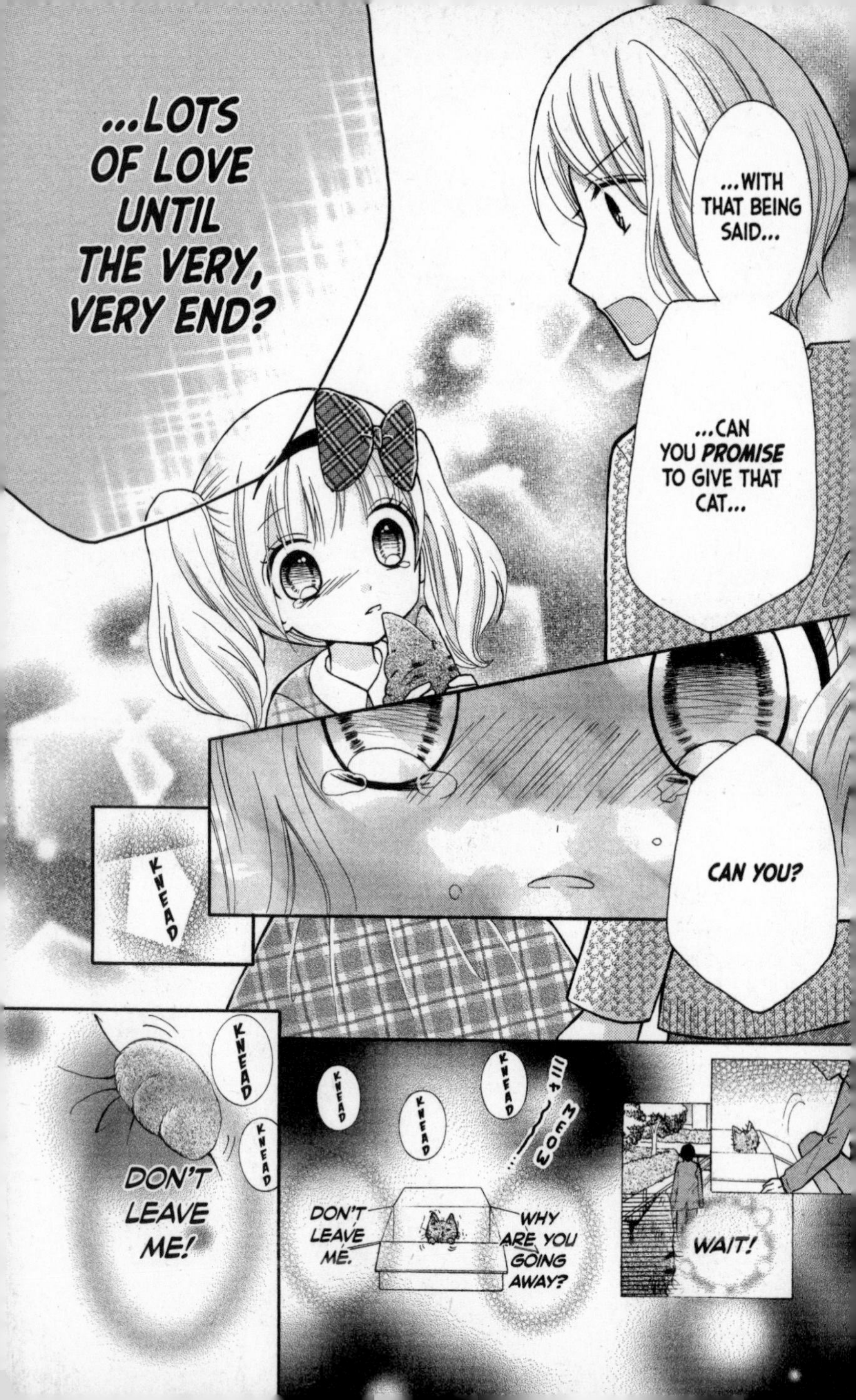
...WITH THAT BEING SAID...
...CAN YOU PROMISE TO GIVE THAT CAT...
...LOTS OF LOVE UNTIL THE VERY, VERY END?
CAN YOU?
KNEAD
WAIT!
KNEAD
MEOW
KNEAD
KNEAD
WHY ARE YOU GOING AWAY?
DON'T LEAVE ME.
KNEAD
KNEAD
DON'T LEAVE ME!

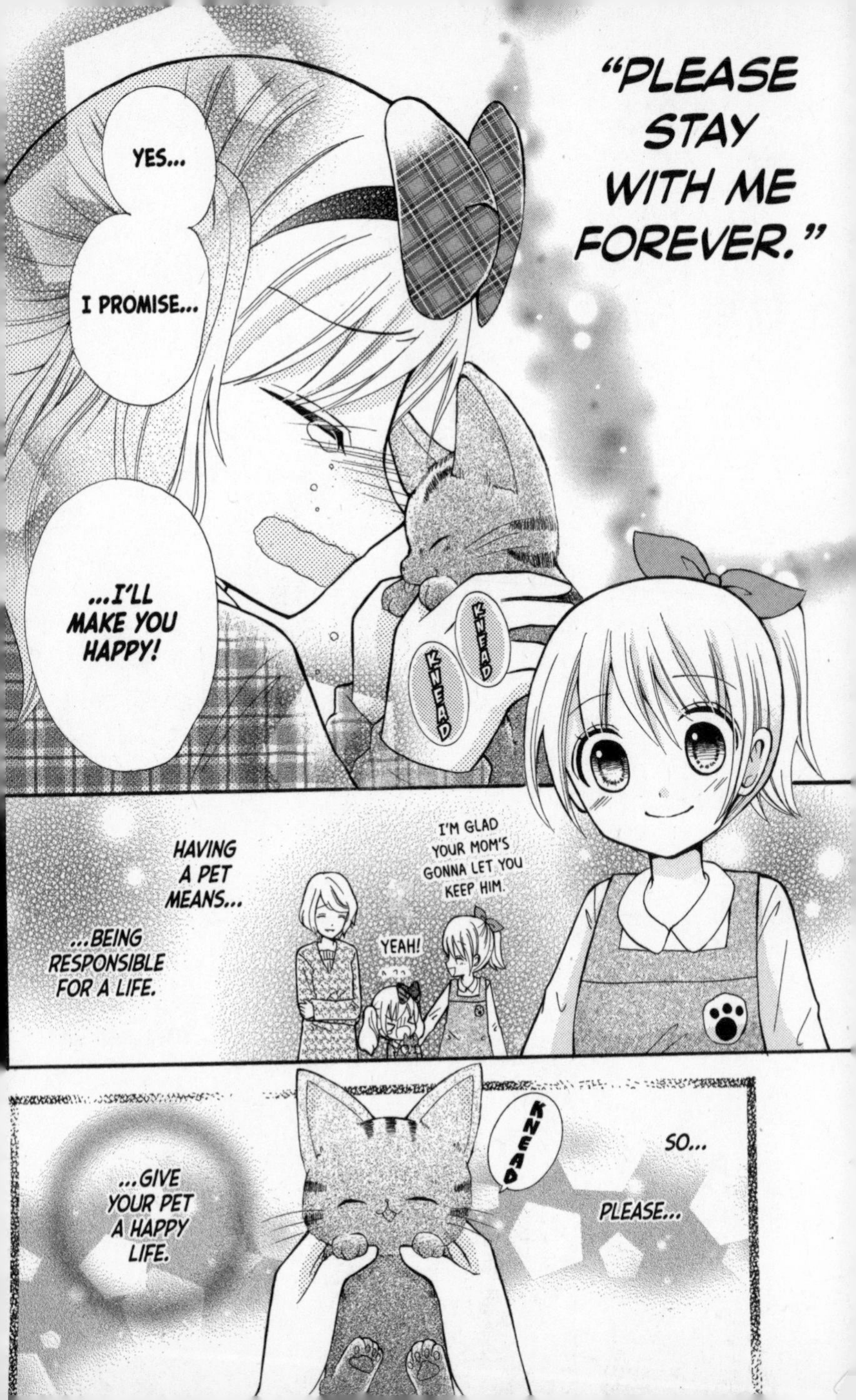
"PLEASE STAY WITH ME FOREVER."
YES...
I PROMISE...
KNEAD
KNEAD
...I'LL MAKE YOU HAPPY!
I'M GLAD YOUR MOM'S GONNA LET YOU KEEP HIM.
HAVING A PET MEANS...
YEAH!
...BEING RESPONSIBLE FOR A LIFE.
SO...
KNEAD
PLEASE...
...GIVE YOUR PET A HAPPY LIFE.

To be continued in volume 3

WOOF★

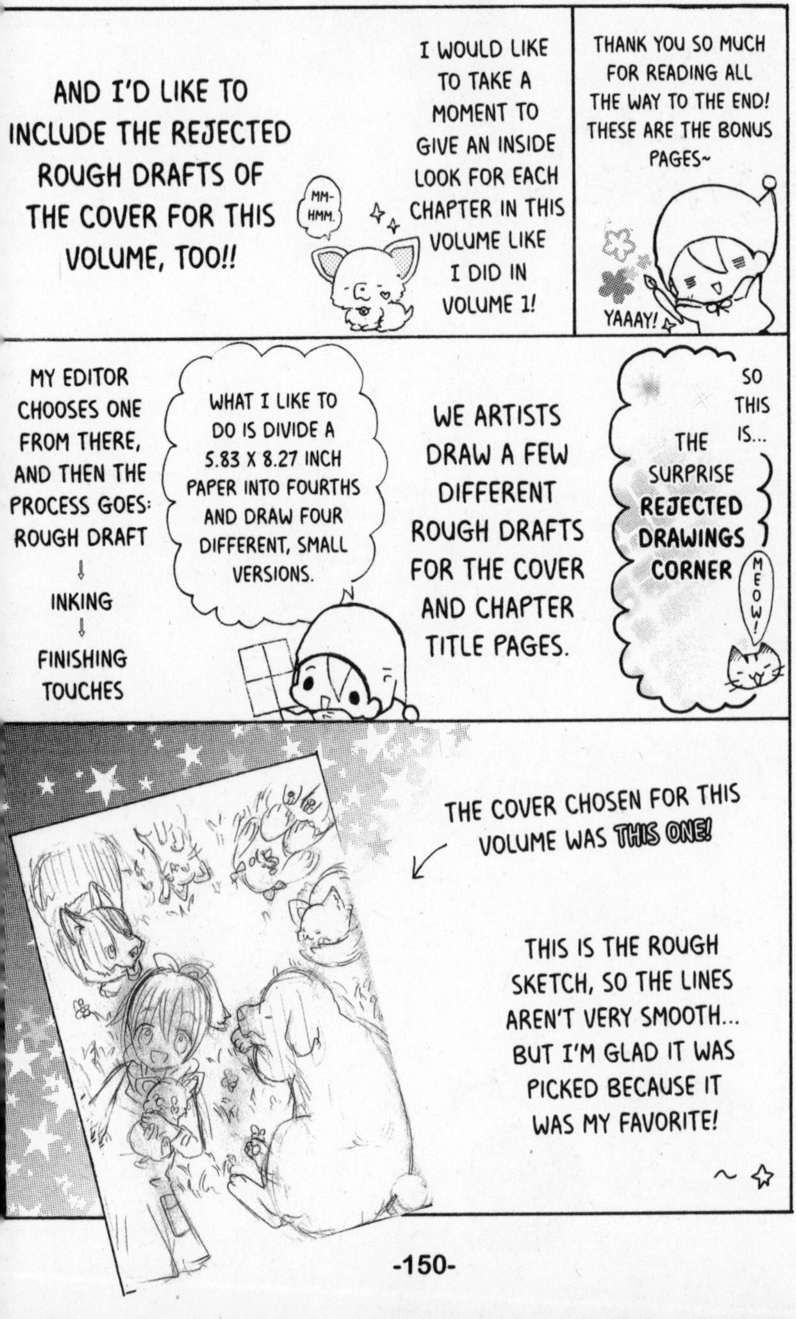
THANK YOU SO MUCH FOR READING ALL THE WAY TO THE END! THESE ARE THE BONUS PAGES~
YAAAY!
I WOULD LIKE TO TAKE A MOMENT TO GIVE AN INSIDE LOOK FOR EACH CHAPTER IN THIS VOLUME LIKE I DID IN VOLUME 1!
MM-HMM.
AND I'D LIKE TO INCLUDE THE REJECTED ROUGH DRAFTS OF THE COVER FOR THIS VOLUME, TOO!!
SO THIS IS...
THE SURPRISE REJECTED DRAWINGS CORNER
MEOW!
WE ARTISTS DRAW A FEW DIFFERENT ROUGH DRAFTS FOR THE COVER AND CHAPTER TITLE PAGES.
WHAT I LIKE TO DO IS DIVIDE A 5.83 X 8.27 INCH PAPER INTO FOURTHS AND DRAW FOUR DIFFERENT, SMALL VERSIONS.
MY EDITOR CHOOSES ONE FROM THERE, AND THEN THE PROCESS GOES: ROUGH DRAFT ⇩ INKING ⇩ FINISHING TOUCHES
THE COVER CHOSEN FOR THIS VOLUME WAS THIS ONE!
THIS IS THE ROUGH SKETCH, SO THE LINES AREN'T VERY SMOOTH... BUT I'M GLAD IT WAS PICKED BECAUSE IT WAS MY FAVORITE!
~☆

SOME OF THE REJECTED DRAWINGS

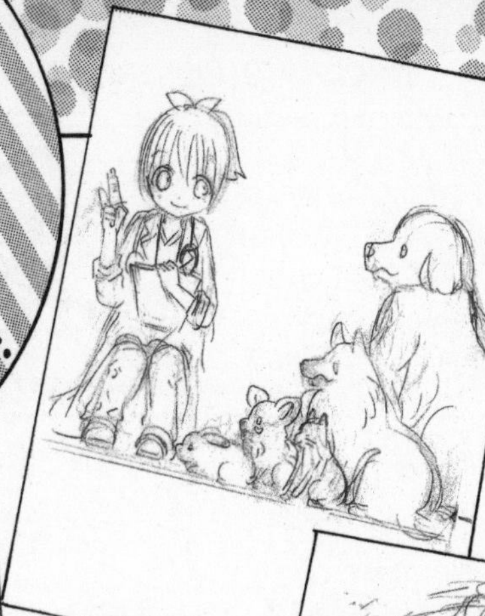

IF THE ANIMALS WERE WAITING THEIR TURN FOR YUZU TO GIVE THEM THEIR CHECKUP.

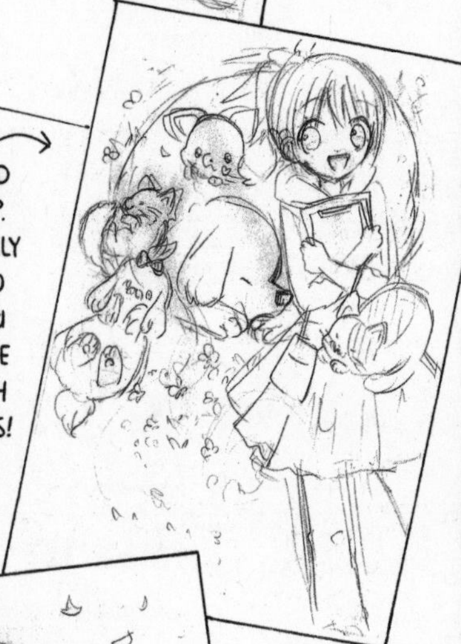

THE SECOND RUNNER-UP. I JUST REALLY WANTED TO DRAW YUZU LYING IN THE GRASS WITH THE ANIMALS!

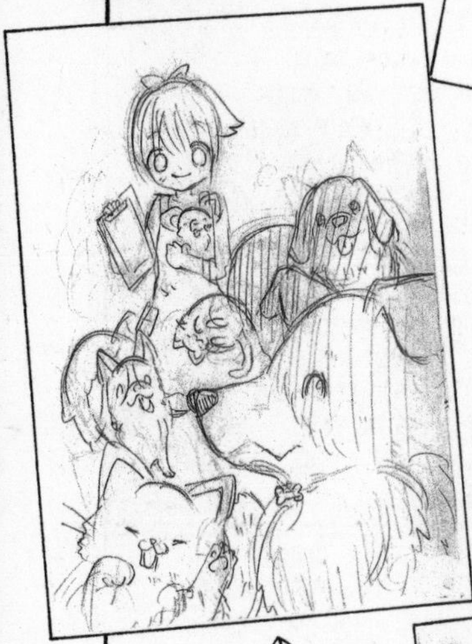

I TRIED **SQUISHING** ALL THE ANIMALS TOGETHER. THERE ISN'T REALLY ANY SPACE FOR THE TITLE THOUGH...

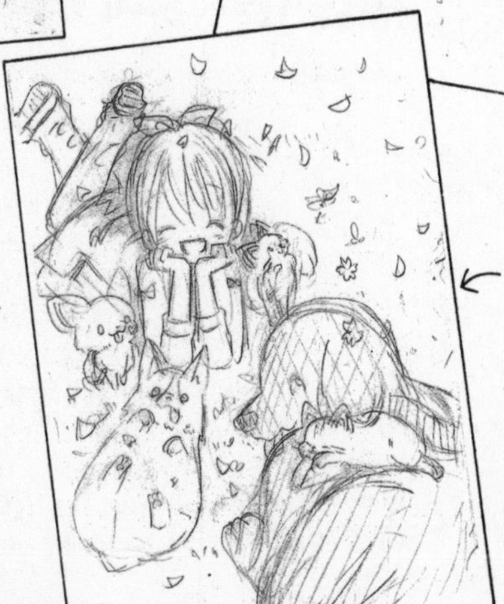

I LIKE HOW THE CAT'S SLEEPING ON THE DOG'S BACK. I LOVE PAIRING BIG ANIMALS AND LITTLE ANIMALS TOGETHER!

THE NEXT PAGE HAS A BEHIND THE SCENES.

BEHIND THE SCENES!!

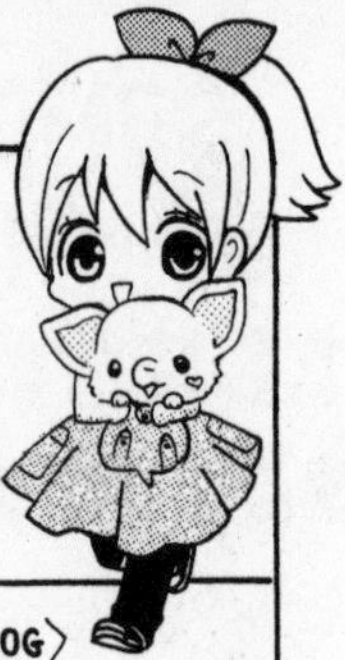

I WROTE THAT THIS IS SUPPOSED TO BE A BEHIND THE SCENES, BUT IT WOUND UP BEING MORE ABOUT MY MEMORIES! I HOPE YOU READ IT WHEN YOU'VE GOT TIME.

CHAPTER 5

⟨LUKE THE GUIDE DOG⟩

JUST A LITTLE BIT BEFORE I STARTED WORKING ON THIS CHAPTER, I SAW A GUIDE DOG AT THE MALL. EVEN THOUGH PEOPLE WERE BEING SO LOUD, THE DOG WASN'T BOTHERED AT ALL, AND WORE A DETERMINED LOOK AS IT WORKED. THE DOG LOOKED SO COOL, I USED THAT AS THE BASE FOR LUKE.

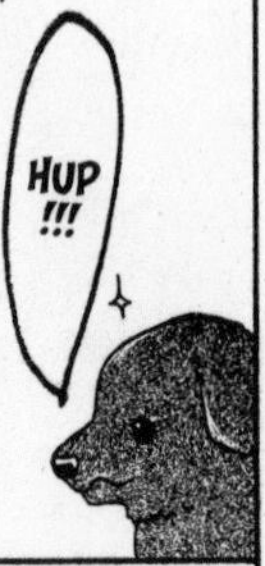
HUP!!!

CHAPTER 6

⟨KOMACHI, THE DOG WHO CRIED WOLF⟩

KOMACHI, THE DOG THAT GETS EASILY CARRIED AWAY, WAS VERY EASY TO DRAW. IT WAS REALLY FUN DRAWING THE HEE-HEE FACE~ I'M HAPPY THAT A LOT OF MY FRIENDS REALLY LIKED THIS CHAPTER.

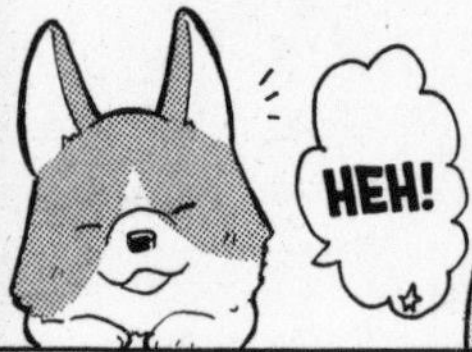
HEH!

CHAPTER 7

⟨CHACHA THE RABBIT BOSS⟩

WHEN I WAS IN ELEMENTARY SCHOOL, I ALSO GOT ANIMAL CARETAKER DUTY LIKE YUZU! I REMEMBERED LOTS OF THINGS AS I WORKED ON THIS CHAPTER—LIKE HOW I WENT TO THE CAFETERIA TO GET CARROTS FOR THE RABBITS, AND HOW WARM AND FLUFFY THEY WERE! THIS CHAPTER REALLY BROUGHT ME BACK!

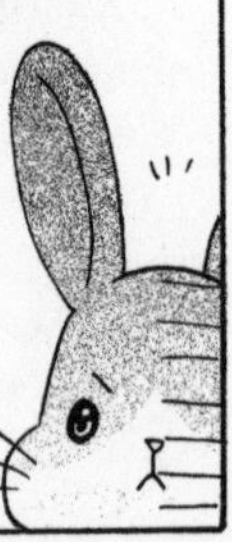

CHAPTER 8

⟨PEANUT THE ABANDONED CAT⟩

THIS IS THE MOST EMOTIONAL CHAPTER IN THIS VOLUME AND PERHAPS THE ONE I WANT EVERYONE TO READ THE MOST. "HOW DO YOU KNOW YOU'RE READY TO BE A PET OWNER?" WAS A REALLY DIFFICULT TOPIC TO TACKLE, SO IT WAS HARDER THAN THE OTHER CHAPTERS TO WRITE. I WANT PEANUT TO LIVE A HAPPY LIFE, TOO!

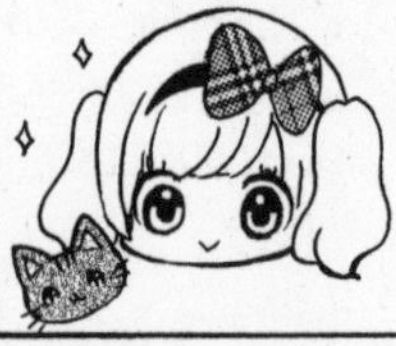

SPECIAL THANKS

🐾 IN COLLABORATION WITH NIPPON COLUMBIA CO., LTD.

🐾 SUPERVISOR: TAISEI HOSOIDO

🐾 EDITORS: NAKAZATO
        NAGANO

🐾 DESIGNER: KOBAYASHI

🐾 EVERYONE FROM NAKAYOSHI'S EDITORIAL DEPARTMENT

🐾 MANUSCRIPT ASSISTANCE: CHIRORU AOZORA
                         NAOCHAN
                         MEIRA ISHIZAKA
                         KOUTEI PENGUIN DX
                         BONCHI

I'D BE REALLY HAPPY IF YOU SENT ME LETTERS WITH YOUR THOUGHTS, ETC. ABOUT THE MANGA!

ADDRESS: MINGO ITO
KODANSHA COMICS
451 PARK AVE. SOUTH, 7TH FLOOR
NEW YORK, NY 10016

BLOG MINGOROKU
http://ameblo.jp/
itoumingo/

twitter
@ itoumingo

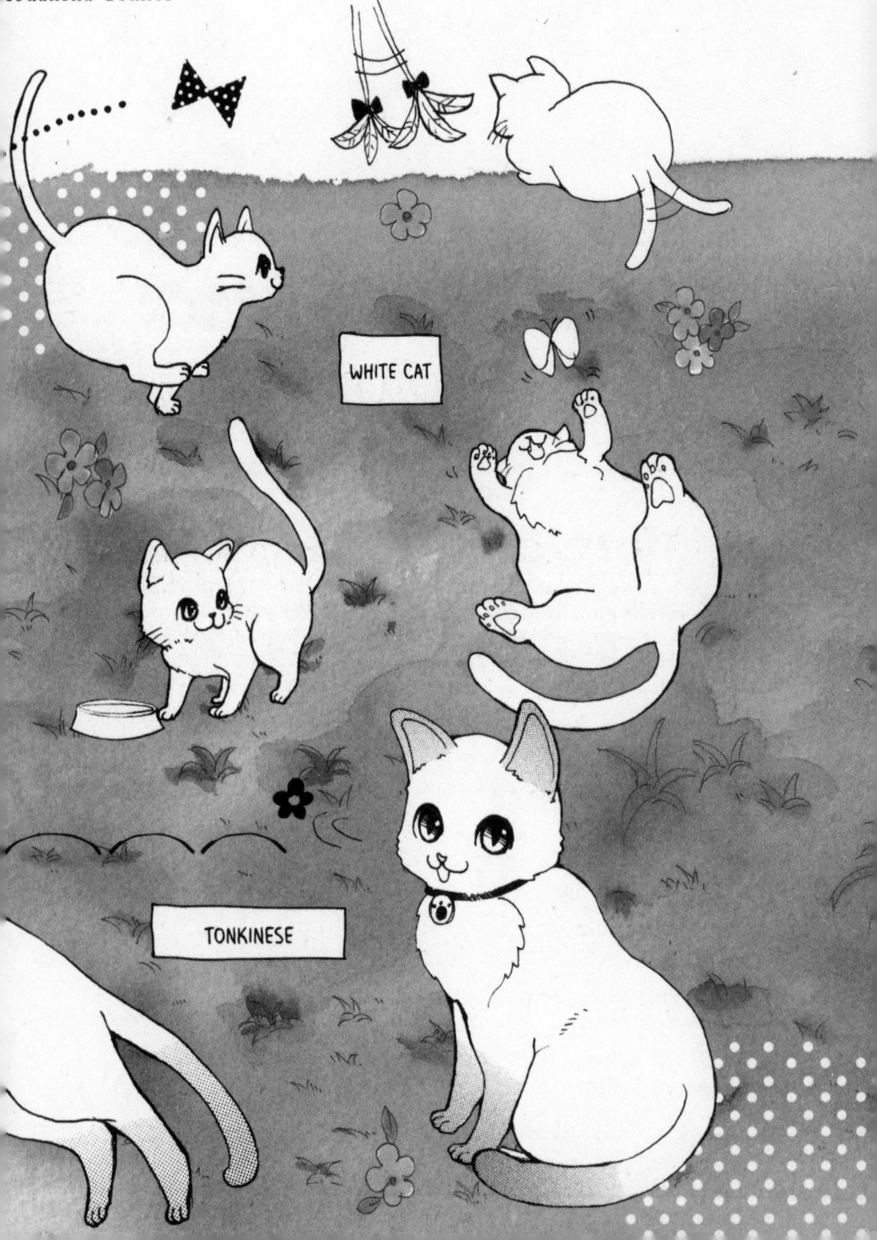
WHITE CAT
TONKINESE

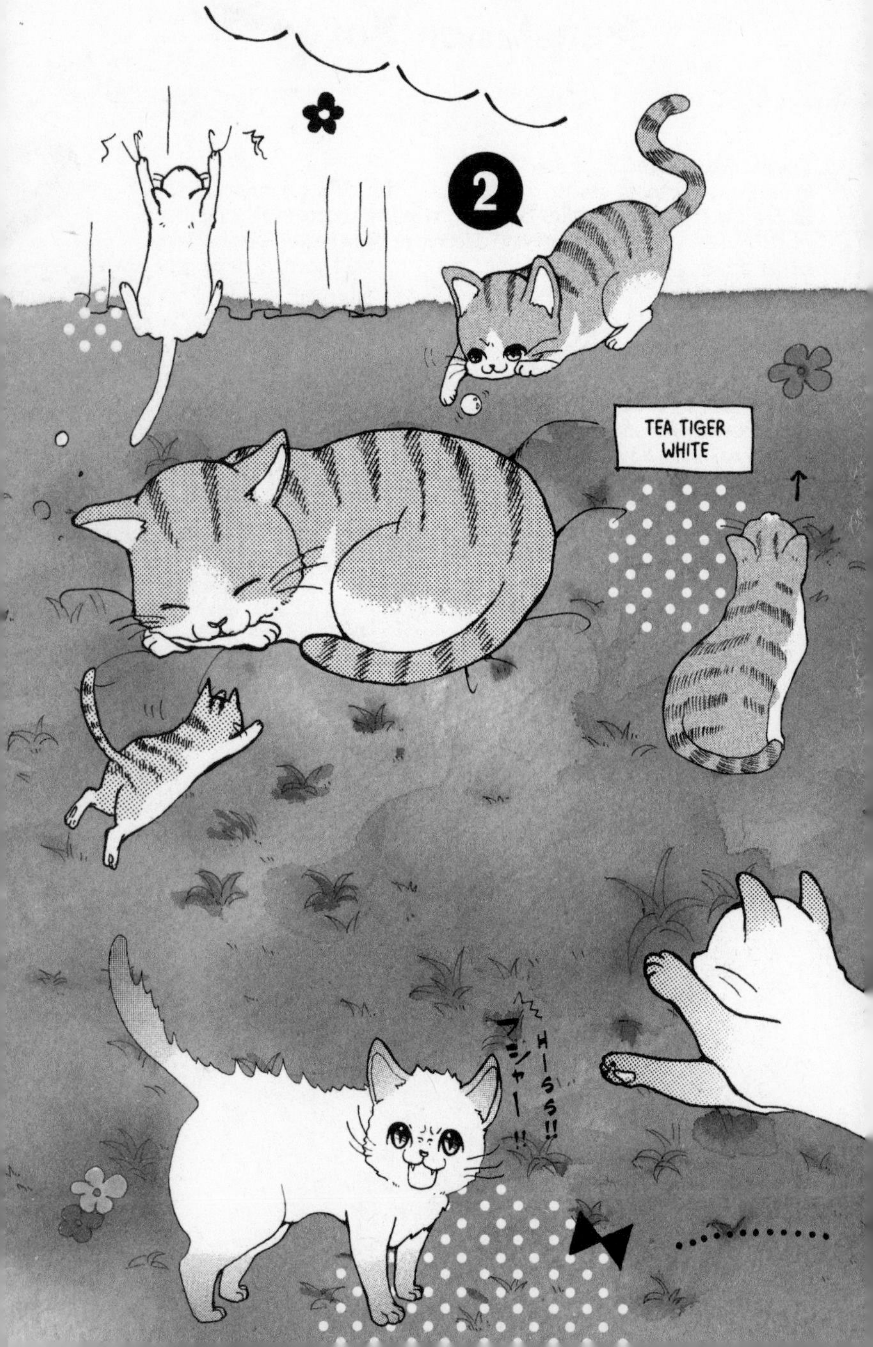
2
TEA TIGER WHITE
フシャー!!
HISS!!

Translation Notes

Class duties, page 79
In Japanese schools, students have designated roles or duties. This is intended to help students be engaged in the school environment, or pursue their interests, all while learning about responsibility. Some other duties can include tending to the communal garden, or assisting in the library.

Mikoto and Yuzu, page 79
In the original Japanese, Mikoto hesitates to call Yuzu by just her first name. This is because in Japanese, to be polite, you usually refer to acquaintances or strangers with their last name, plus an honorific. For example, "Morino-san" or "Miss Morino" for Yuzu. Here, in order to be friendly, Yuzu insists on being called just "Yuzu," and Mikoto feels the same way!

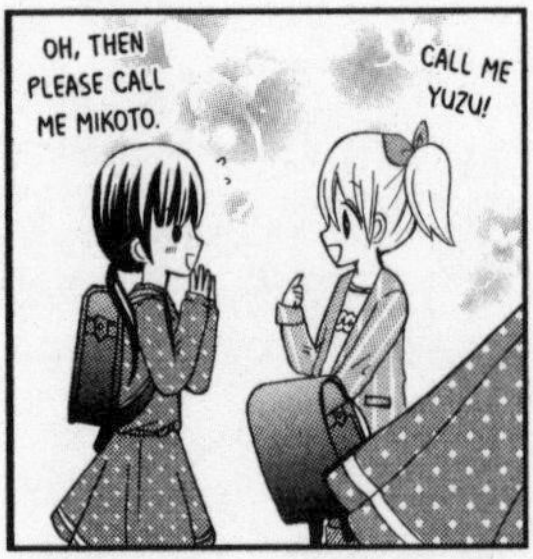
CALL ME YUZU!
OH, THEN PLEASE CALL ME MIKOTO.

A Kodansha Comics Trade Paperback Original

Yuzu the Pet Vet 2 copyright © 2017 Mingo Ito © 2017 NIPPON COLUMBIA CO., LTD.
English translation copyright © 2020 Mingo Ito © NIPPON COLUMBIA CO., LTD.

Published in the United States by Kodansha Comics, an imprint of
Kodansha USA Publishing, LLC, New York.

Publication rights for this English edition arranged through
Kodansha Ltd., Tokyo.

First published in Japan in 2017 by Kodansha Ltd., Tokyo
as *Yuzu no Doubutsu Karute ~Kochira Wan Nyan Doubutsu Byouin~*, volume 2.

ISBN 978-1-63236-974-1

Original cover design by Tomoko Kobayashi

Printed in the United States of America.

www.kodanshacomics.com

9 8 7 6 5 4 3 2 1
Translation: Julie Goniwich
Lettering: David Yoo
Editing: Haruko Hashimoto
Kodansha Comics edition cover design by Matthew Akuginow

Publisher: Kiichiro Sugawara
Vice president of marketing & publicity: Naho Yamada

Director of publishing services: Ben Applegate
Associate director of operations: Stephen Pakula
Publishing services managing editor: Noelle Webster
Assistant production manager: Emi Lotto, Angela Zurlo
Logo and character art ©Kodansha USA Publishing, LLC

HOW TO READ MANGA

Japanese is written right to left and top to bottom. This means that for a reader accustomed to Western languages, Japanese books read "backwards." Since most manga published in English now keep the Japanese page order, it can take a little getting used to—but once you learn how, it's a snap!

Here you can see pages 24-25 from *Yuzu the Pet Vet* volume 1. The speech balloons have been numbered in the order you should read them in.

Page 24—read this page first!

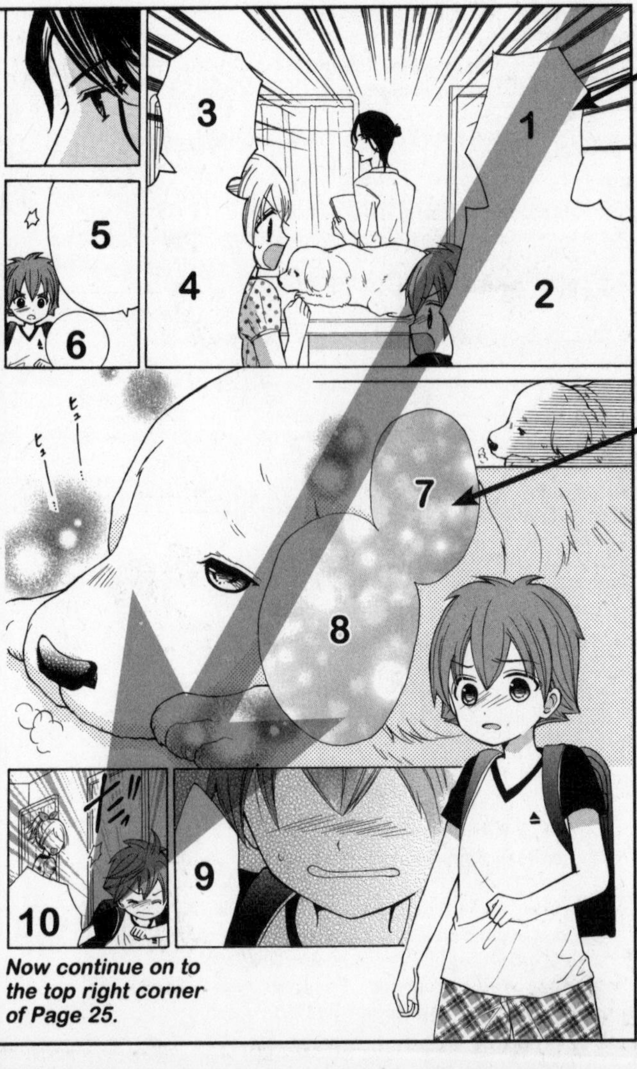

1
2
3
4
5
6
7
8
9
10

Start here, at the top right corner of the right-hand page.

Read right to left, then top to bottom.

Now continue on to the top right corner of Page 25.

After a few pages, you'll be reading manga like a pro!

Page 25—read the page on the **right-hand side** first!

Start at the top right corner for this page, too!

Don't forget to move back to the right side.

This is the bottom left-most panel, so it's **read last.**

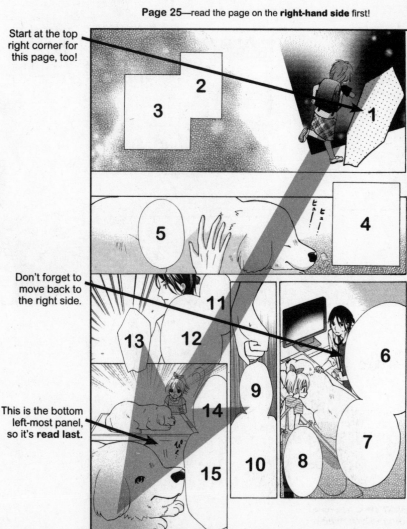

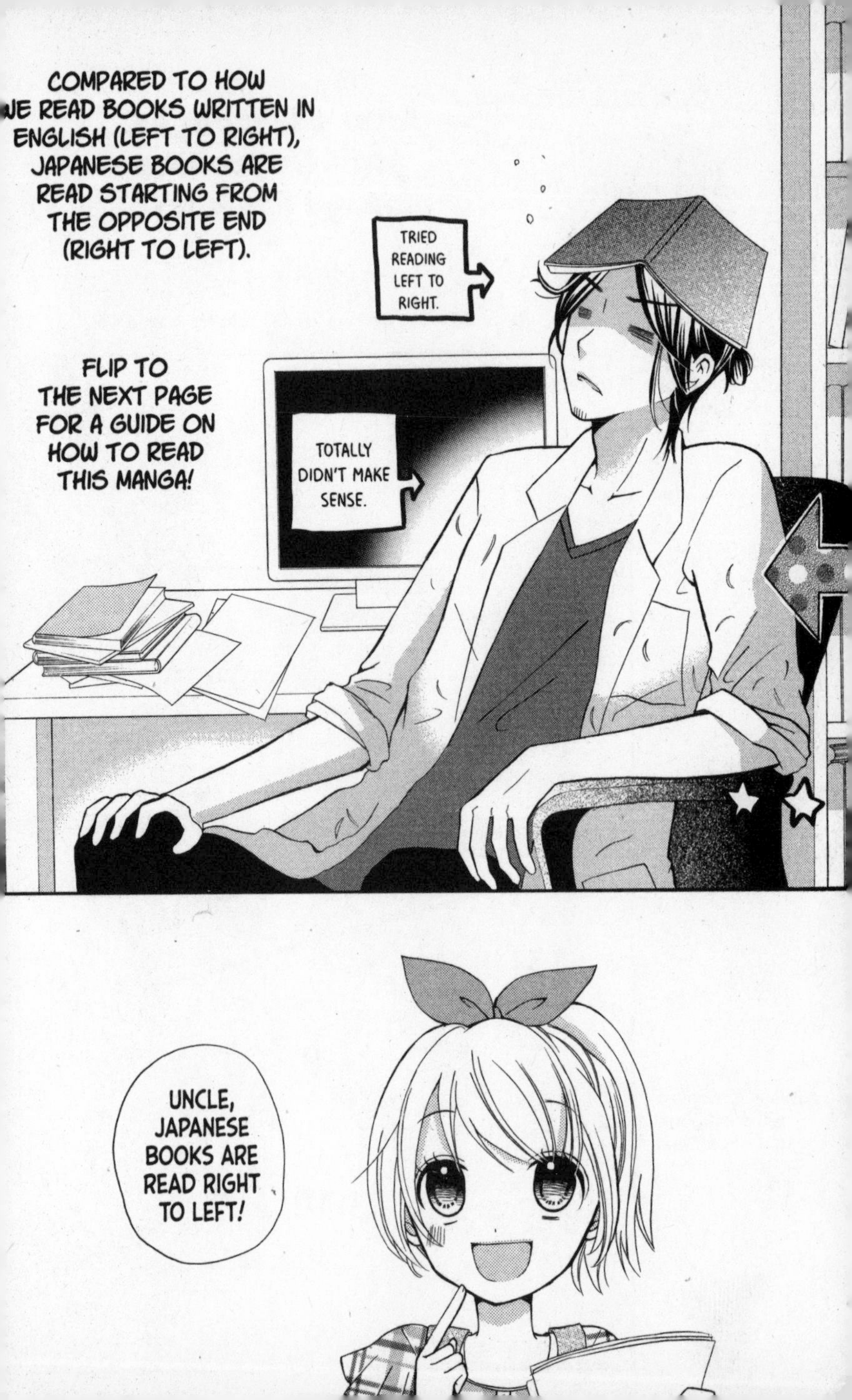
COMPARED TO HOW WE READ BOOKS WRITTEN IN ENGLISH (LEFT TO RIGHT), JAPANESE BOOKS ARE READ STARTING FROM THE OPPOSITE END (RIGHT TO LEFT).
TRIED READING LEFT TO RIGHT.
TOTALLY DIDN'T MAKE SENSE.
FLIP TO THE NEXT PAGE FOR A GUIDE ON HOW TO READ THIS MANGA!
UNCLE, JAPANESE BOOKS ARE READ RIGHT TO LEFT!